THE PRACTICE OF POLITICS IN POSTCOLONIAL BRAZIL

PITT LATIN AMERICAN SERIES

George Reid Andrews, General Editor

Catherine M. Conaghan, Associate Editor

Adriel I. Cepeda
16 - 02 - 06

THE PRACTICE OF POLITICS IN POSTCOLONIAL BRAZIL

Porto Alegre, 1845–1895

Roger A. Kittleson

UNIVERSITY OF PITTSBURGH PRESS

Published by the University of Pittsburgh Press, Pittsburgh, Pa., 15260

Manufactured in the United States of America
Printed on acid-free paper
10 9 8 7 6 5 4 3 2 1

Library of Congress Cataloging-in-Publication Data

Kittleson, Roger Alan.
The practice of politics in postcolonial Brazil : Porto Alegre, 1845-1895 / Roger A. Kittleson.
p. cm. — (Pitt Latin American series)
Includes bibliographical references and index.
ISBN 0-8229-5897-X (pbk. : alk. Paper)
1. Porto Alegre (Brazil)—Politics and government—19th century. 2. Political participation—Brazil—Porto Alegre—History—19th century. 3. Social movements—Brazil—Porto Alegre—History—19th century. I. Title. II. Series.
F2651.P8K58 2005
320.08165'09'034—dc22

2005020902

The people are in the end the opposite of all that they could and should be, if they knew how to claim their rights, to stay within their limits, . . . and if they refused to stand for much of what is done in their name.

O Século, 13 November 1881

Contents

	Acknowledgments	ix
	Introduction	1
1	"Our Compatriots Are Vagrants": Work, Morality, and the Shaping of a New *Povo*, 1845–1880	12
2	The Immigrant Solution and Its Problems, 1846–1880	46
3	The Politics of Everyday Life in the City	74
4	Blurring the Lines of Public Politics: Abolitionist Projects, 1879–1888	118
5	"A Strange Vision of Popular Movement": The Emergence and Limits of a New Politics	149
	Conclusion	183
	Abbreviations	189
	Notes	191
	Bibliography	227
	Index	257

Acknowledgments

THE years that went into this book revealed to me, among other things, the rather banal truth that writing is a social activity. Not only must writers communicate with audiences, but in all but the most exceptional of cases, they must rely on friends and colleagues for conversations of various kinds. Although obvious, this lesson was something I long resisted, despite the best efforts of those around me. My stubbornness and the persistence with which they helped me overcome it render me all the more grateful to those who have made this book possible.

My first thanks must go to those who were present in the earliest stages of the project. At the University of Wisconsin, my constellation of graduate advisors—Florencia Mallon, Steve Stern, and Francisco Scarano—challenged me to sharpen my ideas and prose. At a much more important level, though, they provided wonderful models of how to think historically and how to be imaginative, engaged scholars in this world. In Madison, I benefited also from the friendship and insights that my graduate school colleagues generously shared. Sarah Chambers, Joel Wolfe, Anne Macpherson, Karin Rosemblatt, Eileen Findlay, Sinclair Thomson, Seemin Qayum, Nancy Appelbaum, René Reeves, Greg Crider, Marisol de la Cadena, Ann Lewis-Osler, Laura McEnany, and Ben Labaree were lively influences, and some remain dear friends to this day. All were fundamental in my training as a historian.

As I was researching and writing the earlier versions of this project, many others made invaluable contributions to my work and my life. Though I was only able to study with Tom Skidmore for one year before he left Madison for Brown University, he has continued to bless me with his always thoughtful and usually humorous advice. Probably more than any other scholar, he has shown me how to link my lifelong affective ties to Brazil with the intellectual and political enterprise of historical study. In my two stays at

Northwestern University, Frank Safford was a model of the insistently logical and generous-spirited mentor and colleague. Besides Tom and Frank, others have shared their time and acuity in readings of papers or chapters that became components of this book. Joel Wolfe, Sueann Caulfield, Peter Beattie, Jeff Lesser, John Chasteen, Eileen Findlay, Eric Van Young, Tom Holloway, Martha Esteves, Silvia Arrom, Hendrik Kraay, Thomas Whigham, Diana Paton, Pam Scully, Tom Kohut, and Barbara Weinstein helped improve my work through their critiques of preliminary stabs at sections of the project. Joel has, in fact, always been ready to comment on any piece I might send his way, as well as offer sage advice on personal and professional matters. Sueann has likewise been a source of wisdom and kind support in this work and other developments over the past decade. Peter, Karin, and Nancy have lent their very different comic senses and analytical abilities to my cause for many years.

In Rio de Janeiro, São Paulo, and Rio Grande do Sul, many more friends and acquaintances made my research productive and my life enjoyable. Carlos and Arno Vogel and their families in Rio and São Paulo are more like kin than friends; in ways both personal and professional, they have made me feel like much more than a Brazilianist. Shared days in the archives and shared evenings and weekends elsewhere in Rio forged friendships with Sueann Caulfield, Peter Beattie, Martha Esteves, and Sidney Chalhoub; their enthusiasm and kindness have propped me up on many occasions. In Porto Alegre, Paulo Roberto Staudt Moreira, Silvia Arend, Cláudia Mauch, Adhemar Lourenço da Silva Jr., Joan Bak, and the late Décio Freitas shared archival lore, theoretical and research insights, *chimarrão*, and other invaluable commodities. Despite his inexplicable predilections in *futebol*, Paulo's intellectual drive and exuberant camaraderie have always been energizing.

During my various trips to Brazil, I have enjoyed the gracious assistance of the skilled staff and researchers at the Arquivo Nacional, Biblioteca Nacional, Casa de Rui Barbosa, and Instituto Histórico e Geográfico Brasileiro in Rio de Janeiro; the Biblioteca Rio-Grandense in Rio Grande; and the Arquivo Público do Rio Grande do Sul, Arquivo Histórico do Rio Grande do Sul, Arquivo Histórico Municipal de Porto Alegre, Solar dos Câmaras, Biblioteca Pública, Instituto Histórico e Geográfico do Rio Grande do Sul, and Museu de Comunicação Social Hipólito José da Costa in Porto Alegre. Their kindness and ability to overcome (or simply *driblar*) obstacles have been fundamental to my research.

That research has been made possible by financial, editorial, and technical support as well. I am grateful for the Tinker Foundation Field Research Grant, the Fulbright-Hays Doctoral Dissertation Research Grant, the Wisconsin Alumni Research Foundation Dissertation Fellowship, and the sustained research funding from Williams College that gave me the chance to put this book together. Nathan MacBrien and Cynthia Miller at the University of Pittsburgh Press have been exemplary editors; my thanks to them and to the book's anonymous reader for thorough, constructive readings that helped me make new sense of my arguments. Sharron Macklin of Williams College patiently shared her expertise in the production of maps to meet my needs.

I have relied most heavily and consistently on my family. My parents, Russell and Jean Kittleson, and my brothers, Gary and John, backed me even when none of us was sure when the manuscript would emerge as a book. My late grandmother Gladys Clayton shared her own love of reading and history, and my aunt Ann Clayton has given me much more than tips about fishing on Gilbert Lake.

Finally, I dedicate this book to Zayde Antrim, with whom I have formed a new family. Zayde has both the keenest mind and the warmest heart I have ever known. I hope that our beautiful son, August, will one day read this and know the joy that he and his mother brought me during the latter stages of its writing.

THE PRACTICE OF POLITICS IN POSTCOLONIAL BRAZIL

Rio Grande do Sul in the early Republic.

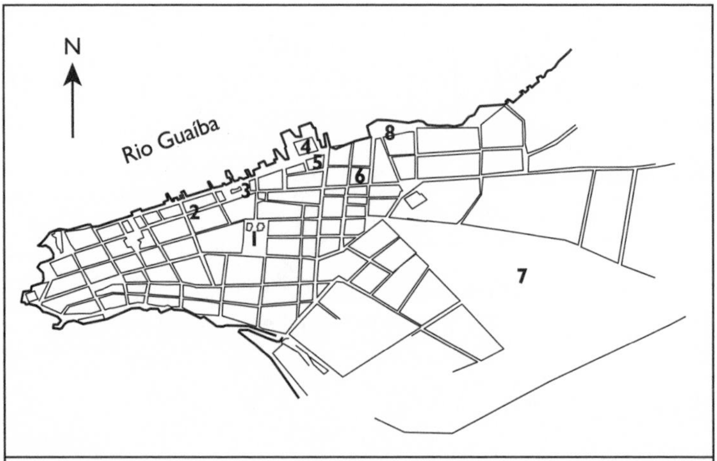

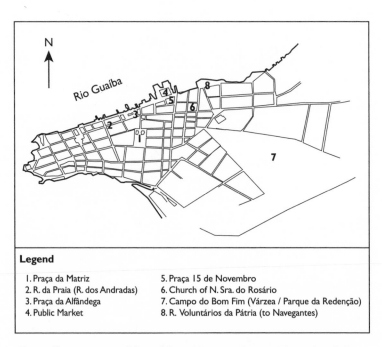

Legend

1. Praça da Matriz
2. R. da Praia (R. dos Andradas)
3. Praça da Alfândega
4. Public Market
5. Praça 15 de Novembro
6. Church of N. Sra. do Rosário
7. Campo do Bom Fim (Várzea / Parque da Redenção)
8. R. Voluntários da Pátria (to Navegantes)

Porto Alegre, c. 1881. Adapted from Henrique Breton, *Planta da cidade de Porto Alegre*, 1881.

Introduction

THE Republicans who fought their way to power at the end of the nineteenth century in Porto Alegre, Rio Grande do Sul, tirelessly proclaimed the conservative nature of their programs. Fervent admirers of the thought of Auguste Comte, they shared the French philosopher's abhorrence of revolution and sought to shore up existing social hierarchies in their city and state. Implicit in their plans for strengthening the social order, however, was the promise of great changes in Gaúcho politics and society.[1] Under the direction of the only group with the requisite "scientific" understanding of historical processes —their own political party, the PRR (Partido Republicano Rio-Grandense, or Rio Grandense Republican Party)—the state was to carry out a broad "civic education" of a novel, if abstract, sort. By "modifying men, humanizing capitalists, pacifying workers, making the strong more sympathetic toward the weak and the weak more resigned, respecting and not hating the strong as now occurs," this effort would produce more submissive, and thus presumably more productive, members of every social class. In short, their simple yet sweeping proposals envisioned "a complete change of opinions, a new regime of ideas."[2]

This book is a study of the emergence of the Republicans' "new regime of ideas" and the political and cultural transformations in which their Positivist initiative participated. As such, it is in one sense a local study of the ascendance of what Charles Hale has labeled "scientific politics" across the Americas in the second half of the nineteenth century.[3] Indeed, Porto Alegre provides a striking case of the shift from Liberal to Positivist dominance. Into the 1880s, Liberals in this southern provincial capital maintained remarkable local control over their region's politics in the highly centralized structures of the Brazilian Empire. Moreover, after years of partisan vitriol that culminated in a notoriously bloody civil war (the Federalist Revolt) in 1893–95, Positivists in Porto Alegre gained more of a direct hand over government than did their "co-religionaries" anywhere else in the New World.[4]

In another sense, this book addresses a broad and persistent problem in Brazilian history—namely, that of continuity. Running through much of the canonical scholarship on postcolonial Brazil is an almost tragic feeling that, despite such events as independence from Portugal in 1822, the abolition of slavery in 1888, and the substitution of the imperial state by the First Republic in 1889, certain core hierarchical structures or values remained in place. The maintenance of these traits, furthermore, preserved the elitist and exclusionary nature of the political system. As historian José Honório Rodrigues has written: "The ancient things lingered on and nothing ever became new, because the leadership never reconciled with the people. It never saw in them creatures of God, never gave them recognition, for it wanted them to be what they are not. It never saw their virtues nor admired their services to the country; . . . [it] denied their rights, crushed their life, and as soon as it saw them grow and, little by little, deny it approval, it conspired to put them once again on the periphery."[5]

The grand generalization I evoke through Rodrigues's words is not, however, meant to deny the methodological variety among, much less the historicity within, classic works of Brazilian historiography; this conglomeration of texts includes narratives of the country's failure to follow different paths to such divergent, presumably emancipatory goals as socialist revolution or the "true" implantation of Liberal values in the Brazilian nation-state.[6] Instead, I suggest that a marked frustration informs the interpretations of scholars who, despite their often contrasting analytical and political stances, nevertheless argue in some way that patronage, personalism, and profound inequalities lived on, through domestic revolts, international wars, and a succession of regimes and legal codes that presented ostensibly new rules of the political game.[7]

One of my goals, then, is to measure how heavily a "conservative conscience," to borrow historian Paulo Mercadante's phrase, weighed on the history of Porto Alegre—and thus, to a certain degree, of Brazil—in the second half of the nineteenth century.[8] To what extent, that is, did the PRR's projects break with the ideals and practices of power relations in Porto Alegre? Although I leave the examination of the ultimate outcome of the PRR's statist and idealist initiatives—its "new regime of ideas"—to other scholars, my aim is to explore the nature and limits of changes in political culture in and around this city from the pacification of a regional revolt, the Farroupilha Revolution, in 1845, through the Republican victory in the Federalist Revolt fifty years later.[9] This chronological focus runs counter to the still-common (if often lamented) tendency to treat the abolition of slavery or the fall of the Empire as the starting or stopping point for studies of social and political tendencies in modern Brazil.[10] For the purposes of examining transformations in power relations, the advantage of this periodization is clear, for it encompasses myriad occurrences of both national and regional significance, from the consolidation of the imperial nation-state at midcentury, through the war against Argentine dictator Juan Manuel de Rosas (1851–52), the Paraguayan War (1865–70), and the various steps toward slavery's legal end and the rise of the First Republic.

Looking at this slice of Gaúcho history, however, contains a hidden danger: precisely because it is so full of "high" political drama, it threatens to restrict our attention to incidents of formal politics. As even the earliest of the works referred to above demonstrate—and as more recent historiography on the nineteenth century elaborates—official politics were but one aspect of the hierarchical relations of power that characterized post-Independence Brazil. In order to get at the question of the reproduction of elite control in Porto Alegre, we must indeed consider what anthropologist Marc Abèlés has called "the multilayered complexity of political reality."[11] By thus casting our analytical net widely—by considering plebeian as well as elite political cultures—we see that the shift from Liberal to Positivist rule in Porto Alegre was part of a transition toward a more inclusionary but also more authoritarian practice of politics. While it did not amount to the full-blown "new regime of ideas" that the PRR desired, the change that overtook Porto Alegre by the 1880s and into the 1890s was a complex reformulation of hierarchical power relations—one that brought new segments of the elite to the fore, mobilized and engaged new sectors of the *povo* (people, here understood as the popular classes) in partisan politics, and still managed to hold off anything approaching revolution.

Liberalism and Postcolonial Brazil

Revolution is what the construction of an independent Brazil most notably did not involve. The almost bloodless separation from Portugal in 1822 left the new country with a dominant class of planters and merchants; the legal enslavement of about half its overall population; and the preservation of monarchy, with a member of the Portuguese ruling family on the throne in Rio de Janeiro. Unlike the former Spanish colonies on the mainland Americas, Brazil maintained its territorial unity and, seemingly, the bases of social and political legitimacy.

The myth of Brazilian exceptionalism, as scholars such as Emília Viotti da Costa have argued, obscures the strains and denies the violence that underlay the first decades of the consolidation of a Liberal nation-state.[12] Beginning before the break with the metropole, but continuing with greater vigor into the 1830s and 1840s, groups and regions outside the elite concentrated in Rio put forward their own interpretations of what independence could and should mean. Reflecting the weak integration achieved under colonial rule and the variety of regional social conditions, these propositions ranged from small-scale conspiracies quickly squelched to armed revolts crushed with the loss of tens of thousands of lives. Some, but not all, of these movements rejected slavery; some denied racial and other hierarchies in military and political institutions; some sought to throw off the political centralization the young imperial government was attempting to impose.[13] All, however, made reference to Liberal thought of some kind; at the beginning of this empire, as novelist and playwright José de Alencar observed, "to be liberal meant to be Brazilian."[14] The Liberalism that emerged triumphant from the battles of the first half of the nineteenth century was fraught with internal contradictions, so much so that some writers have denounced it as a set of "misplaced ideas."[15] However artificial it may now seem to have been in the context of a hierarchical slave society, this Liberalism—which I will call "seigneurial" Liberalism—came to set the terms of national debate in the Brazilian Empire. The manner in which it attained this status, furthermore, demonstrates that what seemed colonial vestiges in post-Independence Brazil were in fact the results of a series of highly contentious battles. Liberalism, that is, became an ideology justifying not only the dismantling of Portuguese restrictions on Brazilian trade and independence but also the ambitions of an elite class to stave off threats to slavery, patronage, and hierarchy.

Rather than a peaceful procession, then, the creation and consolidation of the Brazilian nation-state represented a hard-won victory by certain groups over others. The ultimate winners were the men who dominated the slave- and latifundia-based export economy of the Center-South provinces (Rio de Janeiro and sections of São Paulo and Minas Gerais), along with their political allies. Indeed, as Ilmar Rohloff de Mattos suggests, it is best to think of that class and the imperial state as having constructed each other by the late 1840s.[16] The losers ranged from regional elites in Rio Grande do Sul and elsewhere—who felt their local autonomy diminish in this same period but who generally retained their preeminence in their home provinces—to the free and enslaved poor who found that the Liberalism of the Empire was profoundly antidemocratic. At least until the electoral reform of 1881, a surprisingly high percentage of the free male population may have participated in the theater of elections, as Richard Graham has elegantly argued, but the triumphant ideals and practices of Liberal politics were elitist and exclusionary from the first years of the nation.[17] The Empire's Liberalism was, to adapt the words of W. E. B. DuBois, a "freedom to destroy freedom."[18]

Maturity and Decay of the Brazilian Empire

As much as Independence, it is the Second Empire (1840–89) that has led many observers to portray Brazil as fundamentally unlike the rest of Latin America. During the long reign of Dom Pedro II, after all, the country enjoyed a comparatively stable political system, while many Spanish American nations found themselves mired in internal strife. In Brazil, two major political parties managed the system of patronage that constituted virtually all formal political practice. Given their underlying commitment to the imperial system, moreover, disputes between Liberals and Conservatives rarely seemed threats to the political or social order; the parties' ideological flexibility, in fact, led to a host of contemporary witticisms about their essential similarity. Much of the scholarship on the period has seconded these adages, striving to show more analytically that, as the Viscount of Albuquerque noted, Liberals and Conservatives "all seem to belong to the same family. We live very well together on the same boat, and we do not have any conflicts of opinion."[19]

The image of the nation as a family—with the emperor as the ultimate patriarch—was indeed a powerful conceit in the seigneurial Liberalism of the second half of the nineteenth century. Elites like Albuquerque might describe the political class as a family, but in fact the language of the family ran through society as a whole, from the household and out into the webs of power relations that extended from it. This paternalist discourse was part of a culture of clientelism and hierarchy in which elites and nonelites alike—though with varying degrees of desperation—sought to maximize their personal power by trading loyalty and service for protection and favor.[20] The result was a cultural ideal in which vertical relations between patrons and clients dominated. As historian Sidney Chalhoub sagely advises, though, we must treat this image carefully, for horizontal solidarities persisted among the free and enslaved poor, as well as among elites, and the seigneurial ideal could never be fully achieved.[21] Primarily, though, in spite of the sense of community that family imagery might suggest, the culture promoted a degree of atomization, particularly among "those less favored by fortune," as the more genteel frequently referred to the poor. With few exceptions, the mature Second Empire was spared major challenges to its order "from below."[22]

Political and social patterns began to shift noticeably, however, by the early 1880s, and disorder loomed both on plantations and in the cities. The intramural political battles of the elite had begun to take on a sharper tone after a ministerial crisis in 1868, which spurred the formation of new parties, most of which called themselves Republican.[23] This trend worsened in the years that followed, so that the unity of the ruling bloc seemed in doubt during the struggles over abolition in the 1880s. In part, the new divisiveness reflected the changing fortunes of different regions of the Empire. Whereas regions that had always been less dependent on slave labor in their principal economic sectors—such as Rio Grande do Sul in the South and Amazonas in the North—and others that were experiencing the decadence of slave-based export production—such as Ceará in the Northeast—were more open to gradual reforms to end slavery, the old, declining coffee zones of Rio de Janeiro, Minas Gerais, and eastern São Paulo clung tenaciously to the institution. Meanwhile, the newer and wealthier coffee zones of western São Paulo had the means to buy slaves from the North and South and supported slavery until the very eve of abolition. At that point, convinced that they could afford a switch to legally free labor and exhausted by years of massive flights of captives from their plantations, western Paulistas did an about-face, allowing emancipation to pass in the form of the "Golden Law" of 13 May 1888.[24] Also at work in the transitions of the later Empire was the appearance of true ideological diversity among the elite.

Beginning in higher education, and among the military and some self-titled Republicans, Positivism supplied a powerful language through which to lodge complaints during this period.[25] The Positivist theorist with the greatest impact in Porto Alegre and across Brazil, Comte, was a thinker obsessed with categorization and progress. He believed that the sciences, first of all, existed in a hierarchical order, moving from the simpler and more abstract to the more complex and empirical; the study of society—"sociology," a term he is credited with coining—was at the apex of the sciences. Societies, which he saw as based on systems of ideas, also moved through history from the more general to the more specific, as their foundational principles moved from the theological to the metaphysical to the positive, or scientific. A truly scientific knowledge of society, and an administration informed by that knowledge, were necessary for humankind to achieve its ultimate and highest state. Bearing as it did the seeming objectivity and progressiveness of science, this philosophy gave disaffected elite and more middling segments of the population a discursive tool to use against entrenched interests and the received bases of their power.[26] This tendency fit well with the growth, in size and complexity, of city populations. The "Vintem" riots that broke out in the imperial capital, with some Positivist encouragement, as Rio de Janeiro passed from 1879 into 1880 signaled that these urban groups might constitute new political forces outside the elite.[27]

Although segments of the urban nonelites participated in emancipationist activism in various regions, it was really the coming of the Republic that promised to bring these young groups into public politics.[28] The removal of the monarchy after sixty-seven years (1822–89) left much up in the air; as Renato Lessa has written, the change forced the country to consider such basic questions as "who was part of the political community, what would the relations be like between *polis* and *demos* or between the central power and the provinces, how would the parties be organized and how would political identities be defined."[29] The new regime was not the product of a popular uprising, however, but a largely military coup d'état. Moreover, the presence of urban masses in political manifestations on the streets of the national capital faded by the mid-1890s, when a civilian, oligarchic Liberal government took hold; despite episodic bouts of serious labor unrest, the First Republic was to be an elitist and exclusionary state.[30]

Porto Alegre from Empire to Republic: Looking at Postcolonial Brazil from "Below"

Porto Alegre and Rio Grande do Sul were at once examples of and exceptions to the broad developments outlined so far. Digging into the rich case of the Porto Alegre region, at the far southern corner of Brazil, can therefore help further the contributions of scholars working outside the Center-South, decentering the history of postcolonial Brazil in the geographic sense.[31] At least as important, however, the strategy taken here is to locate formal politics as just one realm in a political-cultural universe, thus decentering the political history of the Second Empire and early First Republic in a more theoretical manner. The detailed examination of the place of "the political" within the larger set of relations of power in this regional society will give a new perspective on the evolution of political culture in one city and, with some careful speculation, in Brazil more widely.

To begin with the more abstract, theoretical decentering: anthropologist John Gledhill has identified the supposed autonomy of official politics from other realms of society as "one of the key *ideological* dimensions of Western 'modernity.'"[32] Certainly in Porto Alegre, as in the rest of postcolonial Brazil, the distinction between, on the one hand, the "high" Politics of elections, parliaments, and constitutions and, on the other, the "low" politics of relations of power experienced in the daily lives of men and women was assumed to be so basic as to go undiscussed; it was simply commonsensical. As Antonio Gramsci suggested in the early twentieth century, however, those ideas that seem "common sense" lie at the core of worldviews.[33] In fact, the history of the construction of a categorical boundary between "the political" and other cultural practices is crucial for an understanding of the 1845–95 period in Porto Alegre and Brazil.[34]

Both the Liberals who dominated Porto Alegre up to the 1880s and the Positivists who followed them in control of the region were antidemocratic, but the transition from Liberal to Positivist rule signified a profound cultural and political shift. Whether or not they had been among the originators of modern nationalism—as Benedict Anderson has famously described North and South American elites in the late eighteenth and early nineteenth centuries—these Gaúchos adapted North Atlantic conceptions of the nation that assumed that only part of the population was rational and civilized enough to rule.[35] During the period of seigneurial Liberal dominance, this notion underlay policies of generally excluding other segments—all women and slaves, as well as most free poor men—from public and official practices of governance.[36] The white European immigrants who began to arrive in significant numbers after 1845 presented a quandary, in this respect, for essentially clientelist Liberals. As we shall see, local elites looked to these Germans and Italians as bearers of the European values so widely admired in Brazil; at the same time, however, such values might enable the immigrants to cross the border into full and active citizenship. As Europeans and new arrivals, the immigrants thus represented a potential challenge from outside the culture. Those already relegated in Brazil to comparatively lowly, "subpolitical" positions in the country, moreover, might become threats from below.

Because of the risks involved in attempting to gain full membership in the official nation, few plebeians in Porto Alegre became revolutionaries, those who, in Octavio Paz's paraphrase of Ortega y Gassett, try "to correct the uses themselves rather than the mere abuses of them."[37] Clearly, they were all *political* beings, choosing various tactics as they negotiated power relations in all their dealings with others; as Carlos A. M. Lima has argued, daily life *was* political life for those excluded from official politics.[38] We cannot, however, assume that breaching the walls around official citizenship was a goal for plebeians in Porto Alegre or elsewhere in Brazil after the consolidation of the nation-state and during the Second Empire; indeed, the evidence suggests that it was not. Rather, nonelite women and men usually strove to engage the ideals and practices of seigneurial Liberalism in attempts to maximize autonomy for themselves and their families in a culture of patronage and favor. More specifically, each wanted individually to become as much of a *sovereign*—in Carl Schmitt's sense of "he who decides on the state of exception"—as his or her status would allow.[39] Thus, while apparently staying within seigneurial relations, plebeian initiatives always contained, as an undercurrent, plans of change, which as a rule meant persuading patrons to respect as *rights* the physical mobility, family unity, or working and living conditions that had begun as privileges or concessions. If this did not make plebeians into fully sovereign actors, it promised at least to lessen their absolute dependence on patrons. Elites themselves realized that this reinvention of seigneurial relations could be a threat to their power; legal commentator Francisco Luis warned in 1885, for example, that an inferior's assumption of rights in his relationship with a *senhor* would tarnish the latter's power: "As soon as a superior is constituted as being in obligation to his inferior, to his subaltern, the superior will lose his moral force, that independence and liberty of action which he should have over his inferior; and at the same time the inferior will lose the obedience and respect which he should have and hold toward his superior."[40] With the rare exceptions of those who sought to destroy or definitively flee their society, the plebeian men and women of Porto Alegre thus tried to make adjustments to seigneurial Liberalism, to constitute obligations on their patrons from within existing relations of power.

The orientation of both elite and nonelite strategies was, however, undergoing a visible transformation by the 1880s, one that accelerated after the conflictive rise of the Positivists in the Republic. The increasingly complex urban population, along with open demonstrations of elite fractiousness on the subject of slavery and other matters, as well as some elite groups' new willingness to involve sectors of the *povo* in formal political spaces and actions, redrew the cultural possibilities for plebeians. Elite men strove to guard the borders of "the political," but they began to allow certain women or specific, organized segments of the nonelite population to cross, temporarily and conditionally, into this realm. The Positivists' project for a "new regime of ideas" did not seek to overturn social hierarchies; rather, the PRR aimed at the creation of a more centralized, authoritarian government, albeit one that would mobilize plebeians to combat partisan rivals and, more grandly, to realize the very Comtean combination of "order and progress." The circumstances of the period, though, also spurred previously excluded groups to claim more of a recognized and influential place in the official nation. If they normally showed obeisance toward powerful partisan leaders, they were nonetheless seeking a kind of inclusion—perhaps a "quotidian exercise of citizenship," as historian Eduardo Silva would have it—that they had not publicly pursued before.[41] This new condition might then give them even greater sovereignty, more like that enjoyed exclusively up to this point by wealthy and well-connected men. In the process, formal, no longer merely contingent and de facto, rights emerged as a goal for plebeians.

Tracing the history of the line between quotidian relations of power and formal *P*olitics thus allows us to gauge the changes that occurred in Porto Alegre over the course of the second half of the nineteenth century. Both elite and plebeian political cultures had undergone significant revisions. By considering these shifts in terms of the place and the definition of "the political" in this particular case, as mentioned earlier, we can achieve a decentered perspective on the history of postcolonial Brazil. The manner and timing of the specific transformations in Porto Alegre suggest that an inclusionary style of politics may have appeared earlier in at least one part of Brazil than scholars have previously argued; if it was not yet full-blown mass or populist politics, the Positivist Republican culture that emerged in the early First Republic clearly involved a wider swath of society in the spaces and practices of official politics than had the years of seigneurial Liberalism. Moreover, the experience of political change in Porto Alegre shows that Positivism—generally and correctly taken to be an elitist philosophy—could help create the political opportunity for an incipient incorporation of plebeians into the formal *P*olitical realm—a role that Liberalism had played in late eighteenth- and early nineteenth-century Brazil and, as several authors have argued, in other Latin American nation-states.[42]

Finally, the conclusions drawn here dare to complicate the majestic, if tragic, narratives of modern Brazilian history with which scholars like Sérgio Buarque de Holanda have graced us. Adopting a thematic and chronological focus on the contending parties and key issues in the negotiation of "high" and "low" politics in Porto Alegre from 1845 to 1895, this work casts doubt on Buarque de Holanda's dark judgment that "the apparent triumph of a principle has never meant in Brazil—or in the rest of Latin America—more than the triumph of one personalism over another."[43] If the Positivists in Porto Alegre were not able to restructure society with their "new regime of ideas," their rise brought about more than just the annointing of a new ruler, more even than the irruption of plebeian voices in spaces previously closed off to them. It represented the potential start of a new system of rule, one that did not bring revolution or another form of emancipation, perhaps, but that recast relations among the elite, the state, and the *povo*. This broad transition, and the interplay of plebeian and elite initiatives within it, forms the central theme of this book.

1

"Our Compatriots Are Vagrants"

Work, Morality, and the Shaping of a New Povo, *1845–1880*

> The rude populace does not admit reason, commits crimes left and right, for which motive we should do what is best for the people, but not what the people want.
>
> *João Machado de Bitencourt, Domingos Roiz Ribas, Bernardo dos Santos Menezes, and Alexandre de Abreu Valle, 11 February 1828*

In 1845, as they pondered the reconstruction of their province after a decade of civil war, elites in Porto Alegre faced the same tough, practical questions that had confronted their counterparts after other regional revolts flared up across Brazil in the 1817–45 period—indeed, the same questions that plagued the country's still-young national government when the final major rebellion (the Praiera) was quelled in Pernambuco just three years later. How could they restore production on plantations and ranches, many of which had been devastated in Rio Grande do Sul's Farroupilha Revolution and other violent regional uprisings? How could they protect or even strengthen social hierarchies when tens of thousands of plebeians had stepped outside old relationships of dependence—and many perhaps retained the dreams, and even the arms, of their rebellions? What sort of political arrangement would result from the central government's triumph over challenges from the provinces?

These problems did not allow for easy or definitive answers. Indeed, the new peace suffered nagging tensions after midcentury, despite the undeniable victory that the imperial state had achieved in Brazil—and the firm hold that planters and merchants of the Center-South had established over that state by the later 1840s. This was true in provinces such as Pará and Bahia, where uprisings had threatened to break out into generalized revolution through the 1830s, and held even more clearly in Rio Grande do Sul, where antigovernment rebels had generally maintained control over their plebeian followers. The comparatively weak threat from below in Rio Grande do Sul, as José Honório Rodrigues has pointed out, meant that the "pacification" of the Farroupillha carried with it little of the vindictive brutality often implied by the term in Brazil and elsewhere.[1] Indeed, in Porto Alegre, the chief of imperial forces, Luiz Alves de Lima e Silva (then Baron, later Count and then Duke of Caxias), used the "natural" language of the family to proclaim in 1845 not only the end of the Farroupilha but also the dawning of a stronger national union: "The brothers against whom we fought rejoice with us today and already obey the legitimate government of the Brazilian Empire. His Majesty the Emperor has ordered . . . that we forget the past, and very positively recommended in the same decree that those Brazilians not be juridically or in another manner persecuted for the acts that they may have committed during the time of revolution. . . . From this day forward, may unity and tranquility be our banner!"[2] Even as Caxias welcomed his wayward "brothers" back into the national family, however, resentments simmered on, in Porto Alegre as throughout the Empire.[3]

The political centralization that accompanied national consolidation fueled some of the lingering bitterness, as provincial elite factions fought among themselves and against the Court (as the imperial capital of Rio de Janeiro was known) for greater influence and resources. The Gaúcho Liberal politician Félix Xavier da Cunha expressed such sentiments when he denounced the Empire's behavior toward his province as verging on the scandalous: "I say with all frankness . . .that, in relation to the Court, the province of Rio Grande do Sul can be considered a bastard son, to whom is denied a share in the social benefits that, if they are scarce for other provinces, are even more so for our own. . . . And yet we are happy . . . because at least they leave us, in compensation (because they cannot take it away from us), the glory of being the heroic bulwark of the Brazilian nationality."[4] Da Cunha's words exemplify the specific rhetoric that Gaúchos employed in their claims —based on the "tribute of blood"—that their province, strategically located on the frontier with Argentina, had paid historically.[5] Beyond that, though, they also suggest that not all regional elites were satisfied with the place allotted them in the imperial family as it was reconstituted under the national patriarch, Emperor Dom Pedro II, in the 1840s and 1850s.[6]

Other threads of discourse in the post-1845 years hint at anxieties not about centralizing elite factions in Rio de Janeiro but about other, much humbler, sectors within the province. While working out the details of the new peace, elites in Porto Alegre and across Brazil also strove to implement projects to refashion their society's plebeians—"the last class of society," as Caxias described them—into a populace more to their own liking.[7] Like their peers in the rest of Brazil, Gaúcho elites evaluated the character and potential of their regional *povo* according to European standards—and found their compatriots wanting. Indeed, given the existence of flourishing colonies of German and other European immigrants just upriver from Porto Alegre, these Gaúchos could reasonably hope for an influx of European immigrants who might improve, if not entirely supplant, the less worthy Africans and Brazilians then forming the popular classes of society. This is not to say, however, that elites neglected the non-European majority. On the contrary, much like elites throughout the Empire, Gaúcho leaders devoted significant time and energy to questions involving such so-called national workers. Throughout the period from 1845 to 1880, elites in Porto Alegre, in fact, debated a series of measures designed to turn the plebeians they had into a people that was, as legislator Dr. João Pereira da Silva Borges Fortes described it in 1851, "well-behaved [*morigerado*], hardworking, industrious, respectful of the laws and of the authorities charged with enforcing their execution."[8]

This ideal people would not, it must be noted, form a body of politically active individuals; the redeemed popular sectors would remain a *povo* (or perhaps, *povão*, with the greater sense of rudeness that the augmentative adds in the Portuguese) of dependent plebeians, and not a Tocquevillean, democratic "people." After all, Borges Fortes's list of attributes to be cultivated among the "national" poor stressed, more than anything else, compliance with the demands of employers and officials. At most, as historian Angela Alonso has observed of the Second Empire generally, ruling groups might entertain the fiction that common men's "political representation was made through the *paterfamilias*" (with women and the enslaved lacking even this ostensible voice).[9] For all except the paterfamilias, then, little remained—or should remain, in the dominant view—except dependence; resisting this status or merely trying to make it a negotiable relationship, from an elite perspective, amounted to "vagrancy." This "ideology of vagrancy" (*ideologia da vadiagem*), as such scholars as Laura de Mello e Souza and Lúcio Kowarick have labeled elite attitudes toward their social inferiors, gave elites a language with which to address the troubling initiatives of slaves and free workers who refused to take their places in a seigneurial idyll.[10]

Only sporadically, however, did elite efforts to build new tools of "moralization" have tangible results. In Porto Alegre as in the rest of the country, politicians' lofty schemes for systems of schools, churches, agricultural and military colonies, and new police corps produced at best slow and uneven growth of such institutions.[11] One of the topics that brought forth some of the most heated and at the same time most thoughtful debates in the Gaúcho capital was precisely a failed plan to both help and refashion the *povo*. The Beggars' Asylum (Asilo de Mendicidade) project of 1857 was not the most sweeping reform proposed in these years; it simply called for the construction of a charitable establishment to care for the beggars of Porto Alegre.[12] As the newspaper *Correio do Sul* noted, however, the project achieved remarkable prominence in the political discourse of the day: "The galleries [of the Provincial Assembly] fill up and follow assiduously the debates that portray social life in all its aspects, all of its folds, all of its mysteries, now discovering the plague that infects it, . . . now the means that science has imagined to combat [the illness]." The nature of the discourse led the debates far beyond the issue of the Asylum itself; describing the addresses in the Assembly, the *Correio*'s editor marveled at "the persistence with which the generally young [deputies] . . . descend carefully to all the details of social arithmetic, to look for a possible solution to those great questions attached to the current state of civilization."[13] The Asylum provided, that is, an opportunity for political elites in Porto Alegre to expound upon their broad visions of society and its component classes. The Asylum debates will therefore serve us here as a window into more general elite positions. In order to understand the dominant elite attitudes toward the *povo*, we will examine the sets of questions with which the discussions of the Asylum resonated most strongly—regarding slavery and vagrancy—after a brief look at the political, social, and economic setting of reform initiatives in midcentury Rio Grande do Sul.

The Context of Reform Projects, 1845–1880

Porto Alegre and its province were undergoing massive changes by the middle of the nineteenth century, so much so that the city could seem "entirely new" to a Belgian noblewoman visiting in 1857.[14] From a Portuguese colonial outpost against the threat of Spanish encroachment from the Río de la Plata region in the south, Rio Grande do Sul became in the early nineteenth century one of the fastest-growing economic regions in Brazil.[15] In both its formative and mature stages, Rio Grande do Sul was in essence a secondary economy within Brazil, mainly producing goods for consumption in the export agricultural centers of the Northeast and Center-South regions.[16] In the early eighteenth century, this activity had centered on raising mules and livestock that were sold for use on the plantations of the Center-South and especially in the then-booming mines of Minas Gerais.[17] The trail that snaked its way from Gaúcho pastures over the *serra* (highlands) into Santa Catarina and finally up to the market town of Sorocaba, São Paulo, was one of the marks of the integration the mining economy fostered across most of colonial Brazil. By the second half of the eighteenth century, with the mining economy in decay, Rio Grande do Sul would have to find other products to export to Brazilian markets. At a time of a general boom in commercial agriculture across Brazil—and spurred by the imperial government's introduction of Azorean colonists—wheat became a key crop for Gaúchos, making the province the "breadbasket" (*celeiro*) of Brazil before imports from the United States, along with the political uncertainty of the era, crushed Gaúcho wheat production.[18]

As wheat production fell off, that of *charque* (dried beef) and other pastoral goods emerged as the great economic motor of Rio Grande do Sul. Purchased mostly to feed slaves in plantation zones in Brazil and abroad, *charque* transformed the province.[19] Although always vulnerable to competition from rival producers in Buenos Aires and the Estado Oriental (present-day Uruguay), its production cemented the dominance of the extensive latifundia in much of the province and led to the rise of the cities of Rio

Grande and Pelotas, focal points of *charqueadas* (*charque*-producing plants) and commerce, as the economic centers of Rio Grande do Sul.[20] The wealth from *charque* and derived goods—the trade especially lucrative when internecine wars in Argentina or Uruguay cut those countries' exports—would create what geographer Stephen Bell has called a "tallow aristocracy," as well as a large slave-labor force serving that class, in Pelotas.[21] Despite the sandbar that made transportation from its docks a risky proposition, Rio Grande would in turn blossom as the gateway for pastoral exports from and manufactured imports to Pelotas; Rio Grande, in the enthusiastic words of one provincial president, served as "the emporium of all commerce in the province."[22]

It was the awkward position of the cattle and *charque* elites that ultimately pulled the province into the regional revolt of the Farroupilha. Emerging as a dominant class in the southern tip of Brazil, the ranchers and *charqueadores* (owners of *charqueadas*) of the *campanha* (rolling cattle lands, or pampa) and southern littoral of Rio Grande do Sul were frustrated by the greater power of other elites in the newly independent Empire. By the early 1830s, powerful planters and merchants from sugar- and coffee-exporting provinces had proved unsympathetic to the demands of their Gaúcho colleagues. Tensions escalated over a number of issues that were vitally important to the pastoral elites in the South, from tariffs on the imported salt used in *charqueadas* to duties to protect domestic *charque* from the cheaper products of Argentine and Uruguayan competitors. Although *charqueadores* and ranchers would not form a united rebel front—most of the former chose to side with the government—enough of these pastoral elites would rise up with their dependents and other armed supporters to create a serious threat to Brazilian territorial integrity.[23]

In contrast with the pastoral zones of the province, the economic might of Porto Alegre, which had been tied to cereal agriculture, declined in the first decades after Brazilian Independence. Impressive gains awaited the close of civil war in 1845.[24] This development grew largely in relation to the emergence of the so-called colonial (i.e., immigrant- or *colono*-based) economy of the highland region of the province. Although navigation between Porto Alegre and the ocean was complicated by the natural obstructions at Rio Grande, the provincial capital enjoyed a good transportation system in the network of rivers that fanned out from the city up into the highlands.[25] Its location often inspired observers like provincial president João Lins Cansansão

Sinimbú to enthusiastic forecasts of prosperity: "When I contemplate the situation of this beautiful City located at the mouth of the majestic rivers before it, when, following their course, I see the good lands that border on them in the valleys they form, when at a greater distance I discover those great highlands, which are a true treasure, I find reunited the three principal conditions for the life and progress of agricultural colonies: productive lands, easy and cheap transportation, and a certain market."[26] Beginning with a colony of German immigrants the imperial government established at São Leopoldo in 1824, this zone received thousands of European immigrants throughout the rest of the century. From the last year of the Farroupilha until 1863, a total of 13,167 Germans arrived in the region. This ethnic group would maintain its predominance until the mid-1870s, after which point Italians formed the largest component of immigrants to the province.

What was critical for the Porto Alegre economy was that the communities of Europeans and the small to medium-sized farms outside them moved from subsistence agriculture to the production of surplus for markets in Porto Alegre and elsewhere by the 1850s. In fact, the war years of 1835–45 gave an important early impetus to this trade; with the capital often cut off from other suppliers, the colonists of São Leopoldo found in Porto Alegre eager buyers of whatever foodstuffs they might take there.[27] In the decades after the war, colonists and their descendants moved into other forms of production, and again the provincial capital would benefit from their dynamism. Porto Alegre remained the center of trade for artisanry and simple manufactures, as well as agricultural goods, from the colonies. In 1863, in fact, one Porto Alegre newspaper lamented only that the colonists could not produce enough to build up export trade to other nations.[28] To meet demand from the capital, the opening of new transportation systems between Porto Alegre and major colonies tightened the links between the city and its hinterlands after midcentury. Even small-scale commerce by canoe had been a profitable venture for enterprising individuals through midcentury (and would continue on for decades); now, the introduction of steamship routes (in 1852) and rail lines between the capital and the highlands (in 1874, between Porto Alegre and São Leopoldo, extended to Novo Hamburgo in 1876) vastly expanded the possibilities of profitable trade in the subregion.[29]

As it grew, the urban economy also diversified; soon it had its own substantial sector of artisans and small-scale manufacturers. At the onset of the Paraguayan War (1865–70), one of several international disputes that touched Rio Grande do Sul over the course of the century, the city of Porto Alegre proper housed some 81 *fábricas* (factories), with another 480 in surrounding districts. Despite their small size (they averaged just 3.5 workers each), these establishments reflected the emergence of a more complex urban economy.[30] The conflict that ranged briefly onto Gaúcho soil—with the Paraguayan invasion of the western part of the province in 1865—gave further impetus to primitive manufacturing, most notably with the expansion of the workshops of Porto Alegre's War Arsenal, which would come to employ well over two hundred men by 1867.[31]

Even though it could not overcome the dominance of cattle and *charque* at the regional level, the colony-based economy thus refashioned Porto Alegre. In 1858, the traveler Robert Avé-Lallemant captured the importance of the colonies to the capital's expanding economic might when he wrote, "Everywhere you hear it said, from Brazilians and from Germans: 'What would Porto Alegre be without São Leopoldo?'"[32] With the immigrant colonies, Porto Alegre became a bustling metropolis from midcentury on. Its major downtown streets and plazas teemed with local residents and visitors doing business; other roads were extended out of the old city to link the farms and commercial enterprises springing up on the outskirts of the urban center.[33] The economic activity burgeoning in and around the city nearly matched the political clout concentrated in the Praça da Matriz, the central plaza lined by the symbols of established power—the city council, the Provincial Assembly, the palace of the provincial president, and the cathedral—along with a sign of the increasingly cosmopolitan self-image of the Porto Alegre elite, the Teatro São Pedro.

Economic growth and immigration also had obvious effects on the population of Porto Alegre. At the turn of the century, Porto Alegre had been just one of several small cities in a diplomatically strategic but sparsely colonized corner of Brazil. Porto Alegre appears in an 1803 census with a population of 3,927, overshadowed by the city of Rio Grande's 8,390 and not much larger than towns like Rio Pardo (3,739), Triunfo (3,037), and Cachoeira (3,283). After midcentury, however, Porto Alegre began to outpace these cities, a tendency that would only become more accentuated by the end of the Empire in 1889. The census of 1890 reported populations of 52,421 for Porto Alegre; 41,591 for Pelotas; and just 24,653 for Rio Grande.[34]

1 Population of Porto Alegre and Its Province

Year (source)	*Porto Alegre*	*Rio Grande do Sul*
1803 (a)	3,927	59,142
1808 (b)	6,035	
1814 (a)	6,111	70,656
1846 (a)	12,355*	149,363
1856 (c)	17,226	
1858 (a)	16,313	285,444
1858 (d)	29,723	282,547
1862 (e)		370,446
1863 (e)		392,725
1872 (f)	43,998	446,962
1890 (g)	52,421	897,453
1900 (h)	73,674	

Sources:

(a) FEE, *De Província*, 49–51, 60, 66, 79–83.

(b) Magalhães, "Almanak," 69.

(c) "Quadro Estatistico da Cidade de Porto Alegre, Capital da Província de S. Pedro, organizado no mes de abril de 1856 pelo Chefe de Polícia interino da mesma província, Dr. Luiz Alves Leite de Oliveira Bello, Estatística," m. 2, l. 532, AHRS.

(d) RS, Pres., *Relatorio* (1859), 76 and annexo.

(e) Camargo, *Quadro Estatistico e Geographico*, 75.

(f) *Recenseamento da população . . . 1872*, 17: 205–6.

(g) *Synopse do recenseamento*, 103, 107.

(h) Hahner, *Poverty and Politics*, 7.

*Includes free persons only.

Along with this growth came a richer ethnic mixture in the capital. Many Germans and Italians stayed in Porto Alegre rather than trekking up into colonies in the interior; later on, many more immigrants and their descendants migrated down to the city in search of brighter economic prospects.[35] The foreign observers who remarked approvingly that Porto Alegre seemed "in a manner a German settlement," however, overstated matters.[36] Despite the region's subsequent image as racially "whiter" than the rest of Brazil, Porto Alegre's population exhibited tremendous ethnic and racial diversity.[37] The imperial census of 1872, for example, reported that 54.8 percent of the population was *branco* (white), 25.9 percent *pardo* (Afro-Brazilian), 16.9 percent *preto* (black, a term usually reserved for slaves and ex-slaves), and 2.3 percent *caboclo* (of mixed Amerindian-European race).[38] Africans and Afro-Brazilians thus represented significant elements of the city's populace. Indeed, the percentage of the population that consisted of the enslaved was comparable to that of the more famously Afro-Brazilian cities of Rio de Janeiro and Salvador. To a great extent, the members of such groups maintained separate ethnic identities. Not only Africans and their descendants but also Germans, Portuguese, and other groups formed social and cultural associations based on ethnic identities. This diverse populace thus had lines of ethnic and racial division running through it.[39]

These distinctions among members of the *povo* should not, however, keep us from seeing the features they shared in the experience of their daily lives, as well as in broader terms of social power. Immigrants, free and enslaved Afro-Brazilians, and other plebeians inhabited the same tenements (called *cortiços*, or "beehives") on the same dirty city streets and alleyways. Slaves often worked outside their master's home or business, rented out by their *senhor* to work in a particular place (as an *escravo de aluguel*) or seeking temporary employment on their own (as an *escravo de ganho*). Whether *de aluguel* or *de ganho*, such slaves would remit part or all of the wages they received to their *senhor*.[40] The range of jobs that slaves performed was vast. A visitor to Porto Alegre in this period would have seen slaves working as porters at the docks; as domestic servants in the houses of the better-off; as agricultural workers on the *chácaras* (small truck farms) that dotted the edges of the city; or as sailors, street vendors, or in any number of other occupations. In 1872, by far the greatest number of the city's enslaved inhabitants (8,155 in total) toiled as domestic servants (2,978), with an almost equal number performing miscellaneous forms of labor (with 2,117 listed as "without profession" and 853 as servants and day laborers) and some 1,498 engaged in agriculture.[41] Much of their work put them side by side with free laborers. This was especially true of work in artisans' shops, where slaves frequently served in the less noble trades, such as shoe repair and tailoring. So great was the number of slaves in artisanry, in fact, that in 1850 one German promoter of colonization felt compelled to advise potential immigrants that "metalworkers . . . manage good earnings, because their job is one of the few in which slaves are almost not employed."[42]

The 1864 survey of *fábricas* referred to above attests not only to the rise of artisanry and simple manufacture but also to the mixing of ethnicities in the workplace. Of the total of 1,944 workers in the ceramic and other work-

2 Slave Population of Porto Alegre and Its Province

	Porto Alegre		*Rio Grande do Sul*	
Year (source)	*Slaves*	*Percentage*	*Slaves*	*Percentage*
1814 (a)	2,312	37.8		
1856 (b)	5,146	29.9		
1858 (c, d)	4,443	27.2	70,880	25.1
1872 (e)	8,155	18.5	67,791	15.6
1883 (d)			62,138	8.9
1884 (f)	5,790	14.5		

Sources:

(a) FEE, *De Província*, 50.

(b) "Quadro Estatistico da Cidade de Porto Alegre, Capital da Província de S. Pedro, organizado no mes de abril de 1856 pelo Chefe de Polícia interino da mesma província Dr. Luiz Alves Leite de Oliveira Bello, Estatística," m. 2, l. 532, AHRS. This census lists an additional 2,664 residents of the outlying areas (*subúrbios*) of the city but does not break that figure down by legal status.

(c) "População da província no fim do anno de 1858, segundo o mappa tirado pelas listas de familias," Estatística, m. 1, l. 531, AHRS.

(d) Bakos, *RS: Escravismo e abolição*, 18.

(e) *Recenseamento da população . . . 1872*, 17: 205–6.

(f) Monti, *O abolicionismo*, 156.

shops surveyed, 27 percent (526) were free Brazilians, 10 percent free foreign-born, and 63 percent slaves.[43] In fact, within Rio Grande do Sul, the *charque* plants were the only large-scale export production centers that relied centrally on slave labor.[44] Elsewhere, on the cattle ranches of the southern plains and in cities like Porto Alegre, slavery was a constant presence, but nowhere near the economic pillar that it was in the coffee- and sugar-plantation regions of the country. In Porto Alegre, slaves represented just one distinct element in a heterogeneous urban working class; the enslaved and free poor, as Thomas Holloway has argued for Rio de Janeiro in the same years, "were considered by the coercive arm of the emerging state to be in a similarly hostile relationship with the dominant class."[45] They fell, that is, on the same side of what one Gaúcho military man identified in 1859 as the fundamental division between a "class . . . of well-off citizens" and a "class of those less favored by fortune."[46]

The seigneurial Liberal political culture that these groups made and remade together was, as noted earlier, elitist and exclusionary. The politics of

3 Slave Populations in Other Brazilian Cities

City	*Year (source)*	*Slaves*	*Total*	*Percentage*
Salvador				
	1835 (a)	27,500	65,500	42.0
	1855 (b)			27.5
	1872 (c)	16,468	129,109	12.8
Rio de Janeiro				
	1838 (d)	37,137	97,162	38.2
	1849 (d)	78,855	205,906	38.3
	1872 (e)	48,939	274,972	17.8

Sources:

(a) Reis, *Slave Rebellion*, 6

(b) Andrade, *A mão de obra escrava*, 29

(c) *Recenseamento da população . . . 1872*, 3: 508–12

(d) Karasch, *Slave Life*, 65–66

(e) *Recenseamento da população . . . 1872*, 19: 1–2.

those legally included in the nation came to be dominated by Liberalism not only in its general ideological orientation but also in a more particular, partisan sense. (The political culture of the officially excluded will be examined in chapter 3.) Except for the ultimate hegemony of the Liberal Party, developments in Porto Alegre generally paralleled those at the more exalted levels of imperial politics in the period of relative partisan peace that followed the Farroupilha. In the regional as well as the national capital, that is, the year 1852 began a decade or so of declared cooperation between the Liberal and Conservative Parties that had taken shape over the course of the 1840s. In Porto Alegre, however, the situation involved, as it often did from Independence to the end of the nineteenth century, somewhat more internal conflict. While leaders of the local Conservative and Liberal Parties—namely Pedro Rodrigues Fernandes Chaves (Baron of Quaraim) and Israel Rodrigues Barcelos—had joined together in the Liga (League), supposedly so that the province could present a stronger, more unified voice in national debates, a Contra-Liga (Counter-League) sprang up almost immediately to oppose the abuses of patronage that "Liguistas" were allegedly committing. At the same time, the Counter-League, most of whose members soon re-formed as the Partido Liberal Progressista (Progressive Liberal Party), engaged in its own personalist politics under the leadership of Manoel Marques de Souza (Baron of Porto Alegre). Finally, by 1863, Félix Xavier da Cunha, together with the two men who would dominate the Liberal Party in Rio Grande do Sul for decades (Gaspar Silveira Martins and Manuel Luís Osório), felt compelled to call for a more exact, and ideological, definition of parties; foreshadowing the appeals that the Positivist Republicans would issue in the 1880s, da Cunha and others demanded a new "politics of ideas." Although a similar split was occurring nationally, unlike their counterparts in Rio, the Gaúcho Liberals behind da Cunha and his allies insisted their followers proclaim exclusive loyalty to their new "Historical" Liberal Party.[47]

By instilling a strong sense of party discipline and harping on the injustices that Rio Grande do Sul suffered at the hands of the central government, these new Liberals managed to construct a formidable partisan machine. They could not always overcome the obstacles that the Empire's centralized system erected, but they were able to win elections in their province and its capital even when Conservatives held the reins in Parliament—a sign of the unusual support they had built up in their province, since the party that dominated Parliament also enjoyed tremendous control over electoral mechanisms in the Empire.[48] Gaúcho Liberals held on to their power through profound changes in Rio Grande do Sul, from the early 1860s up to the challenges of the new politics that took shape in the 1880s and 1890s.

The Asylum Project: Beggars False and True

As could be expected of legislative debates on a proposed social program, the arguments over the Beggars' Asylum touched on both partisan and logistical matters. From the beginning, however, the august figures on both sides of the question elevated their rhetoric to the level of social critique. With a systematic logic unusual in Provincial Assembly oratory, they attempted to define the nature of the poor, the means by which their misery might be diminished, and the relations that should prevail between rich and poor in Gaúcho society. As we shall see, their analyses of such questions formed part of elites' general approach to the *povo* in the period under study here. At its most basic, this approach boiled down to the intent to repress the larger share of the *povo* while retraining whatever small fraction elites deemed to be "salvageable." By that means a new *povo*, one that would more readily accept a dependent position in this seigneurial society, might emerge.

The lofty tone and general thematic structure of the Asylum debates became apparent in an early exchange between Félix Xavier da Cunha and José Antonio do Vale Caldre e Fião. Da Cunha expressed sympathy for the unfortunate members of society; after researching the plan for the Beggars' Asylum, however, he warned his colleagues in the Provincial Assembly not to be "seduced by the religious feelings of charity." Based on a careful morphology of beggars, he argued, the only rational option was to oppose the Asylum. In his explication of this position, da Cunha divided the potential recipients of charity into three categories. First, he pointed to the class of the "able-bodied beggars" (*mendigos válidos*), which he defined as those "who, desiring to put into use their active faculties, wishing to live nobly by the product of their efforts and industry, cannot satisfy this desire because of the . . . impediments that civilization itself brings them." In other words, *mendigos válidos* had the will and capacity for labor but through no fault of their own were not able to procure employment. This class, he averred, did not exist in Brazil; it was, rather, a product of large-scale industrialization such as had been taking place in Europe. The introduction of mechanized industries of the type that "generate pauperism" in France and England had not yet occurred in Brazil. Next, he defined the group of the able-bodied poor who, in spite of their ability to work, refused to seek out gainful employment. Much to its detriment, he explained, Brazil had this class in excess. Finally, he described the third category, that of the "invalid beggars" (*mendigos inválidos*), as consisting of poor persons who "because of the state of their health cannot seek the means of providing for their own subsistence."

The conclusions that da Cunha drew from this classification of possible Asylum beneficiaries were harsh. In his estimation, the first type of able-bodied poor, those who actively sought to work, was absent. The second class, physically able but unwilling workers, he deemed unworthy of charity. If they refused to work for a living, da Cunha asserted, they must be persuaded to change their minds, and the government should not spare force in accomplishing this. He argued that it would be more "convenient" for military recruitment to target "those individuals who do not want to work" than "to remove useful hands from agriculture or other industries"; the latter option would only hurt production and families at the state's expense. The invalid poor, finally, would not in da Cunha's view benefit from the Asylum. Taking them away from their families and placing them to vegetate in such an institution would instead do them harm. If they required official assistance, he concluded, they should receive help in their own homes.[49]

Other speakers would soon respond to da Cunha's stinging criticism of the Asylum and the people it might serve; several would provide fireworks of their own. Caldre e Fião, a physician, novelist, and early abolitionist, emerged as one of da Cunha's principal rivals. Caldre e Fião's analysis was much more generous than that of his opponent, but it also centered on preserving the social order through improvement of the poor. He agreed with da Cunha that society was suffering from the growing numbers of poor infesting the streets; Caldre e Fião even specified "slaves abandoned by their masters" as a particularly troublesome group. Like da Cunha, he recognized further that among this population existed a class of "false beggars," those "vagrants . . . who, able to acquire means of subsistence through their labor, do not do so," those who sought charity only because they wished to avoid work. These observations led Caldre e Fião, however, to point to the Asylum as the great answer to the social problem at hand. He declared, first of all, that the province already had the police corps, recruitment, and other means to take care of the most disobedient vagrants. Taking issue with da Cunha's classification, Caldre e Fião went on to assert that not all of the able-bodied beggars were to blame for their condition; the province, he argued, had its share of "honest poverty"—the poverty of those families who persistently sought work, even the lowliest, most menial jobs, but were unable to get by. Like the physically incapacitated, these workers not only needed but deserved official aid. Indeed, he argued that the Asylum could also become useful with regard to common vagrants. Residents of the Asylum would, he explained, be put to work; the recalcitrant and the infirm alike would perform whatever tasks their physical abilities allowed. In this way, Caldre e Fião supported the creation of an institution that would combine charity with vocational training—more a workhouse than a shelter.[50] In his conception, the Beggars' Asylum would thus include not only humanitarian care for the unfortunate but also a program to put all available bodies to work.

Over the course of the debates, other voices would join in. Whether taking sides with da Cunha or with Caldre e Fião, these speakers would share with those representatives a profound concern with social order, a sense that the poor were threatening that order, and the feeling that the *povo* must be altered to keep the social peace and further the material and moral progress of their province. Running through the speeches by such legislators as Felippe Neri, José Cândido Gomes, and Dr. Manoel Pereira da Silva Ubatuba was a horror at the refusal to work—or to work in a properly obedient way—on the part of many members of the lower classes of Gaúcho society. Indeed, for much of the debates this side of the question overwhelmed any consideration of the issue of charity; the problem of vagrancy, so obviously central to the analyses of da Cunha and Caldre e Fião, would dominate discussions of the Asylum. Plebeians' unwillingness to remain dependent—a phenomenon elites derided as a lack of "love of work"—blew the real *povo* up into a force that threatened to become a "black cloud" over the Empire.[51] The signal importance of the Asylum idea for the elite debaters of 1857 was the potential (or lack thereof) the project held for effectively addressing what seemed to these legislators to be the problem of the *povo*.

Slavery and Abolition

In elite considerations of what they thought of as an essentially vagrant *povo*, slaves and the prospect of abolition held a restricted but privileged place. The assessments elite politicians made of the end of slavery—and the problems such a development might entail—linked abolition very closely to the issue of vagrancy. Like vagrancy in general, slavery and abolition raised fears among the elites of a possible breakdown of social hierarchies; as with the broader issue, their preferred responses to the disorderly potential of slavery's decline combined careful elite control of plebeians with reeducation projects to turn some of them into productive and loyal subordinates.

To begin with, one type of freedperson figured in the definitions of potential beneficiaries of the Beggars' Asylum. Caldre e Fião was far from the only Assembly member to point to ex-slaves as a significant portion of the province's indigent population, but he was the strongest champion of the Asylum as a means to help needy freedpersons. This institution would have no higher purpose, he argued, than to care for "the man who . . . [had] passed his entire life in slavery, often serving a barbarous man who calls himself master and abandons him at the end of his days, when because of his dedication, his zeal, his love, he could rightly hope for other recompense."[52] Neri shared this sympathy for the miserable ex-slave but felt compelled to pardon many of the masters who had rid themselves of the expense of maintaining an elderly and unproductive slave. Families who had purchased slaves in periods of affluence but then watched their fortunes decay, he explained, often faced a bitter choice—whether "to let themselves or their slave die of hunger." Even as he thus disputed the barbarity of the *senhores* who sent their slaves into a free life of begging, however, Neri agreed that the government had to address the problem of these "invalids."[53] Despite their minor disagreements, these and other speakers thus treated a specific type of former slave as part of the formula by which to identify the population that deserved official charity.

Slavery also entered into the broader concerns of the Asylum debates and, indeed, of other elite discussions in midcentury Porto Alegre. Elderly ex-slaves reduced to begging worried Caldre e Fião and his colleagues not just as charity cases but also as symbols of the difficulties of the transition from slavery to free labor. The discussion of these freedpersons, for example, led Neri and several other of the Assembly representatives to speak out in favor of legislation to regulate emancipation in the province. Ubatuba looked at the fate of the infirm former slaves and pondered how his society might achieve a just emancipation; "I do not want," he declared, "liberty just in words or writing, I want liberty in practice." This relatively bold statement was a call not for immediate abolition but for a strengthening of the paternalistic strain of master-slave relations. The emancipation of slaves too old to support themselves by their labors was for Ubatuba an illegitimate form of liberation, because it represented a simple abandonment of former dependents by their patrons. Proud of his treatment of his own slaves, he wondered how the province might ensure that all masters show similar responsibility toward the slaves they held and those whom they were going to liberate. The question thus involved not only taking care of unfortunate freedpersons but reinforcing a proper paternalism.[54]

The focus in these 1857 debates on an orderly and paternalistic emancipation, which ran through elite discussions to the end of the 1870s (and beyond, as we shall see in chapter 4), was at once a product of nationwide developments of the 1850s and of provincial conditions. Before midcentury, elite criticisms of slavery and projects for abolition had appeared in Rio Grande do Sul, but they had come from individual and exceptional voices. Perhaps the most forceful abolitionist appeal was that of Antonio José Gonçalves Chaves, whose 1823 *Memórias econômo-políticas sobre a administração pública no Brasil* damned slavery as a multifaceted evil in Brazilian society.[55] Necessarily inefficient, since "the slave, who can by no means expect a reward for his labor, interests himself in consuming without working," slave labor in Gonçalves Chaves's view also held back the Brazilian economy in other ways and poisoned the institutions of family and government. With agriculture turned over to slave labor and foreign imports restraining the development of industry in Brazil, he argued, a large part of the free population fell into "softness, cowardice, ineptitude, and other vices that are fatal to nations."[56] At the same time, the position of slaves in the economy and the immoral spectacle of captivity also prevented the immigration of Europeans who might, with the families and capital they would bring, contribute to the progress of the Empire. The horrible treatment that *senhores* gave their slaves, moreover, could only serve as an unhealthy example for the children of the slave-owning class; out of such a milieu, only a people educated to live in despotism could arise.[57] To stem the damage slavery had inflicted, Gonçalves Chaves concluded, Brazil needed to reduce and ultimately remove slavery itself. No radical, he proposed simply that the government ban the further introduction of slaves into the Empire and regulate public sales of slaves. Given the slave population's inability to reproduce itself, these measures would lead to a gradual and careful diminution of slavery in Brazil. With further caution, the state would also promote voluntary emancipation of slaves by philanthropic associations "when we are certain that our force exceeds that of the black race." Anticipating the "whitening" ideal that would emerge among racial theorists of later generations, he hoped miscegenation would wash away the vices he associated with the enslaved Africans and their surviving progeny.[58]

Despite such determined arguments, projects like that of Gonçalves Chaves held little sway in Rio Grande do Sul until the 1850s.[59] Events at midcentury forced revision of elite attitudes, pulling the abolition of slavery toward the center of political discourse. Key to the sea change in attitudes was the termination of the slave trade with Africa. Most notably in 1831, authorities had previously signed international agreements to end this trade. Until 1850 or so, however, antislave trade legislation had been almost entirely *para inglês ver*—just for show, or literally, "for the English to see." When pressure from England became more than merely diplomatic in the 1840s and 1850s, with British ships chasing slavers into Brazilian waters, the Brazilian government at last pursued effective enforcement of these treaties.[60] Particularly since it came at a time when the expansion of the coffee economy in the Center-South region was creating new demands for slave labor, the end of the slave trade in the early 1850s spurred more serious consideration of the institution of slavery itself. Brazil's was "a naturally decreasing slave population" that depended on the influx of enslaved Africans to maintain its numbers.[61] By shutting off the entrance of new slave workers, the abolition of the African trade forced many Brazilian elites to ponder the ultimate destruction of the entire system of captive labor that was to a great extent the basis of their wealth and status. In 1850, Joaquim José Rodrigues Torres, a leading Conservative politician from the province of Rio de Janeiro, demonstrated such concern when he warned his fellow members of the dominant class that "if we do not take some measure to protect the interests of agriculture, the only industry of Brazil, we will quickly be reduced to the proletarian class."[62] Albeit with variation among regions, elites across Brazil shared Rodrigues Torres's anxiety; the abolition of the African trade was so monumental an event that it spread fear throughout the Empire's ruling classes about preserving social hierarchies.

Gaúcho elites participated in national discussions of slavery and the transition to some as yet undefined system of free labor, but their interest in the matter reflected local circumstances as well as national-level currents of thought. Both the Asylum debates themselves and related discourse in the period after the Farroupilha showed that elites in Porto Alegre worried about the possibly unsettling elimination of slavery. In Rio Grande do Sul and elsewhere outside the economically booming coffee zones, elites may have felt more deeply the possibility that slavery's elimination was now inevitable. As Robert Slenes has demonstrated, the interprovincial slave trade that intensified in the wake of the African trade's abolition did not produce an immediate and massive shift of the slave population within the Empire; still, the new Brazilian trade "constituted a substantial and constant drain of the slave labor force" out of the northeastern, northern, and southern regions.[63] Dominant groups in Rio Grande do Sul thus had to confront the dilution of their slave population. As we have seen earlier, even without a growing slave-based economic sector, the region around Porto Alegre relied heavily enough on slaves for this development to present elites with the prospect of unsettling change. It was for this reason that Neri argued in 1854 for measures to transfer the remaining slaves out of urban occupations and into agriculture, where he felt the need for their labor was more pronounced.[64] Out of a similar concern,

Ubatuba warned in 1851, "It is imperative that we occupy ourselves with the substitution of African hands, which from one day to the next are disappearing among us, and if we do not attend conveniently to this necessity, we will soon have to see the province in a truly lamentable state and will have to suffer the censure of unforgivable lack of foresight."[65] More involved discussions of the implications of the end of the African trade followed Ubatuba's 1852 presentation of a bill that called for a steeper duty on slaves being sold out of the province; the income from this tax was to be used to subsidize the importation of European colonists. His idea met resistance in the Provincial Assembly, but even opponents agreed that elites had to plan carefully for the transformation of the workforce on which their wealth depended. Reacting to his critics, Ubatuba insisted that, while he had no wish to deny the "thought of the century," he was convinced that elites had to preserve their slave force until a new labor system was firmly established. To do otherwise, he averred, would be to "plunge a dagger into our industry, tear up the sources of wealth in our nation."[66] This exchange, then, demonstrated even more vividly than the Asylum debates elites' concern over the apparently inevitable end of slavery. Differences over plans like Ubatuba's did not go beyond divergences of method; elites in Porto Alegre agreed overwhelmingly on the core aim of moving in an orderly fashion away from captive labor.

Cementing elite consensus on this goal was a second local circumstance that shaped attitudes toward slavery in the province (and that will be examined in detail in chapter 3): plebeians' attempts to put their own interpretations of social relations into effect. Although discussed only obliquely in the Asylum debates, the consistent appearance of plebeian resistance provided a backdrop to elite discussions throughout the period. Elite consideration of popular initiative was undeniably most direct and obvious in the actions elites took and the comments they made in response to slave rebellions and other dramatic instances of plebeian unruliness. Discussions of slavery in the Provincial Assembly, newspapers, and other public forums tended to skip over slaves' actions and focus on the economic and, to a lesser extent, moral aspects of the question. Even in such rhetoric, however, elites in Porto Alegre revealed their concern with slaves' initiatives.

Most often this concern took the form of moral denunciations of slaves as vice ridden. At its core, elite antislavery feeling in this period focused on the poor performance of slaves as laborers. For elites in Porto Alegre, this was as much a moral as an economic matter. Some trained their eye on the financial side of the question. One 1853 editorial held, for instance, that slave labor contributed to the backwardness of Brazilian agriculture by tying up capital that could be otherwise applied and by providing only the poor services of "slaves [who were] unintelligent and enemies of work."[67] This last quality—opposition to labor—was for most commentators of the period the principal moral damage that slavery inflicted on Brazil. In explaining why he had opposed the importing of new slaves, Ubatuba made this stance explicit; previously, he related in 1852, many Gaúchos had bought slaves in large numbers, only to see many of them "become lazy in the province, highly immoral workers."[68] As they turned to European immigrants as their preferred substitutes for slave laborers, Gaúcho elites sought to prevent slaves' immoral antagonism toward work from poisoning these new hands. An 1848 proposal to establish a colony near Pelotas, for example, stipulated not only that the *colonos* not bring slaves into their settlement but also that their lands never be cultivated by slave hands.[69] Similarly, the first article of Provincial Law 183 in 1850 prohibited "the introduction of slaves into territory marked for existing colonies and those formed in the future in the Province."[70] Indeed, as we shall see later (in chapter 2), moral qualities like dedication and "love of labor" that elites in Porto Alegre attributed to European workers were part of the appeal of immigration. This moral discourse provided a language with which elites could discuss slaves' resistance. Rather than going into the many forms of troublesome initiatives emanating in the slave population, that is, elites treated the entire issue of resistance as a generalized moral flaw; the spectacular as well as the mundane forms of resistance within popular political culture became in this way reduced to slaves' laziness and lack of affection for their work.

Shaped by the difficulty of maintaining their slave population and the persistence of slave resistance, elite attitudes became ever more critical of the institution of slavery in the 1850s–70s. Increasingly, elites in Porto Alegre were moving toward reformist emancipationist positions, arguing that they had to find mechanisms to exterminate slavery gradually and without endangering the social order. This growing antislavery feeling was clear even in the 1850s and 1860s. Even as they argued that slavery was a necessary evil, elites like Ubatuba clearly recognized its negative characteristics. In 1851, Ubatuba himself proclaimed the need "to take measures to extirpate the canker of Brazilian society, slavery."[71] The later 1860s and early 1870s would introduce new elements into the rhetoric on the evils of slavery. The first innovation of the late 1860s consisted of more explicit projects for abolition. In 1869, for example, a reinvigorated Liberal Party issued a manifesto calling for a series of reforms. Although it had no "intimate relation to the principal object of the program," emancipation was, the manifesto asserted, "a great question of the day, an imperious and urgent necessity of civilization since all States have abolished slavery, and Brazil is the only Christian nation that preserves it." Part of the "mission of the Liberal Party" was in fact "the reclamation of the liberty of so many thousands of men who live in oppression and humiliation." The means proposed to achieve abolition were essentially those that the Conservative Rio Branco cabinet would adopt and pass into law two years later—namely, that all children subsequently born to slave mothers would be free.[72] Other voices would rise before 1871 to support these mechanisms and afterward to criticize their poor implementation.[73] Although somewhat less concrete, calls for voluntary abolition by private citizens also became a common part of antislavery discourse in these years. Newspapers and clubs were eager to praise those *senhores* and organizations that took it upon themselves to grant liberty to slaves. In 1869, for example, *A Reforma* heralded the noble act of a citizen who had honored his wife's birthday by freeing a slave, writing: "Our congratulations to those friends for such beautiful conduct. May they find imitators, and the practical difficulties against which the generous idea of emancipation fights will be dispelled."[74]

The second new thread of antislavery rhetoric that appeared in the late 1860s and 1870s was a more emotional type of appeal. Some of the antislavery positions in these years included condemnations of slavery's influence on the morality of free Brazilians, recalling Gonçalves Chaves's earlier criticisms.[75] The period's sentimental attacks on slavery's effects on the enslaved were, by contrast, unprecedented. Concern over the conditions of ex-slaves had, as we have seen, appeared in the Asylum debates in 1857. It was only in the late 1860s, however, that elites in Porto Alegre made the harm that slavery did to slaves a pillar of their proemancipation arguments. When they decried the "degradation of man" that slavery inflicted, elites now often meant the "enslaved martyrs."[76] Foreshadowing the 1883–84 abolitionist campaign in the city, Caldre e Fião and other elites used private organizations to express their disgust with the suffering captivity inflicted on slaves. Caldre e

Fião, who had been an eager voice for the abolition of the slave trade in Rio de Janeiro before moving back to his home city of Porto Alegre, published an example of this position in the *Revista do Parthenon Litterario*, the journal of one of the organizations that were pushing for gradual emancipation. His poem "O escravo brasileiro" (The Brazilian Slave) not only pointed out the barbarities that slaves endured but also looked forward to a future when such injustice might cease:

> When did I say that I was not free,
> That my country I would not defend,
> . . . .
>
> They deny me all, my brothers in this nation,
> Even the forum of civil rights,
> Honor, pride, noble sentiments,
> That lofty inhabit Brazilian chests.
>
> But be you unjust—even though I
> Pay you with this brotherly heart;
> In industry and arts, in progress together,
> I will be with you in communion most holy.

Writing in the years of the Paraguayan War, a national effort in which thousands of slaves or ex-slaves served, Caldre e Fião attributed to the slave "noble sentiments"—first of patriotism, honor, and pride but also of forgiveness; the slave would be willing to pardon previous crimes against his valorous nature.[77] By portraying the slave in this way, "O escravo brasileiro" provides an extraordinarily strong example of the sentimental emancipationism that marked this period.

The poem's mention of a "communion most holy" of both free and ex-slave Brazilians makes it, however, something of an anomaly in the debates of the period; this element most likely reflects the perceived need for social harmony during the Paraguayan War. Generally, discussions of slavery made almost no mention of a place in society for the new group of freedpersons that abolition, even in its most cautious and gradual form, would necessarily create. In fact, until the end of the 1860s and beginning of the 1870s, elites offered little hope that ex-slaves would be incorporated into society. Caldre e Fião, on the other hand, spoke explicitly of slaves' joining their freeborn compatriots one day in a social "communion." We should not, however, confuse this more inclusionary stance toward slaves and former slaves with a nonhierarchical vision of social relations. Caldre e Fião may have been willing to accept into society certain ex-slaves, but only on the condition that they become obedient and productive members of the working classes. Caldre e Fião's main goal in this poem was to make the idea of emancipation palatable to his elite audience. To achieve this, he portrayed the slave as not only a harmless but also a potentially model plebeian.[78] In doing so, the author suggested further that ex-slaves could be worthy of uniting with freeborn citizens in a new social union, one that would center on the patriotic feelings the former slaves supposedly shared with their free compatriots and on the labor the two groups would perform in the pursuit of progress. Popular classes with the loyalty and productivity posited in the poem would be ideal from an elite point of view, for they would work hard and mind their place in society. By depicting slaves as capable of joining this kind of peaceful union, Caldre e Fião might thus have assuaged the fears of elites anxious about releasing Afro-Brazilians from the bonds of slavery. Rather than acting as a simple vision of liberation for the enslaved, the poem worked more as an assurance to elites that they would be able to manage the process of emancipation to meet their own interests. To slaves (neither his intended nor his likely readership), Caldre e Fião offered only the chance to mold themselves to elite desires and gain acceptance as a new kind of subordinate.

Outside of "O escravo brasileiro," few other elite voices proposed the inclusion of persons coming out of slavery. Rather than freedpersons, however, these other projects focused on the free children born to slave mothers after the Rio Branco (Free Womb) Law of 1871. The aim behind these plans was similar to that of Caldre e Fião's verse—to incorporate the productive segments of the slave population, or here, their descendants. Rather than assuming that these children would have the qualities that would make them useful free workers, however, such projects argued for the establishment of "asylums of liberty" (*asilos de liberdade*) in which the new generation would receive training to forge them into acceptable plebeians. An 1872 article in the journal of the Parthenon Litterario, for example, proposed the creation of such asylums to give slaves' offspring "the education of labor." Rather than abandoning such children to the "education of the slave quarters and to servilism" until they reached the age of twenty one, the state would do much better to place them in "houses of moral education and vocational training in agriculture or industry."[79] Such an education, the author believed, would turn slaves' children into "agricultural or industrial workers to plow vacant lands or establish shops or factories." From the shame of slavery, that is, the state could create "honest working citizen[s]."[80]

A similar project discussed by the Sociedade Libertadora (Liberation Society) of Porto Alegre was described in the Liberal Party organ *A Reforma* at the end of 1871. With the vehemence of a party that had seen its own emancipationist plan co-opted by its political enemies, the editors of *A Reforma* attacked the Rio Branco Law as incomplete. Although this legislation was essentially a version of the ideas Liberals had been championing, the paper condemned the law for neglecting the free children of slaves (*ingênuos*); the provisions of the law handed the *ingênuo* over either "to charity or to the avarice [*cobiça*] of the *senhor*. Both of these cases give rise to vices that it is necessary not to encourage. . . . Depravity [*hediondez*], crime, [and] sin according to Christian philosophy will be the result of the law's lack of foresight." To correct this flaw, society needed institutions like the one the Sociedade Libertadora was planning that would oversee the education of the children of slaves. If city governments would copy this idea, *asilos de liberdade* in the province would produce "the regeneration of an extensive class of men moralized by work and by the severity of their directors." Thus we see once more in this project the hope that training in labor would salvage "a perfected worker, a citizen who participates neither in vices nor in the immoral qualities of his predecessors." From a society based on slavery, an immoral institution that led a large part of the population into laziness and other bad habits, the province might thus move to a society whose lower levels were inhabited by productive and "moralized" plebeians.[81]

What was missing from the Beggars' Asylum proposals, of course, was a clear notion of the destiny of those who had been born slaves. Aside from "O escravo brasileiro" and its vision of a rather limited communion between freed and freeborn persons, this exclusion of the majority of the enslaved was the rule in elite thought in the post-Farroupilha years. It is as though Gaúcho elites, while coming to an agreement on the desirability of emancipation, hoped it would rid them not only of the institution of slavery but of the enslaved themselves. While the end of slavery would remove a large portion of the province's labor force, rather than worrying about incorporating previously captive workers into society, elites concentrated on saving only the *ingênuos*. Elites held few if any hopes that they might turn these children's parents, whether enslaved in Africa or born as slaves in Brazil, into acceptable free plebeians. As they gained their emancipation, such freedpersons would have the freedom mainly to get out of the way of progress.

Vagrancy

The Gaúcho society that elites envisioned emerging after midcentury would not, however, rest exclusively on a working population of carefully trained children of slaves. These *ingênuos* represented, rather, the small segment of slavery's human legacy that elites felt could productively and safely be educated into proper elements of the *povo*. A much larger portion of the *povo* that elites wanted to construct was to consist of nonslave national workers. As the dispute between Félix Xavier da Cunha and Caldre e Fião made clear, these free workers were far from unproblematic in elite eyes. Indeed, free, Brazilian-born plebeians seemed to be essentially vagrant and troublesome. In the Asylum debates and more generally, elite attitudes toward this free population resembled in most respects the position taken toward slaves and former slaves. As with the enslaved or freedpersons, elites regarded the free poor as marginal candidates for participation in the new *povo;* such plebeians required, as elites saw it, careful repression. With the application of new educational programs, some part of them might be transformed into workers sufficiently obedient and hardworking to be included in society. The differences between this approach and the one elites took toward slaves and *libertos* (freedpersons) consisted, as we shall see, of differing emphases within the same overall scheme.

As was also true with regard to slavery, changing conditions in the post-Farroupilha years gave elites in Porto Alegre good reason to reevaluate the question of the free national poor. With the slave population draining out of the province after the cessation of the international trade with Africa, and with remaining slaves continuing to press their own agendas, elites looked anxiously for new foundations upon which to build their *povo*. As we shall see in the next chapter, elites usually pointed to European immigrants as the ideal replacements for slave workers. They could not, however, keep their gaze focused too serenely on Germany and Italy; the free poor, who made up the largest part of the local population, demanded attention. These plebeians' attempts to gain relative freedom in their lives, as we shall see, made them a troublesome presence in Rio Grande do Sul throughout the period under study. In the 1850s and then again during the Paraguayan War, the disruptions and destruction that warfare inflicted on the economy gave plebeians some greater room in which to pursue their interests, while also convincing elites that the province was entering a labor crisis.

It is essential to see the connections between these two phenomena—plebeians' initiatives and elites' complaints about labor—in order to make sense of an apparent paradox that marked elite rhetoric about the free working population in these years. It often seemed that elites were concerned by both a shortage and an excess of free workers. Declarations that a "lack of hands" (*falta de braços*) was impeding economic progress ran through the period but peaked during the 1850s and the Paraguayan War. The large-scale slaughter of livestock during the Farroupilha Revolution, together with the reappearance in the early 1850s of competition from Argentina and the Estado Oriental, had put the province's cattle-raising and *charque* industries in a difficult position. For many elites, one of the most daunting obstacles to the recovery of pastoral production was precisely an insufficient number of workers. Speaking particularly of *charqueadas*, for instance, the provincial president noted in 1858, "The lack of hands tends to break down the force of this industry."[82] In 1864, another president asserted that the province was far from developing a manufacturing sector, since "labor and capital are still insufficient to satisfy the needs of the cultivation of the soil and other branches of agriculture."[83] The war during the second half of the 1860s brought forth similar worries. The city council of Porto Alegre lamented the economic effects of the removal of men to the front. The production of manioc and manioc flour, the council reported in 1867, had fallen into a "somewhat decayed state, because of the shortage of workers, [the] sole foundation of its development."[84] An earlier complaint, however, brings us to the other side of elite discontent with the free working population. On the eve of Brazil's entrance into the Paraguayan War, the Porto Alegre newspaper *O Mercantil* described the "contortions" the new provincial president would face in Rio Grande do

Sul. The hostilities then underway across the national border had already paralyzed the Gaúcho economy. The main threat, the author argued, was not that a "shortage of hands" would slow down an economic recovery but rather that the mobs of the newly unemployed might damage social hierarchies. The workers who had been used in agriculture, livestock raising, and commerce, "the poor landowners in the midst of wealth, that unoccupied and vagrant population, all are dangers, all are elements that the combustion in the neighboring country might reach."[85] This sort of anxiety, which had also appeared during the 1850s, may suggest that the problem was merely one of employment.[86] When the province's main industries prospered, they sought more workers than they could find, and complaints of labor shortages appeared. When production levels dropped, employers dismissed workers whom authorities then treated as threats to social order.

In fact, the question is more intriguing than that, for worries about dangers posed by the number of vagrants were not limited to periods of economic downturn. As Sandra Pesavento has argued, elite concern with vagrants and attempts to control this all too prevalent population of individuals characterized the entire period, from midcentury to final abolition in 1888. Elites' repeated attempts to compel the vagrant, whom Pesavento aptly defines as any plebeian who "refused to enter the world of labor," do not, however, contradict the image of a shortage of workers.[87] The two descriptions of the free *povo* were very much part of the same phenomenon. Especially (though not exclusively) during periods of warfare, elites in Porto Alegre worried about the availability of good workers. When they saw too few hands or too many members of a mob, they were looking at the same mass of free plebeians. It was the lack of plebeians willing to submit to an employer that caused both impressions. In the second case, elite observers merely felt a greater fear of what those plebeians might do while outside positions of dependence and submission. At times anxious about social threats, at others worried more immediately about their own wealth, Gaúcho elites thus developed their own version of the "ideology of vagrancy," in which Brazilian elites branded as vagrants all those free poor who would not become passive and productive workers for elite patrons.

The conception of plebeians' independence as vagrancy was central to Gaúcho elites' approach to the issue of the free national poor from midcentury on. This found strong expression, for example, in the Asylum debates. Contrasting Brazilian-born workers with European immigrants, Ubatuba even offered the blanket statement that "our compatriots are vagrants." Mariante seconded that observation with his claim that free national plebeians "do not have a love for work."[88]

The ideology of vagrancy did not, however, rest on a belief that the national poor were irredeemably vagrant. This is not to say that elites did not impute congenital defects to such plebeians. The presumed racial inferiority of Africans and Afro-Brazilians, for example, was a major reason Gaúcho elites spoke so highly of European immigration. Discussing the necessity of establishing settlers over "the vastness of the empty lands" of the Empire in 1847, for instance, provincial president Manoel Antonio Galvão said, almost in passing, that the Assembly members "undoubtedly do not want to populate with blacks."[89] When speaking of the free poor as a whole, however, elites more commonly supposed that plebeians' unruliness and lack of "love of work" were the results of a flawed education. Here elites understood "education" in an extremely broad sense to include all of the processes by which members of the *povo* were socialized. Elites thus demonstrated ambiguity about the innate nature of the "flaw" of vagrancy. In any case, they believed the *povo* could be saved from that vice through education. What is most important about this view of vagrancy is that it left open the possibility of retraining the free national poor into a better *povo*.

Education for the *povo* was one of the causes that most attracted elite attention and reform proposals after the Farroupilha. To a great extent, this reflected Gaúcho elites' use of western Europe and the United States as models of progress to be emulated. Marveling at the political, economic, and social development of these other regions, leaders in Porto Alegre focused on education as one of the chief pillars of European and North American civilization; although it represented an imposing deficiency, education might, with the proper reforms, be made to propel Rio Grande do Sul to North Atlantic levels of progress and cultural sophistication. In keeping with this tendency, elites frequently asserted the vital importance of improvements to the provincial educational system. In 1847, for example, the deputy Sá Britto declared in the Provincial Assembly that education was "the basis of the civilization and morality of a people."[90] Indeed, for many elite observers in the period, the "backwardness" (*atraso*) of Brazil's educational institutions relative to those of Europe and the United States called for immediate action.[91]

By raising once again the issue of retraining the free poor, Caldre e Fião's fleeting reference to the Asylum returns us to the *povo* as a problem for elites in Porto Alegre. For while the instruction of the *povo* was part of a broader treatment of education as a step toward European-style civilization, it was in a narrower sense also a means of fashioning something useful out of the often troublesome free national workers in the region. Given plebeians' struggles for autonomy, such a reconstruction effort would not, of course, be easy; elites realized the need for forceful and persistent efforts in a variety of areas.[92] The instruction (again, broadly defined) required to salvage part of the free poor had to encompass various fields of action; depending on the context, elite observers disagreed on the primacy of one or another of these types of education. Some, like provincial president Tenente General Francisco José de Souza Soares de Andrea, in 1849, concentrated on religion as "the strongest guarantee of public order."[93] Others, like provincial vice president Luís Alves Leite de Oliveira Bello, in 1855, concentrated on the importance of the use of force against unruly plebeians; for Oliveira Bello, the only sure way to control the disorder common among the lower classes was "the certainty of punishment."[94] Increasingly, moreover, elite attentions came to focus on education for work as a central force for reshaping the free poor. Through both traditional schooling and training through cautiously overseen labor, "the diffusion of enlightenment," as one eager orator put it in 1862, would form useful and more civilized workers out of the province's free plebeians.[95] Most often, however, elites treated these distinct fields of popular training as intimately related efforts.

Although elites did not see the different areas of instruction as mutually exclusive, they came to focus their attentions on building up the apparatuses of repression and education. The first of these spheres of action, which has been studied at some length by Paulo Moreira, involved primarily the improvement of the various police corps that were charged with the enforcement of order in Porto Alegre.[96] As Moreira has noted, the period after the Farroupilha demonstrated "a growing preoccupation with police organization, seen by elites as a privileged strategy of intimidation and control of the plebeian classes." The years 1846 through 1878 saw, in fact, five new sets of regulations governing the provincial police (in 1857, 1860, 1866, 1869, and 1873), as well as numerous reforms of specific provisions of these rules.[97] Although they tended to be underfunded, inconsistently implemented, and continually resisted by plebeians, these measures of reorganization revealed elites' desires to fashion the police force into an instrument with which they might "moralize" the free poor—turn them, that is, into more obedient workers in the region's new order.[98]

To do this, elites attempted to shore up the moral behavior of the police themselves, an effort that inevitably failed. The regulations of the police corps customarily expressed a preference for recruits to be men of "good conduct, not having committed a crime for which they suffered defaming punishment," and stipulated harsh penalties for crimes they might carry out while serving in the police.[99] These agents of order, however, frequently showed themselves to be a ubiquitous source of disorder in the streets of Porto Alegre. For one thing, both the police and the military drew their rank and file from the same popular segments they were supposed to be repressing. Second, even after receiving their uniforms, these plebeians continued to inhabit the same spaces they were charged with patrolling. Finally, elites' efforts to insert their agents into not only the streets and plazas but also the taverns, tenements, and other semipublic spaces of the city ensured that the police would intrude in areas plebeians considered their own. Together, these circumstances meant that the agents and the objects of repression maintained an intimate coexistence in which tensions could easily break out into violence. The number of such instances of conflict suggests that the police generally did not rise above what the elite saw as the *povo*'s moral misbehavior.[100]

However limited their success, the attempts to establish police control in "those dangerous places where are found only paths that lead to misery, degradation, and infamy" clearly represented a planned expansion of state power.[101] We should not, however, be too quick to assume that this intention meant an increase in government control at the expense of the power of individual elites. On paper, the police regulations and municipal codes that politicians legislated into being in the decades after the Farroupilha took over the punishment of plebeians' public behavior. Those who lived under the power of a *senhor,* however, continued to have their lives regulated by their master. As Thomas Holloway has asserted about Rio de Janeiro in the 1830s, "While punishment was reserved to the state, the master was still allowed and expected to exercise disciplinary control."[102] The apparent growth of the state's role in controlling plebeians did not, that is, necessarily imply any reduction of seigneurial power.

The second area on which elite projects of the post-Farroupilha years concentrated was that of plebeian instruction. This could include formal, classroom education, like the classes on "calligraphy, reading, arithmetic, national grammar, geography, [and] drawing" that a Masonic lodge provided in 1875 for "poor boys and those whose daily labors only permit them to study at night."[103] In general, however, it was another type of instruction, one that involved training for and through work, that elites had in mind when they planned the reeducation of the national poor into a more acceptable *povo*. In some conceptions, the need was for "industrial instruction," teaching the methods of modern industrial manufacturing to worker and capitalist alike. By setting up establishments "where those dedicated to the industrial life go to receive enlightenment [*receber luzes*]," such plans could create what one plan referred to as "a beautiful native technological personnel."[104]

These projects turned out to be exceptionally forward-looking, even utopian, given the lack of resources available to governments in Porto Alegre in the 1846–80 period. Speaking in the Provincial Assembly in 1854, Caldre e Fião stuck to more immediately practical work instruction: agricultural training for the national poor. While many of his colleagues asserted that bringing in hardworking foreigners would be enough to transform Brazilians into efficient and obedient laborers, Caldre e Fião argued, "Simply the example that we want to give of labor and the peaceful actions of the colonists will not be enough." What was needed, he continued, was "to give an agricultural education to the people." He urged his colleagues to set up a system of "internal colonization," placing Brazilian-born plebeians on plots of land and founding "practical schools" to instruct these native colonists in the efficient use of the land. By doing so, he concluded, "we will improve the customs of our countrymen," producing efficient farmers and at the same time cutting the incidence of crime among the *povo*.[105] Similar projects appeared proposing that colonies combine national and immigrant workers to create a "model *fazenda* [plantation]" to train "children of poor farmers or of people worthy of public assistance."[106] Such colonies or plantations would instruct members of the national poor to be good workers, precisely by putting them to work in carefully controlled settings. Such was the faith that elites put in instruction in the rigors of labor that they suggested this vocational training would mold an orderly, as well as industrious, *povo*.

Forging a new and acceptable *povo* through an education in labor also appeared, as the case of the Beggars' Asylum demonstrates, in elites' projects for charitable institutions in Porto Alegre. Caldre e Fião and his supporters, it will be remembered, wanted to set former beggars to work in the Asylum; even the infirm would produce according to their abilities. Other houses of public assistance demonstrated a similar orientation. The Establishment of Minor Apprentices, attached to the national Army Arsenal in Porto Alegre, provides the most obvious evidence of this tendency. Created by the imperial government in 1846, this institution took in orphans and children of indigent parents and trained them to be manual laborers. "There they receive education in primary letters inside the Arsenal itself," the provincial president noted in 1853, "and in the workshops they learn the mechanical art for which they demonstrate the greatest aptitude."[107] In 1848, the provincial government followed the central government's example by setting up its own division of "minor apprentices" to supplement the imperial one. The provincial branch would provide unfortunate young boys with "an education as elevated as that which good fathers should give their children"; again, this paternalistic scheme involved carefully monitored training in artisanal trades.[108] In 1867, it was reported that twenty-two of the forty-two apprentices were learning carpentry, while another eleven were apprentice tailors, four were apprentice blacksmiths and gunsmiths, three were apprentice saddle-makers, and two were apprentice tinsmiths.[109]

In nineteenth-century Porto Alegre, such occupations were very much reserved for men. Other charitable institutions provided a very different working education for poor girls. Both the Asilo de Santa Leopoldina and the Colégio de Santa Tereza aimed to make "useful for society" the "orphan and exposed" girls under their care.[110] As the internal regulations for the former institution, drawn up at its founding in 1857, make explicit, elites thought poor girls' utility to be quite different from that of poor boys. The wards of the Santa Leopoldina were to receive "the education, the teaching of labor and domestic industry appropriate for women."[111] They would be put to work, but at tasks in keeping with the specific position of their gender in society—cleaning and organizing a household and carrying out "handiworks" such as embroidery and sewing.[112] Later on, as the state moved to expand the public school system, girls at the Santa Leopoldina and the Colégio de Santa Tereza were encouraged to study to become schoolteachers. Although the provincial government appreciated the proceeds from the sale of the girls' needlework, officials continually stressed that the overriding aim of both establishments was "to create perfect mothers."[113] Education in this womanly brand of work would achieve that goal. Elites' projects for the retraining of the free poor were, therefore, based on gendered visions of the work plebeians should perform.

Whether male or female, however, these members of the popular classes would have to work in an orderly and obedient manner if they were to fit into elites' plans for the province's progress. In the various ways they sought to reshape a part of the existing populace, elite projects demonstrated a proactive character; elites' failure to implement most of their proposals should, however, remind us that Porto Alegre in 1846–80 had not yet arrived at the more statist policies that would arise during the Old Republic (1889–1930).

As they debated projects to fashion a *povo* appropriate to their grand plans for the province, elites had to take into account the projects of the plebeians already around them. Whether as maids or farmhands, street vendors or artisans, the members of the real *povo* of Porto Alegre performed the work on which the city's economy was based. As they went about their lives, these plebeians struggled in myriad ways to carve out some space of at least imperfect autonomy for themselves. Elite rhetoric effectively hid these initiatives from view by blurring them together as a troublesome moral failing on the part of the popular classes; elites conceived of the persistent creativity of plebeians, that is, as laziness or vagrancy that, in the best of circumstances, might be educated out of part of the working population. Through repression, religion, and other kinds of instruction, elites might thus be able to include a fraction of the national poor in the new Rio Grande do Sul. To be sure, this inclusion would not mean incorporation of popular elements into the politically active, ruling groups; rather, the redeemed national poor would be allowed to participate as an improved type of subordinates. The only plebeians who might take part in any more significant and political manner, as we shall see in the next chapter, were European immigrants. In this way, the threats that plebeians' alleged "defects" represented for elites only reinforced the tendency for members of the dominant classes to look to Europe as a model and source of progress.[114]

2

The Immigrant Solution and Its Problems, 1846–1880

> What is lacking for Porto Alegre to become in a short time one of the principal cities of America? A system of colonization.
>
> *João Lins Vieira Cansansão de Sinimbú, 1853*

In the first week of March 1853, José Cândido Gomes, the intrepid social columnist who wrote under the pseudonym "O Estudante," reported the destruction of a *quilombo* (runaway slave community) near the city of Rio Pardo. The area, an easy boat trip upriver from Porto Alegre, had been the site of many *quilombos* over the years. The arrival of the former *quilombolas* (*quilombo* residents) in Porto Alegre, in the custody of police soldiers, served as the point of departure for one of Gomes's ironic observations:

> This Friday we all learned that the runaway fathers are setting up colonies: Just look at that *quilombo* in Rio Pardo! Warehouses of food, clothing, tobacco, and I don't know what else. If left alone a few more months the black colonists would set up their balls [*bailante*], their theater, and the other little pleasures of those who want to live an Anacreontic life far from the world and its vanities.
>
> This is so that you see how our land is well-policed there in the *campanha* [a zone of rolling hills]. "Colonies" of all sorts are made and subsist 6 to 8

> years, and no one knows about them. All of a sudden we're going to discover there some great city of foreigners that we don't see on the map.[1]

What made O Estudante's ponderings humorous in the Porto Alegre of the 1850s was the juxtaposition they made of runaway slaves and colonies. Clearly for O Estudante the levels of civilization associated with slaves and European immigrants presented a contrast that verged on the absurd. Black colonists! The very idea would have been ridiculous to O Estudante and, presumably, his readers; in their view, if Africans and Afro-Brazilians had really been on the same level as the immigrants who were arriving to set up farming nuclei in the province, European colonies might not have been necessary. The references to high culture—dance, theater, a Greek poet—merely give a final honing to the barb of O Estudante's irony.

The passage is not, however, without its complications. After all, if they had not yet built a theater, the *quilombolas* had certainly shown themselves capable of establishing well-stocked and organized communities. The force of O Estudante's image of a city of foreigners in the midst of Rio Grande do Sul, moreover, did not fall solely on his imaginary super-*quilombo;* this was a vision that ran through elite discourse of the years 1846–80, but one that more commonly referred to the *colônias* (immigrant colonies) proper. The frequently expressed fear of communities of strangers springing up in the heart of the province was, as we shall see, most often an expression of strong ambivalence toward European colonists, not runaway slaves. Although O Estudante's primary intended target was the *quilombo,* some of his bitter comedy thus spilled over onto the Europeans who in the post-Farroupilha period were becoming a dynamic force for change in the region centered on Porto Alegre.

Throughout the years 1846–80, in fact, elites in Porto Alegre gave these "blond compatriots"—to use another of O Estudante's loaded phrases—a much more deeply mixed reception than might be expected. As was generally true in Brazil and much of Latin America, ruling groups in Rio Grande do Sul eagerly hailed European immigration as the answer to a series of problems that beset nation-states under construction across the region in the nineteenth century. Through their economic, cultural, and moral contributions, white immigrants were expected to help pull young nations closer to the levels of prosperity and civilization their home countries in Europe enjoyed. More to the point here, Gaúcho elites assumed European workers would conform to a more acceptable, more civilized model of relations between elites and *povo* in their new homeland in the south of Brazil. Because of the qualities attributed to them, these immigrants would supposedly serve as the foundation of a new *povo* that would fill the subordinate strata of Gaúcho society while at the same time bringing in elements of civilization very much on a par with what the elites enjoyed. Elites, that is, wanted European immigrants to be more modern, civilized, and productive than the "national" workers in the province.

This idealized vision contained, of course, a profound contradiction that only intensified as it came up against the reality of European immigration in Rio Grande do Sul. The underlying aim of immigrationism was to attract an influx of workers whose levels of culture would very nearly equal elites' own but who would nonetheless occupy the lower rungs of society quite contentedly. As Germans and other Europeans settled in their colonies, in the cities, and elsewhere in the province, however, they demonstrated the independence of spirit of which some minority voices in the Gaúcho ruling elite had warned. Throughout the period 1846–80, members of the dominant group struggled with a realization that had not been part of their more optimistic immigrationist visions—namely, that the interests of the new colonists would often run counter to those of the native elite. More troubling still was the recognition that many immigrants would demand formal political responses to, and ultimately representation of, their interests. The resulting doubts about the benefits of European colonization did not, however, lead Gaúcho elites to reject immigration. They ultimately clung to the ideal of the white European immigrant as a pillar of the *povo* they wanted to construct, although their final embrace of that ideal was always somewhat uncomfortable. Elite anxieties about some of immigration's effects thus demonstrated that even their ideal plebeians—white, hardworking, European—could become threats to social hierarchies by pressing into the realm of official politics.

The Nearly Universal Solution of European Immigration

The introduction of white Europeans furnished Gaúcho elites, as well as most of their peers across the Brazilian Empire, with a source of tremendous hope from the mid-nineteenth century on.[2] Despite their positions of dominance in regional and national society, elites felt themselves sorely pressed by a series of economic and social problems. As they cast about for solutions to their difficulties, they often fixed on European immigration as something of a miracle cure. Gaúcho elites were no exception in this regard; despite their reservations about immigration, they looked to the injection of a bit of Europe to cure inherited ills and build their province's social and economic progress.

The "Canaan of free labor" that European immigration represented took on distinct meanings for the Empire's different regional elites, given the unique set of social, economic, and political conditions each confronted.[3] In order to begin to understand Gaúcho elites' particular concerns, it is instructive to compare briefly the meanings that elites in the Center-South region of Brazil gave to immigration. The dominant classes of that zone—Rio de Janeiro, Minas Gerais, and São Paulo—consisted primarily of coffee planters and merchants. Their wealth and power derived from their position in the richest economic industry in the Empire—the production of coffee for export. Heavily invested in a plantation system based on slave labor, planters started to give serious attention to the question of European immigration in the 1840s and 1850s, when the abolition of the African slave trade seemed a very real possibility. Their approach to the immigration question showed, as Emília Viotti da Costa has argued, definite subregional variations. Individual elites from the Paraíba Valley, where coffee agriculture had boomed earlier in the nineteenth century, were ready by the last two decades of the Empire to consider the creation of *núcleos coloniais,* nuclei of independent colonist-farmers. The most extreme among them even called for an end to the latifundia system that monopolized land tenure in so much of Brazil. Such views were, however, not representative of the coffee-planter class as a whole and reflected, as Costa has suggested, the attitudes of a fraction already well supplied with slave workers and with no great need for (or later, capital to spend on) immigrant laborers.[4] The dominant tendency of the coffee elite instead belonged to the wealthy planters of the newer areas of the western São Paulo coffee frontier—namely, the conception of European immigration as a potential source of free workers to replace slaves on the *fazendas.* For Paulista planters, colonization proper—that is, the creation of nuclei of freeholders—was not merely without benefits for their wealth and position but was perhaps even a threat.[5] Certainly they greeted the formation of colonies with hostility.

Denouncing the establishment of independent smallholders in a plantation zone, the provincial president of São Paulo argued, for instance, that immigration's chief function should be to provide dependent workers: "It would be useless to increase the number of inhabitants of the Empire, if we did not take pains to make agriculture prosper, to make fruitful that source of public wealth. . . . Therefore I understand that all efforts should for the most part converge in order to aid the establishments, the plantations, already assembled, because only in this way will the colonists provide some immediate utility."[6] Running through this and similar rhetoric of Paulista *fazendeiros* (plantation owners) were the intimately related desires to protect their control over landholding and to ensure a dependent labor force. At midcentury, several planters installed Germans, Swiss, and other Europeans as contract laborers on their coffee plantations (an arrangement known as *parceria*). Accustomed to treating their enslaved workers with brutality, these elites in the late 1850s backed away from their early experiments with European plantation workers when the immigrants proved to be as demanding and restive as any native Brazilian laborers. This hesitancy faded later, however, when the abolition of slavery itself became a more immediate probability. The coffee planters thus ended up holding to a vision of Europeans as immigrant plantation workers rather than colonists.[7]

In Rio Grande do Sul, by contrast, the main emphasis was from the very beginning on Europeans as colonists rather than dependent workers. When the Empire inaugurated its official immigration efforts in São Leopoldo, up the Rio dos Sinos from Porto Alegre, it was with the explicit aim of creating a settlement of smallholders. With the long history of territorial disputes with Spain and later Argentina in the region, Brazilian authorities were eager to take more definitive possession of the lands of Rio Grande do Sul. A population of farmers, they believed, represented the most efficient means toward this end. At the same time, such a system promised important secondary advantages. It might prevent the *estancieiro* (estate-owning rancher) class already occupying the rolling hills of Rio Grande do Sul's ranching zone from gaining enough power in the region to become a threat to imperial control. Colonization might also produce foodstuffs that the Center-South of the country would need as it moved more exclusively to export agriculture.[8] Albeit with some additional goals in mind, authorities in Porto Alegre adhered to the ideal of smallholder colonization for the remainder of the imperial period. In 1854, provincial president João Lins Vieira Cansansão de Sinimbú made this orientation explicit. After outlining the two main systems of immigration—the *parceria* system that influential planters like Nicolau Vergueiro were then attempting in São Paulo and the colonization system used in São Leopoldo—this prominent figure in national politics declared the second preferable, even going so far as to argue that *parceria* was "merely a means of transition to arrive" at a regime of smallholders. It was only through such a condition, he concluded, that Rio Grande do Sul could "populate and give value to its lands."[9] The following year his successor seconded his opinion and expressed satisfaction that the system of "*parceria* has never been practiced here."[10] Indeed, for the rest of the century, the Germans and later Italians who constituted most of the immigration to Rio Grande do Sul entered into an exclusively "colonial" pattern.[11]

The dominance of the colonization pattern in the province did not, however, mean that Porto Alegre elites' goals for immigration were simple ones. On the contrary, these elites looked to colonization to accomplish a wide range of vital and at times contradictory objectives. To begin with, colonization was seen as a certain boon for both the agricultural and the "industrial" sectors of the economy. The development of these two sectors would lend greater diversity to a regional economy dominated by livestock raising and the processing of hides and jerked beef. The troubles the pastoral industries experienced in the years after the Farroupilha only heightened elites' interest in other areas of production. Dr. Manoel Pereira da Silva Ubatuba, for example, declared in the Provincial Assembly that colonization was of "sufficient transcendence [that] it can by itself make the crisis in which the province finds itself and which allows us to predict a grim future, change completely . . . [by] contributing to the creation of new industries that have to this point been forgotten here and that can replace the province's principal industry, which has been so punished [that] it will soon disappear."[12] This was a wildly optimistic statement when Ubatuba made it in 1851; subsequent events, furthermore, demonstrated that the pastoral economy would maintain its predominance into the twentieth century. Precisely because of their exaggeration, however, Ubatuba's words exemplified the inflated hopes regarding colonization's economic impact in the province.

At a more specific level, elites in Porto Alegre expected colonization to spur agricultural production by replacing an old slavery-based system with one founded on the labor of free Europeans. Rarely, as indicated earlier, did Gaúcho elites call for a direct substitution of slaves with immigrants. When Saião Lobato de Ulhôa Cintra and other political leaders spoke of "the necessity of promoting foreign colonization to substitute the lack of forced labor," they were not referring to an actual placement of Europeans as subordinate workers under *senhores* who had previously used slaves.[13] Rather, they had in mind a reorientation of production itself, away from larger *fazendas* using captive labor to smaller farms cultivated by free and independent owners. The benefits that such a shift was to provide for agriculture, "the mother industry," were several.[14] The end of agriculture's dependency on slavery would, first of all, ease worries about the dwindling population of slaves in the province after the 1850 cessation of the African slave trade; as one provincial president remarked rather bluntly in 1856, "The extinction of the traffic [in slaves] produced the . . . need for colonization."[15] Energetic Europeans would also bring new lands into cultivation; only they, the argument went, could be counted on to perform "the heavy labors of plowing the forests" and thus increasing the base of the province's agricultural production.[16] Most important, European colonization would install better, more productive workers on the land. In its contemporary condition, elites argued, agriculture was inefficient and locked in a backward "routine" of production.[17] A writer in *O Mercantil*, for instance, described the "decadence of Brazilian agriculture" in 1853 as the result of outdated techniques and the use of slaves. "Contaminated with vices," he argued, agriculture had become "little productive for farmers." Besides "the vices of the system of planting, harvest, and preparation of the products," he identified "the service done by slaves [who were] unintelligent and enemies of work" as one of the main causes of the pitiful state of things. A shift from slave to immigrant labor would, moreover, free up capital with which to remove the first set of "vices."[18] Ubatuba offered a very similar evaluation of agriculture's "stationary" condition in 1851. In his eyes, the blame for the industry's poor performance lay in the fact that it "has been carried out by routine and unintelligent hands that, without hope of a better future, work mechanically without any method." Although presenting some social explanation for the brutishness with which slaves worked—namely, that they had no incentive to do otherwise—Ubatuba here again pointed to the installation of free workers as the solution to agriculture's ills. "Being done by free hands," he concluded, agriculture "will without doubt develop."[19] Europeans would, elites presumed, arrive with not only more modern technical knowledge but also the mental capacity and incentive to incorporate further improvements in production later on. Some elites also expected colonists to bring a "certain sum of capital" with them.[20] The financial ability to invest in machinery and new techniques would complement colonists' intellectual abilities and thus create a much more highly productive farming population.

Agriculture was not, however, the only economic sector elites expected colonization to transform. The desire was that the various colonization schemes being tried out would turn Rio Grande do Sul, in the words of Antonio Ângelo Christiano Fioravanti, into a veritable "theater of industries."[21] While colonization was always primarily an agricultural venture, elites like Fioravanti expressed hopes that it might also stimulate artisanal and small manufacturing production throughout the province. Certainly the example of São Leopoldo, the first and most successful of the region's German colonies, gave them solid reason to believe in such secondary economic effects. Despite receiving no new immigrants from 1830 to 1844, and very little constructive attention from provincial authorities in the first half century of its existence, São Leopoldo was by the 1850s fast building a prosperous and diverse economy.[22] First- and second-generation colonists were branching out into not only artisanry of all sorts but also transportation, commerce, and the production of tanned leather, beer, and other simple manufactures.[23] The factors that elites thought would enable *colonos* to spur these other industries were virtually the same as in agriculture. The technical know-how and capital immigrants presumably brought with them, that is, would blossom forth into the development of a range of nonagricultural activities.[24] In their discussions of these economic fields, elites made virtually no mention of the importance of moving from slave to free labor. It was certainly not that they considered the transition unimportant for the development of these other industries; rather, elites assumed the shift to be so essential that it did not require mention. Despite the presence of slaves in urban artisanry and a variety of other economic activities in the province, the rise of a diverse economy based on slavery would have been practically inconceivable to elites in Porto Alegre.

Even when merely implicit, the contrast upon which such ideas rested was never too far below the surface. European colonists, that is, represented for elites the very antithesis of reticent Brazilian workers who, free or enslaved, hindered the economic progress of the province. The contrast drawn between the *colono* and the "national" worker, moreover, revealed the true breadth of the colonization ideal for elites. Members of the dominant classes in Porto Alegre certainly felt that an influx of European *colonos* would invigorate the provincial economy. Such improvements in nonelites' contributions to economic progress were, however, just a small part of the question. Beyond the spread of agricultural techniques or even free labor, colonization was to effect a much greater transformation: the establishment of *colonos* in the region was to bring about the reconstruction of the *povo* itself, on terms of elites' choosing. All of the *colonos'* positive traits—which were often understood through contrasts with those of Brazilian plebeians—would help create the kind of *povo* Rio Grande do Sul deserved and needed in order to progress.

We have seen that Gaúcho elites viewed the free and enslaved plebeians of their province as constituting, in a basic sense, a lazy and vagrant mass. European *colonos*, on the other hand, seemed to offer a cure for the plague of vagrancy. Indeed, in the vision of the elite, the colonist would be able to meet every vice of the Brazilian plebeian with a corresponding virtue; the ultimate result of the injection of Europeans into Gaúcho society would thus be a replacement of the existing *povo*'s unacceptable character with the triumphant nature of the European.

The first and most often praised characteristic of European colonists was their work ethic. The Germans and other white immigrants who were carving out farm lands in *colônias* in the region around Porto Alegre were, elites believed, imbued with precisely what the national plebeians lacked—the "love of work." In the Provincial Assembly's debates over the Beggars' Asylum (examined in chapter 1), Antonio Joaquim da Silva Mariante drew this comparison in clear terms that greatly favored the *colonos*. Amid discussions of a project to open a new colony near the town of Santa Cruz, Mariante asked some of his "countrymen" why they did not go to the area and try to obtain some of the lands set aside for new farms. Their response, according to him, demonstrated the lack of enterprise among the national poor: "These lands are in the middle of the forest; what are we going to do there?" Thus, in Mariante's telling, while the Germans cleared away trees and overcame other grave obstacles to create new, productive farmland, the Brazilian poor were content to remain idle.[25]

It was not only Mariante who conceived of *colonos'* role in their new society as in part a moral one. As we have seen, leaders in Porto Alegre thought of plebeians' refusal to submit passively to elite control as to a great extent a moral failing. Tainted by the flawed instruction that a slave society had given them, the national poor had fallen into vices, one of which was precisely their unwillingness to accept subordination without resistance. European *colonos*, on the other hand, appeared in elite rhetoric as a positively "moralized" force. So highly did elites esteem them in this regard that even O Estudante felt compelled to apologize for his "rude jokes" (*chalaças*) at their expense. After poking fun at a group of German immigrants who had served as soldiers in Porto Alegre, he endeavored to make clear his true opinion of them. "Our compatriots," he wrote, "handled themselves like good citizens: very well-behaved [*morigerados*], obedient toward their superiors, zealous in their duties, they became worthy of our highest praises."[26] More serious rhetoric supported this general position. Throughout the period 1846–80, Porto Alegre's elites consistently described *colonos* in their province as paragons of moral behavior and respect for order, as well as industriousness. Unlike the troublesome members of the Brazilian-born popular classes, European colonists were in elites' view so morally trustworthy that they would give the province "many other defenders of public order."[27] Once again, we must not forget, these tributes to *colonos'* morality did not exist in isolation from praise of their labor; indeed, the two were inseparable elements of these Europeans' civilized nature. Their devotion to a peaceful social life, to the care of their families, and to law and order might have been cause or consequence of *colonos'* industriousness; what is crucial here, however, is to recognize that for elites discussing colonization in midcentury Porto Alegre, hard work was part of a people's moral character.

A final and obvious contrast that elites made between *colonos* and the national poor was racial. In relation to the question of colonization, elites' racial views emerged in two main ways. First, individual political leaders occasionally made passing reference to the undesirability of Africans, Afro-Brazilians, and Asians as settlers of new lands in the province. In 1854, for instance, Fidêncio Prates asked his colleagues in the Provincial Assembly to consider what might be "the means of populating" the country's vast territory. "Certainly," he began in explaining his proposal, "the noble Deputy will not want us to continue to populate it with inhabitants of the coast of

Africa."[28] Similarly, seven years earlier, the provincial president had introduced the topic of colonization by speaking of "the vastness of the deserted lands, which you will doubtless not want to populate with blacks."[29] When the national minister of agriculture proposed the importation of Chinese contract laborers in 1869 as a means of furnishing docile plantation workers for coffee *fazendas*, the Porto Alegre paper *A Reforma* attacked the project. Pointing first to the economic success of German colonization in Rio Grande do Sul —"the only [immigration] that until today has brought real advantages to the nation"—the editor denounced the idea of Chinese immigration in racial terms as well. With a few government measures, Brazil could receive thousands more Europeans, "who with their labor, with their intelligence, with their very blood will contribute to raising the country out of the state of prostration in which it finds itself." Like the Africans before them, the so-called Chinese coolies would on the other hand be a source of unhealthy racial mixture. "No, a thousand times no," the article continued, "we do not want new slaves [from the] bastardized races of inferior Asia."[30] This statement stands in stark contrast to the other expressions of elite racism in the 1846–80 period; it demonstrates, that is, an exceptionally virulent form of hatred based directly on a conception of another people as a race, in the pseudo-scientific biological sense.

A Reforma's call for "a strong immigration of people from perfect races, capable of working, intelligent, and able to help us in the progressive march of civilization," did not, however, represent a complete break with the racial tenor of colonization rhetoric.[31] As evident in the remarks above that dismiss out of hand the idea of African *colonos*, elites in mid-nineteenth-century Porto Alegre had clear preferences for white European colonists. These immigrants, they believed, would bring intelligence, industriousness, and the other constructive traits that we have examined so far; their whiteness was simply another positive characteristic associated with the others. Elites' manner of expressing that preference, however, suggests that racism was for them a somewhat vague but shared assumption.[32]

The critique of Chinese immigration in *A Reforma* was not, however, based solely on racial criteria; the editorial's secondary argument brings us back to the general question of elite goals for colonization in Rio Grande do Sul. When the anonymous author of that 1869 article denounced a "new slavery" of Chinese workers, it was not only the allegedly racial traits of the potential workers but also the idea of continuing slavery that provoked his ire. The dangerous effects of replacing the African with a Chinese "de facto, if not de jure, slave" would, in other words, not be limited to a new miscegenation; just as prejudicial would be the preservation of the old social system of slavery. What the country needed, the writer asserted, was in fact a transition away from the slave-based latifundia to a system of smallholdings like that which German *colonos* had produced in the South.[33] Given the dominance of large planters in the imperial economy and polity, this was a radical proposal; if implemented, such a transformation of agriculture would have profound implications for the nation's social hierarchies. For that reason, the dominant factions of the Empire were loathe to consider plans like the one *A Reforma* put forward.[34]

The regional elites in Porto Alegre, by contrast, adhered to the colonization model of immigration throughout the period under study here. As we have seen, these Gaúcho figures attributed many invigorating effects to colonization. They fully expected that the influx of European *colonos* would refashion the *povo* of their province. By introducing not only greater productivity but also positive moral and racial qualities, colonization would create a harder-working and less threatening lower class while also stimulating the economy.

Locating Colonos in Gaúcho Society

> Still they [the German colonists] preserve the warmest recollections of the Fatherland and in language, sentiment, and traditions are as true to their native land as if only travelers in a strange land.
>
> *Michael G. Mulhall,* Rio Grande do Sul

Despite their habitual praise of European colonization, from the close of civil war in 1846, elites in Porto Alegre expressed serious misgivings about the Germans and Italians who were occupying the eastern highlands of their province. Elites tended to attribute so much power and so many meanings to immigration that it was perhaps inevitable that reality would not measure up to their ideals. The problem, however, was not so much that the *colonos* were failing to meet specific elite expectations; even critics of government support of immigration agreed, by and large, that colonization had brought tremendous benefits to the region. Rather, the source of dissatisfaction lay in elites' own uncertainties about the place immigrants should and would occupy in their new society. If elites looked to the introduction of Europeans to remake the popular classes, they also realized that such a transformation of the *povo* would most likely necessitate broader shifts in elite-*povo* relations. Establishing tens of thousands of independent producers in the region and expecting their spirit of enterprise to plant seeds of artisanry and manufacturing would lead to certain change in Gaúcho society. Perceiving that such change might threaten their positions of wealth and seigneurial dominance within the province, elites began to criticize certain of colonization's attributes; these attacks would continue until the late 1870s, when factions of the elite felt that they could integrate segments of the immigrant population into their own bases of power.

General ambiguities about the social position European immigrants would hold in Brazil were not exclusive to Rio Grande do Sul. The coffee planters of São Paulo reached a basic consensus on the economic role they wanted Europeans to play; as we have seen, these powerful elites of the Empire's richest region wanted immigrants to serve as dependent workers on coffee *fazendas*. The political status of European immigrants posed a more complicated problem, however, for the Empire. Clearly, the São Paulo planters had little if any interest in extending political power to dependent workers. From the very beginning of official colonization programs, the central government, on the other hand, displayed a great deal of ambiguity in this regard. The contracts Germans signed to come to the first colonies in Brazil in 1824 (Nova Friburgo in the province of Rio de Janeiro and São Leopoldo in Rio Grande do Sul) contained concessions designed to integrate the *colonos* quickly and effectively into their new society. Besides financial support and grants of land, these agreements provided for the *colonos* to gain Brazilian citizenship and enjoy full freedom of religion. Both of these latter articles, however, were in clear contradiction of the constitution that the Brazilian emperor had promulgated in March of the same year. While establishing Roman Catholicism as the state religion, this founding document granted limited freedom of worship. The Empire would tolerate the private practice of other faiths but would not recognize non-Catholic marriages or the legitimacy of the children such unions produced. Moreover, the 1824 constitution stipulated that foreigners could only be considered Brazilian after naturalization; legislation regulating naturalization was to follow at a later date. When a naturalization law appeared in 1832, it did little to change the status of early colonists. By requiring a four-year residence in Brazil before foreigners would be eligible for citizenship, and by setting up complex and costly bureaucratic processes for applying, the law effectively left the residents of São Leopoldo and the other colonies in a state of political exclusion. Subsequent legislation eased the restrictions on foreigners' participation in the nation only very slowly. In 1861, for example, the civil marriages of Protestants gained legal recognition, and in 1881 non-Catholics received the right to vote. A highly specific law of 1846 conceded immediate naturalization to all *colonos* residing in São Leopoldo, but without extending this status to other foreigners in Brazil. Another national law reduced the residence requirement for naturalization; now immigrants only had to live in the Empire for two years rather than four before they could become citizens. This 1850 legislation introduced a new constraint, however: immigrants not only had to reside in Brazil but also had to live on and work their plots of land in the *colônias* to qualify for naturalization.[35] Although a decree would lift that restriction in 1871, it was, in the words of Jean Roche, "necessary to wait for the Proclamation of the Republic [in 1889] for naturalization, religious freedom, and civic equality to be conceded to immigrants and their descendants."[36] While welcoming European immigrants with rhetoric about the "Brazilian family," the imperial government in practice did not facilitate *colonos'* full membership in that body.[37]

Such ambivalence might be expected of a government dominated by representatives of the agricultural export interests of the Center-South. It was improbable, after all, that the latifundia holders would hasten to grant full political rights to European workers when they and other elites across Brazil had striven to deny such rights to the Brazilian-born labor force. Planters wanted Europeans to be a dependent class; their political participation on a par with elites would contradict such subordination. A different response from the elites of Rio Grande do Sul, however, might have been foreseen. In contrast to the system of *parceria* in São Paulo, the colonization the Gaúcho elites hailed would not introduce Europeans into the zones where the latifundia was dominant. The great cattle economy had its base in the southern plains, not in the eastern highlands that would be home to most of the European colonies. There was no real possibility of Germans or Italians filling in the labor force on the ranches of the pastoral zone or in the *charqueadas* that processed the ranching elite's cattle.[38] Europeans would then be free to set up their farms and other activities in an area that Luso-Brazilians had not previously developed. Elites tied to the regionally dominant pastoral economy expressed no trepidation at the rise of colonial production in the central and northern parts of Rio Grande do Sul; isolated in the highlands, this new economy seemed to pose no threat to the institution of the ranch or the economic power of the wealthy rancher.

As noted earlier, however, it was precisely the issue of *colonos'* isolation that came to bother the provincial elite. Most authors who have analyzed the phenomenon of elite disapproval of German *colonos* have explained it in terms of the prejudices of the Luso-Brazilian dominant classes. With an at times obviously ethnic partisanship, some have argued that the elites simply failed to recognize the merits of the European *colonos* and discriminated against them out of unreasoned cultural biases. Subtler explorations of this question have examined *colonos'* responses to the negligence and hostility of the local elites to show that the distance between elite and colonial groups was a bilateral creation.[39] The integration of the *colonos* and their descendants was not, however, merely a matter of elites' overcoming their prejudices. While certainly not free of stereotypes about Germans and Italians, elites in Rio Grande do Sul acted toward these *colonos* for understandable social and political reasons. Eager to reap the benefits of a transition to free labor and the construction of a more acceptable *povo*, members of the Gaúcho ruling classes were nevertheless uncertain about how arriving Europeans would change the balance of power in the regional society. If the *colonos* were to form a crucial part of the new *povo*, they would have to be a subordinate class. As such, they would have a difficult time achieving political rights in their new homeland. As we have seen, Gaúcho elites could only conceive of incorporating a small fraction of the existing popular classes into their province's future; even this inclusion, however, would not entail full political integration into the nation. Those plebeians judged suitable for elites' plans would continue to live outside formal politics. The problem the *colonos* raised was this: having the qualities to make up a better *povo*, would these Europeans then be deemed worthy of achieving a more complete citizenship than that which elites had granted the national poor? In other words, as João Capistrano put it in the Provincial Assembly, "Are those Germans Brazilians or not?"[40]

Nevertheless, in the decades after the Farroupilha, elites in Rio Grande do Sul demonstrated conflicting feelings on this matter; by the end of the 1846–80 period, many in the dominant classes would move to a more inclusionary position. By the later 1870s, that is, significant portions of the elite would actively seek greater political incorporation of their province's immigrant communities. To understand how this shift occurred, we must first look at the anxieties elites in Porto Alegre showed toward colonization at midcentury. In large part, these worries revolved around the isolation of the colonies, the "Great Wall of China" (in the words of the era's greatest champion of German immigration and immigrants' political rights, Carlos [Karl] von Koseritz) that seemed to separate *colonos* from Gaúchos.[41] By approaching the question in this way, we can see that for some elites in Porto Alegre the European *colonos* represented a vague social threat. This was not the same challenge that the national poor posed; the Brazilian plebeians were a problem from below, but largely within existing hierarchies. Despite their presence within Gaúcho territory, on the other hand, Germans, Italians, and the descendants of both groups seemed to represent a threat from outside the hierarchies that defined this regional society.

It was not only the end of the 1835–45 civil war that occasioned elite discussions and doubts about colonization in midcentury Porto Alegre; changing government policies brought the issue into public debate. Three years after the Treaty of Ponche Verde that concluded the Farroupilha, imperial legislation allowed the creation of provincial colonization projects. Law 514, signed on 28 October 1848, ceded to each province thirty-six leagues of central government land on which local authorities could establish immigrant smallholders. *Colonos* would gain ownership of their plots only after clearing and then farming them for five years. In 1850, the imperial government modified this scheme somewhat; in a measure that definitively turned land into a commodity in Brazil, the Land Law banned further concession of lands to *colonos*. From this point on, immigrants could only obtain their lands through purchase. With some minor adjustments, this set the basic legal framework for colonization until the end of the Empire in 1889.[42]

The creation of these guidelines gave elites in Porto Alegre an opportunity to express their somewhat contradictory assessments of colonization in

Rio Grande do Sul. As we have seen, political leaders in the province maintained a strong faith in the ideal of colonization and in the benefits it would bring. From the late 1840s on, however, some in Porto Alegre questioned whether the reality of colonization merited great official support. Once again it was José Antonio do Vale Caldre e Fião who presented one of the most colorful formulations of these doubts. While stressing that he understood "the necessity of foreign immigration for our rural or artisanal industry," he argued that the province should now move away from official colonization projects; the ideal would be either "spontaneous" colonization, immigrants arriving of their own account, or private colonization, wealthy Brazilians sponsoring immigration projects. The system of government subsidies that the government had used previously, he argued, had resulted in a ridiculous situation: "Up to now we gave lands, lent all sorts of help. . . . When they arrived here [*colonos*] did not even need to chew their food; we watched over them as if they were our best-loved brothers, even more, as if they were our children; they had no work, we did everything for them."[43] Although the imagery was his alone, Caldre e Fião was here expressing a feeling many of his colleagues shared. Colonization was, they all insisted, an almost indisputable good, but it did not deserve the full financial backing of the provincial government.

Along these same lines, others argued for scaling back subsidies. In 1852, for example, Israel Rodrigues Barcellos asserted that Brazil should follow the lead of the United States. Acknowledging that nation to be the greatest success story in immigration—a judgment that Gaúcho elites almost unanimously shared—Barcellos urged his fellow politicians to promote colonization through rather more indirect means. Instead of purchasing lands to grant to immigrants, this self-proclaimed devotee of colonization wanted the province to obtain *terras devolutas* (empty lands) like those that the Empire had given the province in 1848 and, after marking out individual plots and building roads to the colonial zones, sell the farmland to *colonos*.[44] Some in the 1850s would go even further. One of the province's most stringent critics of subsidized immigration, João Jacintho de Mendonça, felt compelled to praise the former colony of São Leopoldo (an 1846 government decree had raised it to the status of *município*, or municipality) but otherwise came as close to denying colonization's benefits as any Gaúcho elite of the period. Indeed, he claimed that outside of São Leopoldo colonization had not been a great success. If the case of this ex-colony were exceptional in some way, he intimated, perhaps the province should not take out loans or otherwise commit itself financially to large-scale colonization. Even if the province should support immigration, he reminded his colleagues, "I do not believe that colonization is our only necessity." In other words, he accepted the example of São Leopoldo while urging caution in attempts to extend that model to much more of the province.[45] Like a number of political leaders in the 1850s and 1860s, Mendonça did not criticize the ideal of the introduction of Europeans but protested against what the newspaper *O Mercantil* called "colonization at the price of gold."[46]

Mendonça and the others who called into question subsidies for colonization did not escape without criticism. Elites like Luís Alves Leite de Oliveira Bello argued that eliminating the cost of official immigration represented an ideal that Rio Grande do Sul was yet prepared to achieve. In a sharp tone, Oliveira Bello denied that the United States was an appropriate model for Brazilian immigration policy. Several factors, in his opinion, made the U.S. case distinct from the Brazilian one. The North American republic's greater economic prosperity, larger support networks for German residents, lack of slavery in much of its territory, and true religious liberty combined to give immigration to the United States a character Brazilians could not hope to replicate in their own country.[47] In the end, the realities that elites like Oliveira Bello mentioned (along with others, such as the greater expense of traveling from Europe to Brazil) would win the day, and provincial leaders would adhere inconsistently to policies of governmental support for colonization schemes until the early 1870s. By 1874, however, the battle would be against defenders of subsidies; criticisms of official funding of colonies would at that point lead provincial governments to return control over immigration to the hands of the imperial authorities.[48]

What is important about the criticisms of subsidy programs is not, of course, the financial but rather the social and cultural evaluations on which they were based. Beneath the assessments of the costs of colonization programs, that is, lay elites' criticisms of colonization itself. Despite all of their grand rhetorical celebrations of São Leopoldo and other immigrant settlements, many elites in Porto Alegre were not satisfied with the way colonization was taking shape in the province. In essence, their discontent derived from a sense of incomplete control over the new immigrants residing in the highlands. Championing the idea of smallholding agricultural colonization, elites became frustrated when German and German-Brazilian *colonos* refused to remain passively where Brazilian planners wanted them to be. One form this feeling took was an irritation with *colonos* who left their farm plots. In 1852, João Pereira da Silva Borges Fortes, for example, expressed desperation at the failure of colonization to meet the province's need for workers. It was not sheer numbers that had caused the shortfall, he assured his fellow members of the Provincial Assembly; rather, it was *colonos'* tendency to drift off the lands the province had given them. "The noble deputies know," he thus declared, "that these hands, when they arrive here, ordinarily take destinies different from those for which we had them come."[49] Similarly annoyed by *colonos'* independence was Fioravanti, who explained in 1857 that he understood the *colono* to have "the duty of dedicating himself to the work for which he was contracted." Unfortunately, like Borges Fortes, he found *colonos'* pattern to have been "the dispersal of men for ends other than those for which they were introduced into agriculture."[50] Given the benefits that virtually all Gaúcho elites associated with colonization, such mobility seemed to men like Borges Fortes and Fioravanti an affront to the province that had made great efforts to import European immigrants. That abandoning the colony might have represented the very spirit of enterprise they praised in Europeans seems not to have occurred to these elites. Their anger at immigrants' refusal to stay in their place overran any more sympathetic reading of *colonos'* actions.

The Germans who remained on their lands in the colonies presented other exasperating tendencies to elites in Porto Alegre. As they cataloged the concessions the government had made in the interest of immigration, elites often described *colonos* as ungrateful and demanding. In 1854, for instance, Ubatuba warned that the Provincial Assembly had to use great caution in drawing up any legislation on colonization. "The entire house knows," he argued, "that *colonos* are very demanding." If a law promised to defray "some small expenditures," he continued, "the *colono* can understand that the entrepreneur [of a private colony] has the obligation to give him good cigars from Havana, beer, and champagne, because they are small expenditures."[51] Other members of the Gaúcho elite expressed their irritation with *colonos'* "bad disposition" (*mau gênio*) in less sarcastic ways; the spirit of Ubatuba's complaint was, however, common at midcentury.

The most serious and frequent elite criticisms of *colonos* targeted the very foreignness of these immigrants. Elites in Porto Alegre very rarely derided German customs or culture in this period; rather, they centered their hostilities on German *colonos'* alleged resistance to assimilation into their new social surroundings. Looking up into the highlands or even around the streets of the provincial capital, many of these elites saw what most foreign visitors also observed there—a "semigermanization."[52] Indeed, for many, this phenomenon made Porto Alegre seem "in a manner a German settlement."[53] Particularly galling for Luso-Brazilian leaders was *colonos'* tendency to maintain control over education within their communities; as a result of this control, many schools both public and private in colonial areas were taught exclusively in German. In 1857, German-language schools made up, in fact, fully 86 percent of all educational institutions in São Leopoldo.[54] The director of the former colony, a German himself, reported in 1851 that inability to speak the national language was generalized there: "The Germans and their descendants who inhabit this Colony . . . absolutely ignore the idiom of Brazil . . . ; a multitude of individuals between the ages of 20 and 25, born in Brazil, are so ignorant in that respect that they require an interpreter when by chance they are obligated to appear before any Court."[55] The image of first- and now second-generation immigrants unable to speak Portuguese was deeply troubling to elites in Porto Alegre, for it suggested that the *colonos* constituted "a Germany that exists among us."[56]

Often political leaders warned that immigrants who would not adopt the language or customs of Brazil would not be loyal to the Empire. In 1854, for example, José Bernardino da Cunha Bittencourt ventured the opinion that "there is no son or even grandson of a German *colono* who fights for [*pugne pelo*] Brazil as though he were fighting for his fatherland; because of the examples of his parents, they look at this land more as a stepmother than as a mother."[57] With somewhat more kindness, others made allowances for the first-generation immigrant, while demanding "that the children of immigrants, those who were born in Brazilian territory, be Brazilians, feel with their feelings [*sintam com o sentir*], with their life, and with their spirit that they . . . share the common rights of Brazilians of the Portuguese race."[58] Although the position of the colonial zone in the highlands, removed from the pastoral economy and the ranchers who dominated it, may have rendered *colonos* less direct threats to the latifundia in Rio Grande do Sul than they might have been on the coffee frontier of São Paulo, these European arrivals clearly seemed a threatening force to many elites in Porto Alegre. Their sheer difference and apparent persistent cultural independence made Luso-Brazilians perceive them as dangerously autonomous.

This climate of suspicion of Germans' loyalty to the Empire contributed to the outbreak of three days of rioting in Porto Alegre in January 1863. When locals looted the *Prince of Wales*, a ship that had wrecked on a reef off the farthest southern coast of Rio Grande do Sul in 1861, and three officers of another British vessel found themselves arrested while on shore leave in Rio de Janeiro, the incidents set off a fiery international conflict that ended with a break in diplomatic ties between Brazil and Britain. As Richard Graham has argued, the so-called Christie Affair (after the British minister to Brazil, William Dougal Christie) developed against the backdrop of Brazil's continued efforts to establish its sovereignty against British influence; it was little more than a decade, after all, since the intervention of British warships had forced the end of the African slave trade to Brazil.[59] Of more immediate impact for Gaúchos in the 1860s was the reaction to a column in a German paper in Porto Alegre. When the editors of *Deutsche Zeitung* dared question the legitimacy of the Brazilian position in the dispute, they sparked what the provincial president delicately labeled an "excess of patriotism."[60] Police records suggest that some of "the most illustrious [*gradas*] people of the City, many of whom held important public offices," gathered in protest outside the home of *Deutsche Zeitung* the first day, but the presence of the chief of police calmed spirits. Soon, however, tensions spread, and the "less enlightened" joined in, leading to efforts to destroy the newspaper's printing press, minor conflicts between Germans and non-Germans, and the trampling of several onlookers by army horses. In the end, officials repeatedly stressed, not even "the smallest resentment" remained; the third day, apparently, witnessed Germans and Luso-Brazilians marching arm in arm as a show of reconciliation.[61]

Despite such ostentatious displays of harmony, misgivings about Germans' alleged isolation persisted, impelling elites in Porto Alegre to adopt a range of responses. The most sympathetic supported projects to bridge the gap between *colono* and Gaúcho through education. The editors of *A Reforma* went so far as to praise the German-language newspaper *O Kolonist;* before its demise, *A Reforma* noted, that journal for *colonos* had been extremely useful "since it carried to ten thousand *colonos* forgotten in their fields some awareness of what was happening in the world and above all of the laws of the Empire, which those ten thousand *colonos* are required to obey."[62] Others promoted a more effective extension of the province's school system up into the highlands. Some were even willing to admit instruction in German if no qualified Portuguese-speaking teacher was available; what was crucial was bringing the next generations of *colonos* into the structure of the dominant society.[63] A more complex and hostile reaction took the form of projects to increase the use of other national groups for colonization. Several influential political figures debated a shift from German to Portuguese colonization in 1854, for example. Before finally concluding that the Portuguese were not truly given to agriculture, these elites focused on the relative cultural similarities between the peoples of Brazil and its former metropole as a prime reason to consider this new stream of immigration. Bittencourt, for instance, argued this point forcefully: "The *colonos* that can for all reasons be most useful to us are undeniably the Portuguese. In addition to the habits, customs, and language similar to our own, we see that the second generation of Portuguese among us, Gentlemen, are already Brazilians." Such assertions faced direct denials; Fidêncio Prates, in fact, interrupted Bittencourt to claim that the most useful *colonos* were still Germans.[64] Even so, that the issue of non-German colonization was raised reflects the anxieties "cultural isolation" was causing elites in Porto Alegre.[65]

It was this same worry that led other elites to suggest what would have been a very different kind of colonization—one that used Brazilian plebeians rather than European immigrants. The 1850s in particular witnessed the emergence of a variety of proposals to install Brazilian workers, either exclusively or in combination with Europeans, in new colonies. Fioravanti in 1857 declared "national colonization" to be his particular aim. He would have the government "seek within the Empire the elements of the aggrandizement of the provinces [and] later import tons of diverse customs."[66] Caldre e Fião was another enthusiastic supporter of "internal colonization" projects, despite his professed respect for the "external" type. In a clear display of chauvinism, he argued that the provincial government should supply national workers with education and land that would allow them to compete with German *colonos*. Compared to the native Brazilians, "deprived of all resources," the immigrant faced "almost no difficulty to overcome" in Rio Grande do Sul.[67] In their formulations of plans to use Brazilian plebeians as *colonos*, elites like Caldre e Fião provided, however, few details. They left unanswered vital questions as to which plebeians would be used, how elites might choose them, and whether elites would set these Brazilians up as free smallholders. Given the reluctance such elites demonstrated with regard to incorporating national plebeians into their visions of progress, these vague projects of internal colonization seem to have served essentially as protests against German immigrants' persistent independence.

One more uncommon elite response in these years was trying to comprehend the motives behind what elites considered *colonos'* isolation. German immigrants and their descendants were indeed constructing their own cultures and systems of social relations in and around their colonies. What elites down in Porto Alegre rarely seem to have considered, however, is that these initiatives were reactions to conditions *colonos* faced in Rio Grande do Sul and not mere ingrained obstinacy.[68] Culture and society in the *colônias* were by no means static or homogeneous. At such basic levels as language and religion, the colonial communities were highly diverse collections of different forms that had come with immigrants from Europe. As soon as they found their way to their new residences, *colonos* engaged in dual processes of adaptation and change, creating German-Brazilian cultures that mixed different German patterns with Brazilian ones.[69]

Elites were to a certain degree correct in their assertions about *colonos'* attitudes toward the official society of their new home regions; they simply ignored the reasons behind the immigrants' positions. Both Germans and Italians proved eager to demand that the government fulfill its promises to them. After the imperial government cut its funding of colonization programs in 1830, for instance, Germans in São Leopoldo repeatedly petitioned authorities, seeking the payment of subsidies stipulated in their contracts.[70] Much later, Italian immigrants would stage a "strike," marching from the colony of D. Isabel (now the city of Bento Gonçalves) "alleging a lack of resources."[71] Rather than their "bad disposition," such protests revealed *colonos'* justifiable anger at authorities' negligence. Indeed, for most of the post-Farroupilha period in particular, the *colonos* of the highlands had minimal contact with the official world centered in Porto Alegre, and what little they had often seemed threatening to them. *Colonos'* construction of social clubs, German-language schools, and religious congregations was due primarily to the institutional vacuum into which official colonization programs had placed them. As a few elites in Porto Alegre recognized, neither the provincial nor the imperial government had done much to try to foster Germans' assimilation into Brazilian society. There were no cultural associations in which *colonos* and Luso-Brazilians could interact and virtually no agencies to provide social assistance to newly arriving Europeans. The state, moreover, established too thin an educational network in the area to accommodate immigrant parents who wanted their children to enter into formal studies. Religion was an even more problematic area. Neither the Roman Catholic minority nor the Protestant majority in São Leopoldo (in 1845 the proportion was 36 percent Catholic to 64 percent Protestant) and other colonies had ready access to clergy or institutions of their faith. Lacking official priests and ministers, these German-Brazilians created their own systems of worship, in which religious authorities were selected from within the community. The modifications of both ritual and dogma that accompanied the development of these varieties of popular Catholicism and Protestantism would lead to tensions when religious hierarchies tried to take more direct control of the colonial zones of Rio Grande do Sul. Indeed, open, bloody conflict broke out when the largely poor and illiterate followers of one insular sect, the so-called Muckers, refused to bow before religious and civil officials.[72]

Authorities gave German immigrants little reason to pursue integration into the Brazilian polity. As we have already observed, government policy made naturalization a difficult procedure. Beyond that, the citizenship official Brazil had to offer did not have obvious advantages for foreign-born residents of Rio Grande do Sul. Naturalization did not legally represent a grant of full political rights. Only the Brazilian-born, for example, were eligible for election to most government offices. At the same time as it denied naturalized citizens some rights, government legislation also imposed heavy obligations on them. Most notoriously, the achievement of Brazilian citizenship carried with it vulnerability to recruitment into the military or the National Guard. Non-Catholics were, moreover, denied not only legal recognition of their marriages and their children's legitimacy (until 1861) but also political rights (until 1881).[73] Official policy, in sum, treated *colonos* as at best "second-class Brazilians."[74] Facing so many obstacles and with limited potential rewards, relatively few Germans and German-Brazilians sought to join the political community of the province.

If the indifferent or at times hostile face of the government inspired much of German *colonos'* "isolation," this was not the full explanation. Not only Germanic but also other ethnic groups that came to occupy the *colônias* of

Rio Grande do Sul displayed a tendency to try to preserve their groups' heritage.[75] As noted above, this phenomenon was far from a simple continuity; blending elements from different European and local Brazilian cultures, *colonos* produced their own Teuto- or Italian-Brazilian beliefs and behaviors. These processes of construction did not, however, simply derive from authorities' negligence. Particularly after 1850, when different types of German immigrants began to arrive in the province, Rio Grande do Sul witnessed occasional expressions of "Germanism," or German chauvinism. The generation that would nurture these feelings was led by Germans who left Europe after the failed revolutionary movements of 1848. Known collectively as the "Brummers" (understood in Rio Grande do Sul to mean "grumblers" or "complainers"), these immigrants tended to come from more highly educated and politicized classes and immediately began to foster new attitudes among the Teuto-Brazilian community in Porto Alegre and the *colônias*.[76] In the late 1870s and into the 1880s, the foremost Brummer, Carlos von Koseritz, was championing German contributions to the province. Even after the close of provincial government-sponsored immigration in 1874, Koseritz called for measures to create a more massive immigration of Germans to Rio Grande do Sul. In justification of this project, he argued that Germans had in fact a special "cultural mission" in the world; Brazil would do well to bring in the carriers of the "religion of labor" and "German enlightenment."[77] While it is difficult to judge to what extent common German-Brazilians adapted them, the ideas of Brummers like Koseritz show that some manifestations of *colonos'* separateness went beyond direct reactions to authorities' institutional neglect of their communities; by the 1880s, certain tendencies had clearly gone beyond protectionist stances and burst forth into avowedly Germanist positions.

Ironically, just as these more pro-German attitudes were gaining strength, many Gaúcho elites were moving toward a greater inclusion of *colonos* in provincial society and politics. The socioeconomic development of the *colônias* and their accompanying gains in potential political power were key factors in this transformation. From the 1840s on, the colonial economy became increasingly articulated into that of Porto Alegre. The isolation of the capital during the Farroupilha had, as noted earlier, sparked the production by *colonos* in São Leopoldo. From 1846 onward, this commercial orientation proved to be decisive for São Leopoldo and other colonies located on the river system that converged on Porto Alegre. While thus linked to the provincial economy, the *colonos* otherwise remained in their relative isolation. With relatively little interference from outsiders, merchants in the colonial zone began to increase their wealth and power at the expense of the simple agricultural smallholder. Thus, along with the booming prosperity of the region came the growing impoverishment of much of the colonial population.[78] Nonetheless, demographic and economic growth in the colonies led the provincial government to begin to grant them status as *municípios*. As regular political units of the province, the former colonies became sources of potential support for leaders looking to gain or consolidate their power in politics.

By the mid-1870s, in fact, the colonies were becoming ever more integrated into the political system based in Porto Alegre. Individual members of the emerging *colono* elite were, moreover, succeeding in establishing themselves as figures of some importance. Despite the disincentives explained earlier, the number of *colonos* becoming electors had been increasing since midcentury. Beginning in São Leopoldo, these new voters were able to force out many of the nonimmigrant politicians who had previously dominated local politics in their areas.[79] Frederico Haensel became the first naturalized citizen elected to the Provincial Assembly when the law changed in 1881; three years later, Koseritz took his own place as the first non-Catholic in that body.[80] The increasingly hierarchical, class-differentiated society of the colonies was producing its own political leaders, and these men were, in small numbers at least, beginning to join the representatives of the dominant classes in the province.

For some nonimmigrant politicians, this development coincided with their own partisan struggles. In the 1850s and 1860s, formal politics in Rio Grande do Sul, as we have seen, were marked by a hazy definition of parties. A series of electoral and personal alliances had led to the creation of new political groupings that eroded the Liberal-Conservative distinction characteristic of the 1845–52 period. By 1860, however, the formation of the Historical Liberal Party marked the reemergence of a more familiar form of partisan conflict. Arguing for a stricter ideological conception of political parties, leaders like Félix Xavier da Cunha, Gaspar Silveira Martins, and Manuel Luís Osório promoted the cause of an elitist reform Liberalism. Da Cunha's 1863 manifesto, for example, called for the political decentralization of the Empire, the adoption of direct elections, greater individual liberties, and other projects that characterized Liberal programs of nineteenth-century Brazil.[81]

Religious freedom was perfectly in keeping with this Liberalism. When the Liberals were forced out of power at the national and provincial levels at the close of the 1860s, they picked up on this issue as part of a reinvigorated reformism. Their more energetic calls for change were perhaps more a maneuver to win back positions of power than a heartfelt demand for restructuring the nation's political and social relations.[82] Whether or not the ideologues of Rio Grande do Sul's Liberal Party believed in the justice of political rights for non-Catholics and the foreign-born, they certainly could make good use of the issue. Not only could Liberals like Silveira Martins take advantage of debates on the matter to denounce Conservatives as tyrannical and reactionary, but they might also win new electoral support if they achieved immigrants' political enfranchisement.[83]

Liberal overtures toward potential colonial supporters in the 1870s and 1880s did not mark the end of elite suspicion of German and other European immigrants, nor did they guarantee the continued loyalty of immigrants and their progeny to the Liberal Party. World wars, immigrants' participation in the labor movement, and other developments provoked subsequent revivals of nativism in Porto Alegre.[84] Moreover, by 1888, some Gaúcho legislators were asserting that immigrants were becoming Conservative in their electoral behavior.[85] Liberals' willingness to link colonization to the increasingly conflict-ridden partisan politics of the post-Farroupilha period suggests, however, that the hostility elites had evinced toward an isolated *colono* community was fading. If not exactly matching the ideal of the enterprising yet obedient, civilized yet subordinate *colono* that elites had conjured up at mid-century, immigrants were nevertheless proving to be less of a direct threat to social hierarchies than were the national poor.

In yet another newspaper column early in 1853, O Estudante displayed great amusement at the sight of German immigrants trying to become *gaúchos*, the cowboys of Rio Grande do Sul's vast ranching region: "As there are now in the city two friends who have Bucephaluses to rent and there are many blond compatriots who have sworn by their Gods either to break their noses twenty times or become horsemen, I saw many races in the streets and even saw several families bury themselves behind their daddies so that the blond compatriots would not ride right over them."[86] Although the cowboy figure of the *gaúcho* had not yet become the romantic symbol of the province, these wild riding lessons certainly represented for O Estudante a humorous example of German *colonos* attempting to adapt to their new homeland. Just as certainly, in the chronicler's view, the endeavor was not going well. Elsewhere members of Porto Alegre's elite evinced similar interest in, but much less tolerance for, immigrants' difficulties in fitting into their society.

European immigrants provided an easy symbol of the progress that elites in Porto Alegre hoped to realize in their province in the years 1846–80. To the eyes of an elite beset with all too familiar resistance from "national" plebeians, the *colonos* arriving in the highlands near the Gaúcho capital seemed carriers of many of the traits that had made their home nations centers of economic prosperity and civilization. Their presumed hard work, orderly habits, racial superiority, and even investable wealth all would spur Rio Grande do Sul toward not only increasing economic prosperity but also a more acceptable social formation. *Colonos* would, in the dreams of regional elites, replace or reform troublesome national plebeians.

These same elites vacillated, however, on just what space they wanted European workers to occupy in Gaúcho society. As was to be expected, the powerful in the region were not anxious to lose any of their dominance to new competitors. That these potential challengers came from nations Brazilian elites considered models of progress must have made the immigrants that much more intimidating. By the end of the period, as they discovered potential sources of strength in the increasingly stratified and decreasingly remote communities of the colonial zone, elites in Porto Alegre would begin to experiment with greater integration of *colonos* into the province's dominant social relations—and even into formal politics. The perceived threat of these foreigners within Brazil had faded so much that greater incorporation of *colonos* and their descendants became an issue in the increasingly heated partisan politics focused in Porto Alegre.

3

The Politics of Everyday Life in the City

We cannot all be masters, nor all masters
Cannot be truly follow'd.

William Shakespeare, Othello

In the early 1830s, Arsène Isabelle, a French businessman who later came to know Porto Alegre well, expressed surprise that the harsh conditions of slavery in the city did not lead the enslaved to rebel. Isabelle was no lover of the blacks and mulattoes whom he saw working in servitude on the streets of the city; "They are necessarily brutes," he wrote, "vile usurpers of the name of men." It was, however, principally the treatment they received at the hands of their *senhores* that appalled the traveler. To the question of how Porto Alegre's masters treated their slaves, Isabelle answered: "Like we treat our dogs! They begin by insulting them. If they do not come immediately, they receive two or three from the delicate hand of their mistress, metamorphosed into a harpy, or a rough punch, a brutal kick from their rude master." Still, he asserted, those slaves who only felt punches and kicks were lucky; other masters whipped their captives hundreds of times and even rubbed pepper into their victims' open wounds. In light of such depravity, he remarked, "It is astounding how the blacks do not revolt against the whites!"[1]

If Isabelle found the apparent dearth of slave resistance in Porto Alegre inexplicable, the most influential scholar of slavery in the region certainly did not. Indeed, in *Capitalismo e escravidão no Brasil meridional*, a work first published in 1962, sociologist (and later president of Brazil) Fernando Henrique Cardoso placed the blame for slaves' supposed inaction on the nature of the slave regime itself.[2] Taking slavery as a system of material and social production, Cardoso argued that it created in the enslaved a sense of themselves as less than human. This process of objectification (*coisificação*), he theorized, limited slave initiatives to primitive and unthinking negations of their captivity, "gestures of desperation and revolt" that expressed their "vague desire for freedom."[3]

Several generations of scholars have challenged Cardoso's depiction of Gaúcho slaves as individuals reduced by their captivity to prerational status.[4] The documentation under analysis here—particularly the 427 criminal court cases (*processos crime*) and the police and government records that constitute the base of my research—renders his thesis insufficient in several regards. Cardoso does not account, first of all, for the richness of overt, dramatic rebellion; black slaves did revolt against white masters, if only out of Isabelle's range of vision. Second, and much more tellingly, Cardoso's thesis fails to recognize the creativity, political savvy, and persistence that Gaúcho slaves demonstrated as they read the changing power relations in which their lives were embedded and then acted on their interpretations. The enslaved, that is, practiced a wide range of subtle forms of resistance in their daily relations with their *senhores* and other social superiors. As Cardoso's most eloquent critic, Sidney Chalhoub, has argued, *Capitalismo e escravidão* performed a crucial historiographical task by emphasizing the violence of the system of slavery. Because it exaggerated the effects of that brutality on the enslaved, however, Cardoso's book ended up denying slaves' political capacities.[5]

These popular projects point to the existence of something unthinkable in Cardoso's analysis—a vibrant and complex popular political culture in mid-nineteenth-century Porto Alegre. Indeed, the types of slave resistance that scholars have found lacking in *Capitalismo e escravidão* merely formed a part, if a central one, of that political culture. Participants in that culture, to begin with, included the free as well as the enslaved. Slavery constituted a basic division within the popular classes, often compelling the enslaved to pursue different strategies than the free poor. This distinction was not enough, however, to prevent the formation of solidarities or deny broad parallels in the projects of the enslaved and the free. Moreover, the universe of popular political understandings and initiatives encompassed projects that were not primarily or exclusively reactions against elite power or its quotidian manifestations.[6]

Rather than attempting a cataloging of popular political strategies, this chapter will lay out the motivations behind the most common strategies non-elites employed. Teasing out plebeian attitudes is never, of course, uncomplicated; proceeding with care and an awareness of sources' limitations, however, we can arrive at reasonable reconstructions of plebeian aims. In the documentation examined on Porto Alegre during the 1845–80 period, we see that men and women of the *povo* struggled to achieve the trappings of personal sovereignty: physical mobility; family continuity; improvements in living and working conditions; and, more abstractly, gains in power relative to their social superiors and their fellow plebeians. Playing with seigneurial social relations, they attempted to turn ideals of paternalism into models with clear responsibilities and, most important, *rights* for dependents and *obligations* on patrons.[7] Extreme strategies of revolt, the formation of *quilombos* (runaway slave communities), and definitive flight (often over the border into Argentina or another country) were options available to plebeians and undoubtedly lurked in the consciousness of masters as well. Such radical efforts were, however, highly risky and therefore also rare.[8] The usual pattern was instead to try to manipulate seigneurialism. Given the range and ingenuity of plebeian initiatives, it is more apt to describe this as working *with*, rather than merely *within*, the dominant cultural patterns of seigneurialism.

Engaging Masters and Mistresses

Some of the complexity of Porto Alegre's plebeian political culture emerged in the case of the freedwoman Benedita, who made use of patron-client relations in the mid-1880s. A former slave of the Baroness of Cahy, Benedita had a son, Felipe, who was in constant trouble with the police. Only twelve years old, Felipe was said to gamble and wander the streets. When he confronted Manoel, a fellow Afro-Brazilian minor, about a gambling debt, a fight ensued (one witness supposed it to be *capoeira*, a martial art) in which Felipe fatally wounded Manoel. In the course of the investigation of the crime, it came out that Benedita, though now free and apparently living away from her *senhora*, had put her son back in the service of the baroness. According to one witness, this was neither a way for the boy to gain money nor the fulfillment by Benedita of some obligation to her ex-mistress; rather, the mother had put her son in the house where she herself had served, hoping the baroness would "take charge of him since she [Benedita] cannot control him due to his bad behavior."[9]

Coming in an era that saw innumerable efforts by slaves and freedpersons to win the manumission of their kin, this is an extraordinarily suggestive story. Even if she had maintained an amicable relationship with her former owner, the decision to place her son in the service of the *senhora* must have torn at Benedita's heart. Whatever the nature of her emancipation had been, Benedita now lived and raised her son on her own. Making use of the baroness as she did would have restricted not only the boy's freedom but perhaps that of Benedita herself; Felipe's entry into the *senhora*'s household, that is, might have appeared as a favor that Benedita would later have to return in some manner. The question of putting limits on Felipe was, of course, precisely what Benedita seems to have been after here. Pressed by difficult circumstances, Benedita seems to have seen in the baroness's control the possibility of more effectively disciplining her son. Her strategy here reminds us again that Porto Alegre's plebeian political culture was not simply a culture of resistance. Benedita may have been trying to achieve the kind of family solidity that her own conditions made improbable, but the means she used would in practice most likely have supported social relations in which she and other plebeians held positions of relative weakness.

As Benedita's experience points out, the patron or *senhor* was a figure of supreme importance for plebeians. Of course, the free and enslaved poor also confronted the police and other social superiors on a daily basis. Several scholars have traced the growth in the social-control functions of the police and judicial systems in Rio Grande do Sul in the second half of the nineteenth century; as historians Paulo Moreira and Valéria Zanetti have argued, this phenomenon represented the extension of state power into elite-*povo* relations in Porto Alegre and its province. The intervention of the state was, however, restricted primarily to those relations that took place in the public spaces of the capital city, as we will later see in relation to popular religious practices.[10] The line between state and seigneurial control was indeed shifting and indefinite in midcentury Porto Alegre. On the one hand, masters commonly used state apparatuses as instruments with which to discipline their own slaves. Protests against this practice from even before the Farroupilha did not stop masters from sending slaves to the police to be whipped in the city jail into the late 1870s.[11] On the other hand, city officials (like their counterparts in the national capital) enacted but rarely enforced regulations concerning seigneurial treatment of slaves. Again, efforts to impose humane standards of comportment on masters appeared early in the independent Brazilian Empire. In 1824, for instance, Porto Alegre's municipal council noted that it had received an order from the national government to set up a code to fine "*senhores* who, forgetting the sacred duties of religion and humanity, punish their slaves or give them bad treatment."[12] The intent of these laws was not to impose uniform regulations on the master-slave relationship. The aim was rather to prevent the worst tyrannies of slaveholders, which might tarnish the paternalist sheen that legitimized patron-client relations in the region.[13]

The legal proceedings involving Antonio Gonçalves Carneiro and his slave André demonstrate, moreover, that in the final instance, the state would bow before patronal control even in cases of horrific abuse. In 1852, André stayed away from his master's house for three days. As an *escravo de ganho*, André worked as a shoe repairman, bringing back to his *senhor* part or all of his wages.[14] It was the loss of one such paying job that led to André's temporary flight; as his fellow slave Aniceto later testified before the police, "having been fired from a cobbler's shop, fearing to return to the house of . . . his *senhor*, who would punish him," André absented himself. Whether he hoped that a few days' time would cool his master's anger or simply give him the chance to find new employment, André's ploy did not work. Shortly after arriving back in his master's control, André suffered beatings that would ultimately cause his death. As André lay dying in his tiny room, begging for water, his master merely complained that the slave would not go immediately to work in the garden. So scandalous was this case that it reached the Council of State (Conselho de Estado), an appointive body that advised the emperor directly on the highest matters of state. The council found, however, that the *senhor*'s right of property outweighed the government's duty to prevent excessive cruelty and even murder in master-slave relations.[15] In this and less notorious cases, the limits of the expansion of state power into master-slave relations—particularly in residences and other spaces defined as private—were evident.[16] As late as the early 1880s, in fact, authorities would fail to keep *senhores* from using state institutions and personnel as instruments in the domination of their dependents. Throughout this period, that is, masters would continue to send their slaves to the public jail to receive whippings.[17] The role of the state in disciplining the poor indeed expanded from midcentury on, but *senhores* held on to their position of primacy in elite-plebeian relations. Plebeians would thus have to respond to the police while devoting more direct and careful attention to their patrons.

The importance of the *senhor* did not lie exclusively in his role as the hand of discipline. Certainly, as the case of André suggests, seigneurial power rested firmly on the application of violence; no consideration of paternalism should overlook the centrality of physical violence to patron-client and master-slave relations. Punishment was, however, merely one part of the complex relations between *senhores* and their dependents, a means by which one side might try to enforce its claims on the other. Patron-client relations were essentially informal pacts of mutual responsibility and, in a sense, dependence. Patrons controlled vital resources, doling them out to clients in exchange for obedience and loyalty. The parties in such relations did not, of course, hold equal power. *Senhores* might frame granting access to land or protection as paternal benevolence, but such acts were certainly not donations; patrons expected their wishes to be fulfilled in return and were willing to back up their expectations with threats and eventually violence.[18]

In the urban setting of the Gaúcho capital, masters offered both economic opportunities and protection to their clients. Porto Alegre's *senhores* could, first of all, provide access to land and stable work situations. Indeed, when the slave João Antonio dos Santos and the free day laborer (*jornaleiro*) Manoel José Sanhudo attempted to buy a piece of land for themselves in 1874, several more prominent landowners marveled at this "extraordinary" event. As follows from our earlier analysis of the "ideology of vagrancy," the very idea of plebeians' setting up independent production around the city met with elite disapproval.[19] For this reason, as well as a relative lack of viable alternatives, even those who fled intolerable situations of subordination often ended up toiling for a *senhor.*[20]

More important for patron-client relations in the city, however, was the defense *senhores* could offer their dependents, particularly against incursions by the state. Influential patrons could support those involved in legal problems. Whether as authors or targets of legal cases, plebeians commonly used their links to such *senhores* to support the honesty of their character and assertions. Accused of robbery and assault in 1853, for example, the carpenter Dionísio José put forward as evidence of his innocence the fact that "he had never been disorderly, as he can prove with very distinct Persons of this city."[21] Elsewhere opponents pitted the prestige and power of their patrons against each other, often presenting written statements these *senhores* had signed on their behalf.[22] At other times, elites entered the courtroom as patrons in a more direct manner. "Attending the entreaties and requests of the wife and several friends of the supplicant," for example, the Baron of Cahy withdrew a complaint against the day laborer Tristão Pires de Lima in 1877; the phrasing of his proclamation makes clear that the supplicant and his allies were to understand his act as one of seigneurial generosity, with the likely implication of future compensation by Tristão.[23] Other patrons served as the legal representatives of accused criminals; perhaps the best example of this is provided by *senhores* who tried to prevent their slaves' condemnation. One lawyer ventured to declare this more than a legal right of *senhores:* "It is certain," commented Serafim dos Anjos França in 1851, "that the *senhor* is the natural *curador* [legal defender] of the slave."[24]

Patrons' protection of their clients extended, of course, beyond the confines of the police station or courtroom. Indeed, as we shall see, *senhores* could help keep their slaves or other dependents out of the hands of military recruiters. Service in the army, National Guard, or navy was technically required of all Brazilian men. The law provided so many exceptions, however, that troops were largely raised through forced recruitment. In practice, the wealthy and powerful manipulated this system to keep themselves, their sons, and their dependents out of the army and the lower ranks of the National Guard. Military service thus fell mainly on the unprotected poor.[25] Much the same can be said of harsh police vigilance: members of a failed slave revolt in Gravataí resorted to searches for new *padrinhos* (literally, godfathers; figuratively, patrons) to shield them against the police in their reintegration into slave society, suggesting the extent to which patron-client relations were key in this society.[26]

Important here is not the full scope of such relations in Gaúcho society but rather what this represented for dependents. Although assuredly not the equals of their *senhores* in social status or power, plebeians tried to impose political meanings on their relationships with patrons.[27] Slaves and the free poor put forward their own constructions of the respective roles and responsibilities of patrons and clients. These plebeian interpretations turned on an understanding of patron-client relations as contractual, with rights not only for the *senhor* but also for the dependent. Plebeians considered any *senhor* who failed to meet the obligations contained in the popular vision of patronage a bad master; as one slave put it in 1872, such a *senhor* was "very impertinent."[28] It was through this general strategem that plebeians in Porto Alegre sought the various components of the experience of autonomy that were accessible to them within their society's hegemonic seigneurial relations.

One of these much desired conditions associated with independence was the maintenance of solid and lasting family ties. The ability to live with or frequently see close relatives emerges in the documentation as a common demand of plebeians; this is precisely what makes Benedita's case so heartrending. After the slave Maria ran away from her *senhor* in 1846, for instance, the only aspect of her life she mentioned as a possible justification for her flight was that her master had recently sold off two of her three young children.[29] The emancipation of relatives was a related concern for slaves in Porto Alegre, as we shall see; here we need only note that at times the attempt to win freedom for family members was also a way to try to bring them closer. The complaint Dona Damazia Joaquina Ferreira made against the *pardo* tailor's apprentice Antonio Clemente Suzano in 1850 provides a suggestive example of this motive. Dona Damazia alleged that Antonio had been trying to spirit away Libania, a slave of hers. Producing two letters supposedly in the defendant's handwriting, the slaveholder further argued that Libania's mother had in fact sent Antonio to Porto Alegre from Rio de Janeiro specifically to carry out this task. The first of the letters supported this charge, Antonio reporting to the mother that he would have to wait in Porto Alegre "a little while longer until I have money for her ticket and mine, since it does not suit me [*não me convem*] to send her alone." The factual truth of the case is, as ever, impossible to ascertain; a judge ultimately dismissed the charges against Antonio on technical grounds having to do with police procedure in the case. Still, Antonio admitted to knowing Libania and her mother and to having sheltered the slave during a previous flight. At the very least, then, the case suggests that this family friend, possibly on orders from the girl's mother, was looking out for Libania.[30] Even this less remarkable alternative, however, shows plebeians' concern with the care of their family members, whether they were close at hand or several days' travel away.

Brought before the authorities to explain their actions in and around the city, plebeians often mentioned the very down-to-earth conditions of their service to patrons as a primary motivation. With tactics such as temporary flight, work slowdowns, and even physical threats, plebeians sought to improve the conditions of their working lives. Insufficient food or excessive workloads, for example, at times were given as reasons for flight or aggression. In 1869, the African slave Felipe explained to police that he had run away from the pottery factory where he worked because of the unacceptable conditions there; "the cause" of his flight, he averred, was "his work in the factory [*olaria*], in which he then found himself, very heavy, and the food given by his *senhor*, so tiny that it would not sustain a man even if he were not working, since it is just a portion of *charque* with potatoes that is distributed at noon . . . , only infrequently varying from potatoes to beans."[31]

At other times, plebeians struck out at overseers (*capatazes* or *feitores*); in this regard, as in others, these individuals may have served as substitutes for or representatives of their patrons. Indeed, since overseers often had much greater contact with workers and more direct control over subordinates' lives and work, they were natural targets of negotiations in general and violence in particular.[32] The very choice of an overseer could thus be one of the most important circumstances in a plebeian's life. For that reason, workers tried to influence their *senhores*' selection of a *capataz*.

In 1863, on a *fazenda* near Taquari, frustration at the reversal of a decision about an overseer led slaves to rise up. Eighteen-year-old Manoel, one of the slaves involved, later explained to the police in Porto Alegre that he and his fellows had not really "revolted." They certainly had been angry, however, at the return of a hated overseer; fired twice by the slaves' *senhor*, the overseer returned at the behest of the *senhor*'s son. The slaves' complaints about the overseer revolved around basic issues. One slave had apparently complained to the *senhor* about the food rations the overseer provided; he allegedly gave them only peas and at times took away their food and threw it to the dogs. It was seemingly because of their circumvention of his authority and his probable fears of dismissal that the overseer had sworn vengeance against the slaves. Although he had not yet punished any of the slaves, they clearly anticipated beatings; it was because of the inevitability of punishment, Manoel and his colleague Francisco explained, that some of them had tried to flee and others had resisted arrest. In this instance, then, slaves' violence was less offensive than defensive; they appear to have been protecting themselves. But here, too, this violent confrontation formed part of a longer process of bargaining; what most irked these slaves was that the gains they had made in negotiations with their elder *senhor* had so unfairly been taken away from them. They felt, that is, that the younger *senhor* and the overseer had unjustly revoked their hard-won privileges or rights.[33]

The case of the slave Fortunato illustrates how plebeians read their personal political surroundings while pursuing goals related to working conditions. At a moment when his *senhor*'s financial well-being and authority seemed in doubt, Fortunato tried to create some changes in discipline at the sugar refinery where he worked. According to his master, a Portuguese immigrant named Francisco Caetano dos Santos, the slave had become more disobedient in the months before the final eruption of violence. This change was not due to any increase in punishment or deterioration in rations or other living conditions, but rather to the slave's perception of a change in the balance of power in his relationship with Francisco. The owner of the sugar refinery Francisco administered also noticed this, saying that until recently Fortunato had "always been of good conduct and very submissive." After Francisco fell into financial difficulties, even having to pawn some of his belongings, that submissive behavior gave way to audacity. Fortunato began trying to control his own time. The administrator was having breakfast with a friend at seven o'clock A.M. when Fortunato came down from bed. When Francisco asked, "Is this a time for you to get up?" Fortunato defiantly responded, "Yes, it is." Aware of the administrator's poor financial situation and knowing also that his skills as a sugar refiner were valuable, the slave dared Francisco to sell him. When Fortunato went on to call Francisco a bad master, however, he pushed too far and soon faced an irate overseer armed with a club. Ultimately, then, Fortunato's attempt to profit from a changing political scene backfired, leaving him with two broken arms and other injuries.[34]

The moderation of an initiative was not, then, a guarantee of its success; Fortunato dragged his feet and insulted his master but did not flee captivity or physically assault his owner. Still, in almost all possible ways, plebeians pressured *senhores* and other figures of authority, hoping that at least some of their efforts might bring them more of the autonomous conditions that lay within their reach. Two of the most highly charged of their goals in this regard involved punishment and emancipation. Touching on masters' rights to treat their workers as they saw fit—even as property, in the case of slave workers—these issues struck at the very heart of the power relations between *senhores* and plebeians in Rio Grande do Sul. Because of this, popular efforts to make their positions on punishment and emancipation count were the most politically volatile of plebeian initiatives within Gaúcho society. Perhaps also because of the centrality of the issues involved, slave efforts here focused especially on appeals to new protectors, whether public officials, previous masters, or neighbors. Usually these appeals had as their stated aim the removal—most commonly through sale—of the slave from an abusive master or overseer.

This strategic tendency is telling. As they shook two of the pillars of seigneurial authority—the rights to punish and hold in bondage—slaves thus attempted to enlist the help of alternative authority figures against their patrons. In doing so, moreover, they revealed the complexity of their political machinations within the hierarchical relations that characterized their society. Insofar as they were searching for a new patron-protector, they worked very much within accepted patterns and, indeed, often rhetorically supported the rights of elites to hold and punish slaves.[35] After all, they were not—or did not want to appear to be—rejecting subordination to a *senhor* but merely seeking what they considered to be a more just master. At the same time, however, by trying to turn that new authority against their old patron, they took on more independence of action than elites desired. If not as radical as slave rebellion or escape across the border, these manipulations of hierarchy were much more politically complex and, at least when they worked as planned, perhaps more strategically astute than more dramatic incidents.

Charging a *senhor* with excessive brutality was not without its own risks and drama. Any slave who ran to the police or to a presumably sympathetic private citizen to make such an allegation in the hope of forcing transfer to another master was taking a serious step that could easily lead to the intensification rather than alleviation of intolerable punishments. The slave Estácio, for example, reported in 1869 that he had been beaten for a previous complaint he had made to the police about his master's cruelty.[36]

The most impressive aspect of these efforts, however, is the assertion of a plebeian vision of what was proper in relations between master and slave. National and provincial legislation had, once again, tried without great success to regulate the punishment of slaves. As the Council of State made clear in its review of the case of the slave André and his master Antonio Gonçalves Carneiro, however, final authority over punishment lay in the hands of the master.[37] In spite of such official attitudes, slaves argued that excessive or unfair beatings justified outside intervention in their relations with a *senhor*. In 1863, the slave Estácio complained not only of repeated beatings but also of threats of being beaten for a week straight; like other slaves, he resisted being put in irons.[38] Perhaps the most famous such incident took place in 1874, when Luiza, a slave of one of the most powerful and renowned political figures in the province, Gaspar Silveira Martins, presented herself to police in Porto Alegre and alleged that her mistress mistreated her horribly. The case would gain greater notoriety in later years, when another of Silveira Martins's slaves died because of alleged mistreatment; in the early 1880s, the Liberal leader's political opponents would bring the first incident to light again in an attempt to discredit Silveira Martins.[39]

When they went to the police to denounce their *senhor* for cruelty, the slaves Genoveva, Leopoldina, and Rufina likewise concentrated not on the fact of punishment but on the use of offensive types of punishment. Their master's punches, particularly the one that was said to have caused the fifty-year-old Genoveva to lose sight in her right eye, had led them to make their allegations, they told the police.[40] Within the classification of unfair punishments, slaves included beatings for deeds they had not committed. Indeed, phrases such as "for no reason at all" feature prominently in slaves' testimony about unacceptable punishments; often, that is, they denied having given their masters any reason for the beatings or tortures they suffered.[41] Similarly improper, some tried to argue, were punishments from anyone but their owners. In 1880, for instance, the twenty-two-year-old *crioula* slave Silvana responded to a beating with the declaration that "it is not this way that you put your hands on others' slaves." Her aggressor was not her mistress, Maria Luiza Nelson, but rather a public functionary who had slapped Silvana in the house where she worked.[42]

Silvana's action suggests, further, that slaves appealed to their legal owners when the *senhores* who had rented their services proved too quick to punish. This pattern appeared again in separate incidents that occurred eleven years apart. In each case, a thirteen-year-old girl, first the slave Eva and then the former slave Rita, justified a horrible crime with reference to her failure to convince her *senhora* to remove her from brutal renters. Each girl's mistress had rented her out to serve as nursemaid in another household. Their frustrations with conditions in their new homes led both Eva and Rita to wreak terrible vengeance not on their masters but rather on the more vulnerable figures of their masters' children. Both Eva and Rita made clear that they understood their acts to have resulted from failed attempts to negotiate their way out of workplaces they did not like.[43]

Implicit in some such arguments was, however, a recognition of the proper application of mild corrections for slaves' actual misdeeds. The slave Verediana explained in 1874, for example, that her *senhor* mistreated her frequently; what is intriguing, however, is that Verediana admitted that she had made mistakes in her service. Her anger at her master derived from his violent reaction to less significant mistakes; she alleged that "he punishes her frequently, for the most minor fact that she commits."[44] Similarly, the *crioula* Luiza charged in that same year that her mistress beat her for "futile" causes, while the *parda* Leopoldina declared in 1865 that "she never fled nor committed serious faults [*graves culpas*], and that her *senhor* mistreated her for light mistakes."[45] At least implicitly, then, these slaves argued that punishment, when not extreme and when following serious transgressions, was intrinsic to their relations with *senhores* and perhaps unavoidable. As long as they refrained from serious offenses like flight, according to this plebeian view, slaves should enjoy freedom from seigneurial excesses. In making this point, slaves like Verediana, Luiza, and Leopoldina argued, in effect, for de facto if not de jure limitations on masters' authority over slave workers.

Slaves' petitions to authorities on matters of emancipation followed a broadly similar pattern. In point of fact, the right of slaves to put together a savings fund, or peculium (*pecúlio*), which would not be subject to the control of their *senhores* and which slaves could use to buy their freedom, received legal recognition only with the 1871 passage of the Rio Branco (Free Womb) Law by the national parliament.[46] Before this legislation, such a distinguished legal authority as Perdigão Malheiro could note, as he did in 1866, "Among us, no law guarantees to a slave the peculium, and even less so the free disposal [of such a sum]." The only exceptions he noted were customary and not juridical. The concession of a peculium, however, had become common: "Even in cities and towns," he wrote, "some permit their slaves to work like free persons, giving them [the masters], however, a certain daily wage; the excess is their peculium." As was his general tendency, Perdigão Malheiro underlined the ultimate authority of the *senhor* in relations with his captive workers. Whether or not granting the right to a peculium was wise, he cautioned that this was a decision that lay with the master: "If the *senhores* tolerate" a slave's use of a peculium, "it is a fact that must . . . be respected."[47] As Manuela Carneiro da Cunha has argued, such a formulation of the question of self-purchase participated in a conception of manumission that, until 1871 at least, left power over emancipation in the hands of the *senhor* and not of government authorities. By allowing individual slaveholders to control the granting and revocation of liberty, the "silences of the law" thus helped masters foster subservient behavior among both those aspiring to freedom and the newly freed.[48] This kind of construction did not, however, preclude the manipulations of slaves and freedpersons. Indeed, the enslaved plebeians of Porto Alegre consistently demonstrated a willingness to put forward their own interested understandings of their rights in the question of self-purchase.

The construction of emancipation with which Gaúcho slaves confronted seigneurial power revolved around a contractual understanding of master-slave relations. Not only after the Rio Branco Law but also before it, slaves in Porto Alegre claimed a degree of legal personality that they did not in the strictest formal sense have. They asserted, that is, the right to compel (or better, to have the authorities compel) their masters to respect their ability to put together a peculium and apply it toward their freedom. What is more, they demanded that *senhores* be made to respect agreements on this matter.[49] Indeed, despite its clear provisions in this regard, the passage of the 1871 law did not free slaves from the need to fight for their right to purchase their manumission. Slaves who had been able to build up their savings and convince their owners to set a price for their liberty later had to seek out authorities to enforce the agreements. An individual named Belisário wrote to the chief of police in 1872 of one such case. "Managing from his ex-*senhora* a letter of manumission for the quantity of 400$000," he related, he had paid some 192$000 in monthly installments. Unfortunately, he wrote, some unspecified illness (*molestias*) had prevented him from making later payments, and his *senhora* had had him jailed "as if he were a slave." Outraged, Belisário argued that a simple lapse in payments meant only that he was "his ex-mistress's debtor" and certainly not that "because of this he stopped being a free man."[50]

Two aspects of Belisário's argument here merit attention for the manner in which they address slaves' rights. Belisário begins, first of all, by implying that the agreement regarding his liberty was something he had wrested from his mistress. Like other such petitions, this suggests a level of slave initiative that Perdigão Malheiro's construction of manumission and similar arguments simply ignore or deny. Clearly slaves like Belisário were in active pursuit of their emancipation. Achieving an agreement with a *senhor* on self-purchase, moreover, made Belisário free in his own eyes. He understood the later troubles over payments toward the final cost of manumission as mere difficulties between two free persons—his owner and himself—over a debt. In this way, Belisário's petition adds a final twist to the rights slaves claimed with regard to their emancipation through self-purchase. Even while enslaved, the implicit general argument went, these individuals had certain rights; the most important of these were their rights to put together a peculium and to buy their freedom with it. Belisário's case suggests, furthermore, that some slaves wanted their full enjoyment of the rights of liberty to begin not with the completion of the purchase but with setting the contract for that transaction. Finally, by protesting his imprisonment, Belisário was claiming for himself freedom from the absolute control of his former owner; he might still serve her, as in fact he did, but under new terms that did not include the right for his mistress to order his arbitrary incarceration. Thus he asserted not only the slave's right to enter into a contract with his or her *senhor* but also the right to a certain freedom from seigneurial control after the concession of such a contract.

In a slave society like that of nineteenth-century Rio Grande do Sul, such assertions of rights represented constructions of social relations that would challenge the freedom of elites in patron-client relations. This is not to say that individuals like Belisário, Maria, and Manoel intended to reject outright the hierarchical nature of their society or that they were claiming a place among the powerful minority of Brazilians who enjoyed the full rights of active citizens. Rather, they attempted to reformulate the model of master-slave relations in ways that would narrow the gap in power between the two parties.

Engaging Officials of the State

Although it did not supplant the authority of the individual *senhor*—or even try to do so—the state was also a nagging presence in the lives of plebeians. The harassment—at times through acts of violence but generally passive, through the use of teasing nicknames, for example—that policemen and other state agents received at the hands of plebeians gives some sense of popular resentment of official incursions into the lives of common Portoalegrenses. At the same time, appeals to authorities on such matters as emancipation, examined above, suggest that plebeians could look at the power of the state as a potential tool in their personal struggles.

To understand the richness of plebeians' strategies for protecting their autonomy, even as they maintained contact with *senhores* and government figures, the realm of popular religiosity deserves special consideration. Religion, in fact, appeared in courtroom discourse as both means and motive for plebeian initiatives in the city, factoring in to relations with private authorities as well as with the state. To illustrate the first of these points, we can look to the charges leveled against slave "sorcerers" (*feiticeiros*) who supposedly applied their dark lore against *senhores*. In 1871, the *liberto* Joaquim Vieira da Cunha, for example, stood accused of being a "sorcerer, who knew how to tame [*amansar*] *senhores* and . . . furnished slaves with powders and other objects to place in the food and drink of their *senhores*." Furthermore, rumors suggested that the defendant promised that using his "witchcraft" would allow slaves to free themselves from their masters.[51] In such cases, popular religion appeared as a mechanism in plebeian struggles within patron-client relations.

Three years later, another case suggested that religion might serve not as the alleged instrument of conflict between master and slave but rather as its cause. Indeed, the means of struggle here were much more direct. The defendant, José, an elderly slave whom two witnesses described as highly trustworthy, explained that in a sudden outburst of frustration and irritation, he had killed his master with three thrusts of a knife. Like many other plebeians, when a *senhor*'s punishments became too brutal, José lashed out violently. As he explained, he "killed his master . . . because he continually mistreated his slaves, so much so that he killed four, named Belisário, Adão, Domingos, and Vicente, the last of them being hanged in the chapel." While José's reaction to his *senhor*'s tyranny was not unusual, his explanation of the event that provided the final spark was. According to José, the victim "neither had religion nor counted on God the Father"; when he wanted to commemorate Holy Friday by fasting, José added, "he was for that reason atrociously beaten by his *senhor*." It was purportedly in response to this final injustice—refusal to allow the celebration of a religious holiday—that José killed his master. Against a backdrop of brutality, it was thus the repression of a religious practice that set José in action.[52]

What is unusual about these cases is the role religion played in master-slave relations. Outside of such court cases, the era's documentation reveals few other visible instances of religion factoring directly in to such relations. The freedom to practice religion, along with related freedoms of movement and sociability in the city, was, however, a core concern in Porto Alegre's popular political culture; such concerns brought this culture into frequent, if often unwanted, confrontation with representatives of the state. We may well suspect that religion figured into patron-client relations more frequently than records indicate; what the surviving documents, products of government officials, point to is the fact that religion led plebeians into contact with both religious and police authorities. This does not, however, deny a general similarity between plebeian struggles for religious independence and other efforts to win the autonomy usually granted, strictly speaking, to those holding higher stations in society. As in their other initiatives, men and women of the *povo* attempted to gain religious or cultural autonomy by playing off the dominant hierarchies in their society. With regard to religion, then, as more broadly, autonomy did not mean living free of all control for most plebeians.[53]

Any cultural autonomy that members of the *povo* managed to guard was necessarily limited and fragile. The principal reason for this is obvious; elite efforts at social control of the *povo* served as constraints on the appearance or survival of practices deemed "disorderly," in the sense of opposing the existing social order. Municipal codes and police actions throughout the mid–nineteenth century provide a wealth of examples of administrative efforts to repress popular culture and recreation. The city's *códigos de posturas* (municipal codes) tried to clamp down on dances and other cultural expressions not only directly but also indirectly, by prohibiting the mixing of slaves and other plebeians in certain privileged places, such as dances, loud parties, gambling, cockfights, and other "illicit gatherings."[54] Afro-Brazilian dances received special attention; an 1857 reform of the *posturas* included the complete prohibition of "*candombes* or *batuques* [terms used in the region to refer to any sort of Afro-Brazilian dance or religious gathering], and dances of blacks in the field on the edge of the city, *chácaras* [truck gardens or small farms], or any other place."[55] Even the songs and chants to which slave and ex-slave stevedores and carriers gave voice in their arduous labors were banned by the codes.[56] Other regulations sought to cut off such social activities before they could begin. Several laws were intended to prevent slaves and other plebeians from gathering in spaces outside the control of elites. Thus the municipal codes banned slaves' living on their own (with penalties for the slaves' *sen-*

bores and the landlords involved), loitering inside or at the entrances of bars and shops, being on the street after curfew without the written permission of their masters, or simply gathering with other slaves.[57]

Throughout the nineteenth century, members of the police showed particular enthusiasm for breaking up "illicit meetings," especially, it seems, when these included large numbers of free and enslaved Afro-Brazilians. In one week in 1833, for instance, police drove "one civilian, 3 or 4 *minas* [Africans of the Mina "nation," a constructed African ethnic group], and 2 cavalry soldiers" out of a bar at two in the morning and arrested eight free black men, eleven male slaves, and six female slaves for taking part in an unspecified gathering at one of their houses.[58] Enforcement of the codes regulating the operation of bars—particularly restrictions on their hours and the serving of slaves—seems to have been more inconsistent. The city's police certainly cited bar owners for ignoring curfew, for buying stolen property, and for accepting slaves as patrons. The frequency with which members of the police mixed with the enslaved and others in taverns, however, must have complicated the application of municipal laws in these establishments.[59]

Ironically, of course, accounts of the suppression of dances and other events also suggest the vitality of popular culture in the face of elite projects.[60] The need for police action and for the repetition of legislative prohibitions arose precisely because of popular refusals to accept passively elite projects to reshape the *povo*. Plebeians in mid-nineteenth-century Porto Alegre continued to occupy social spaces that elites had labeled dangerous and to engage there in activities of which elites disapproved. Because of the ineffectiveness of repressive measures, it is impossible to measure trends in popular frequency of those places that authorities tried to close to them. What is certain, however, is that plebeians still appeared in these dangerous spaces.

At the same time, of course, such persistence consisted of assertions of plebeians' rights to their own cultural practices. Once again, we must keep in mind that popular culture did not exist in complete isolation from elite culture. Confronted with a dominant culture, and with the *posturas* and other attempts at regulation of popular life, members of the *povo* had in large part to carry out their cultural practices in dynamic tension with elites and their preferences.

Although necessarily only capturing that fraction of religious activity of which authorities were aware, the documentation for the period 1846–80 reveals an impressive range of forms of popular religiosity. Much of this took place in a Roman Catholic context. Porto Alegre's was of course a Catholic society, although there is no evidence of Gaúcho masters' diligence in providing for the instruction of their slaves and dependents in the Catholic faith. The events of the Roman Catholic Church's calendar dominated social life in the city, and contemporary descriptions make clear that plebeians participated heavily in Church activities.[61] Much more than any civic holiday, religious processions marking saints' days and other key moments in the Catholic year provided the main social events of the municipality. With Church and State tightly linked in imperial Brazil, such Catholic celebrations were, in effect, the city's principal civic festivities. While revealing disdain for slaves' capacity to grasp Church teachings, the German traveler Joseph Hörmeyer was nevertheless impressed by the tremendous presence of enslaved Afro-Brazilians in these events: "The many holidays, the processions and fireworks displays linked to them, and the days of rest that slaves receive because of them, make these [slaves] the most fervent adepts of the only true Church, even without their understanding much; rarely does the procession of one of the Saints contain fewer than 2,000 slaves of all shades, chattering and screaming."[62] The memorialist Antonio Álvares Pereira Coruja noted not only the existence of *pardos* in processions but also some rivalry between these Afro-Brazilians and members of white *irmandades* (lay Catholic brotherhoods). The procession was, to an important degree, not only an adoration of God or a particular saint but also a performance of social hierarchies. To occupy a leading position within such a performance was thus to assert and display one's high social rank. When, in the incident Coruja described, the *pardo* brotherhood of Nossa Senhora da Conceição (Our Lady of the Conception) insisted on carrying a saint's image, it thus provoked a white brotherhood into open conflict.[63] At the same time, a contemporary chronicler was struck by another feature of processions—the simple mixing of classes and races that marked the mass of participants. As José Cândido Gomes remarked, in the body of believers marching through the city, "all cats are gray" (*todos os gatos são pardos*).[64] Although even the followers might not escape racial tensions, they clearly represented a coming together of plebeians and other members of society under Church auspices. Most dramatic was the overwhelmingly Afro-Brazilian character of the procession honoring Our Lady of Travelers (Nossa Senhora dos Navegantes). As Dante de Laytano has documented, Afro-Brazilians in Porto Alegre essentially took over this festivity over the course of the late nineteenth and early twentieth centuries, turning it into a central social and religious event for members of their community.[65]

Popular participation in the formal rituals of the Church was not, however, limited to processions. Many of the most important institutions in the city's official religious life included plebeians. The clearest example of this is provided by the lay brotherhoods, several of which were distinctly Afro-Brazilian organizations. The Irmandade da Nossa Senhora do Rosário (Brotherhood of Our Lady of the Rosary), for example, had African as well as Brazilian, free as well as enslaved, and female as well as male members. In 1786, at the time of its founding in Rio Grande do Sul, this *irmandade* had 220 members, 104 of whom were slaves, 16 of whom were *libertos*, and 100 of whom were free Afro-Brazilians. Ninety-three of these original "brothers" were also women.[66]

Like brotherhoods in other parts of Brazil, the Rosário of Porto Alegre served as a dynamic center of Afro-Brazilian culture and mutual-assistance efforts. Its social activities included not only the celebration of its patron's saint day (26 December until 1845, when it was moved to the second Sunday in October) but also Afro-Brazilian dances and other events of which the Catholic hierarchy disapproved. Writing in the 1880s, the memorialist Coruja recalled that Church officials' censure of such dances was one reason that leaders of the Rosário worked to build their own church.[67] The brotherhood's internal regulations called for its officers to apply portions of the group's income to the relief of brothers who had fallen into poverty and of families of deceased brothers. Members also made contributions each year to purchase the freedom of one of their slave brothers, chosen by lottery in the *irmandade*'s church.[68] Such charitable activities, together with the religious and social events the brotherhood promoted, made the Irmandade da Nossa Senhora do Rosário a key consolidating institution for the Afro-Brazilian population of Porto Alegre.

The *irmandades*, moreover, were not only foci of religious and cultural activities for members of the African popular classes but also contributors to the institutional Church in Porto Alegre. They helped organize processions with other *irmandades*, overseeing the celebrations of Our Lady of the Rosary, Our Lady of the Immaculate Conception, Saint Benedict, and other saints who were important as patrons or in other roles. They also maintained their own chapels within the city's central cathedral. The Rosário brotherhood,

View of the Church of Our Lady of the Rosary, c. 1860. From Ronaldo Marco Bastos, *Porto Alegre: Um século de fotografia*, 1997.

commonly known as the *irmandade* of the blacks, went further, constructing its own church in downtown Porto Alegre. The Church of the Rosary, opened in 1827 after eleven years of strenuous fund-raising and planning, served as physical evidence of Afro-Brazilian plebeians' presence in official religious life and, according to one scholar, a source of great pride for persons of color in Porto Alegre.[69]

Such pride may have contributed to the social-control function that foreign observers attributed to the Church in mid-nineteenth-century Rio Grande do Sul. For both Hörmeyer and John Luccock, that is, Catholicism served to keep members of the lower classes, and particularly slaves, in submission to their social betters. Writing in the first half of the century, Luccock was none too sanguine about the moral state of the Gaúcho populace but did see religion as a positive force toward social order. "It is true," he opined, "that, here as in Rio de Janeiro, the principles of good morality seem to exercise minute influence; the same lack of loyalty, of honor, and of confidence exist here. Religion contributes by scaring some toward the good path, while a vigilant police restrains and compels a great number."[70] Nearly forty years later, Hörmeyer likewise believed the Church to provide a means of control over "such a numerous mass of slaves."[71] Neither Hörmeyer nor Luccock was explicit about how he perceived Catholicism as helping to control non-elites. The clearest suggestion here comes in Luccock's description, with its implication that Church doctrine persuaded plebeians to act in appropriately moral ways. Hörmeyer's description of slave participation in processions (see above) adds the hint that the festivity and release from work that Church rituals made possible may have won over slaves; slaves beaten publicly for misbehavior, he noted elsewhere, might not be allowed to take part.[72]

By channeling popular religiosity into approved spaces, official Catholicism may indeed have limited its autonomy. Instigating and accepting popular participation in its institutions and rituals, the Church may, that is, have served to help define the terms of cultural conflicts (or potential conflicts) between elites and the *povo* in Porto Alegre. If some plebeians came to be proud of their active membership in Church institutions, that sense of satisfaction may—ironically, in elites' eyes—have represented a popular pride in occupying a position very much to elites' liking and benefit.

The constraints official religiosity placed on popular beliefs and practices were, however, never close to complete. Indeed, those plebeians following a holy image through the streets of Porto Alegre or attending meetings of their *irmandade* probably did not often see their presence in such elite-sanctioned spaces as restrictive. This was, rather, one facet of their full—spiritual, social, and political—lives. Their relationship with official Porto Alegre, and the contentiousness inherent in that relationship, would have been as present in this as in other aspects of their lives.

With specific reference to religious practice, this meant that plebeians continued to hold beliefs and perform rituals that could only have been seen as heterodox from the point of view of the official Church. At the same time, they presented their own variations on orthodox practices. Thus, plebeians turned the seemingly restrictive spaces of official, institutional Catholic practice into arenas for their own cultural creativity. As the example of the procession of Nossa Senhora dos Navegantes in particular demonstrates, members of the *povo* could make orthodox events their own. In other activities, these people brought elements of heterodox belief and ritual into official religious space and practice. As they blended such beliefs and forms, members of the *povo* in Porto Alegre and across Brazil created syncretic new religiosities.

After visiting Porto Alegre in the early 1940s, Melville Herskovits reported the discovery in a Rio Grande parish church of a statue he described as "a female figure of artistic distinction in terms of West African patterns."

For the U.S. anthropologist, this carving, presumably placed in the church in the early nineteenth century, represented not only "the existence of living African beliefs and techniques" in the past but also "at least the basis for the Afro-Catholic syncretisms" that, he argued, marked Porto Alegre in the twentieth century.[73] For our purposes, the figure can also serve as a symbol of the presence of distinct and heterodox popular religion within the official Church. While recognizing syncretism in the juxtaposition and mutual influence of African and Catholic religiosities, this reading of the carving goes beyond Herskovits's interpretation. Where Herskovits saw merely evidence of mixture, we can also see the vestiges of power struggles within a field of cultural practices. Rather than being neutral in regard to elite-*povo* relations, that is, religious syncretisms were also in part subversive political initiatives. In acts like placing an African-style carving within a Catholic church, Gaúcho plebeians of the nineteenth century asserted the validity and demonstrated the creativity of their own cultures within the dominant framework of their society.[74]

The record of popular religious practices in and around Porto Alegre shows plebeians not only performing this kind of "embedded" cultural-political act but also creating and perpetuating more independent beliefs and customs. Africans and Afro-Brazilians brought their own non-Catholic practices into their *irmandades*. Indeed, brothers and sisters of the Rosário performed Afro-Brazilian dances, some with religious meanings, in their group's seat. Dances by members of various "nations," for example, formed part of the celebrations of Christmas and other official holidays.[75] Such activities must have seemed to the Catholic Church, as they later did to the scholar Ottilia Gresele, unfortunate "superstitions."[76] For free and enslaved Africans and Afro-Brazilians in Porto Alegre, however, dances in the *irmandades* were just one part of close and complex, lived associations between official Catholicism and popular religious forms. The links between these traditions were strong enough to extend beyond the brotherhoods' buildings and into the public spaces of the city. In December 1850, the Mina freedman Francisco sought police permission for one of such event, "desiring to celebrate Our Lady by the holiday of Christmas, with the dances of his *nação* [nation] in his residence on the rua do Arroio."[77] One year earlier, the creole Eduardo had written to the police of his need "to go out with his group on Sunday afternoons until the day of Our Lady of the Rosary because of a promise they had made to that saint" to raise money by performing *cocumbi* dances, of which he was leader.[78] In their petitions, plebeians like Francisco and Eduardo were, it is true, at least superficially accepting the authority of police officials over their religious practices. Even as they thus worked within legal boundaries, however, these Afro-Gaúchos were asserting their right to conduct their own rituals. As long as they obeyed the normal dictates of maintaining public tranquility (i.e., as long as they did not disturb others too much), they felt that official Porto Alegre should respect or at least tolerate their distinct religious customs.[79]

The *cocumbi*, generally associated in Rio de Janeiro with the Congo nation, was but one example of African rituals present in mid-nineteenth-century Porto Alegre. In fact, Africans and Afro-Brazilians of various nations conducted different kinds of these theatrical dances, also known by such names as *ticoumbis* and *congadas*. No elite observer recorded the details of *congadas* in Porto Alegre, so we lack even the Eurocentric descriptions of their content that exist for other regions of Brazil.[80] What we have for Porto Alegre are merely a few petitions from community leaders to the police. Those of Eduardo and Francisco explicitly link *cocumbis* with Christian holidays. Others speak only of the desire to collect alms for various mutual-assistance programs. The free black Maria José, for example, explained to authorities in 1850 that the "blacks of the Angola nation and the other nations" wanted to "play on Sundays and holidays . . . , as has always been their style, resulting from this innocent pastime the advantage of collecting alms for their celebrations, burials, and mutual aid in cases of sickness, all of which is well-known and public." This declaration does not mention any religious significance that the dance may have had. After Maria José personally tracked down a police official to press her case, it became obvious that the authorities knew her to be a *rainha ginga* (Queen Ginga), a central figure in *congadas* whose title refers to a famous seventeenth-century ruler of the West African state of Matamba.[81] The fact that a self-identified Angola sought permission for her own nation and others to perform a Congo ritual suggests the mixing of African ethnicities occurring in Porto Alegre. Given the notorious vagueness of nation categories—often based on the African port from which slaves had been shipped to Brazil and not on their origin in a linguistic or cultural group—concrete conclusions in this regard are impossible. Without more specific knowledge of their content or of the ethnic composition of their performers, we can, however, see the *congadas* of Porto Alegre as part of the Afro-Brazilian religion plebeians created in the city. At least in the 1850s, furthermore, plebeians of African descent seem to have adapted cultural forms to the ethnic environment in which they lived in Porto Alegre. At the same time, they asserted their right to present these forms in public on select occasions.

Authorities would not always be receptive to such assertions. As we have seen, municipal legislation banning Afro-Brazilian religious rites and dances was in existence even before the Farroupilha. Around the time of the Paraguayan War, moreover, police leaders urged a crackdown on *batuques*, *candomblés*, and dances. In May 1872, the provincial chief of police repeated for Porto Alegre what his predecessor had declared five years before for another Gaúcho city: officials were no longer to permit Afro-Brazilian dances.[82] The reason for this change in policy is not entirely clear. It may have been a vestige of wartime anxiety about activities and potential subversion from among the *povo*. In any case, it certainly did not bring about the end of Afro-Brazilian religious practice in the city. Afro-Brazilian members of the *povo* had never taken elite tolerance of their *batuques* for granted. The individual petitioners we have examined were, as noted, asserting their religious rights. In doing so, however, they were not making absolute claims. They always felt compelled to justify their dances. Besides appealing to simple custom by saying they had long performed their dances, they played to the question of order, always a central concern for the police. Maria José, although a queen in her group's ritual, justified a *congada* with great deference, "assuring . . . Your Lordship [the police chief] that these games [*brinquedos*] are innocent . . . , and there will be no disturbances."[83] This careful presentation of a customarily asserted right contains some rather obvious analysis of the attitudes of elites and the chances of being able to put this right into practice without police interference.

At other times, members of the *povo* did not attempt to win formal elite acceptance of their rituals. Their motivations here probably varied. Believing such approval to be unlikely, some may not have thought the process of seeking it worth their while. Others may indeed have feared that a petition on behalf of a *cocumbi* might alert hostile authorities to the location of the forbidden event, bringing repression. Still others may simply have preferred the power and independence that secrecy might lend them. Whatever their precise drives, plebeians would have had to consider the politics of their religious practices; any practices not part of the dominant Catholicism were sources of potential conflict with elites. Despite the example of a "civilized *batuque*" that caught the attention of the columnist O Estudante by its presence in the city's central plaza, plebeians much more frequently led their spiritual and social lives in ways that would keep them out of the sight and away from the sanction of official Porto Alegre. Thus, perhaps anticipating police reaction to their ceremonies, Afro-Brazilians tended to hold their *candomblés* and dances in the less densely populated fringes surrounding the city center or simply in secret locations in the middle of Porto Alegre.

The *várzea*, or Campo do Bom Fim (later the Parque da Redenção), a field to the west of the city's core, was one preferred site. In fact, so common were the *candomblés* held there that they became part of Porto Alegre's folklore. The *candomblé* of Mãe Rita was for chroniclers like Coruja and Athos Damascena Ferreira one of the defining features of nineteenth-century society. As Coruja explained, "There on Sunday afternoons gathered blacks of various *nações*, who with their drums, *canzás*, *urucungos*, and marimbas [all musical instruments], sang and danced, forgetting the grief of slavery, without causing problems for the police." Returning us again to the links between *candomblés* and official Catholicism, Coruja also noted that "in that *candomblé* they also rehearsed the *cocumbis*" that members of the *irmandade* of Nossa Senhora do Rosário performed at Christmas.[84]

Because of the secrecy many plebeians preferred to keep, authorities—and through them, historians—only became aware of many religious sites by accident. It was often only in responding to complaints of a loud party or gambling den that police discovered religious rituals and cult leaders of the *povo*. One such occurrence in 1858 brought to elite eyes the existence of a *terreiro* (ritual house) of *candomblé*. Investigating events at the house of the *preta* Matildes Lebania Pereira dos Santos, the police found "profane objects of all sorts, to which are vulgarly given the name of witchcraft [*feitiçarias*], and ridiculous vestments that are foreign to the Divine religion." These objects, despite the police chief's judgment that "they have nothing to do with prayers to God," revealed a vibrant center of Afro-Brazilian religion. Under interrogation, Matildes declared that the "images" had belonged to her mother. Now, under Matildes's care, others came to her home to practice religious rituals: "the aim of all of this was the adoration of the said Images, . . . which was done by her relatives who, dancing, made use of the aforementioned instruments and clothing in the practice of that same adoration." Without responding to questions about the size of the meetings in the house, Matildes went on to explain that "the gathering was for prayer, to seek help from God and even to find luck with gambling, with women, and to cure certain illnesses." The only financial benefit that accrued to the house came from the sale of some medicines that "had previously been found in the hands of the Nagô [nation]." Her repeated assertions that prayer was at the center of their activities may have been an attempt to present the *candomblé* in a favorable light; surely, she may have thought, the police would be likely to tolerate purely spiritual pursuits. Clearer still is her attempt to defend the ritual house by giving the names of the "many good people" who frequented it. Despite his claim that he had only come to buy candles, the arrest of the Portuguese Manoel Fernandes Talhada in the house even suggests that it was not only the Minas, Gegês, and creoles that Matildes listed who attended rituals there. Whether true or not, Manoel's denial of any but the most coincidental contacts with the *batuque* may also indicate that persons from outside the Afro-Brazilian segment of the *povo* would have tried especially hard to hide their participation in these proscribed rituals.[85]

Despite the judgment of police officials, the rituals practiced in Matildes's house were not witchcraft, properly speaking, but rather *batuque* or *candomblé*. Although various forms existed in the nineteenth century—and have evolved into the twenty-first—*batuque* can be characterized as the worship of African *santos*, or deities. The term *santos*, literally "saints," hints at the syncretism that permeated *batuque;* its rituals contained elements drawn from not only various African religions but also indigenous American and Catholic traditions. The types of "witchcraft" that existed in Porto Alegre—with their spells, charms, and other practices to effect directly some action—may also have been the product of mixed cultural traditions. Certainly it was not only African societies that included practices that European and Euro-Brazilian elites labeled as witchcraft; the folk Catholicism of early modern Portugal and the wider European world contained such tendencies as well.[86] In the Porto Alegre that official documents of the mid–nineteenth century present, however, witchcraft was largely associated with Afro-Brazilian culture. One *processo* from 1853, for instance, records the practice of *adivinhações*, or divinations, among free and enslaved blacks. In this case, a free *preto* accused a runaway slave of having stolen some money from the former's house. From the various testimonies, it appears that when accused by the plaintiff, the slave João agreed to go with him to the house of another *preto*, Sebastião Americo, so that the latter would perform "the divination of the sieve" (*a adivinhação da peneira*) to determine whether João was guilty of the theft. João seems to have participated in the rite freely, apparently accepting it as a manner of settling disputes. Later in the *processo*, however, he retreated somewhat; after being pointed out as guilty by Sebastião, he said, he went off with the plaintiff and others (supposedly to lead them to the money) only because they had obliged him to "in view of the divination of the table" (*adivinhação da mesa*).[87] Besides divining, practices such as blessings (a common form was known as a *benzedura*) and spells to affect other people's feelings, behavior, or health were common among members of the *povo*.[88] In one case, a slave frustrated in his attempts to win his freedom responded with vague threats against his master and a neighbor, saying, "they were all cooked by a witch" (*cozidos por um feiticeiro*).[89] Rarely, however, did members of the *povo* appear to bring their dealings with the divine into the view of official Porto Alegre, which would treat it, in one lawyer's phrase, as just so many "illicit proceedings."[90]

For the most part, then, members of the *povo* purposely kept their distinctive popular religious practices to themselves. This was not because they necessarily saw their African, Afro-Brazilian, or syncretic beliefs and rituals as contradicting Catholicism. While some undoubtedly maintained exclusively non-Catholic faiths, many others probably considered themselves Catholics while also participating in very different religious systems.[91] What anthropologist Norton Corrêa has written of contemporary adepts of Afro-Brazilian cults in Porto Alegre may well have held true for their nineteenth-century predecessors: "every initiate in Batuque calls himself Catholic, because many ceremonies of the former include Catholic locations or rites."[92] At the same time, they had to be aware of the official disapproval with which their *batuque* or other practices might meet. Whether openly, in full view of the authorities, or secretly, away from prying eyes, continuing these rituals was a political act. The ways in which plebeians performed their variations of Catholic rites, their Afro-Brazilian dances and ceremonies, and their divinations and spells varied, of course, but all demonstrated that these members of the *povo* in Porto Alegre were trying to preserve some space of relative social autonomy in which they might carry on with the religious aspects of their daily lives.

Engaging Fellow Plebeians

Religious practices brought some solidarity to the lives of many Gaúcho plebeians, whether in the dark "damned places" of which authorities complained or in the heart of institutional Catholicism.[93] In its institutionalized forms, popular religiosity undeniably reflected some of the hierarchicalization of the society in which it existed. Whereas Gaúcho *irmandades* of the mid–nineteenth century were less strictly defined in ethnic terms than the Afro-Brazilian brotherhoods of colonial Bahia and other regions, for instance, their broadly Afro-Brazilian ethnic identity did not remove all trace of rank from their organization.[94] Internal rules dictated that certain offices be open only to whites or only to blacks; the board of directors, furthermore, tended to be made up exclusively of the free.[95] Even if these divisions represent some imposition of hierarchies within the brotherhood, however, they do not deny the real solidarities that associations like *irmandades* provided for members of the *povo*.

As we have seen, there was much in the seigneurial culture of the nineteenth century to impede the spread, and political use, of such solidarities. Individual plebeians simply had to expend much of their political energy dealing with their *senhores* or agents of the state. At the same time, however, popular political culture in Porto Alegre also contained strong, sometimes violent attempts to increase individual power over other nonelites; a kind of plebeian seigneurialism peeks out from the documentation of the period. Plebeian residents of Porto Alegre did not have a single system for ranking themselves and their neighbors hierarchically. Rather, they referred to a variety of traits, most of them intimately associated with honor, to measure and assert their status, or *condição*.[96] In their appeals to different factors, we can see that the lines of tension among plebeians in the city were largely gendered and racial/ethnic.

Members of the *povo* could try to wield their ties to a powerful *senhor* or to state authorities in their relations with others. The case of Marcelino, an African (of the Gegê Mina nation) slave of a German master, presents an example of one such effort to make instrumental use of a *senhor*. According to witnesses, Marcelino entered into trouble soon after entering a *venda* (a shop that might also be a bar) where the young, free man Manoel Francisco da Silveira sat eating oranges with a friend. The owner of the *venda* reported that Marcelino arrived already cursing and looking for trouble; other witnesses declared that the slave drank some *cachaça* (unrefined rum) before the conflict began. Apparently all agreed, however, that Marcelino provoked Manoel to anger by climbing on the counter and starting to "dance in the manner of his land with his hat on his head." In the telling of three witnesses and Marcelino himself, it was this last detail, the hat, that sparked trouble. Manoel took the slave's refusal to uncover his head as an affront, at one point grabbing the hat and shouting "that it was thus that he should do at the feet of whites." Marcelino returned the hat to his head, however, and continued his dance, justifying his impudence by saying that his *senhor* had given him the hat. This appeal to "the German" showed Marcelino attempting to use his link to his *senhor* in relations with other free men. Strictly on the basis of this link, Marcelino seems to have acted toward a man generally understood as his social superior with a brashness that he could not otherwise begin to justify; even here, his daring ended up in violence, with the slave ultimately killing his free antagonist.[97]

Particularly after the Paraguayan War, during which national propaganda represented military service as an "act of patriotism" rather than "a humiliation," a military record could support claims to respectable status and, in certain situations, even citizenship of a kind.[98] To demonstrate his orderly nature, for instance, the former cavalryman Salomé Suzano Escalara presented a judge with his discharge, which contained "just two correctional arrests" and thus showed "he was never disorderly nor committed any criminal act for which he had been punished."[99] Others to whom the postwar years had not been particularly kind tried to make similar use of their service in the war. Manoel Francisco da Cunha, for instance, who lamented that a "lack of means" had led him to become "the *agregado* [dependent, resident peon, or servant] of Fermino Martins de Oliveira Prates," asserted his "many years" of service "to the state" as a source of status.[100]

Still others pointed to wartime experiences to make more confrontational, and less orderly, claims on status. In late March 1874, on rua Voluntários da Pátria (Volunteers of the Fatherland Street), the busy commercial avenue in Porto Alegre that had been renamed in honor of his Paraguayan War comrades, Antônio da Costa e Oliveira, veteran of his nation's Twelfth Infantry Battalion, entered a bar and "began to recount the deeds that he had performed in Paraguay." When the volume and bravado of his stories began to irritate other patrons, the tavern owner, Felipe Lopes de Bittencourt, tried to quiet Antônio. Likely nervous about losing business, Bittencourt heeded the wishes of several English customers and repeatedly ordered the troublemaker to stop his harangue. Antônio bristled at this perceived challenge. As four witnesses recalled afterward (with slight variations in the exact wording), he accused the tavern owner of being "a false Brazilian since he stood up more for the interests of the English than for those of a soldier who had gone to Paraguay in defense of the fatherland" and added menacingly that "there [in Paraguay] he had committed many murders and here he could kill one more." Not content to issue such threats, Antônio then vaulted the bar to attack Bittencourt; his advance fell short, however, when the bar's clerk grabbed a pistol and shot Antônio, first in the abdomen and then in the forehead. The resulting wounds proved fatal and brought to a close Antônio's enraged search for status.[101]

Antônio was, moreover, far from the only veteran to carry his experience in the Paraguayan War back to the streets, taverns, and residences of the city. So, too, did men such as João Alves Pedroso, who returned from the war to stir up life in Aldeia dos Anjos. Indeed, witnesses in Pedroso's 1874 trial for murder said the defendant had come back from the front a changed man. One of João's lifelong acquaintances explained that whereas his friend "until going to Paraguay was worthy of esteem . . . for his beautiful qualities," he was now given to provoking police and neighbors alike; indeed, the witness averred that Pedroso's "behavior has been such that today in the Aldeia there is no one, except perhaps some relative, who has not been offended by him." The defense lawyer in the case, while attempting to soften Pedroso's image, pointed out the key—and for residents of Aldeia dos Anjos the most problematic—characteristic of this and other veterans' behavior: their experience had left them with an "independence of spirit" that caused friction with the hierarchies of peacetime society. Against the promise of wartime propaganda, Pedroso and others found that their military backgrounds did not help them escape the norms of dependence in their seigneurial society.[102]

Nevertheless, in part because of the potential power that veterans' discourse of service to the fatherland represented, men of the armed forces and civil authorities were particularly appalled by the fraudulent use some plebeians tried to make of the war. The illicit distribution and sale of military gear had long been part of the contraband trade for which Porto Alegre's shops and taverns were infamous.[103] In the 1870s and even into the 1890s, this took on new dimensions and meanings, as men who were not serving, and had not served, in the military sold and wore army uniforms in the streets of Porto Alegre and other Gaúcho cities.[104] The provincial chief of police felt it necessary to warn his block inspectors of such practices shortly after the end of the war in 1870, and notices of individual desertions at times made the obvious point that men escaping the military took their uniforms and arms with them.[105] Authorities could not, however, stop such abuses. Perhaps hoping to share in the sense of authority that his friend enjoyed as a soldier in the light cavalry, for instance, the unemployed clerk Pedro Firmiano da Silva appeared in 1878 "dressed in military clothes without being a soldier."[106] Even slaves attempted to take on the power of the uniform; that same year, one such slave, Guilherme, was said to have fled from his master in a soldier's "pants and shirt of blue cloth."[107] For military men like the commander of the Sixth Infantry Battalion, of course, only soldiers deserved to wear such symbols of honor; in late 1871, that officer ordered his men to arrest any civilians found wearing military uniforms, "principally black slaves, belittling the military class."[108] This particularly strong reaction to slaves in uniform is far from surprising; the degradation of slavery was the opposite of the discourse of heroism and service to the nation on which veterans in this period were hoping to capitalize.

Although it might seem self-evident, the distinction between slave and free was not always a clear one in the daily lives of plebeians. In many respects, the experiences of slavery and free poverty exhibited more similarities than differences in Porto Alegre. Slaves who "lived out" inhabited the same shacks and tenements as the free poor, often in fact sharing rooms; frequented the same bars, parties, and religious processions; and worked alongside free laborers of every racial category. Medical experts charged with inspecting the general health situation during a scarlet fever epidemic in 1850, moreover, reported little difference in the material conditions of life among the enslaved and the free poor.[109]

Most important, the free as well as the enslaved faced the problems of dependency on patrons. Without being identical, the domination that marked the lives of both free and enslaved was parallel enough for some to evince confusion about the distinction slavery made.[110] As was true across Brazil, freedpersons often had to attend to their *senhores'* whims; some even said that they continued to be hired out as though they were still property.[111] A show of disobedience or disrespect could technically result in reenslavement.[112]

The fact that reenslavement was perceived as a threat, however, is a clue that legal status mattered to plebeians; indeed, the energetic efforts by many to win their emancipation provide definitive proof of this. In part this was a matter of concrete living conditions, as the case of the *parda* Delfina suggests. As was common throughout the nineteenth century, Delfina's mother had placed her with other persons. Delfina was not, however, as lucky as those children whose adoptive parents (*pais de criação*) raised them like biological sons and daughters.[113] As her patron explained in court, Delfina had lived in his house, "serving there always without earning anything, . . . just subsistence." What finally drove Delfina to flee, in her own telling, were the beatings that her patron and his common-law wife (*amásia*) had inflicted on her. This brutal punishment—and the cries of agony it caused—led some neighbors to assume she was a slave.[114] The link between physical violence and slavery was a vital one in Porto Alegre; neighbors who heard wails of pain in other circumstances also unthinkingly took them to be the result of *senhores'* beatings of slaves.[115]

The association between physical punishment and slavery was also one source of the stigma attached to slavery. Being subject to whippings and other violent "corrective" measures, that is, was a mark of lowly status that plebeians hoped to avoid. To establish one's identity as a free or freed individual might not only lessen the chance of feeling a master's whip but would also place one above the condition of slave. Thus freedpersons and free plebeians would react sharply and resentfully to the use of a whip (*chicote* or *relha*) on their bodies, and free Africans and Afro-Brazilians might speak of slaves as untrustworthy in order to distance themselves from their former legal condition.[116]

With regard to race and ethnicity, it is crucial to distinguish between points and sources of conflict. Members of the *povo* often used racial or ethnic criteria to assert their own superiority to others. Whether highly charged or seemingly casual, such references to race often fueled escalations of conflict. In none of the cases I have examined, however, did race or racism serve as the sole and independent cause of violence. Racial epithets appeared in the criminal court cases instead as "fighting words," the final spark that turned potential explosions into real ones. By no means does this relegate race and ethnicity to a plane of secondary importance; the observed uses of racial epithets do not, that is, imply that race and ethnicity were mere functions of class or of other, somehow more fundamental contradictions among plebeians. In fact, the role of fighting words may imply that race was one of the factors that extended across popular society; so strong were the feelings associated with race and ethnicity that they could appear in and transform any potentially tense confrontation between members of the *povo*. If not the cause of specific violent acts, race and ethnicity were thus underlying currents of tension that could be tapped into at any time.

The expression of antiblack remarks demonstrates the role of race and ethnicity in conflicts among plebeians. In June 1850, for instance, the young tavern clerk Luiz referred to race to try to enforce propriety at his place of employment. When José Joaquim, one of the rowdy Garcês Cabelleira brothers, rode his horse into the tavern and demanded wine, the clerk refused to serve him. Instead, with obvious disapproval of the man's behavior, Luiz led the horse outside, adding the jab that "this wasn't the shop of Manoel of the mulattoes." It may not have been this insult alone that set off José Joaquim's angry reaction. As three witnesses who were in the tavern mentioned, Luiz grabbed the bridle of José's horse; in the macho culture of Rio Grande do Sul, this may have been taken as a slight to José's masculinity. José and his brother Francisco would also assert that they had long had a relationship of "enmity" with the tavern owner. What is clear, in any case, is that the racial reference pushed the situation toward its climax. Shown the door with an insult but no wine, José discharged his pistol—toward the bar, Luiz's boss would allege—and rode off.[117]

Elsewhere antiblack racism found more virulent forms. A lack of respect for racial hierarchies was one of the conditions that galled eighty-five-year-old Luiz Manoel da Silva Rosa on the farm where he worked. When his fellow employees Luiza and Sofia, both creoles, told him to go buy meat, Luiz Manoel responded sharply "that he didn't serve blacks [*negras*]," adding that Sofia should go since "she wasn't better than he and . . . he was white." In Luiz Manoel's version of events, the boss of the three then stepped in to reprimand him; the two women grabbed Luiz Manoel's arm, and in the confusion a knife found its way into the *senhor*'s chest. The elderly Luiz Manoel had other grave problems with the way his *senhor* ran the farm; before the jury he declared that "he didn't like [his boss], because he usually fed him just once per day, and . . . he [Luiz Manoel] found himself obligated to beg in the city." This resentment burst out into violence over a question of race; mistreated by his patron, Luiz Manoel could not tolerate becoming a subordinate of his creole colleagues.[118] As these two cases suggest, racial tensions could crystallize, and catalyze, already explosive circumstances.

With the presence of European immigrants increasing in the province after the Farroupilha, racial and ethnic tensions could also turn on European identity. The case of Luiz Weber, a Prussian immigrant, demonstrates that German ethnicity, for instance, could make one the target of ridicule. Having come from the German colony of São Leopoldo to attend some horse races on the outskirts of Porto Alegre, Weber ended up killing Ignacio Furtado Fanfa in front of a bar. The witnesses and later the jury agreed, however, that Fanfa had provoked the hostilities by directing "indecent words" at Weber. The offensive terms the court scribe recorded were mainly references to Weber's ethnicity. Seeing the Prussian dismount, with sword and pistol visible to all, Fanfa had greeted Weber with a sarcastic remark: "Even a blond goes about armed!" Calling to the new arrival ("Come here, João Alemão, son of a . . ."), Fanfa continued to taunt Weber. Once again racial or ethnic insults alone did not lead to violence; in the welcome he gave Weber and in later jabs at Weber's "valor" and bravery, Fanfa wove challenges to Weber's masculinity in with ethnic references. Fanfa thus succeeded in implying that Germans, or "blonds," were somehow less manly than Brazilians. Ethnicity, then, was part of the combination of insults that delivered to Fanfa the fight for which he had allegedly been looking that day at the races. As Fanfa lay on the ground outside the bar, the Prussian he had pushed into violent confrontation rode off, slipping past the three mounted men who tried to capture him. If he had lived, Fanfa might have seen the foreigner excelling on the very masculine terms on which he had been challenged.[119]

Constructions of masculinity and femininity were, in fact, at the heart of the most important line of tension and conflict among plebeians in Porto Alegre. In a more immediate sense than race or ethnicity, personal honor was the measure of a man or—by different criteria—a woman. To question the extent to which a man or woman fit the standards of honorability as socially defined for his or her gender was to venture into dangerous territory. So central was honor to the construction of a person's worth in society that casting doubts on it could lead to violent reprisals.

The manner in which challenges to honor arose tells us something about the definitions of plebeian honorability itself. Honor was at the same time intensely personal and public. As we shall see when we further dissect its components, the quality of honor was based not only on an individual's particular characteristics but also on his or her fame for having these traits. As a result, honorable persons had to guard their reputations vigilantly. When someone began to spread rumors about another's dishonorable deed, the object of the gossip might very well appear to seek redress. Thus the butcher Izidro de Souza confronted his ex-roommate when he heard that the man "continued to talk and intrigue about" him.[120] Rumors might take other forms as well, showing up in newspapers or in anonymous lampoons (*pasquins*). What was most galling to the shopkeeper who assaulted a musician for sullying his good name in such lampoons was precisely that he felt his honor mocked in public.[121] At the same time, most of the cases that gained the attention of the authorities involved face-to-face challenges. The most serious of these cases—and the ones most assuredly headed toward violence—were those that took place in front of onlookers. Even with an audience consisting of the challenger alone, however, the gravity of the question of honor meant that violence was a strong possibility.[122]

With or without spectators, plebeians' behavior in the private yet public matter of honor contained elements of theater. For both women and men of the *povo*, attaining and preserving honorability meant responding to certain defined roles they were to fill *as* women and men. Although (as we shall see) they would not always take on these roles in the precise manner that dominant notions of femininity and masculinity prescribed, they had to react to common gender conceptions.

This necessity could be highly constricting for both women and men, but the latter, male case better illustrates my point here. In the post facto (and at times postmortem) stories they told in the courtroom, men implied that the demands of maintaining masculine honor could lead instantly and automatically to open conflict, even between plebeians who had known each other for years or who considered themselves friends.[123] In fact, at times men made it seem that the weighty demands of honor left them no choice but to act in aggressive, macho ways. A slave who killed his coworker in 1852, for instance, expressed regrets over his act. When João Fidelis discovered his wife, Felicidade, engaged in sexual relations with Manoel, he pulled out a knife and attacked his colleague. "It was not by his will that he killed his partner," João later explained. Recuperating from a few days' illness, João had gone out to help Felicidade in their small garden plot; to his horror, he saw her there "lying with his partner Manoel." While his wife drew away, Manoel buttoned up his pants and asked of João, "What will you do?" There was little reason to ask the question, João's testimony implied; the facts had given him no option but to fight Manoel.[124]

Although matters of honor provoked what Steve J. Stern refers to as "a certain touchiness about masculinity," the path from having one's honor questioned to physical confrontation was not as direct as João Fidelis hinted.[125] (And, of course, João's version was highly self-serving: if the murder was unavoidable, he could hardly be blamed for committing it.) Even criminal records, which by their nature overrepresent violent incidents in plebeians' daily lives, show that the escalation to bloodshed was not automatic. Before striking out at Ignacio Furtado Fanfa, Luiz Weber had, after all, tried to avoid the man and then ignore his belittling remarks.[126] In other situations, plebeian men seem to have looked for others to intervene when they felt circumstances moving quickly toward conflict; insofar as it took the matter out of their own hands, such intervention would save potential combatants from having to choose between two dangers—fighting and thus risking injury or death or backing down and thus appearing cowardly and dishonorable in front of others.[127]

This is not to say that João Fidelis did not feel a real compulsion to attack his colleague but to propose that the theater of gender relations—especially with its public playing out of personal disputes over honor—was open to complex, improvised performances. The stabbings, beatings, and other brutal events that fill the criminal records were not, that is, products of inflexible codes of behavior (or, for that matter, of some collective, violent psychosis among the *povo*).[128] Rather, they arose out of contentious, contingent relations among plebeians, relations through which these members of the *povo* would in large part define themselves as honorable men or women. We might speculate further that the lowly positions such plebeians held in society would have given a special charge to tensions over gendered honor; with relatively poor chances of gaining recognized power or status in wider society, efforts to establish themselves as honorable might have held special importance for plebeians.[129]

The meanings of honor took on distinctly gendered forms for Portoalegrenses, just as they did throughout the Americas. The court cases under examination present a difficulty in teasing out these meanings, for the only access they allow to relations among plebeians is through testimonies before officials. Here, then, hints about offstage behavior emerge only from carefully scrutinized onstage communications. As we shall see, this feature of the documents can turn out to be a window into popular initiatives. What matters at this point is merely the observation that what plebeians professed to believe about female honesty and honor varied according to context; as Martha Esteves found for members of the popular classes in Belle Époque Rio de Janeiro, plebeians held to versions of an elite code of honor and shame in their appeals to authorities but seemingly acted on different codes in their daily lives.[130]

This contradiction between the constructions of female honor that plebeians professed in court and those they appeared to live out in their daily lives—what Esteves refers to as "ambiguities between what was to be fulfilled and what was fulfilled"—emerged in courtroom testimony.[131] When they were appealing to the judicial authorities on their own behalf, men and women of the *povo* made reference to a code of honor for women that approximated the classic honor/shame complex that generations of scholars have described as dominant throughout Latin America.[132] Early in 1850, for example, a young woman named Zeferina Maria da Conceição sought protection from the police. A neighbor, José Ferreira Santos, had deflowered her, she explained, and now her adoptive mother wanted "to punish her severely." The rhetorical strategies that Zeferina and José followed in making their opposing cases bring up some of the key elements of the honor/shame code. As was the pattern in cases of sexual crimes, the honesty of the alleged victim was central to the trial; although this case lacked the vicious attacks on the victim's honesty that marked other *processos*, in effect, Zeferina, not José, was on trial here. Accordingly, the girl (doctors who examined her estimated her age to be thirteen) testified that she had been a virgin prior to the incident in question. In fact, she averred, she had remained at home with her adoptive mother, who never let her leave the house alone. The mother, furthermore, was chaste, living alone with no male companion. Finally, the girl swore that the "carnal relations" (*cópula carnal*) with José had occurred against her wishes; the man had entered the house surreptitiously through a window, grabbing the girl and putting his hand over her mouth to prevent her from screaming, as she wanted to, while he forced himself on her. Even as he was raping her, Zeferina added, José promised to marry her; indeed, as he continued to visit her in this way, he repeated this pledge. For his part, José swore that he had never had sexual relations with this daughter of a friendly neighbor who "owed him many obligations and money." Rather, the girl had sought him out one night, claiming her mother wanted to kill her and seeking his assistance. He had, he explained, simply returned her to her own house.[133]

The case of Zeferina and José was not the most highly contentious sexual case in the years after the Farroupilha. Its relatively simple arguments illustrate, however, the use of the honor/shame complex that plebeians made before authorities. To begin with, nonconjugal sexual relations were ostensibly forbidden to women. For young women like Zeferina, this meant preserving their virginity until marriage. As other cases make clear, breaking this rule made a woman dishonest; unless she were "intact," she had little if any presumed legal protection against seducers and little claim to an honorable marriage.[134] Zeferina's statements about her mother's care suggest, moreover, that mothers were to help shield their daughter's virtue; again, other *processos* give evidence that men—whether fathers or brothers—were also essential guardians of the chastity on which the honor of "their" women rested.[135] Honorable girls remained, according to the ideal, isolated by these figures from the dangers of the street—that public space with no defense against other men. Indeed, the ideal was the modesty attributed to a girl in another case; a witness described her as "honest, so much so that she does not even go to the window."[136]

If a woman were to fall prey to a man's advances, certain circumstances might lessen her subsequent dishonor. Maintaining secrecy about the carnal act—or even a resulting child—was a practical option for some women, but not an ideal component of the honor/shame code.[137] Instead, a woman guilty of sex before marriage might expiate that shameful deed by demonstrating that she had not performed it out of her own physical desire; like Zeferina, a woman taking this tack might argue that her lover had taken her by force or deceit or had promised marriage.[138] Indeed, an actual wedding might transform the premarital sexual act into nothing more than an early consummation of the marriage that followed. A girl who agreed to have sex would not face dishonor, except in the absence of a marriage with her lover that would legitimate the act. In her assertions, Zeferina brought together several of these strains of moral thought; the combination of force and a pledge of marriage was the justification that would protect her honor from the stain that her sexual relationship with José might otherwise represent.

The honor of José and other men was not, by contrast, at great risk in these cases. Rather, a double standard, which presumed but did not censure men's advances on other men's women, pertained.[139] From a male perspective, what was very much at issue in cases of sexual crimes was the honor of the female victims' men—those men, especially husbands and fathers, who were defined as the women's protectors. The sexual honesty of a woman, that is, was the basis not only of her own honor in the honor/shame schema but also that of her husband or other male guardians. In two cases, we see young fatherless boys trying to take on this role. As evidence of his proper conduct, witnesses testified that Lourenço Luiz Vieira had stepped in to protect his mother from an assault; neighbors elsewhere reported approvingly that Joaquim José dos Santos had worked to provide his sister with a trousseau so that she might have a proper marriage.[140] To be honorable, men had to be able, physically and otherwise, to protect the women supposedly in their care.

Aggressive, violent behavior, or the threat of violence, could thus be a source of honor for men. One case in 1851 links the construction of male honor based on a wife's sexual honesty with a man's own financial honesty. Antonio Joaquim dos Santos, a poor sailor from the Cape Verde Islands, faced the charge of assaulting a member of the National Guard. As the defendant explained in his testimony, the entire dispute revolved around the alleged victim's claim that Antonio owed him money. As he pursued Antonio, even following him by boat to an island in the Guaíba, the Guard member insisted that the immigrant fulfill his financial obligation and insulted the honor of Antonio's wife by asserting she was unfaithful. Whether or not a fight actually followed (Antonio denied it), the defendant's strategy in the courtroom is suggestive of his definition of honorability. He carefully tried to answer both of his accuser's challenges; not only did he not have a debt that he was neglecting, but he also had a wife who was loyal to him. After one witness finished his response to the judge's questions, Antonio (or his legal representative) pushed the latter issue, leading the man to declare that "he knows with certainty that the accused is married and that his wife has always been very honest."[141]

Although Antonio's example supports the common conception of the macho sense of honor, we should not be too quick to assume that plebeians always lived by these rules. For one thing, the court cases show men who did not always obey this code. At least some plebeian men appear not to have held women of their class to the strict limits of the code. We see, for example, a husband who did not seem to mind that his wife allowed another man to spend the night with them. He went off to sleep, leaving the two alone; shortly thereafter, at least by his telling, it was the other man, a *pardo* policeman named Satiro Antonio José da Rocha, and not her spouse-guardian, who pleaded that the woman "at least respect her husband."[142] Moreover, other stories seem to show that men did not label as dishonorable women whose sexual life went beyond relations with a single legal partner. As Esteves suggests, the fact that defendants in trials for sexual crimes applied stereotyped notions of gendered honor and shame when face to face with judicial authorities might mean that they were trying to anticipate and manipulate these officials' attitudes. Outside the presence of judges and scribes, such men may have been less strict in their imposition of the classic definition of female honor.[143]

The existence of other codes of gendered honor, outside the classic honor/shame ideology, must largely, however, remain a tantalizing possibility here. The court cases give only faint suggestions in this regard. For example, some men showed little concern with their women's fidelity to them; more commonly, plebeian men worried less about women's previous sexual histories than about monogamy during a formal or common-law marriage.[144] Despite such relatively more forgiving attitudes on the part of some men, the court cases under study reveal a great deal of conflict over gendered constructions of honor, particularly over control of women's sexuality.

As some of the cases examined earlier reveal, perceived threats to masculine honor were sources of verbal and physical violence. In 1869, four years after the outbreak of the Paraguayan War, an outburst on the rua Arvoredo reflected this tendency. A neighbor boy had irritated the African street vendor (*quitandeira*) Joana Guedes de Jesús. Trying to cut down a line that Joana had strung up behind her house, the child drove the woman to complain to his mother; in spite of the "good peace" in which they had always lived, the woman responded harshly to Joana's appeals. Some days later, the boy's father sent an employee, the *preto* José dos Passos Júnior, to confront Joana; as José began "to provoke her," Joana explained, "the only thing she said was that he [should] stop the show of bravery [*valentia*], that our government needed brave men for the campaign." This challenge ended in a beating as José ran after Joana, giving her "various offenses" with a whip.[145]

Threats to masculine honor came particularly in acts and words that suggested a man could not control his women. Clearly, some men strove to keep women's sexual and material lives under some version of patriarchal dominance. One of the most tragic of these cases involved a poor workingman's attempts to control a woman who no longer wanted him. Even after Clara Joaquina da Conceição had broken off her relations with her common-law partner, Manoel José Vieira, the man hounded her, appearing in her house and trying to assert his patriarchal authority. Coming to her house one day with some provisions, Manoel declared that "from that day forward, no one would govern in that house but him." When Clara opposed him, he set upon her with a knife. In his defense before a jury, he claimed that he had in fact merely been defending himself. Perhaps feeling this argument to be insufficient, he then attacked the honesty of Clara and the neighbor who had supported her; like many of their friends, he averred, the two women were nothing but prostitutes.[146]

Tragic though they were, such incidents do not demonstrate that the honor/shame code functioned in perfect, monolithic form among plebeians. Men of the *povo* were not able effectively to live up to the ideals of this code. We must remember here that men's desires to act according to what now seems the classic formulation of honor in Latin America should not be assumed. Even for those men who sought to be good patriarchs in classic terms, this honorability was difficult to achieve. In one sense, the concept of honor commonly ascribed to Brazilian and other Latin American societies contained a certain democratic potential. Any man who lived as a patriarch, protecting and dominating the members of his extended family, might gain honor. In practice, however, this potential was as unequally distributed as were wealth and power among social classes. Poor men did not enjoy access to the resources richer men had. Without the wealth and influence that would enable him to attract dependents and keep his women isolated at home, a poor man's chances of attaining honorability suffered.[147] It is this very undemocratic association of honor with "social precedence" that gave meaning to allegations that the poorest individuals were, by virtue of their social position, unworthy of trust and incapable of honor.[148]

Complicating the situation of such men of the *povo* was the behavior of poor women. Even if they wanted to, women like Clara Joaquina could not remain ensconced in some idyllic home set apart from the outside world; they had to work, and their work took them out onto the streets and into other people's homes. As throughout the nineteenth century, plebeian women also appear to have often lived on their own. With or without children to raise, these women rented rooms by themselves or moved among living spaces they shared with friends, employers, or lovers. This mobility was not without costs; women and their children suffered from poverty and predatory males' advances.[149] At the same time, living without patriarchal protection could also mean a degree of independence. As Paulo Moreira has observed, some women even turned their residences into centers for gambling, dances, or other festive gatherings. In the process, their homes became privileged spaces of popular cultural activity.[150] For Clara Joaquina and many more women of the *povo*, however, mobility meant being able to do without the dangers that macho patriarchs like Manoel José posed. Beyond this degree of escape from such men, women took more direct control over their sexual and material lives. Indeed, the court cases provide a few examples of women fighting to keep certain men. In May 1870, for instance, two freedwomen (one African and the other Brazilian-born) came to blows over a certain Bernardino, husband of the defendant, Andreza do Rosário. Furious that Bernardino had abandoned her to go live with Semiana Joaquina de Souza, and with "suspicion . . . of spells cast by the victim [Semiana] on the husband of the accused," Andreza set upon Semiana as she walked by.[151]

In light of such actions by women of the *povo*, cases like those of Clara Joaquina and João Fidelis may provide less proof of plebeian men's patriarchal control than of something quite different. Their violent efforts to impose themselves on the sexual and material lives of "their" women may, that is, demonstrate the difficulties these men had in living up to a classic patriarchal code of behavior. The violence into which plebeian men fell may reflect not male domination but rather women's success in maintaining some relative independence in adhering to their own, distinct codes.[152]

Through their efforts to dominate the women in their lives, men of the *povo* attempted to establish a version of patriarchal honor. As noted previously, the distribution of material resources and power in Gaúcho society erected obstacles to these men's achievement of such honor. As we have also seen, it is far from certain that plebeian men and women in Porto Alegre fully accepted the dominant code of honor and shame. Quite possibly, this moral code was subject to as many popular interpretations and manipulations as were other ideological constructions. What is evident, however, is that conflicts over questions of honor pervaded the lives of plebeian women and men in mid-nineteenth-century Porto Alegre. Together with tensions along the axes of legal condition and race/ethnicity, honor thus contributed to a sense of anxiety and a definite potential for violence within the *povo*. At the same time, honor, legal condition, and race informed struggles over status. These factors, that is, could define a person's social position vis-à-vis others —and play a role disputes over such definitions. Insofar as they set plebeians against one another, such disputes represent the atomizing effects of seigneurial and hierarchical ideas among members of the *povo*.

In the decades after the Farroupilha Revolution, plebeians confronted and applied versions of seigneurial ideals in their daily lives. In relations with their patrons, the authorities, and their fellow nonelites, members of the popular classes did not seek full citizenship; this goal may have seemed unrealistic. Instead, poor men and women, both free and enslaved, worked to maximize personal sovereignty in myriad ways, from playing *senhores* off one another to simply playing the role of *senhor* themselves. At heart, though, Porto Alegre's plebeians wanted greater control over the conditions in which they lived their lives—an aim that pushed *senhores* and officials alike to debate projects for creating a better, more submissive *povo*.

4

Blurring the Lines of Public Politics

Abolitionist Projects, 1879–1888

> Emancipators can be as coercive and oppressive, in subtle ways, as enslavers.
>
> *David Brion Davis,* Slavery and Human Progress

ON 10 February 1884, just eleven days after his five *senhores* granted him a letter of emancipation, José Velho broke into a storeowner's house; stole a watch, a golden medallion, and other objects; and fled. Seeing José depart and then noticing a door and some drawers forced open, the storeowner's clerk took off as well, chasing down José and taking him to the police. Questioned by the police, the prisoner did not deny his crime but rather tried to justify his actions by explaining the pressures of working for his *senhor.* Even when technically free, José had continued to serve, in effect, as an *escravo de ganho,* a slave who worked and often lived outside the master's home or business and turned over his rent or salary to his *senhor.* Police notations and José's testimony at the arrest show that José worked as a cart driver, transporting various goods through the streets of Porto Alegre in a cart he had rented. By removing the former slave from the direct supervision of the master, such a situation might have produced a relative looseness in the relations between

José and the one *senhor* with whom he seems to have had active dealings, Marcos Antonio da Costa.[1] The fact that José had four other *senhores* as well (who together with Marcos had acquired José through inheritance) might also suggest a diffusion of seigneurial power that José could have exploited. Nonetheless, the situation had become intolerable to José. While stricken by an illness, he explained, he had fallen 26$000 réis behind in his payments to Marcos. Whether José had actually been incapacitated or had feigned disability to cover over attempts to withhold money from his *senhor,* the delay in payments led to a strong reaction from Marcos. From that time on, José testified, Marcos "plagued him with threats." Implicitly then, in this testimony, the theft was not a result of José's criminal nature but of the unjust badgering he had received from his *senhor.*

When his case came up before the jury in June 1884, José chose a different strategy. Dropping the explanations he and later his lawyer had put forward, he now simply denied his guilt. Tantalizingly, however, he added that "he always considered himself the slave of Marcos Antonio da Costa and others and it is now that he knows how to be free." Coming as it did in the face of authority, in the form of judicial and police officials, probably at least one of his former masters, and a jury about to decide his guilt or innocence, this was a striking declaration indeed. What precisely José Velho meant by it is not, however, immediately clear. His statement might have been a bow before the assembled representatives of legal power, a promise that he had learned his lesson and would from then on behave better, serving Marcos with greater dispatch and refraining from committing further crimes. In such a way, he may have been reflecting his understanding of the difference between slaves' and free persons' behavior; now that he realized he was no longer a slave, this would imply, he would comport himself with the responsibility and honesty befitting a free man. Given the hostility toward Marcos that José showed throughout the stages of his arrest and trial, however, it seems probable that he was making a bolder declaration. Perhaps he was merely playing to an assumed or perceived belief about how slaves and free persons behave differently, in an attempt to avoid conviction. He may even have been asserting, in a somewhat cryptic manner, his autonomy in relation to Marcos. José, that is, may, have intended to behave even more independently in the future; being free, he would no longer show as much subservience to his master as he had in the past.[2] More important than any particular reading we make of José Velho's statement is the simple fact that by making it he took on a great deal of subjective power. Whether he was giving in to or defying the authorities present, that is, his declaration represents a claim of profound significance; in saying that he knew how to be free, he asserted his power to give meaning both to his own life and to the concepts of freedom and emancipation.

While José Velho languished in prison awaiting release—which came only after he was acquitted for a second time on 23 September 1884 (the judge had appealed the jury's 11 June verdict of "not guilty")—Porto Alegre witnessed the efflorescence of a dramatic emancipationist movement that proclaimed the city free of slavery on 7 September 1884, almost four years before the declaration of final abolition on a national level. Hailing this "redemption of the captives" as a "great and patriotic act," local politicians, abolitionist societies, and the press claimed authorship of emancipation for themselves.[3] As we shall see, these groups linked the issue with partisan disputes, arguing not only during 1880–84 but even into mid-1888 over the predominance of Republicans versus Liberals, or declared abolitionists versus slaveholders, in the achievement of abolition. At other times, politicians might proclaim that abolition in Porto Alegre and the province had been the work of the "people," but their rhetorical "people" referred to the distinguished ladies and gentlemen, the cadets of the Escola Militar (Military Academy), the priests, and the other respectable citizens who attended the many meetings, benefit dances, and bazaars that made the abolitionist movement in Porto Alegre as much a subject for gossip columns as for political editorials.[4] At its most generous, this conception of abolitionism might include the small merchants, widows, and others who had owned only a slave or two as participants in the movement. Finally, the press at times showed a glimmer of awareness that people outside this tightly defined *povo* could have their own views of abolitionism, as in an 1884 cartoon that depicted a slave complaining to his friend: "The black is up a creek [*Negro está no mato*] with these men who fill their mouths with liberty! . . . Look, my master is one of the bigwigs of some abolitionist conference . . . , [and] meanwhile I'm still a slave."[5] Nowhere in their speeches or writings, however, did these elite groups acknowledge that slaves and other members of the popular classes had any but a passive role in the processes that led to abolition.

In fact, these processes consisted of a series of struggles more complex and contingent than their descriptions by elites recognized. First of all, the course of official abolitionism was politically innovative, for though it excluded slaves and ex-slaves, it brought together sworn partisan enemies and, more novelly, many of the "ladies" of the city's elite in a movement that sought to depoliticize the potentially explosive question of emancipation. Moreover, José Velho was far from the only slave or ex-slave trying to impose alternative meanings on slavery's end and the freedom that was to follow it; the efforts of these plebeians would, in fact, force elites to take further steps in order to protect their place of privilege in the socially tumultuous years of the late Empire.

The Context of the Emancipation Movement

By 1883–84, several conditions offered great potential for reforms to eliminate slavery in Porto Alegre. Although Rio Grande do Sul still had the sixth-largest provincial slave population in the Empire, this population had decreased by as much as 38.9 percent during the previous decade, to approximately 60,136. Porto Alegre itself reported only 5,790 slaves in 1884. Although the part of the population made up of slaves was greater in Porto Alegre than in the province as a whole, this proportion had dropped significantly at both municipal and provincial levels. A quarter century earlier, slaves had made up 25 percent of the population of Rio Grande do Sul and 28 percent of Porto Alegre; by 1884, these numbers had dropped to approximately 8 and 14.5 percent, respectively. Moreover, with the exception of the *charque* industry centered in Pelotas, no major economic activity in the province still relied heavily on slave labor. Slaves in Porto Alegre held a wide array of jobs, with a particularly large proportion working as day laborers and domestic servants; though important in a variety of economic activities in the city, slave labor was not the basis of any large-scale type of production.[6] Finally and most significantly, by 1883 virtually no one in Rio Grande do Sul remained in open support of slavery. All the major political factions agreed on the evils slavery had brought to society and on the necessity of replacing that "vile stigma" with a system of free labor. As English traveler Herbert Huntington Smith noted after spending several months in the province in 1881–82, even if the local and national assemblies were not yet ready to legislate the end of slavery, "Fortunately, the people of Rio Grande do Sul have better sense than those who govern them."[7]

The political leaders of Rio Grande do Sul and its capital city did not, however, easily bring themselves to implement the good sense Smith attributed to the people they governed. The organization of a large-scale movement in support of the emancipation of slaves met with a daunting obstacle—the ideological factionalism that Smith called "party spirit."[8] In Porto Alegre and Rio Grande do Sul in the last decade of slavery, every issue that arose in public debate—from the lighting of city streets to immigration policy—set off a tremendous uproar of charges and countercharges among representatives of the different political parties. Furthermore, to a much greater degree than elsewhere in Brazil, these debates reflected not only jockeying for position within the system of patronage that characterized imperial politics but conflicts between substantially distinct ideologies.[9] Thus, although Liberals, Conservatives, and Republicans all acknowledged the need to end slavery, the depth of the antagonism and factionalism among them meant that it was only with great reluctance that any one group would ally with another—even when they essentially agreed on the matter at hand. These schisms within the male elite, together with the exclusion of women and "womanly" issues from general political debates, led in the 1880s to the feminization of abolition in the city.

The debate over the abolition of slavery—commonly acknowledged to be the most pressing social, economic, and political issue the nation faced in the 1880s—was an extreme case of the acrimony that characterized Gaúcho elites' debates in the last decade of the Empire. Even for a regional elite with few ties to large-scale slave-based production, slavery was the issue that focused the overriding anxieties of the powerful. Through debates over abolition, elites addressed a range of questions of power within national and provincial politics as local groups tried to position themselves with strong allies from outside Rio Grande and against local political competitors. Obviously, abolition also involved the definition of relations between elite and popular groups—not just masters and slaves, but all patrons and their dependent workers—for slavery had long been a central model for all relations between the powerful and the powerless in Brazilian society. When factions of the elite managed, however temporarily, to put aside their differences on an issue that encompassed all of these concerns, it was thus a monumental occurrence in provincial politics. Coming after the accelerated organization of emancipationist sentiment into a movement that swept through Porto Alegre and the rest of the province from late 1883 into 1884, the declaration of abolition on 7 September 1884 represented the conclusion of an intricate process of compromise among disparate political factions of the elite.

In order to understand this compromise, we must first examine the positions of the main elite political factions before and during these "exalted" years of abolitionism in Porto Alegre. Since the late 1860s, the two traditional parties of the Empire, the Liberals and the Conservatives, had maintained wavering commitments to the idea of abolition, and partisan competition had influenced changes in their positions over time. The emergence in 1882 of an innovative and aggressive new player, the Rio-Grandense Republican Party (the PRR—Partido Republicano Rio-Grandense), in that competition gave added momentum to the growth of a proemancipation majority across party lines. So explosive were partisan politics in the era, and so potentially perilous was the end of slavery, however, that the transformation of this majority into an abolitionist movement still depended on the feminization of the emancipation question.

Liberals had been the most powerful partisan force in the province since the early 1870s. Neither while in control of the provincial government nor when the peculiarities of the Empire's centralized patronage and electoral structures pushed it into the opposition did the Gaúcho Liberal Party embrace any but the most moderate reform proposals on abolition or other social issues until the very eve of the emancipationist movement.[10] Indeed, it was only in the late 1870s that Liberals in Rio Grande do Sul urged emancipationist strategies beyond a simple enforcement of the Free Womb (Rio Branco) Law passed by a Conservative ministry in 1871.[11] Another organizational concern reinforced their desire to show that their tentative reform programs were more than mere demagoguery. During the 1870s, the Liberal Party had suffered much internal dissension over the issue of religious freedom for non-Catholics—an important question in a province that was receiving so much German immigration. Abolition thus offered an issue around which Liberals could regroup and overcome potential splits within their ranks.[12]

Even when ready to tackle abolition in the early 1880s, however, Liberals continued to espouse only gradualist solutions. Their proposals for the reform of slavery show that they wanted to accomplish the end of slavery in a way that would hardly affect existing power structures; as the foremost Liberal leader, Gaspar Silveira Martins, argued, abolition was a noble idea but "should be directed in such a way that the enthusiasm for liberty does not become prejudicial to the life of the citizens who constitute the more intelligent classes."[13] These desires received their most telling formulation in Silveira Martins's attack on those who began to press the abolition issue in 1879–80. Admitting the injustice of slavery but evincing great concern for the property rights and financial well-being of slaveholding planters, Silveira Martins declared, "I love the country more than the black man."[14] As late as 1879, this Liberal leader refused to consider emancipation without full indemnification for slaveholders. By 1883, however, Silveira Martins and most of his Liberal colleagues had come to deride as slavocrats those who insisted on monetary compensation for freed slaves. Instead, the Liberals now saw the solution to the abolition question in a scheme of conditional liberty based on freedpersons' continued service to former masters.[15] Any more immediatist plans, particularly those that did not mention indemnification through services, the Liberals denounced as potential sources of disorder.[16]

This emancipationist stance, moderate though it may have been, served as the basis for bitter Liberal attacks on Conservatives. Portraying their rivals as cut off from the spirit of the people and as threatening to disturb social harmony, Liberals demonstrated their desire to turn the emancipationist campaign into a triumph for themselves and a crippling defeat for their Conservative opponents.[17] This Liberal effort had, in fact, a good chance of success, for the slavery issue was threatening to tear the Conservative Party apart at both national and provincial levels. During their party's time in power at the national level and within the provincial executive branch, Gaúcho Conservatives had found themselves weakened by a split over the issue of abolition. On one side stood the "wolves," who opposed abolition, and on the other the "lambs," who supported moderate reforms.[18] This lack of internal cohesion, as well as its historically weaker base of support in Rio Grande do Sul, made the Conservative Party, as a Republican paper noted, "an extremely weak competitor in this province."[19]

Because of this weakness, the hard-line Conservatives lashed out frequently at the emancipation movement that grew so precipitously in 1883–84 and at those who participated in it. The editors of the party organ, *O Conservador,* denounced the hypocrisy of the alliance between Republicans and Liberals within the movement, pointing out that these groups disagreed on the concept of indemnification (the Liberals insisted on indemnification through services; the Republicans renounced indemnification completely), while also criticizing individual abolitionists—usually Liberals—for not living up to their professed ideals.[20] More vehemently, these Conservatives attacked the actions of the emancipationist movement as both inefficient and dangerous to the social order. The nation had entered into crisis, according to this view, and now sat upon a "frightening and dangerous volcano." It followed that the emancipationists, in their exhortations to the slaves, could set off terrible social explosions.[21] To counter this potential catastrophe, hard-line Conservatives offered a strategy of stability and control. Instead of drastic new steps, they called for continued obedience to the Free Womb Law and private, voluntary emancipations by slaveholders. In sum, these Conservatives paid lip service to the justice and inevitability of abolition, while opposing any plan that threatened the rights of *senhores* over their slave property.[22]

Whereas the Conservative "wolves" held out in defiance of the emancipationist wave that swept through Porto Alegre, the party's "lambs" fell into line with the Liberals and Republicans and evinced enthusiasm for direct action in favor of abolition. Proclaiming themselves to be "abolitionist to the core" as early as 1881, they even came to poke fun at the purely rhetorical abolitionism of *O Conservador*, particularly when it hailed the great generosity of masters' liberating slaves in return for large sums of money.[23] Their analysis of the slavery issue—and actions based on this evaluation—offered further contrasts with the "wolves." Instead of trying to head off disaster through adherence to planter-led private initiatives, the dissident Conservatives called for immediate reforms.[24] Within Porto Alegre, they established funds to collect money with which to purchase individuals out of slavery and played leading roles in the organization of the emancipationist movement itself. Miguel de Werna e Bilstein, editor of *O Século*, promoted abolitionist events, and his wife, Miguelina, oversaw the collection of donations for the great benefit bazaar of 7 September 1884.[25]

The party that most energetically pushed for a quick end to slavery was also the youngest one in Porto Alegre, the PRR. Republican ideals of various types had existed in the province since the Farroupilha Revolution and in Brazil since the end of the eighteenth century. Rather than a mere culmination of the growth of Republicanism, though, the PRR was in significant ways an innovative political group. As Celi Pinto has argued, although the families of PRR leaders like Joaquim Francisco Assis Brasil and Ramiro

Barcellos held large ranches in the southern *campanha* region, many other Republicans came from less powerful *estancieiro* (rancher) families in that area or the northern part of the province. Also tending to be younger than their rivals in the Liberal and Conservative Parties, the organizers of the PRR thus represented an alternative to the group of ranchers who controlled the provincial political system.[26] Many of these young militants had studied in other provinces, especially at the Law School of São Paulo, and on their return home brought back to Porto Alegre a fascination with Comtean Positivism.[27] This system of thought quickly became the guiding principle of the province's Republican movement, so much so that Republicans of a more Liberal orientation, like Apolinário Porto Alegre, became disenchanted with what they saw as the dogmatism of the Republican Positivists.[28] At the Republican convention of 1882 and the First Republican Congress the following year, the Positivists overcame such tensions to enjoy moments of triumph, as their leadership attempted to establish a political party and a propaganda machine on rigorous scientific organizational principles.[29]

These principles gave the Republicans a position on slavery that stood out for its radicalism and coherence against the hesitant reformism and divisions that characterized Conservative and Liberal camps. Until 1883, Gaúcho Republicans had followed the federalist line put forward by their São Paulo colleagues in the early 1870s, calling for abolition to be carried out at the provincial level, through indemnification and measures that would "increase the effects" of the Free Womb Law.[30] By 1884, however, the PRR began to move the focus of their proabolition propaganda toward a more universal attack on slavery. Declaring that "abolition should be immediate and prompt, as soon as our assembly receives the necessary powers to legislate on the matter," the PRR stepped up its broad arguments against slavery; abolition must come, Republicans argued, "to avenge defiled morality, redress outraged rights, reclaim freedom criminally suppressed, honor the nation, and get satisfaction for humanity, which has been stained by the cursed black institution."[31]

The PRR's new position on abolition proved to be markedly more radical than those of the existing parties.[32] Using language filled with images of violence and struggle, Republicans chided Liberals, Conservatives, and above all the emperor for neglecting the "national aspiration" of abolition.[33] In fact, the PRR's extremism with regard to abolition went beyond demands for complete abolition, linking the idea of abolition with the overall fate of the Empire and calling for the end not only of slavery but also of the Empire itself.[34] The PRR's members were very careful to point out, however, that they were an "evolutionary" and not a "revolutionary" party; they called for progress through the destruction of the Empire, but they insisted always on the maintenance of social order.[35] Thus, despite their willingness to criticize their partisan opponents and especially the emperor, the Gaúcho Republicans' real target was the political regime rather than social hierarchies.

Overcoming the bitter partisan conflicts among Liberals, dissident Conservatives, and Republicans required a compromise political solution: not complete but conditional emancipation. Slaves would be freed technically but would receive their letters of emancipation with *cláusulas de serviço,* clauses requiring them to continue to work for their former masters for a set period of time (up to seven years, though the average in 1884 was 5.7 years).[36] This conditional emancipation promised to protect the interests of the Gaúcho elite. It would, to begin with, allow an exceptionally self-conscious regional elite to present itself as progressive and civilized, on the leading edge of the abolitionist struggle in Brazil.[37] More important, conditional emancipation would guarantee former slaveholders the further service of their dependent laborers. According to the Rio Branco Law of 1871, new freedpersons (called *contratados,* or contractees, in Porto Alegre) who failed to comply with the terms of their conditional liberty would not lose their freedom but would have to serve the remaining time of their contract in a public establishment or in service to another private employer. In daily practice, many *contratados* who resisted their contractual obligations in Porto Alegre were simply jailed, much as had long been done with particularly unruly slaves.[38] The similarity with formal slavery extended also to the manner in which masters treated their laborers as property. Although no longer selling human beings outright, *senhores* commonly sold workers' time of service. Thus one *senhor* advertised in the *Jornal do Commercio* in 1882 the sale of "five years of a very able female slave, for the service of a family house."[39] Conditional liberty even represented a regression in the few formal rights these recent ex-slaves enjoyed. As nominally free workers, *contratados* lost their ability to buy their way out of service to their masters; under the Rio Branco Law still in force, slaves could gather their savings into a sum (a *pecúlio,* or peculium) that their masters were legally obligated to accept as a purchase price for the slaves' freedom. According to their labor contracts, however, the new freedpersons would have no legal way to control where and for whom they worked.[40] This, then, was very much what elites had in mind when they hoped to achieve a reform of slavery without any disorganization of labor—the glory of declaring the end of slavery in their province, with few of the risks they associated with abolition.

The Organization and "Feminization" of Emancipationism

The 1884 emancipation was not, however, merely the result of the wise selection of a project that would be both favorable to elite interests and politically feasible. The most striking feature of the process of the 1883–84 emancipationist movement was, in fact, the manner in which it "feminized" abolition by shifting the issue out of the realm of formal, partisan politics and lending it a feminine gendered character. That is, in the organizational and discursive processes by which the elites realized conditional emancipation, the conception of abolition as a political or economic problem increasingly—if never completely—gave way to an understanding of abolition as a nonpartisan moral question.[41] This is not to say that abolition ceased to be a topic of partisan struggles; organization and support of the movement drew, to a certain degree, on partisan concerns. Certainly Liberals saw in the increasingly popular movement a chance to shore up their party structure and assert their dominance over Conservative opponents. For Republicans, furthermore, the movement represented an opportunity to project themselves as a serious and cohesive new political force in the province. At this level, the discursive depoliticization of abolition can even be said to have served partisan political aims.

At quite a different level, however, this phenomenon went beyond political factionalism to address the broader question of how to effect fundamental social reform without opening up the social hierarchy to disorder or even revolution. Here the partial removal of such a potentially disruptive debate from the sphere of partisan conflict protected a ruling bloc in a time of crisis. As we shall see, elites tried to manage abolition by associating it with issues and qualities long defined as social and moral instead of political. In terms of organization, they brought to bear the experience and strategies that the genteel ladies of Porto Alegre had developed in their charitable endeavors. In doing so, elites found a language of compromise in existing constructions of "the feminine" and at the same time relied on a familiar, ostensibly apolitical culture of women's social activism in their struggle to enact abolition without endangering existing social hierarchies.[42]

The first signal of the move away from partisan politics was the lead taken by private groups in pushing the emancipation ideal forward. Porto Alegre had for many years hosted a number of charitable and other associations that emancipated individual slaves. These ranged from associations with other aims, like the prestigious Sociedade Partenon Literário (Parthenon Literary Society), the Masonic lodge Luz e Ordem (Light and Order), religious orders, and *carnaval* schools, to entities formed specifically to buy slaves out of captivity, like the Sociedade Emancipadora Rio Branco (Rio Branco Emancipation Society), which cadets of the Escola Militar (Military Academy) established in 1880, and the Caixa Libertadora Mercantil (Mercantil Emancipation Fund), which the newspaper *O Mercantil* set up in 1883.[43] With very few exceptions, the city's emancipationist organizations existed in, and consisted of, elite society. They raised money through contributions, bazaars, benefit auctions, and similar activities.

The Abolitionist Center of Porto Alegre (Centro Abolicionista de Porto Alegre), which took the leading role in the emancipationist movement, serves as an illustrative case here. Founded at a 29 September 1883 public meeting called by the Partenon Literário, the Center emerged as the umbrella organization of the movement during the following year. Its leadership included some of the most prominent politicians of the day; although dominated at its top ranks by Liberals such as Coronel Joaquim Pedro Salgado, its various commissions also counted Conservatives and Republicans among their members. Indeed, although it was a nongovernmental and nonpartisan society, it maintained strong links to the highest political authorities in the province.[44] Still, the Center's activities largely took place outside formal political spaces. Its greatest energies went into organizing the street-by-street liberation of Porto Alegre. After nominating leading citizens to a series of "liberating commissions," the Center assigned them to the various districts of the capital and its outlying zones. Within each district, members of the relevant commission went block by block, attempting to convince *senhores* to free their slaves. Whether it was the moral suasion they wielded or their distinguished members' social prestige—and in spite of the complaints of *O Conservador*—the commissions apparently met with little resistance. Their goal seemed, in any case, more the declaration of emancipation than the realization of complete abolition. Describing the first city block freed—rua dos Andradas, between rua General Câmara and rua do Comércio—the Center's official report proclaimed it liberated of slavery, "except for three or four possessors of slaves."[45] At the same time, the Center organized banquets where orators read abolitionist poetry and made inspirational speeches and charity events to raise money with which to indemnify masters for the loss of their slave property.[46]

In fact, it was because these activities were defined as social and charitable affairs that women's collaboration in them was not a complete novelty. Women had long been involved in charitable causes in the city, administering shelters and schools for orphans, supporting the education of poor workingmen, and taking up collections of money and supplies to aid war efforts during the Farroupilha Revolution and the Paraguayan War. A certain discretion generally characterized such activism; elite women working on charitable and social issues were almost always restricted to supporting roles that kept them out of the more openly debated public questions of the Empire.[47] In one sense, women's emancipationism of the 1880s represented a simple expansion of the established feminine culture and its focus on matters seen as moral and social rather than strictly political. In fact, much of the *senhoras*' contribution to the movement came through the more "frivolous" events that different emancipationist societies held—events of a "purely social character."[48] Women performed music; gave inspirational readings; or simply added an element of festivity, of light fun, to auctions, bazaars, and dances designed to raise money for the purchase of slaves' freedom or to celebrate the liberation of small groups of slaves.[49] At times, prominent individuals would set up social affairs to mark their emancipation of slaves; women were commonly present on such occasions as well. To commemorate his liberation of a slave in March 1884, one Dr. Isidro organized a ceremony at which various women played the piano and "a delightful young woman, daughter of Sr. Júlio Cesar Leal, divinely sang a folk song [*modinha*]."[50]

Although no women's abolitionist societies were formed, as had occurred in other provinces, women in Porto Alegre also contributed with organizational work even before their display of "incomparable devotion" in the final days of the movement.[51] The Abolitionist Center did not include women in its directorate. But when it set up its commissions to liberate Porto Alegre proper, along with the seven outlying districts of Belem and Pedras Brancas, it created separate women's commissions for the three divisions of the capital and one for Pedras Brancas. In these integrated districts, twenty of the Center's forty-three agents were female.[52] Although we do not know the exact mechanics of these commissions, women may have had a particularly important role in their efforts at persuasion; one article described Dona Maria Jesuína Gay (a member of the commission for the first district) as follows: "True angel of charity, she has been directing herself personally and tirelessly to various families, asking for their cooperation in the humanitarian work of rescuing the slaves."[53]

The climactic event of women's participation in emancipationism and of the movement itself was the *kermesse* (kermis, or charity bazaar) held on 7 September 1884. Led by such respectable examples of "the gentle sex" as Dona Maria Jesuína Gay and Dona Miguelina de Werna, emancipationists in the city spent months preparing for this bazaar, and their "campaign all of peace and charity" demonstrated the central role that "decent" women, and the moral and charitable concerns that were their domain, played in Porto-alegrense emancipationism.[54] Drawing on their experience administering charities, *senhoras* worked to turn the kermis into a festivity that also raised the money needed to purchase and emancipate Porto Alegre's remaining slaves. With Liberal, dissident Conservative, and Republican papers trumpeting the progress of their movement and issuing calls for assistance, these "priestesses of Humanity" sought donations of items that could be sold at the booths (*tendas*) they directed in the Praça da Matriz.[55]

On the evening of 7 September, at the end of two days of ostentatious civic rituals, including a meeting at which leaders of the Abolitionist Center offered solemn speeches and a Te Deum that the bishop celebrated in the city cathedral, crowds made their way to the booths, purchasing food and decorative trifles or risking small amounts on raffle tickets.[56] People of humble station participated, but the kermis was above all an occasion for members of high society to commemorate their own generosity and the efforts of prominent *senhoras* while also diverting themselves. Descriptions of the booths reveal the unmistakably elitist tenor of the festivities. The booth named after Conservative politician Severino Ribeiro, to take but one example, offered for sale "perfumes, artificial flowers, objects of crystal, fine porcelain, crystal bottles, beautiful paintings, bijouterie."[57] Men of the elite, meanwhile, tried to outdo each other with exorbitant bids on cigars and other luxuries.[58] The city's press saw in such activities the very essence of charity and attributed the glorious success of the kermis to its female leadership. H. Martins, for instance, wrote of the "zeal, ardor, and abnegation" of the *senhoras* involved, whereas the poet Apolinário Porto Alegre addressed more abstract praise to the *tendeira* (woman in charge of a booth): "Oh, holy prophetess," he rhapsodized, "Your soul synthesizes / The love of charity!"[59] The kermis became a celebration of the noble, charitable spirit of Porto Alegre's elite and especially of the energetic and moral women who shone in this movement as they had never done before in a public campaign.

Unlike the participation of elite girls and ladies in emancipationist salons and dances, the mobilization of women in the Abolitionist Center and later in the kermis brought women out into public to serve the most pressing cause of the day. Dona Maria Jesuína may have been making arguments that were strictly appropriate for a concerned lady of her era and doing so mostly in the drawing rooms of fellow elites, but she and other *senhoras* were also going through the streets of the city to take on the potentially explosive topic of the abolition of slavery. In effect, the positions such *senhoras* held in the emancipationist campaign pointed to two changes that were taking place: Porto Alegre's emancipationism was not only stretching the boundaries of women's activities but also reformulating abolition itself.

The transformation of the emancipationist movement into a social and charitable endeavor involved, after all, more than mere organizational strategies that enlisted certain women. At a discursive level, the construction of the movement as nonpartisan and "feminized" involved the movement of the abolition issue into a realm strongly identified with "the feminine." Part of this consisted of emancipationist appeals to sentimentality and morality, which had long appeared as responses to the brutal treatment of slaves (see chapter 1) but which took on an intensified form in the early 1880s. Expressions of sympathy for slaves could assume partisan trappings, as did the charge that an unfortunate young female slave had been horribly tortured in the house of Silveira Martins—a charge first made in 1876 and then brought up eight years later by Conservatives.[60] Cases of such partisan use of sympathy were, however, few and far between. The vast majority of appeals to sentimentality, which began to appear almost daily as 7 September 1884 approached, were not political in so narrow a manner. The most common type simply railed against the abuse of slaves or freedpersons by masters or the police. Such was the case with "poor Laura," whose mistress "constantly inflicted barbarous punishments on those unprotected by destiny, who had the misfortune of having been born under the despotic pressures of the traffickers in human flesh!" Her *senhora*'s abuse finally drove Laura to "martyrdom," when she threw herself off the roof of her master's house.[61] The imprisonment of slaves and ex-slaves without charging them with a crime became the cause of much irritation in *O Século* in 1884, although such abuses were a long-standing practice of *senhores* of disobedient slaves. After twice noting the presence of such slaves in the jail, the paper cried out in August of that year, "Enough, now, of barbarism!"[62]

Other appeals were more detailed, often involving stories of slaves' difficulties in maintaining a family. Damasceno Vieira described the awful effects of bondage on a slave mother in his poem "A Doida (scena da escravidão)" (The Madwoman [Scene of Slavery]). Fleeing naked and bloody from her master, the slave rejoices in the fact that her child will never know the cruelties of slavery. She fantasizes about her son, grown up, protecting her:

> If you saw me innocent,
> Beaten brutally,
> Mistreated like the dogs,
> You, in a sublime impetus,
> Would kill! There's no crime
> In children's avenging their mothers.

When she sees that her master has found her, she jumps from the rock on which she has taken refuge and, with her child in her arms, seeks in death the peace that slavery had denied her in life.[63] At the triumphal moment of emancipation, poet Candida Fortes projected a happy resolution to the problems of slave families in "Fructo da liberdade" (Fruits of Liberty). In a family that slavery had condemned to poverty and stripped of a male breadwinner, a young girl manages after abolition to find honest employment as a domestic servant and with her salary finally provides for her mother and little sisters.[64]

Newspapers of the period described not only slaves and their families but also slave owners with language of moral degradation. Slavery was depicted as driving elite men and women to acts seen as unnatural in the context of the family. In 1884, O *Mercantil* reported that a slave, caught stealing a chicken, had killed his master's son before the boy could report the crime. At the slave's trial, the master "wanted to avoid a new blow: the LOSS as much of his slave as of his son's murderer." His property in human beings overcame his proper paternal feelings. Having already sold the slave to another *fazendeiro,* and not wanting to lose the money from that sale, he tried to prevent the conviction of the slave. The article's author, Valentim Guimarães, reported happily that the slave went to the galley despite the master's efforts, commenting that "in this country not everything is yet rotten." To his horror, however, the perverse father, despite his lack of appropriate paternal feelings, continued to live "in the sweetest and closest affection" with the dead child's mother.[65] Such accounts, then, portrayed slavery as a threat to the institution of the family as much among the elite as among slaves.

Appeals to feelings of sympathy and charity and fears of moral damage to the family were ways of conceiving of abolition very different from concerns with continued profitability or access to labor; in fact, they linked the question with qualities and duties that were, among the Porto Alegre elite of the 1880s, socially defined as feminine.[66] Recognizing that elite women could play an important role in the emancipationist movement because of their association with the family and morality, elite men in Porto Alegre in effect followed the advice that the great abolitionist José do Patrocínio had offered activists in the province of Ceará: "It is necessary to make the weakness of women into the strongest of forces."[67] In this way, male leaders incorporated women and women's charitable activities into the abolitionist movement and depoliticized abolitionist rhetoric by moralizing and feminizing it. Bringing elite women and the characteristics associated with them into a movement acted out in meeting rooms and even on the street changed the character of such public spaces—moralizing or feminizing them—and provided a gendered language of morality, a discursive way to circumvent the internecine political squabbles that marked more strictly defined political debates in the era and that might have led to the breakdown of social hierarchies. This feminization was, of course, a political development, for it not only involved a maneuver around partisan differences but also played on some of the most basic political constructions in Gaúcho, or any other, society—the definitions of gender roles. It was, however, exactly because women's roles and activism were defined as nonpolitical—and they remained so after emancipation—that the relocation of the abolition issue into a feminized discursive space could be a key factor in the political compromise of conditional emancipationism in 1883–84.

Popular Projects for Abolition

As the case of José Velho suggests, even before the formal declaration of emancipation in Porto Alegre, free and enslaved members of the popular classes were formulating their own understandings of slavery and freedom. Elite hopes to head off challenges from freedpersons and other members of the popular classes faded quickly in the face of popular initiatives. Regarding maintenance of the seigneurial control to which they had been accustomed, elites had a great deal to worry about. For one thing, forms of resistance slaves had practiced throughout the period under study continued into the 1880s in the behavior not only of those who remained slaves (as few as fifty-eight in the final registry, taken in 1887) but also of the new *contratados*.[68] Only one strain of resistance, the establishment of *quilombos* (communities of runaway slaves), does not appear in the documents of the 1880s, the last recorded *quilombo* in or near Porto Alegre having been discovered by authorities in 1879.[69] Another kind of resistance, rebellion on a collective basis, appeared in Porto Alegre only as a rumor in late 1887 that was quickly denied by the provincial police chief.[70]

Without resorting to these most dramatic forms of resistance, slaves and freedpersons persisted nonetheless in efforts to protest against unacceptable work conditions or punishment, protect relations with spouses and relatives, and seek freedom. All of these means by which slaves and *contratados* escaped servitude and made their lives their own represent continuities with the years before the emancipationist movement in Porto Alegre. The rise of this movement, especially the implementation of conditional liberty on a large scale, did, however, bring changes in popular attitudes and behavior. Setting off open conflict within the elite on the very legitimacy of slavery, emancipationism created a new political climate characterized not only by heightened partisan tensions but by a more profound uncertainty about the proper forms of seigneurial dominance.

Slaves and *contratados* began to make use of this change in public attitudes. With virtually all elites speaking out against slavery, and many of them actively and publicly imploring masters to emancipate their slaves, dependent workers tried to take advantage of the openings that such a crisis in slavery's legitimacy might provide. To escape the control of their *senhores*, for instance, slaves and *contratados* increasingly sought out alternative authorities to champion their cause. Counting on the sympathy of journalists who had attacked slavery in print, slaves presented themselves at the offices of *A Federação*, *O Século*, and *O Mercantil*, complaining of the abuses their masters inflicted on them.[71] (It is impossible to know if the slavocrat *O Conservador* refused to make known similar visits it received or if slaves knew they would not find a sympathetic ear there.) At the end of 1887, for instance, *A Federação* reported that the *contratado* Manoel Joaquim had come to its offices "complaining of *sevícias* [excessive cruelties] by his ex-*senhor* Manoel de Souza Ferraz," adding that the *contratado* "had various contusions, from which blood still flowed!"[72] An article in *O Mercantil* likewise noted in 1887 the appearance of Joanna, former slave of the prominent Liberal journalist and politician Carlos von Koseritz, who declared that she could no longer stand "the mistreatment that was inflicted on her not by Sr. Koseritz, but by his wife." According to the newspaper, Joanna's *senhora* "almost crushed her head against the wall of the house, without the patient having contributed to this either in acts or in words." Joanna further declared that she lived in terror, so rarely let out that she "does not know any street of the city." The reaction of the journalist involved is illustrative: "Joanna being a *contratada*," he wrote, "we do not know on what law her ex-*senhores* base their proceeding against her with such rigor, inflicting punishment on a free person, an act that finds penalty in the Criminal Code."[73] In such cases, slaves and *contratados* like Joanna obviously made a correct reading of public opinion and their opportunities for receiving outside help through the press.

Support for slaves also came from the *povo* itself. In a variety of circumstances, crowds in the street or groups of neighbors proved willing to intervene on slaves' behalf. This derived in large part from the long-standing hostilities between members of the popular classes and the soldiers who trained in and policed the city. Something of this can be seen in the murder of a military cadet in 1886; in the middle of a group following a military band through the streets, the *pardo* Manoel Vicente suddenly grabbed the cadet Emílio de Andrade Vasconcellos and—saying "today I'm going to fulfill my judgment; you think that because you're a cadet you don't get a beating"—struck Emílio on the head with a club. Another violent example occurred in

1884, when a soldier told Paulino Ferreira da Silva to quiet down. When Paulino responded by declaring that "he couldn't order him to shut up because he was a Brazilian citizen," the soldier became incensed. This time it was the soldier who attacked.[74] According to the police, such conflicts represented ill will on the part of the *povo*. Exasperated, the commander of the police force related a case of such hostility: a group of policemen, returning from a party, encountered two men "in attitude of battle, one being armed with a knife and the other with stones." When a police corporal tried to separate the men, one attacked him. The fight was not serious, but it led the corporal to reflect that "every day one sees that the *povo* in this and other cases attends these scenes, with the aim only of seeing a policeman wounded."[75]

Even if this police official exaggerated the level of hostility, his comments do point to a real tension that existed between the *povo* and police. If they judged that the police were going too far, members of the populace would at times step in. When soldiers under the command of a police official invaded the house of a woman of the Mina nation, in an attempt to arrest her son, a crowd met them with "vehement protests."[76] A more striking case occurred at the city docks in 1887. An official named Bernardino, hearing that there was a runaway in a nearby warehouse, arrested the slave and tried to take him on board the steamer *Rio Pardo*, in order to return him to his owner in Pelotas. The ship's captain refused, however, to be a party to the capture, forcing Bernardino to move to a small boat. When this boat came near the land, "a murmur started in the middle of the *povo*" present, including "cries of let him go." A police magistrate, hearing the uproar, came to investigate and learned from Bernardino that he had made the arrest on his own authority, with no warrant or other order. The crowd "applauded the noble magistrate noisily with clapping and shouts and made the justice official leave running and humiliated."[77] Although it enjoyed the support of a police official, this event shows that crowds were ready to step in against arbitrary actions by the authorities.

In other cases, we can see that slaves and freedpersons received assistance from individuals, often neighbors. Having broken the chain that bound him to a wall, the ex-slave Antonio, for example, ran from his *senhor*'s house and sought the protection of one Francioni and others who lived nearby. When the *senhor* sent an employee to bring Antonio back by force, these neighbors refused to let him go, taking him instead to the local police chief for an examination of the wounds the *senhor*'s tortures had left on him.[78] Shortly after emancipation, the savage mistreatment of a young servant led her companion to ask a neighbor to lodge a complaint. Although this neighbor did press charges, declaring that it was "notoriously known" that the master "daily beat the minor," the trial ended in the *senhor*'s acquittal.[79]

Slaves and *contratados* also sought out police and legal authorities, the agents of legitimate authority, to hear their appeals. In March 1884, the interim chief of police reported that one slave, Domingos, had come to his office saying that he had been "barbarously bludgeoned" by his master (who lived in São Jeronimo), while another, Antonio, appeared to declare "that his *senhor* had punished him without just cause, in a barbarous manner that produced the wounds that he presented."[80] The conditionally free Damásia did much the same the following year, although in her case, due to a supposed lack of witnesses, the police did not proceed to an inquiry.[81] Still another slave, Paulina, went to the police to complain of the abuses she suffered at the hands of Mariano José do Canto Filho, to whom her *senhor* had rented her.[82] Remarkably, one freedman, Firmino, not only took his complaints to court but did so to prosecute the police *delegado*, Leopoldo Bier. Firmino alleged that Bier had unjustly abused him during an interrogation about a robbery; Bier admitted to having ordered Firmino's palms beaten but said he had been forced to do so "by the said freedman having behaved with audacity and insubordination toward the defendent [Bier]." The rapid dismissal of the case shows that Firmino had misread the tenor of the times; sympathy for mistreated slaves and ex-slaves did not mean acceptance of those who challenged police authority.[83]

A more notorious example of assistance to slaves and *contratados* further suggests the limits of the era's public sympathies. Appeals to alternative authorities, or even to the representatives of state power themselves, could find a welcome in this time of slavery's rejection. When slaves or freedpersons adopted strategies of greater autonomy, however, they might be branded as dangerous; working outside some form of seigneurial power, even in the age of emancipationism, could meet with sharp reprisals. A telling example appeared at the city's fringes, on the property of Joana de Oliveira Eiras. A free woman living in the district of Belém, on the outskirts of Porto Alegre, Joana "took into her house and its dependencies disorderly and ill-reputed individuals," including several slaves and at least four *contratados*.[84] Some of the men and women who rented living space from her seem to have worked in small agriculture around the property, while others seem merely to have slept there—but all had fled the control of their *senhores*. Alleged to have sheltered runaway slaves and other criminals and to have herself ordered a murder, Joana came under police scrutiny and, ultimately, attack. Authorities' preoccupation with this semiautonomous community and its mingling of slaves, ex-slaves, and free poor is clear in official documents describing the raids police soldiers made on the property (raids that only with great difficulty overcame the residents' armed defenses).[85]

All of the strategies by which slaves and freedpersons went outside the bounds of seigneurial authority obviously irritated the masters involved. Two months before final abolition, one master placed an angry advertisement in *O Conservador;* his slaves Victorno, Brazilio, and Jeronymo had run away, and now he "took recourse in the press to protest against those who criminally keep his slaves hidden in their houses, thus depriving [him] of their services and of the right that he has over the same [slaves] in virtue of the faculty that the law regulating property concedes to him."[86] Several *senhores* took pains to respond to accusations appearing in newspapers by themselves going directly to the press. The day after *O Mercantil* ran an article relaying his slave's accusations against him, for example, Luiz Becker went to that paper's office to give his side of the story. Whereas the slave claimed that her master had refused to provide medical care for an injury that kept her from working, Becker convinced the editors of *O Mercantil* that he had in fact seen to her treatment both at the Santa Casa de Misericordia and at home, with a Dr. Heinzelmann.[87] Another *senhor*, charged with torturing his fourteen-year-old servant, angrily declared in court: "Everyone knows that in this country delivered to the dominion of publicity, any individual without distinction can form and feed public opinion, giving news of their inventions, conjectures, or falsehoods. Today, whether by mistake or out of bad faith, any paper gives news; the next day it goes from mouth to mouth."[88] This declaration reveals the resentment of a master who felt his control over his servant eroding. This in turn suggests the effectiveness of the efforts of slaves and former slaves; *senhores* feared the opening of a wedge between themselves and their dependents through interventions by alternative authorities.

The desires and efforts of slaves and freedpersons went beyond simply trying to evade their masters' control, however; they also wanted to control the process and meaning of emancipation in other ways. One of the most remarkable court cases of these years involved a suit instigated by five *contratadas* against the emancipation society to which they had belonged. All of these women had joined the Sociedade Esperança e Caridade (Hope and Charity Society) in 1883, as slaves. Following its statutes, they were to contribute to the Society's emancipation fund. The Society's directors, in turn, would apply this money to purchase the freedom of members, beginning with those who had deposited the largest amounts. If members received their freedom before paying off their full purchase price, they were obligated to continue their contributions until reaching this amount. The five women's account books, presented in court, had notations of the deposits each had made; ranging from 60$500 to 226$000 réis, all were considerable sums.

With so much of their money involved, however, these women refused to be passive participants in the scheme. One of them, Maria Lydia, said that she had sought out the Society's directors to ask about its delay in freeing her, even after she had met the 200$000-réis sum that her owner demanded. Suspecting perhaps that the Society's directors would make off with her money, she complained to her master, who sent one of his associates to inquire about Maria Lydia's emancipation. Told that it would soon occur, the associate let the matter drop. When Maria Lydia and the other four slaves received conditional freedom through other means, they apparently felt the loss of their money. At first they again informed their *senhores*, some of whom seem to have been sympathetic. (One master, on the other hand, said that his ex-slave should instead seek help from the person "who had counseled such an end.") Continuing their pressure, the freedwomen succeeded in getting their masters to approach the Society about reimbursing its former members. Testifying in the suit that followed on the failure of these efforts, one of the *senhores* involved went so far as to imply corruption on the part of the Society's directors; he claimed to have been told that one of the directors, "from a certain time ago, manifests prosperity, both by buying a house in Menino Deus and by advantageously improving his mattress shop." The suit failed; the directors successfully argued that they had not profited personally from the Society's fund-raising scheme and, more important, that the five plaintiffs had stopped their contributions for longer than four weeks. According to the Society's statutes, this meant that they lost their membership status and with it the ability to withdraw the money they had deposited. Although their efforts were thwarted, the actions of the five freedwomen demonstrate their determination to control their lives as fully as possible. Far from being overwhelmed by gratitude at receiving emancipation, they felt that the manner in which their emancipation had occurred left something to be desired. By appealing to their *senhores*, they acted on these feelings, thus attempting to use paternalism for their own ends.[89]

In general, however, a more complete freedom from the control of *senhores* and from seigneurialism itself was central to slaves' and freedpersons' efforts after 1884. In part, this involved the continued efforts of the Irmandade de Nossa Senhora do Rosário, the religious lay brotherhood that included slaves and former slaves among its members, and the Sociedade Floresta Negra, an Afro-Brazilian social and cultural association, to purchase the freedom of remaining captives.[90] Much more dramatic, however, was direct action by individual Afro-Brazilians, particularly the massive rejection of the scheme of conditional freedom that had been at the core of the 1883–84 emancipationist movement. Although apparently without the collective organization that characterized the flight by groups of slaves from *fazendas* in São Paulo, *contratados* set about defining their status within months of Porto Alegre's de jure emancipation.[91] Officials from Porto Alegre and cities of the interior complained of groups of new freedpersons who refused to seek work or obey authority. Provincial vice president Rodrigo de Azambuja Villanova, for instance, observed in 1887, "A large part of the freedpersons of 1885, violating the faith of their contracts and surprising everyone with their ingratitude, precipitously abandoned the houses of their benefactors as quickly as they gained possession of their letters of emancipation; another [freedman] was quickly dispensed as a way of freeing his *senhores* of the irritations of their servant's constant infidelities."[92] Newspapers and daily police reports carried brief notices of *contratados*' arrests. Many were for common crimes, such as theft, public drunkenness, and disorderly conduct.[93] Other charges were more directly linked to the issue of freedom and conditional emancipation. Throughout the final four years of slavery, *contratados* appeared in arrest records as imprisoned for failure to complete the services for which they were contractually obligated. Perhaps frustrated in her attempt to use public opinion and the power of the press against her master's control, the *contratada* Joanna ran away from her *senhor*, Carlos von Koseritz, in May 1887, only to be captured "for being a runaway and denying the payment of services" she owed to Koseritz.[94] Another formulation of this charge appeared in the notice that the *pretos* Lúcio and Antonio Moçambique had been arrested for the "theft of service for which they are obligated."[95]

As Paulo Roberto Moreira has pointed out, such resistance involved more than occasional incidents. Police reports for 1886–87 note seventy-one arrests of *contratados*, fifty-seven of which were for refusal to fulfill service clauses.[96] Unfortunately for historians, these cases never made it to court, so even imperfect records of *contratados*' explanations and justifications of their behavior, if indeed they were made before the police, have not survived. Clearly, however, *contratados*' denial of obligations to their former masters represented a challenging reading of what emancipation would mean. Freedpersons' actions thus dashed elite hopes that service clauses in letters of emancipation would keep their dependent workers within existing paternalistic relations. Elites would have to meet these plebeian efforts with stronger plans of their own.

Elite Responses: Bringing the State into Seigneurial Relations

As in other parts of Brazil, members of the elite expressed serious concern over the alternative understandings of freedom that plebeian initiatives presented in the last years of slavery. Often their preoccupation appeared as a belief that emancipation would represent to the *povo* merely freedom from work, morality, and responsibility. The danger here was that in leaving formal bondage, freedpersons would also break out of their ties of dependence on their patrons and, as Liberal deputy Egydio Barbosa Oliveira Itaqui warned, plunge Rio Grande do Sul into the "horrors of vagrancy and libertinage."[97] What was needed, elites agreed, were measures to turn the unruly ex-slaves living on the real streets of Porto Alegre into the fantastical figures portrayed by Damasceno Vieira, who through the various works that he read at abolitionist meetings became the semiofficial poet of abolitionism in Porto Alegre.[98] In "A Fábrica" (The Factory), for example, he described a group of workers laboring fearlessly and tirelessly, in the midst of the "insane movement" of the factory's machinery:

> They laugh, sing with immense joy!
> They really work! After an instant,

Without great excess in the task,
Drops of sweat shine! diamonds
On the face of the workers of progress![99]

Similarly, in "O Liberto" (The Freedperson) he glorified the worker who, on leaving slavery,

. . . to the flame of the furnace, red-hot, intense,
Brilliant as the violet dawn,
Goes to conquer honored recompense
In the thousand precepts that work teaches.[100]

Coming as it did in a decade when the outcome of abolition was uncertain, it should be clear that this passage was essentially prescriptive; in it, Vieira issued a hopeful vision of the transition to free labor.

Instead of obedience, however, elites found themselves confronting what they considered ingratitude. The solution, elites agreed, was to keep the poor —including the recently freed—at work. Throughout slavery's final years, elites applauded projects to train or educate freedpersons and other members of the *povo* to be good workers, for the common refrain was that the "backwardness of popular instruction" increased disorder among the *povo*.[101] Charitable institutions received praise not only for giving succor to "the thousands of unfortunates who wander . . . in search of bread to kill their hunger" but also for teaching these sad cases to work. Indeed, in the pages of *A Federação*, Felicissimo Manuel de Azevedo declared that, due to "the impossibility of distinguishing between the true poor and scoundrels" or "vagrants," one asylum had done the right thing in setting its residents to "labor proportional to their strength."[102]

This training could also take place in more conventional educational settings. After the announcement that part of the funds raised by the Centro Abolicionista would go to the construction of a building in which freedpersons would receive free education, *A Federação* expressed its approval, adding that it would be only fair to use this money to provide "the practical education that will train them for intelligent work." Such an education was an "indispensable" way to make sure that "freedpersons, just now departed from the tormenting regime of slavery, render their efficient cooperation to society and not constitute a perturbing element."[103] Liberal José Rodrigues Lima, meanwhile, supported the creation of new agricultural and technical schools in the province. The need for this innovation came most immediately from the growing population of new freedpersons: "There is a large part of the [population of] ex-slaves that, recently freed of the chains of captivity, soon will enter into society, stripped, however, of energy, foresight, and perseverance, without initiative, self-control, and feelings of family, therefore incapable of promoting, by themselves, the means of an honorable subsistence."[104] Rodrigues Lima and his colleagues urged the state to exercise, as a provincial president put it, "its moralizing and educational action, obligating the freedpersons to the harsh law of work, perennial source of happiness and morality."[105]

Contratados' rejection of the new dependent condition elites attempted to impose on them, however, lent urgency to the problem; pondering the character of plebeians and the efficacy of education in moralizing them was simply not an expeditious enough response to the contemporary situation. Pushed along by *contratados'* actions, elites would in fact eventually adopt plans to bring the power of the state to bear directly on elite-*povo* relations.

Even so, elites' reactions to popular resistance were neither quick nor efficient. They did, it is true, step up coercive measures throughout the 1880s. The provincial government instituted new nocturnal police patrols in Porto Alegre and approved the formation of private police groups in Pelotas and Rio Grande. In 1886, the Conservative-led government also began to make greater use of regular army forces stationed in the city for police supervision of the city.[106] In general, however, the size of the police force and the money set aside for it remained fairly constant from 1879 through 1888.[107] These military and regular police forces may have contributed to the numbers of runaway *contratados* captured in 1886–87, but they certainly did not prove capable of stemming the tide of popular rejection of conditional freedom. The warm reception the local press gave a new curfew in January 1888 hints at the continued need for such measures to control freedpersons. Commenting on the curfew for *contratados* and for "determined individuals without qualified position," *O Mercantil* declared: "Thus proceeding [the police authorities] render real service to the population, avoiding the continued offenses that have as their setting our beautiful capital. May the same authorities continue to hunt the individuals without occupation that infest the many dens [*espeluncas*] spread throughout the city, and with that a great number of conflicts will be avoided."[108]

The most forceful elite reply to the free actions of ex-slaves came in the 1885–88 campaign to regulate servants (*criados*). In its earliest stage, Republican propagandists proved key to this effort. An article published in *A Federação* in June 1885, for instance, called attention to the need to address the relations between masters and servants. Commenting on the murders of two employers by their servants in Paris, the writer asserted that "Porto Alegre is not exactly the place in the world where servants [*a criadagem*] are exemplary." As evidence of this, he pointed to female servants' common resistance to sleeping in the house of the family they served and "the insolence in [their] responses," which was "the timbre of the majority" of such *criadas*. In the face of this insolence, he urged that heads of good families exercise "courage and the greatest severity in the choice of servants." Without such care, masters put themselves and their families at risk: "We should not be inferior to the employees. Such weakness could cost us dearly."[109] Republicans began to urge legislative attention to the matter the following year.

The initiative here seems to have begun with private individuals, most notably Colonel Taborda Ribas, but *A Federação* contributed by promoting the efforts of such individuals. The Republican paper clearly agreed on the need for organized action, noting that "for a certain time domestic service has worsened in a very noticeable manner in this city, where there are in abundance vagrants of both sexes, who to disguise their vagrancy take the name of servants, and where there are ever more rarely those who occupy themselves in domestic service and there reap the means of honest subsistence." Given the "terrible conditions" of domestic service in Porto Alegre, as well as the fact that the municipal government was not considering this problem, the initiative of persons like Ribas received praise from *A Federação*. In a letter to the paper, Ribas explained that the "disorder" of relations between masters and servants in a period of "transformation of labor" had led him to take action; he saw this disorder as a "legacy of the barbarous institution, which, distorting customs, establishes a profound abyss between labor and capital, making impossible . . . mutual concessions imposed by the new phase." Without a system of regulation, servants with good habits and references suffered by not getting the distinction they deserved; even worse, masters risked introducing "into the home the professional vagrancy that only seeks work to abuse the confidence that many calculatingly try to inspire in the first days, in order to practice in its shadow the usual courtesies."[110]

With these concerns in mind, Ribas and a small group of like-thinking individuals met in the offices of *A Federação*. Out of their deliberations emerged a plan to sign up *senhores* who promised to employ only servants who presented a "testament of conduct."[111] In the first few months after this agreement, *A Federação* published lists of individuals who pledged their compliance.[112] Once again, the paper lauded this project. In fact, it published a statement by Ribas, who declared that despite its limits, the project would "remove in part the disorder" of domestic service, "stimulating the public powers" to take more significant steps, "not only suppressing the deficiencies of the agreement in question but also regularizing labor in general, a momentous measure in the face of the transformation underway in the nation." Such government efforts, he continued, were crucial even "in the advanced nations, where the proletariat, fighting with overawing competition, exerts itself in the development of the various branches of activity to which it applies itself; where the fight for life does not offer the respites that countries that, like ours, find themselves in the initial phase of exploitation, provide; where, finally, there does not exist the class of freedpersons, erected from the mephitic slave quarters and brusquely exposed to social life with sentiments deformed by the abject condition in which the barbarous institution . . . placed them." In a Brazil not yet on a par with these nations, the government had an even greater responsibility to intervene in order to maintain "the harmony between labor and capital."[113] This arrangement, in which a new rationality would be applied in order to reinforce social hierarchies, clearly fit in with Republican scientificist thought.

By September 1886, however, the issue of regulating domestic service was becoming a more general concern in the province. Across Brazil, slavery was crumbling as a model of employer-employee relations. More to the point locally, popular rejection of conditional emancipation in Porto Alegre was emphasizing the fragility of this transitional solution. To try to take control of a situation seemingly headed toward general disorder, and probably inspired by the earlier Ribas-*Federação* efforts, municipal governments in Porto Alegre and other cities in Rio Grande do Sul drew up projects to guide domestic service.[114] The project that Porto Alegre's city council put together and sent to the provincial president for his approval on 22 September 1886 was typical of such proposals. Based on regulations set up by the city council of Pelotas, the Porto Alegre *regulamento de criados* defined domestic service broadly to include anyone who "being of free condition takes for salary the occupation of *moço* [boy] of a hotel, eating-house, or inn; cook, waiter, coachman, gardener, [or] footman; *peão* [peon] of an establishment of agriculture, animal-raising [*criação*], or factory; or wet nurse, nursemaid, [or] in general any domestic service." Giving the secretariat of the police authority over the implementation of details, the city council established obligations on the part of both *criados* and masters. The former were to register with the police, receiving in return a passbook (*caderneta*) with their "number of inscription, name, age, parents' names, national origin, marital state, type of service or occupation, [and the] name and address of the person" they were to serve. Furthermore, *criados* were to present a "certificate of their behavior" given by the last person they had served or by the police in the district where they resided. The regulations even provided models of the contracts employers were to use in hiring servants and insisted that only *criados* with the proper papers could be employed. After a servant was hired, his or her employer also had to conform to set obligations, filling in *cadernetas* and firing servants only with ten days' prior notice or in the case of "grave offenses" against a member of the employer's family or "habitual drunkenness." Servants faced a greater burden of responsibilities. Not only were they barred from leaving a master's employ without ten days' notice (except in cases of physical disability, marriage, nonreceipt of wages, or a legal motion by their lawyer), but they also had to "obey their patrons with good faith and diligence in all that is not illicit or contrary to their contracts," protect "the interests of the patron that are entrusted to them . . . promoting the well-being and comfort of those that depend on them," and pay for any damages they might cause.[115]

After its rapid creation by the city council, this detailed set of regulations would linger for years without formal passage into law or implementation. In January 1887, A. Soares Amaya de Gusmão, president of the council, commented on the need for such a law, noting that the proposed project was still awaiting approval by the provincial president.[116] In a message sent to the provincial vice president on 19 December 1887, the council was still complaining of delay in final approval of the regulation by the Provincial Assembly.[117] Only in April 1888, just weeks before final abolition, did authorities began to hand out *cadernetas;* even then, they did so without the Assembly having acted on the project.[118]

The significance of the attempts to establish disciplined relations between masters and servants does not lie in their effectiveness. Indeed, in terms of instilling a new order into these relations, the *regulamento* proved a failure. The implementation of this careful and long-awaited code could not prevent popular abuses. Even with the proper inspectors in place and *cadernetas* distributed to over fifteen hundred *criados*, the city council informed the provincial president on 2 June 1888: "It seems that the *cadernetas* have been sought out as a safeguard, as a guarantee, by a large number of vagrants. . . . Either on admission or on departure of *criados*, there are constant infractions of these codes, which exactly obeyed could produce beneficial results."[119] Such abuses would continue after the fall of the monarchy in late 1889; officials were still discussing measures to tighten up enforcement of the *regulamentos* in 1890.[120] The problem for elites was that, quite simply, members of the popular classes in Porto Alegre were again refusing to obey legislators' well-thought-out rules—refusing, as Paulo Moreira has noted, to continue in relations that must still have carried the stench of slavery.[121]

This popular initiative suggests what the *regulamentos de criados*, and elite attitudes toward emancipation more broadly, meant for Porto Alegre in the 1880s. In the context of slavery's decadence across Brazil, Gaúcho elites faced challenges from the *povo* within their province and its capital. Like the 1884 scheme of abolition through service clauses, the regulation of domestic service represented an attempt by elites to preempt popular initiatives and interpretations. The report by the city council suggests that the two efforts were similarly ineffective in this regard. What is most compelling about the 1885–88 *regulamentos*, however, is precisely the fact that they represented a broad elite response to popular actions. Because of the extreme rejection of seigneurial power that plebeian initiatives threatened in these years, elites in a time of crisis tried to come together behind a project to interject the power of the state into elite-*povo* relations in a novel manner. In this way, plebeians in Porto Alegre nudged their social superiors toward the type of rule that one elite faction, the Positivist Republicans, would establish as dominant in the years that followed.

5

"A Strange Vision of Popular Movement"

The Emergence and Limits of a New Politics

The correct collaboration of all citizens in public affairs is their most patriotic duty.

A Federação, *3 December 1889*

THE Republic came to Porto Alegre on 15 November 1889, as it did to most of Brazil, via telegrams from Rio de Janeiro. Eight months earlier, Júlio de Castilhos and other powerful members of the Rio-Grandense Republican Party (PRR) had met at the Fazenda da Reserva, a ranch belonging to Castilhos's family, to declare their intentions of ending the Brazilian Empire. Despite their pledges to carry out "revolution," however, Porto Alegre's Republicans had no hand in the military-led conspiracy that toppled the monarchy in the nation's capital.[1] The first rumors of a coup d'état appeared around midday on 15 November, after banks reported sharp fluctuations in currency markets and a commercial firm received the curt message "Neither exchange rate, nor government" from its agent in the Court. Hungry for further information, Castilhos and his fellow Republicans could only wait with their Liberal and Conservative rivals for cables from Rio.[2]

When it came, word of the Empire's demise set off a political earthquake in Porto Alegre. With strong ties to the provisional government forming in

Rio and an unquestionable record of republican militancy, the PRR moved to gain control in the southern capital. Unlike the Republicans who took over in the other states of Brazil, Castilhos and his followers came from the margins of a regional oligarchy; in fact, their tightly organized party was unwilling to share real power with representatives of the traditional elite of Rio Grande do Sul. Thus, proclaiming the advent of the Republic "a victory for the Nation and not the victory of one party," Castilhos and his "co-religionaries" nonetheless set out to establish exclusive PRR control over the reorganization of state and society along Positivist lines.[3] The parties that had ruled under the Empire—the Conservatives and the long-dominant Liberals—disintegrated quickly in late 1889, but many of their leaders refused to leave the political stage. Grudgingly recognizing the new regime, ex-Liberals in particular warned the PRR not to shunt them aside, since their cooperation was "of complete necessity for the regular organization of the new relations established by the current political regime."[4] This partisan saber rattling quickly led to real strife, as the PRR on one side and a series of shifting anti-Castilhos coalitions on the other tried to make the Republic their own. Their contests for supremacy culminated in the notoriously bloody Federalist Revolt, which broke out in 1892–93 and raged across the state until the PRR, decisively aided by the national government, triumphed in 1895.

The transformations these battles fostered in Gaúcho politics went beyond the replacement of one ruling faction by another. For one thing, the disputes of the early 1890s escalated ideological as well as partisan conflict in Porto Alegre. The dogmatically Comtean PRR and its more heterogeneous competitors presented substantially distinct projects for what three former Liberals dubbed "the reconstruction of the fatherland on other foundations."[5] These different projects meant that there would be more in play, in terms of the very social and political organization of the region, in the Gaúcho partisan conflicts of the 1890s than there had been in those of the Empire.

A major reason for the higher stakes was that, in an acceleration of processes that had begun in the 1880s, partisan factions reached out to near-elite and nonelite segments of the urban populace for support as the country moved into the Republic.[6] What made this strategy feasible was a rising tide of activism by small industrialists and entrepreneurs, teachers, artisans and other workers, European immigrants, and Afro-Brazilians from the mid-

1880s into the early 1890s. Both as junior partners in alliances with elite parties and through more autonomous associations and newspapers, these sectors came together behind previously unknown political identities to demand influence in the shaping of government policy. In their efforts to achieve sovereignty of a kind that had been denied them, they became key, if always subordinate, political players in the nascent First Republic and helped effect a reformulation of power relations in Porto Alegre.

New Identities and Forces in the 1880s

The new politics of the Republic in Porto Alegre began to take shape before the Empire crumbled. The last decade of the old regime brought a jolt of associative energy to the Gaúcho capital. The groups that emerged in the public arena, moreover, rehearsed struggles over issues, identities, and strategies that anticipated the much more bitter clashes of the 1890s. While also addressing the quotidian concerns of nonelites—such as abuse at the hands of police, urban sanitation, and the high prices of staple foods—many of these organizations took on grander matters of government. As they weighed in on tariffs and other policy questions, they had to carve out identities for themselves, more or less explicitly, as active members of the body politic—as citizens, in a word. These self-definitions, as we shall see, necessarily involved tensions between inclusionary and exclusionary aims, so that the new political actors effectively contested only the location and not the existence of the boundary around the official political realm.[7] Finally, as they negotiated their passage into that realm, near- and nonelite activists debated the utility of forming ties to existing parties; such collaborations might prove strategically useful, but they might also erode any hopes for autonomy.

Their most inviting but also most controlling allies among the political parties were the Castilhista Republicans. As we saw in the previous chapter, the PRR leapt into the partisan fray in the 1880s, and its development catalyzed the reformulation of Gaúcho politics. PRR leaders built strong party structures to compensate for their relative marginality in provincial power structures; in contrast to the Republican parties of other provinces, the PRR acted like an antioligarchic pretender.[8] In one sense, the Gaúcho Republicans were simply mirroring the Liberals, who had put together a party that their foremost leader, Gaspar Silveira Martins, favorably likened to the Prussian army.[9] Like the Liberal Party, the PRR centered on a dominant figure, Castilhos, whose authority galvanized his partisan constituents and repelled those unwilling to submit to his orders. What set the PRR apart from the Gasparista model was not only the strength that Liberals had established in the late Empire but also the very different character of leadership Castilhos provided. Unlike Silveira Martins, whose eloquence earned him the nickname the "Tribune," the Republican boss's charisma largely remained on the printed page, for he was a famously awkward public speaker. Castilhos's strength lay in propaganda and particularly in the tactical use of a corpus of political ideas —a Positivism based on the writings of Auguste Comte.

The unity and clarity of Republicans' logic, as Nelson Boeira has noted, were key weapons in their challenge of the much larger but less explicitly ideological parties that dominated the region during the imperial period.[10] Rigid in their application of their Positivism in the city, the Castilhistas drove off some early proponents of republicanism in the 1880s (see chapter 4); many more followed after 1889. Indeed, the Castilhistas' insistence on strict adherence to the official party line made the PRR seem to one observer "less a political party than a school of philosophy, a religion. Or, if you prefer . . : a sect."[11] The PRR was, after all, still a small, young party in what had for decades been a staunchly Liberal province. As scholars such as Joseph Love, John Chasteen, and Loiva Félix have argued, Castilhistas faced tremendous difficulties in winning over political bosses who considered themselves well served by Silveira Martins and his Liberal subordinates. To break the bonds of patronage that Liberals had so expertly forged in the Gaúcho countryside, PRR activists could at times be less stringent in their ideological demands on potential supporters. Even if it stemmed from some personal animosity toward a local Liberal enemy rather than intellectual conviction, backing from rural bosses was welcomed—indeed, actively courted—by the Republicans; it need only include some perfunctory public declarations of support for the PRR and its projects in Rio Grande do Sul.[12] Very much in keeping with the style of imperial politics, this maneuvering by Castilhistas won over some former Conservatives and Liberals; it was, however, only with the establishment of PRR control over the state government—shaky up to the Federalist Revolt and only fully consolidated thereafter—that Castilhism created a power bloc across the state that could hold off challenges from ex-Liberals.[13]

Even as they cleansed their higher ranks ideologically, Castilhos and his allies looked beyond the traditional political class for support in the cities and particularly in Porto Alegre. If they could not yet overcome Liberal dominance in the interior, Republicans hoped at least to turn the Gaúcho capital into a staging ground for their ultimate takeover, and refashioning, of politics in Rio Grande do Sul. As Sandra Pesavento has noted, the Castilhista project envisioned Porto Alegre "as a central piece of its program for rule," not a surprising option given Liberal power in the interior and the overrepresentation of cities in Brazilian politics more generally.[14] It was in Porto Alegre, more than anywhere else, that the feeling later recorded by João Neves da Fontoura, himself a product of the PRR political machine, was most pronounced: "the Republican Party of the old Province lacked masses."[15] The PRR sought in part to remove this weakness by appealing to near- and non-elite sectors of Porto Alegre society.

Party members' thinking on this as on all questions drew on Comte's writings about the evolution of society. In their search for allies among social classes previously excluded from official politics, the ideologues of the PRR wanted junior partners who would respond favorably to Castilhista influence. Here the Republicans were attempting to apply Comte's advice on eliminating tensions between workers and employers. Rather than a directly political solution to the "social problem," Comte had urged Positivists to prepare "an influence which is sure and peaceful, though it be gradual and indirect; the influence of a more enlightened morality, supported by a purer state of Public Opinion; such opinion being organized by competent minds, and diffused freely among the people."[16] In other words, Positivists were to create a system of proper education that would engender a "universal ascendancy of morality" and subsequently shape worker and master alike into more contented and efficient members of society; indeed, the laborer would even come to view himself "morally, as a public servant."[17]

Comte's phrase "the incorporation of the proletariat into society," which has often served as a shorthand version of his analysis of the evolution of classes, became a PRR motto. As it did for Comte himself, this concept held antirevolutionary significance for the militants of the PRR, who took it to mean the integration of the urban working classes into the nation not so much to empower as to control them. While still in the Castilhista fold, Demétrio Ribeiro gave a strident formulation of this motto in a speech that presented a dream of the regime to come: "As for the incorporation of the proletariat into society, I should tell you that I consider this a capital question for the Republic. The Republic is the regime of the public good; the public good is prepared by society itself, the main part of which consists of the enormous mass of the proletarians. . . . Thus it is this class of society, disdained until today, that most deserves government attention."[18] Thus Castilhos and his colleagues, as Ricardo Vélez Rodríguez has written, centered their social philosophy on "the idea of the moralization of individuals through State tutelage."[19] But unlike earlier attempts at direct regulation of master-slave or employer-servant relations, the PRR project aimed not to repress vagrants and other troublesome members of the *povo* but to form "better" masters and servants who would accept their place in a rationally organized society and thus avoid the "perennial battle" between capital and labor.[20] Through the actions of Positivist leaders, men whose training and outlook would enable them to transcend narrow personal interests in the formulation of state policy, the *povo* might join the ranks of the "conservative classes."

The intention of the PRR was not, again, to open the gates to all workers' participation in politics; rather, its members began to try to enlist, while also shaping, organizations they deemed appropriate. In practical terms, this first meant cultivating labor groups through the vehicles of Republican propaganda. Thus, in 1887, the PRR saluted the creation of workers' societies as "symptoms of life, which the productive classes have recently shown," and in the last year of the Empire turned over a section of *A Federação* to a "Workers' Column." As long as it was "perfectly disciplined," the Republican editors predicted, the "collective activity" discussed and perhaps fueled by such inclusion in public discourse would be vital to the "progressive march [forward] of our province, with regard not only to questions of a purely material nature but even, and principally, to questions of a moral nature."[21] Organization, as Comte ordained, would educate workers morally, yielding a competent, energetic, yet also subservient *povo*.

The PRR also looked to nurture allies from marginal political associations to help the achievement of its ideals, especially groups that rejected class conflict in favor of more universal social progress. One such society, which announced itself a political party and quickly became a partner of the Castilhistas, was the Agricultural-Industrial League (LAI, or Liga Agrícolo-Industrial). When the LAI came into being at a large meeting in January 1889, it counted several artisans and industrialists, most notably Franz Herzog and João von Steenhagen, among its directors.[22] Claiming to be the sole true representative of the city's workers, the group urged a series of reforms that, its manifesto emphasized, depended on "the union of all agriculturalists, industrialists, and workers, in short, of the working class [*classe operária*] in general."[23] That image of harmoniously combined socioeconomic sectors, whatever inner tensions it may have obscured, was precisely the sort of initiative the Castilhistas wanted to foster. So pleased were the editors of *A Federação* with LAI aims that they changed the title of the "Workers' Column" to "Agricultural-Industrial League" less than three weeks after the League's emergence.[24]

In fact, few of the elements that might constitute the PRR's idealized *povo* could be "proletarian," in any strict sense, in the Porto Alegre of the late Empire and the early Republic. The city was in the throes of striking growth and diversification in the 1880s–90s. As outlined earlier (see chapter 1), the economy of Porto Alegre had benefited greatly from a transition to the production of cash crops and small manufactures in the immigrant or "colonial" zone of its hinterlands. Situated on the Guaíba basin, the conjuncture of the rivers that served as the principal lines of communication for the European immigrant settlements, Porto Alegre was the focal point of a regional trade that expanded steadily in both its volume and its value in the late Empire.[25] In the late 1880s, the shift of economic power to the area that fanned out from Porto Alegre received an additional boost, as the cattle economy of the southern zone of the province entered into crisis.[26]

Within and around the city, the artisanal production of beer, tobacco products, and small manufactures took on a more industrialized tone by the 1880s, and factories turning out furniture and other goods increased the size and complexity of their production.[27] As shown earlier, the Paraguayan War had sparked manufacturing in the city, its clearest effect in this regard the expansion of Porto Alegre's largest industrial establishment, the War Arsenal.[28] Private enterprises emerged as well to meet the demands of the expanding city population, up from 43,998 in 1872 to 52,421 in 1890 (see table 1). By 1892, the largest of the nonstate *fábricas* (factories), the Cia. Fiação and Tecidos Porto Alegre, employed 263 workers in its textile mill, while another factory, Progresso Industrial, engaged 175 in the production of leather goods.[29] It should be noted, though, that most factories were still assemblages of artisans rather than units of mass production; indeed, records of disputes among laborers suggest that at least in some of the factories each worker continued to own and maintain his separate set of tools and was responsible for producing whole units or finished products.[30] Even so, the appearance of the *fábricas* transformed sections of the city. Workshops producing chairs, shoes, and other consumer goods lined rua Voluntários da Pátria, a busy street that ran from the city center northward along the Guaíba.[31] Indeed, this part of the city, stretching out to the neighborhood known as Navegantes, was becoming a corridor of manufacturing enterprises and workers' housing.[32]

The labor for this expanding economy included women and children as well as adult men, but it was a portion of this last group that most interested the PRR and other parties.[33] Indeed, by 1888–89, the Castilhistas and their rivals were making appeals to the same segment of the working populace, a demographic that the Pelotas socialist newspaper *Democracia Social* described in 1893 as "a class of aspirants, our small masters, almost proletarian but with pretensions, as is natural [of becoming] large industrialists, whose interests are not, cannot yet be defined."[34] From this hazily bounded sector came men like Herzog, a German cabinetmaker who became one of three owners of a furniture factory in 1892; Steenhagen, a Dutch machinist, foundry owner, and merchant; Guelfo Zaniratti, an Italian tailor with his own shop; and Francisco José de Mesquita, a civilian worker at the War Arsenal—all of whom appeared in public politics beginning in 1888. Public employees and other skilled workers also filled meetings and wrote for the press in these years.[35]

Categorizing these men was no easy task. Contemporaries referred to activists working outside the official political parties as "artisans" (*artistas*), "workers" (*operários*), "the working class" (*a classe operária*), "the laboring classes" (*as classes laboriosas*), "the proletariat" (*o proletariado*), or "the productive classes" (*as classes produtivas*).[36] Though some are anachronistic and all are vague, these terms give a sense of the variety of identities with which these heterogeneous groups, as well as their real and potential allies among the political elites, were experimenting. Perhaps the greatest novelty of the labels coming into use in the 1880s is that they all derived, with more or less precision, from an association with work; as we have seen, while elites had long hailed labor as a social tonic for the lower classes, they certainly had not conceived of it as a basis for membership in the body politic.

It is, however, necessary also to see what this range of terms left out. This "almost proletarian" group consisted, first of all, of men. Among elites, neither Castilhistas nor their enemies wanted to bring women into official politics; the Positivists, in fact, reemphasized the supposedly domestic essence of the feminine. They may have been laborers, but women who worked in factories or for the War Arsenal (through a putting-out system) found no support among the incipient groupings of workingmen.[37] Moreover, these male activists could, by and large, claim European descent, if they were not from Europe themselves. Even the PRR, which had been the political party most sympathetic to slaves and ex-slaves in the post-1884 years and which celebrated final abolition as "a day on which the humble [were] great," saw the welfare of Afro-Brazilians as a secondary concern in the passage from Empire from Republic.[38] The great cause, in the Positivists' eyes, must be the Republic itself and their rule over it. The repeated attacks in the PRR organ *A Federação* against mobs of "black guards"—ex-slaves allegedly willing to defend the monarchy by force—hint at Republican priorities.[39] Although they at times published complaints against individual acts of racial discrimination, PRR leaders denounced those who planned "to divide the country into castes, planting race hatred in the soil of the Fatherland."[40] Without more complete data about the membership of the associations that emerged in the later 1880s, it is impossible to know the degree of exclusion that Afro-Brazilians faced; the leadership of the new groups and their principal partisan ally, though, suggests at least that it was white, skilled, male worker-entrepreneurs who edged their way into formal politics.

The paths these men took into public political debates were diverse and indirect at first. Along with the economic dynamism of the end of the Empire came an acceleration of associative activity, varying in type but often revolving around occupational identities. Societies of mutual assistance had existed since the organization of the Sociedade Portuguesa de Beneficência (Portuguese Beneficent Society) and the Deutscher Hifsverein (German Beneficent Society) in the 1850s, but they took on a greater public presence and a less elite nature in the last decade of the Empire. Some of the later associations echoed not only the structures but also the ethnic orientations of their midcentury predecessors. Most, though, strove to define themselves in large part by references to their members as workers. This was true, for instance, even of the Sociedade Operária de Mútuo Socorro e Beneficência Vitório Emanuele II

(Victor Emmanuel II Workers' Mutual Aid and Charity Society), which included in its title an homage to the Italian ruler who died in the year of its founding (1877) and named Garibaldi as its honorary president in its statutes, while also making clear that it represented laborers.[41] Other groups sprang up among particular segments of the working population, such as artisans (Instituto dos Artífices, 1880; Grêmio dos Artistas, 1882), shop clerks (Club Caixeiral, 1882), and peddlers (Musterreiter, 1885). Some of these, like the Musterreiter, which later changed its name to the Associação Sul-Rio-Grandense dos Viajantes Comerciantes (Rio-Grandense Association of Traveling Salesmen), seem to have moved away from ethnic requirements for membership, whereas others rejected such criteria from their inception. The statutes of the Artisans' Guild, set up in 1882, for instance, explicitly (and perhaps hopefully) described the organization as consisting of "industrial artisans and in general all people belonging to the laboring classes, without distinction of nationality."[42]

Though it was far from a radical group, the Club Caixeiral (Store Clerks' Club), established in late 1882, was the first of the new associations to present a clear group identity and to raise its voice in public debates. The clerks did not represent innovation either in their identity or in the content of their claims. The figure of the clerk, scheming to inherit or buy out his employer's business and thus rise socially, was a well-known stereotype in the nineteenth century.[43] Indeed, the self-image that the Club Caixeiral revealed in its newspaper, *O Athleta*, certainly gave some credence to this characterization. The paper's insistence on the distance between clerks and the mass of the *povo* was unmistakable. The city's clerks, one article put it in 1885, had chosen education in order "to raise themselves up out of an unconscious life, of a type of servilism"; their efforts, another writer added, had made these clerks into veritable "vehicles of civilization."[44] Moreover, arguments over their main cause, the preservation of the mandatory closing of stores on Sundays, went back to the 1850s at least and did not take the general welfare of the *povo* into account.[45] Still, club leaders were willing to criticize politicians who opposed the clerks' position and to praise those who supported it; in that sense, at least, this sector, while trying to avoid being confused with common working people, contributed to the broadening of public political discourse in the 1880s.[46]

Other voices, by contrast, quite self-consciously took on the general concerns of workers, though still with the hazy definition of that identity described above. *A Federação* reported that as early as 1887 some sixty city residents met to form "an association of workers," and several newspapers advancing the interests of the laboring classes appeared between 1885 and 1889, at least two under the title *O Operario* (The Worker).[47] The first *O Operario* included criticism of police repression of plebeians and poems glorifying the workingman. Its proworker stance was most evident, though, in editorials like the one that complained about the "aristocratic law" that left "us, the artisans, . . . banned from the Brazilian communion." Appealing to military service as the basis of citizenship—much as Gaúcho elites and individual men of the *povo* had done before them—the editors further argued, "In the great crises, in international conflicts, in the supreme moments at which the honor of the fatherland demands that the *povo* fulfill its duty, no other class contributes more powerfully to swell the ranks of combatants than the working class."[48] This grandiose language reappeared in the 1889 *O Operario*, with a significant distinction; this later paper more concretely addressed local political events and pressed for representation of workers in government. As historian Silvia Petersen has noted, the affiliations of the later *O Operario* remain mysterious; it declared in its first issue that it had no "politics except those of class interest."[49]

If the editors of that paper chose to refrain from alliances with "militant parties," other new societies dove into official politics by allying with established parties. In fact, this tendency, which began in the last year or so of the Empire, became commonplace in the Republic and was a central feature of the new politics. By the end of 1889, the Sociedade Beneficente União Operária (Workers' Union) was linked to the LAI, for example, which was in turn allied to the Castilhista Republicans. The first unmistakable episode of such worker-entrepreneurs' partisan action took place in the last year of the Empire's existence, when the LAI put forward a ticket of four candidates—Alfredo de Azevedo, Guilherme Roth, João Maria von Held, and José Manoel da Silva Só—for the 31 December 1888 elections to the Provincial Assembly.[50] In both that vote and a second on 31 July of the following year, Silva Só, widely proclaimed the "workers' candidate," won a position in the Assembly. Had Silva Só truly been a laborer, his victories would have been nearly miraculous, especially since an 1881 imperial electoral reform had restricted suffrage dramatically.[51] He was, however, a capitalist, owner of a foundry that employed from thirty to over forty workers, depending on demand, in the early 1880s; its bronze and copper products, according to the catalog of a manufacturing exposition in 1881, made Silva Só and Cia. "the most important [workshop] in this trade."[52]

How did this industrialist gain a place in the provincial legislature as the "workers' deputy"?[53] This extraordinary occurrence was possible because of a loose definition of workers that, as we have seen, folded skilled laborers in with factory owners and because of partisan competition over ties to an abstract working class. Although not literally a laborer, Silva Só could plausibly fit under the abstract labels given the worker-entrepreneur sector of Porto Alegre's population—certainly as much so as men like the tavern keeper and small merchant Roth, the surveyor Azevedo, or the painter and shop owner von Held.[54] Helping Silva Só, moreover, but clearly complicating matters for both the PRR and the LAI, was the fact that Republicans were not the only political party embracing, in some manner, the participation of actors from burgeoning urban sectors.[55] Shortly after Só's first election and until the end of the Empire, both the Positivists and their collaborators from the "productive classes" vehemently denounced their "betrayal" at the hands of the new assemblyman. Silva Só had thrown in with Silveira Martins, and the Tribune's Liberal political apparatus engineered enough votes to elect the foundry owner.[56] This maneuver apparently came as enough of a shock to the PRR-LAI coalition that its propagandists could only attack it as Machiavellian and fraudulent—one paper charged that Silva Só's vote count had actually been lower than another candidate's—and as contrary to the true interests of workers, industry, and the province as a whole.[57] The PRR and LAI also jointly sponsored candidates—Azevedo in the earlier election and the powerful PRR propagandist Ramiro Fortes de Barcelos in the later one—but still treated Silva Só's union with the Liberals as treason; after all, he was a member of the "productive classes" who in their eyes had split from the authentically progressive forces of the city, the worker-entrepreneurs and the Republicans. After Silva Só assumed his seat, his presence in the Assembly drove Castilhistas and their "worker" allies to fits of rage. They condemned him for voting blindly in favor of any proposal that came from a Liberal and thus selling out his supporters among the real working population. More broadly, they alleged, he merely remained silent and in the background, serving as a compliant dependent of his Liberal patron.[58] Indeed, a photo of the Liberal contingent in the Provincial Assembly in 1889 shows Silva Só standing behind the left shoulder of Silveira Martins, as if offering the quiet support of a faithful client.[59]

Liberal Party majority of the Provincial Assembly, 1889. From Olympio Duarte, *Excavações históricas*, 1933.

Liberal support for this apparently acquiescent, factory-owning "worker" might thus have been a gesture toward the "productive classes" of the city, just as it might have been a purely cynical attempt to preempt Castilhista strategies of including near- and nonelites in partisan battles. In any case, allies of Liberals and Republicans alike tried to use the "worker deputy" to prove their points on one of the key political issues of the late Empire and young Republic: the "special tariff" that Silveira Martins had championed in the national Congress and that, as political scientist Sílvio Rogério Duncan Baretta explains, "came close to transforming the province into an area of free trade." The tariff law of 1888, which reduced or even eliminated duties on an unspecified number of products, was intended to spark pastoral production, which had formidable competition from Argentina and Uruguay. The measure's effects within Rio Grande do Sul were, however, complex; it hurt many merchants and raised the ire of most manufacturers and their employees in Porto Alegre, their jobs now threatened by an influx of cheap imports.[60] It also stoked the flames of enmity between the Liberals and the PRR-LAI coalition. In the new context of 1888–89, this sent both sides scrambling to prove the widespread support for their position on the tariff. Their arguments often counterposed Silva Só against the "workers" of the LAI. Thus, on hearing of Silveira Martins's telegram to the minister of the interior that averred, with implicit reference to Silva Só, "Working class united to Liberal Party, no longer protests against the special tariff," the directorate of the LAI fired off its own telegram to the minister: "Working class continues to protest against special tariff."[61] The terseness of the medium did not, though, signify moderation on the part of the rival forces here. In fact, the dispute over the tariff led at least one faction to take to the streets in the last months of the Empire. On 5 May 1889, a local almanac tells us, "The working class of Porto Alegre carried out a civic procession at night" against the government's tariff policy.[62]

As we shall see, this tariff, along with other fiscal projects, focused much of the political energy of the first years of the early 1890s. Even before these struggles, however, the trajectory of Silva Só, along with the LAI and other entities claiming to represent the "laboring classes" of Porto Alegre, suggests that the rigidly exclusionary political culture of the Empire was weakening before the regime itself came crashing down. Established parties clambered to assert connections to new societies from "the working classes." As this suggests, at least some near- and nonelites had become meaningful sources of support for political parties. The alliances that derived from this development, and the spilling of the tariff issue into common public spaces of the city, signaled a redrawing of the boundaries around the official political realm.

The New Politics in the Republic, 1889–93

The coming of the Republic on 15 November 1889 at first promised to explode politics as they had been known in Porto Alegre. Those who had long ruled the province, particularly the Gasparista Liberals, now felt power slip from their grasp, while the upstart Castilhista Republicans asserted their right to run the new government. With neither able to consolidate its supremacy until the conclusion of the Federalist Revolt, both the Castilhistas and their enemies, moreover, called demonstrations and parades that left, as one observer put it in 1892, "the streets providing a strange vision of popular movement."[63] In fact, with the birth of the Republican regime, it was no longer unusual for plebeians to discuss openly "high" political events or to join in partisan events.[64] The question of the day was not simply, as contemporary scholar Sylvio Romero put it, knowing "which patron to serve"; the very nature of the nation's political culture seemed in doubt.[65] Brazil was undergoing, in the phrase of lawyer and scholar Evaristo de Moraes, an "ideological binge," and nowhere as intensely as in Porto Alegre.[66]

In the years leading up to the Federalist Revolt, a range of actors continued the construction of a new politics, using the foundations laid before the demise of the Empire and responding to the opportunities the Republic provided. What this conflictive evolution reveals is not simply the participation of groups previously assumed to have been left out of or perhaps uninterested in "high" political events—a historiographical corrective that scholars have usefully supplied for many key points in Brazil's nineteenth-century history—but the complexity of plebeian politics and its relationship with the official nation.[67] To be more specific, Porto Alegre in the period from the declaration of the Republic to the outbreak of civil war in 1892–93 experienced the expansion and complication of alliances between men called "workers" and formal political parties but also saw the rise of public voices among segments excluded by these coalitions.

WORKERS AND PARTIES

Once the people of Porto Alegre were confident about the news of the regime change, they acknowledged it with differing degrees of enthusiasm. The PRR and other Republican associations, of course, hailed the Republic and congratulated the provisional government headed by General Deodoro da Fonseca in Rio. Castilhistas also rhapsodized about the "popular jubilation" that greeted the regime in the streets of the Gaúcho capital: "Numerous groups of citizens and families move about the streets and come to rest in the plazas, musical bands play the Marseillaise, thousands of fireworks burst in the air; by night the agitation intensifies in an indescribable manner. . . . The Republican Union [União Republicana, an ally of the PRR] has been in a permanent party, before an enormous multitude."[68] As Ricardo Pacheco has astutely noted, descriptions of events by the PRR organ attempted to remove or reduce the political nature of the support for the Republic by characterizing the populace as engaged in festive social activities. Despite this possible parallel to descriptions of antislavery efforts in 1883–84, the editors of *A Federação* did refer to the crowds as consisting of "citizens," thereby including them as part of the Republic.[69]

The diversity of groups that sought to be citizens in this broad sense became more evident in the greatest celebration of the regime's advent, a "civic march" that students of the Escola Militar (Military School) called for on

15 December.[70] According to *A Federação,* never stingy when estimating the number of Republican followers, as many as ten thousand Portoalegrenses paraded in commemoration of the first month of the Republic's life. Although some took part as private individuals, most seem to have joined in as members of the many associations that made up the main body of the march, each announcing its presence with a flag or banner at the head of its contingent. The list of the participating organizations suggests that the associative energy of the 1880s was booming as Porto Alegre moved into the Republican era. Partisan newspapers presented conflicting accounts of the order of the groups, but all gave a sense of the impressive array of societies whose standards flew in the march that day, including the Military School (carrying the new national flag); the staffs of the newspapers *A Federação, Jornal do Commercio,* and *Folha da Tarde;* army, navy, and police corps; the União Republicana and the Banda Republicana (Republican Band, a new club); the LAI and the Workers' Union; German, Portuguese, and Italian associations; trade associations such as the União Comercial (Commercial Union) and the Shop Clerks' Club; and schools such as the Colégio Rio-Grandense and the Normal School (the latter including female as well as male marchers).[71] At this point, all of these organizations felt empowered to make a public statement about the new regime and thus claim at least some place in it.

Within the first six months of the Republic's existence, members of some of these groups were, however, actively involved in struggles to control and define the regime. Some of the earliest such interventions were relatively small in scale. In late November, for instance, the workers at the War Arsenal in Porto Alegre pledged to donate portions of their monthly salaries to help the new regime pay the foreign debt the imperial government had incurred.[72] Such a gesture, though, had repercussions beyond its effects on some workers' incomes and the nation's finances; it represented a public backing of not just the Republic but also the PRR at a moment when that party was making a grab for power in the state. Castilhos did not assume the governorship immediately after 15 November 1889, but he and his allies worked quickly to establish exclusive sway in the government. The Viscount of Pelotas was named chief executive in Porto Alegre and faced the incompatible pressures of his former Liberal colleagues on one side and of Castilhos and the PRR on the other. The ex-Liberals largely found themselves toothless, however, as their leader, Silveira Martins, went into forced exile and their archenemy, Castilhos, took the vital post of secretary of state. From this position, the PRR chief set about purging his enemies—mostly ex-Liberals at this juncture—from public office and creating a state militia (at first called the Civil Guard and later the Military Brigade) with commanders loyal to the PRR.[73] Both of these efforts by Castilhos infuriated his enemies; the creation of the Civil Guard, moreover, promised to give the PRR military might to go along with its grip on much of the state government and its connections to workers' groups.

The attention party leaders gave to shoring up PRR support among "worker" organizations like the LAI and the Workers' Union suggests the prominence that these groups had won. The national government eliminated the special tariff in early February of 1890, a move that the PRR had promoted and that the LAI and allied clubs received gratefully.[74] Moreover, the Castilhistas benefited from the popularity that Demétrio Ribeiro, the only PRR member to garner a seat in the cabinet of Deodoro's administration, brought them. Ribeiro, as Sandra Pesavento has observed, adopted rather faint prolabor measures while serving as minister of agriculture, commerce, and public works—principally by granting paid vacations to employees of a water utility and a railroad in Rio de Janeiro.[75] A much grander project announced by the finance minister in January 1890, mandating the incorporation of private banks with the right to issue legal currency, provided both Ribeiro and the PRR an opportunity to improve their standing with the new political groups in Porto Alegre. The bank-of-issue proposal, to PRR eyes, violated the federalist principles that the Republic should have been embodying (particularly since one of the banks would be in Porto Alegre) and contradicted the Positivist ban on special privileges for any socioeconomic sector. Privilege was also at the heart of small manufacturers' and workers' opposition to the bank; both segments feared that only the already powerful would benefit from the credit the bank would provide and attacked the provision that would grant tax exemptions and greater access to government contracts to any enterprises set up with such credit.[76] As Finance Minister Rui Barbosa insisted on the bank-of-issue idea, Ribeiro resigned from the cabinet and returned to the Gaúcho capital. There, greeted as a hero by the LAI, Ribeiro took the chance to praise the independent worker-entrepreneurs who formed the League, in the process conflating, as Pesavento indicates, workers and small capitalists as independent producers.[77]

This blurring of categories, already present during the late Empire, proved politically useful for the PRR. In both a street demonstration and a banquet celebrating Ribeiro's rejection of the government's plan, PRR leaders and their allies among the "productive classes" found that this language could be a bridge between them; thus we see not only the Republican Assis Brasil but also LAI director Mesquita declaring that "small producers" of all types would suffer because of the bank. Mesquita went so far as to assert explicitly that there were "no odious differences between citizens who cooperate for the common good, be they military men, workers, [or] large or small capitalists."[78]

In fact, by May 1890, the PRR came to rely visibly on its ties to the "productive classes" of Porto Alegre in its efforts to cement its power in Rio Grande do Sul. Castilhos and his partisan colleagues had emerged victorious from a struggle with the Viscount of Pelotas, first governor under the Republic, in early February. When Pelotas appeared to give in to the demands of his former Liberal colleagues in a nomination for the relatively humble post of customs inspector in February, Castilhos and the PRR rebelled. For the time being, their revolt took a peaceful form. Through local wrangling and appeals to the head of the Republic, General Deodoro, Castilhos triumphed. Offered the governorship, the PRR chief refused it. As at the very start of the new regime, Castilhos allowed someone else, this time General Júlio Anacleto Falcão da Frota, to become the state's chief executive, thereby currying favor with the military while securing for himself a position, this time as first vice governor, that allowed him tremendous say in the actual governance of Rio Grande do Sul.[79] By April, however, the bank of issue was creating an irreparable break between the PRR and Frota, though the governor personally was unsympathetic to the bank plan. Despite the telegrams and even the emissary (Assis Brasil) that Castilhos and his party sent to Rio, the bank project was moving ahead. Here the "worker" allies that the PRR had cultivated since the late Empire proved highly useful. On 28 April, the LAI organized a tremendous public demonstration to be held at a key focal point of the urban economy, the Praça 15 de Novembro (renamed in honor of the proclamation of the Republic).[80] What Governor Frota described in a telegram as "just peaceful representations [by] commercial classes, workers and *povo*," flowed out of the large plaza and wound through the main streets of the city center. First Barros Cassal and later Ribeiro and Castilhos made speeches against the bank.[81]

However moving a spectacle this political protest may have been—and it was as massive a political gathering as the city had ever produced—neither it nor Castilhista diplomacy could halt the opening of the Bank of Emissions (Banco Emissor) on 7 May 1890.[82] Still, the precedent of the mobilization of the masses in favor of a political party was set and only grew in influence over the rest of the period. Indeed, other demonstrations shortly after the installation of the bank led to more change at the top of the state government and bolstered the PRR's influence. Not only Castilhos but several other key Republican Party members (such as Antão de Faria, Ramiro Barcelos, and Barros Cassal) and Governor Frota submitted their resignations on 6 May, in protest against the bank. At the same time, the PRR and the Republican Union called for civic action against this institution imposed from Rio. On the night of 6 May, a large number—probably thousands—of Republicans and their "worker" allies, along with anonymous members of the *povo*, heard Castilhos explain the underlying reason for PRR anger: "The Republic was prepared by the republicans, it was made by the republicans . . . ; yet, however, who is it that governs? Is it the republicans? No! They have the support of the army, the applause of the *povo* . . . ; that is what this extraordinary manifestation demonstrates, but they don't govern!"[83] Spurred on by Castilhos and other speakers, the crowd marched through downtown streets to the bank. Though some stone throwing occurred at the final destination, according to the anti-Castilhista paper *A Reforma*, violence was largely avoided. The following night another large crowd gathered; in the telling of *A Federação*, "representatives of all classes" took part in "one of the most splendid popular manifestations yet realized" in Porto Alegre. Significantly, the PRR organ bestowed the term *citizens* on the participants who listened to Barros Cassal and Ribeiro and added its own enthusiastic voice in favor of the Republicans.[84] Within a week, further Republican mobilization of their "worker" allies in large public actions forced the resignation of Frota's interim replacement, the ex-Conservative Francisco da Silva Tavares (a vice governor holding the governorship until the appointed executive, General Cândido Costa, could arrive from Rio).

Another march, taking place on 13 May, the anniversary of abolition, carried a hint of hypocrisy. PRR directors alleged that the march was simply meant to mark the anniversary of the "Golden Law," but they had done little to address the concerns of former slaves since emancipation. In truth, the demonstration was another show of force by the Republicans, again using mobilization of worker-entrepreneurs and whatever elements of the *povo* they might attract. Events began late in the afternoon, when "a great mass of people" turned out in front of the seat of the Republican Union, where PRR leaders were meeting and at least two (and perhaps as many as six) bands were playing music. Silva Tavares hastily ordered a police unit of sixty or so soldiers to disperse the gathering; it did so, brutally and to tragic effect. The police opened fire on the crowd, injuring several plebeians and one Republican notable, Barros Cassal, and killing a young Spanish hotel employee. Though the planned march was thus prevented, PRR leaders and followers —*A Federação* claimed the participation of large "groups of citizens"—made their way to the governor's palace. There, as a result of the tumult and some backroom politicking between PRR chiefs and military commanders in the city, Silva Tavares publicly renounced his office and General Carlos Machado de Bittencourt took over.[85] Castilhos once again served as secretary in this latest state government.[86]

The option of backing the army's top commander in Porto Alegre reflected the Castilhistas' desires to maintain good relations with Deodoro's government. After all, the PRR had been persecuting its ex-Liberal foes, and the ouster of Silva Tavares only brought their party new enemies. Moreover, the PRR and its allies had taken to the streets repeatedly against part of the administration's fiscal plan. As Castilhos had revealed in his speech on 6 May, the PRR was well aware of its dependence not only on groups like the LAI but also on the army and, through it, the government of General Deodoro. Thus, while General Machado briefly held the governor's post and then passed it on to Cândido Costa, Castilhos was considering how to ensure the friendship of the Republic's chief executive. Shortly after Costa became governor, Castilhos traveled to Rio, where important figures in the regime welcomed him with a banquet and the PRR chief reforged his ties with Deodoro.[87]

Castilhos's allegiance to Deodoro, though, stirred up further controversy back in Porto Alegre. Apparently without consulting his fellow Republicans, Castilhos decided to endorse Deodoro's candidacy in the upcoming presidential elections, the first to be held since the coup d'état of 15 November 1889. Seeing this move as an indication of Castilhos's own authoritarian tendencies, as well as his support for Deodoro's similar leanings, major PRR activists—such as Barros Cassal, Ribeiro, and Antão de Faria—left the party. While in the short term this meant that the PRR controlled the election of delegates to the national constitutional assembly, in the longer term it signaled growing troubles for Castilhos. The dissident Republicans, whose numbers only grew as Castilhos gathered more and more power for himself, became critical opponents of the PRR. Anti-Castilhista forces were already coalescing, as ex-Liberals banded together with the governors forced out by the PRR (Pelotas and Silva Tavares) to found the first formal anti-Castilhista party, the União Nacional (National Union), on 3 June.[88] By the following April, the dissident Republicans and the historic anti-Castilhistas were working together openly, in the Partido Republicano Federal (Federal Republican Party).[89] In terms of the new politics that had been evolving since the 1880s, the departure of Ribeiro in particular from the PRR also led many of the "workers" and some of the military cadets who had supported the party to defect as well.[90]

The dissidence of key Republicans thus led to division among the "working-class" organizations that had entered the partisan political realm. Barros Cassal and Ribeiro took various approaches to winning near- and nonelites over to their side. Ribeiro offered public speeches and edited a new paper, *O Productor* (The Producer), that pledged to eliminate any distinctions among professions, "whether they be considered purely intellectual or exclusively related to industry." In that phrase as in promises for minimal government interference in professions—only "the inspection necessary . . . to repress the abuses of speculators"—Ribeiro was clearly speaking to segments of the population like those that formed the LAI and similar groups. By publishing a separate German-language edition and taking as its aim "construction of a free fatherland, made up of native-born and adoptive citizens," *O Productor/Der Produktor* was apparently also reaching out to German immigrants and German-Brazilians.[91] Barros Cassal, meanwhile, called mass actions in September and October and, like Ribeiro, denounced as fraudulent the elections held under Castilhos's supervision.[92] At the end of 1890, moreover, a new workers' group—this one more pointedly representing laborers and not abstract "productive classes"—emerged. By the names of those present at the meetings that culminated in the formation of the Centro Operário (Workers' Center), including von Held and Zaniratti, it is clear that the PRR had lost some of its principal activists.[93]

Castilhos was, however, nothing if not pugnacious, and he and the PRR fought to offset the damage the dissidents were causing. They supported the organization of another new workers' group, this one called the Liga Operária

(Workers' League), which included among its "principal objectives the preservation of the federal republican government."[94] Among the officers of the new League was the old pro-PRR activist Francisco José de Mesquita. Together with the places that LAI director João von Steenhagen and Workers' League president Joaquim Alves dos Santos Cunha e Silva received on the party's electoral roll, this suggests that the PRR held on to some major supporters as it tried to meet the dissident Republican threat; the remaining PRR leaders, after all, had worked with the dissidents in the construction of links to new political players.[95] The PRR also continued the overtures it had been making to immigrant groups since the late Empire, especially by promoting religious freedom for non-Catholics, though this risked alienating Catholics, and a less controversial "great naturalization" for the foreign-born.[96]

Both sets of Republicans, therefore, made the most of the potential support the new politics of the era could supply. In the end, though, the PRR's control over elections to the state constitutional assembly proved too much for the dissident Republicans and their allies to overcome. If they were in a sense as predictable as the result of the vote (and the charges of manipulation by the defeated candidates), the debates that followed the assembly were also potent indications of the gap between the ever more dogmatic PRR on the one side and its rather heterogeneous rivals on the other.

These debates centered on the product of the 1891 state assembly, a constitution for Rio Grande do Sul that Castilhos himself authored.[97] This document set up highly centralized, authoritarian political institutions through which its leaders were to govern in Porto Alegre. Closely following Comte's proposals, the Castilhistas established a unicameral legislature and restricted its responsibilities to purely budgetary matters. The powers of the executive, on the other hand, were greatly expanded to include most legislative functions. As in Comte's "Positivist dictatorship" (and in a proposal that the orthodox Positivist Apostolate of Rio de Janeiro had made in 1890 for the new national constitution), the president of the state would himself propose laws, disseminating them through municipal authorities for public discussion, and then, after considering citizens' reactions, "maintain the project unaltered or modify it in accordance with [those reactions] that he considers valid." As laid out in the project that became law in July 1891, a Gaúcho version of Comte's dictator would thus enjoy the right to rule virtually by decree.[98] At the same time, though, the constitution made concessions to those outside the small band of Positivists who were to govern. Chief among these provisions was the abolition of any distinctions between state functionaries and civil workers; all would enjoy freedom from government licensing and most other regulation.[99]

For the opponents of the PRR, this constitution not only contradicted the Liberal-inspired national charter approved earlier that year but also dragged the state toward absolutism. Despite the "invincible heterogeneity" that the coalitions of dissident Republicans and former Liberals and Conservatives evinced, their criticism of the PRR constitution was consistent in its claim that the PRR's 1891 state constitution, by concentrating legislative powers in the hands of the executive, would plunge Rio Grande do Sul into an "elective despotism."[100] The "legalized tyranny" of the PRR's rule, according to the Federalists—as the opposition came to be known—clashed with the "sentiment of justice" and respect for individual liberties that they saw as inherent in the people and history of their state.[101] For the most eloquent of the anti-PRR propagandists, the former Republican Assis Brasil, the state needed a constitution that reestablished a parliamentary system and guaranteed individual rights.[102] The Federalists, however, at no time went beyond this general defense of parliamentarianism and individual rights to suggest greater measures of equality in the Republic. Indeed, their project for the Republic closely resembled the imperial system in which they had flourished: a nominally democratic parliamentary regime in which only a small fraction of the population participated officially in politics. In fact, for Silveira Martins, the "maximum leader" of Gaúcho Liberals since the 1870s, even the responsible, male citizens of the elite would have only an indirect say in the election of executives; he rejected direct presidential election on the grounds that "a million ignorant men do not make one sage."[103]

As intellectually dry and generally elitist as they might seem, these arguments took place in the context of the new politics; even the former Liberals showed their willingness to bring "workers" into their ranks. Indeed, in the major events of 1891–92, both sides continued to act within the patterns of the politics that had emerged by that point. The revocation of the special tariff and the inauguration of the Bank of Emissions were no longer the flashpoints of partisan conflict; control over the state government and the living conditions of the *povo* became the issues that set off PRR-Federalist battles.

Castilhos and his remaining colleagues maintained their grip on the state only until November 1891. To a great extent, they managed this simply but characteristically thorough manipulation of state institutions; Castilhos, chosen as governor on 15 July 1891 by the same assembly that had obediently passed his constitution a day earlier, proved always to be an excellent "conductor of men," as historian Sérgio da Costa Franco has put it.[104] He was not, however, able to withstand the flurry of opposition that his sometime patron, General Deodoro, caused in early November by closing the national congress and calling for new elections. The Gaúcho Republican had tolerated Deodoro's prior antidemocratic maneuvers and reconciled himself to this latest one as well, but his situation was untenable. Though he was not, as we have seen, a democrat himself, even Castilhos faced Deodoro's brazen move with some anxiety.[105] His doubts, if Castilhos allowed himself such feelings, proved prescient, for within days of Deodoro's dissolution of congress, open protests broke out in Gaúcho towns, from nearby Viamão, to Bagé, Rio Grande, and Pelotas, and then on to Porto Alegre itself.[106]

Indeed, the critical moments of the November 1891–June 1892 period depended on the behavior not only of politicians and military troops but also of "worker" groups. In the two weeks after Deodoro's 3 November coup attempt, pressures mounted for the overthrow of Castilhos. Clearly led outside the capital by Gasparista ex-Liberals, the movement picked up force when some army units joined it and then again when "masses of the *povo*" crowded its public meetings in Porto Alegre. Although the PRR argued that Castilhos had accepted Deodoro's outrageous behavior only to maintain order, this claim was too late. On the morning of 12 November, *O Mercantil* reported, commerce shut down in the city and "an enormous mass of people came together." At the behest of ex-PRR propagandist Ernesto Paiva, the crowd marched peacefully to the governor's palace to convince the Republican chieftain that "he no longer enjoyed popular confidence." After this declaration, groups made their way to the houses of Barros Cassal and Assis Brasil, cheering these dissident Republicans.[107] The new administration, dismissed by the PRR as a mere *governicho*, a parody of true government, was in fact headed by these two ex-PRR leaders, along with one of the generals who had led the rebellion in Porto Alegre.[108] The *governicho* was "politically unstable," political scientist Hélgio Trindade has written, and necessarily so, given the disparate elements that made up the anti-Castilhista forces.[109] The administration was unable to preserve a unified ruling bloc, particularly after Silveira Martins returned from exile in March 1892 and tried to resume his old position of power. The arrival of the "Tribune" and the founding of a new political party, the Partido Federalista (Federalist Party), electrified his longtime followers but also repelled those anti-Castilhista activists unwilling to submit to the command of the ex-Liberal boss.

Both dissident Republicans and some of their allies among labor organizations balked at Silveira Martins's efforts to reestablish Liberal control under the aegis of the Federalist Party. On 3 March 1892, perhaps two hundred "workers" met in the São Pedro Theater in the Praça da Matriz to form an independent labor party. Called by the editors of a new paper aimed at workers, *L'Avvenire*, the event brought together representatives of the German and Italian communities in Porto Alegre, along with others, like Nicolau Tolentino da Soledade, who had been active in earlier organizations like the LAI and the Workers' Center. Francisco Colombo Leoni, editor of *L'Avvenire*, spoke out about "capitalists and workers," condemning the former for their "arrogance." It had always been his "conviction," Leoni explained, "that by the power of the people, there should emerge . . . a providential law, regulating the rapport between workers and capitalists, establishing the true bases of universal prosperity and, above all, that of the class that to this day has only been disadvantaged and disdained, that of the productive class, of noble workers." Francisco Goerisch, the leader of the German contingent, and Soledade offered discourses of their own, supporting Leoni's idea of establishing a multiethnic party for and by the workers of the city.[110] Though they did not break with the dissident Republicans, the actions of these workers expressed their clear desire to distance themselves from the old political elite.

This expression of doubts about the *governicho*'s coalition occurred between two attempts by Castilhistas to restore the PRR to power. In both instances, moreover, the anti-*governicho* forces made use of supporters from the military and their "worker" allies. In fact, a failed "putsch" of 4 February 1892 revealed just how far not only worker-entrepreneurs but also, as *O Mercantil* put it, "men of dubious looks, that is, of the *povo*," had come in attaining influence on political events in the Gaúcho capital.[111] The massive documentation spawned by the criminal investigation of the February incident sketches an outlandish plot to tunnel into the building of the Bureau of Lands and Colonization; rely on the Civil Guard to neutralize the police; shut down the Telegraph Office; and then move to the governor's palace, where Castilhos would once more take the post to which he had been elected the year before. More intriguing than the improbable scheme that the police claimed to have uncovered is the range not only of participants but also of the reasons they gave for their presence. Against the overall trend, some men of color appeared in the *golpe* (coup d'état) effort. Aside from one vague reference to "some white and *pardo* persons," though, the two Afro-Brazilians mentioned specifically were described as being "of the household of" prominent citizens, implying that they were merely acting as servants—perhaps former slaves—obeying their masters. One Russian immigrant, moreover, asserted that he came—and left early—at the behest of his employer, the chair-factory owner Simão Kappel, suggesting that clientelism drew more than just ex-slaves into the partisan initiative.[112] The rest of the participants ran the gamut from stonemasons, teachers, shoemakers, barbers, and typesetters to merchants, military men, and at least one federal magistrate. The Brazilian-born mixed in the crowd with Portuguese, Argentineans, Italians, and the one Russian woodworker.

Predictably, some of those interrogated denied any ties to the plot or swore they had been elsewhere. More interestingly, many justified their role in the plot with explicit political explanations. Like one Portuguese barber, for instance, several suspects declared simply, "as a partisan of Doctor Castilhos, there [I] was." Others were more specific. One small merchant, after identifying himself as a "sincere Republican," expressed his desire to reunite the PRR with the dissidents who had defected from it. Another merchant, meanwhile, alleged that he did not want to depose the *governicho* but "merely [to] dispute the form of government." What makes these statements remarkable is not their diversity but their mere existence in the records. They show, after all, something that would have been unthinkable for elites in midcentury Porto Alegre: "people of low class" (*gente de baixa classe*) working with their social superiors in open, partisan political action.[113]

By June of the same year, however, discord in the highest ranks of the *governicho*, along with the accompanying fractiousness of the anti-Castilhista "worker" groups, left the government more vulnerable to PRR-led assault. Though the dissident Republicans called a public demonstration to protest the new Castilhista *golpe*, their efforts were in vain. Castilhos had not only a large crowd in the streets demanding his restoration but also the backing of the national government and the militia (now called the Military Brigade) that he had sagaciously created at the very start of the new regime. On 17 June, Castilhos was back in power; once more, though, he stepped into the shadows for the time being by placing national congressman Vitorino Monteiro in the governor's chair.[114] Only with his election as governor that November did Castilhos reject his role as the éminence grise of the Gaúcho Republican regime and become its public face. The long and bitter trajectory from the PRR's first ascension under the Viscount of Pelotas to its recovery of control in mid-1892 had been possible only because of the new politics that had been growing in Porto Alegre since the late Empire. As effective—and ferocious—a partisan fighter as Castilhos was, in other words, throughout this phase of his career he acted within a framework, which he helped build, of increasing political inclusion of plebeians and lesser elites.

A PLEBEIAN PUBLIC

While the coalitions between "workers" and political parties went through the tribulations of the 1889–92 period, a wider, related development was taking place in Porto Alegre. As we have seen, a number of nontraditional organizations achieved visibility and influence in the partisan politics of the late Empire and early Republic. Beyond this "incorporation of the proletariat," as the Positivists put it (or "absorption" of the *povo*, as the ex-Liberals might have it), though, new voices appeared. Some replicated the strategies and aims of the mostly white artisans and worker-entrepreneurs of the "worker" groups, while others proposed new aims.[115] Still others posited a novel "popular" identity more far-reaching than anything that the LAI or its rivals embraced. Finally, a specifically Afro-Brazilian activism and journalism made its presence felt. Though these last two identities—the popular and the Afro-Brazilian—in part represented reactions against omissions implicit in the definition of the near- and nonelite groups of the 1880–90s, in the end, they also contained exclusionary tendencies. They, too, in other words, often treated many of "their own" people as needing improvement before they could be full citizens—much as elite parties had portrayed the *povo* throughout the period under study here. Still, partly because of such strict judgments of the crudest sectors of the *povo*, these voices, together with those of the "worker" groups, constituted a plebeian public, a new realm of open discourse on official matters in the city.

Given the opportunities that their alliances with elite parties gave them, "worker" groups' voices were naturally the loudest elements of this public.

Even here, though, surviving documentation hints at a more variegated segment than one composed of the LAI, the Workers' Center, and the other organizations mentioned above. Labor historians have, for instance, often noted the appearance in 1890 of a manifesto from a Socialist Party in Porto Alegre. Incredibly detailed and in many ways extraordinarily radical—as in its call for the "gradual leveling of fortunes" by taxes on those with incomes above a certain level—the party left no other traces.[116] The year 1892 saw not only the establishment of still more labor groups, like a second Grêmio dos Artistas (Artisans' Guild) and the Allgemeiner Arbeiter Verein (General Association of Workers, a German social-democratic union), but also the first celebration of 1 May in the state's history.[117] Noting the existence of these associations does more, however, than give a fuller accounting of "worker" activism in the period; it also reminds us that some groups pursued their own interests, defining them in class terms, through means other than collaboration with official political parties.[118]

These other means could be the formation of autonomous labor parties, of the sort that Leoni and his colleagues described in their March 1892 meetings. Most obviously, however, these means took the form of a press based on (and, indeed, derived from) new conceptions of plebeian interests. As Partha Chatterjee has argued about historically distant cases, these new public voices, by trying to endow the *povo*, or some part of it, with "the moral attributes of a community," were adding their "irreducibly political" claims to the realm of public debate in Porto Alegre.[119]

The option of asserting "popular" interests in public discourse was most evident in the evolution of the newspaper *A Gazetinha* (though it built on images of an "average Joe" figure, "Zé Povo," that had been common for decades).[120] Of course, in some ways, the construction of different "worker" identities—whether socialist, anarchist, or simply more exclusively laborer-based than the multiclass identities that lay at the heart of the ideologies of the LAI and the Workers' Union—and the emergence of a popular, plebeian-oriented press could be mutually reinforcing. Certainly in practice this was the case in Porto Alegre, where *A Gazetinha* criticized "worker" leaders like Steenhagen, Herzog, von Held, and Tolentino da Soledade; a January 1893 editorial in the paper blasted these men and their like for destroying "the Portoalegrense workers' party" by trying simply "to add the laboring class to the number of adherents of the parties run by professional politicians [*bacharéis*]."[121]

Such precision about, and allegiance to, the identity of laborers was not, however, characteristic of *A Gazetinha*. More frequently, the paper's editors—led by its owner and managing editor, Otaviano Manoel de Oliveira, and its dynamic contributor Francisco Xavier da Costa—presented a broader profile. Though the paper's staff included some of the main socialist activists in the city, it remained, as Cláudia Mauch argues, "much more a 'popular' than a worker" enterprise.[122] In that vein, the paper's columns tended to address the basic, quotidian conditions of the *povo*, though without ever becoming fully detached from political commentary. Thus in April 1892, during the *governicho*, the paper offered open criticism of the direction the Republic was taking. Instead of concentrating their energies on the true progress of the people, the writer contended, Republican leaders had merely demonstrated a "trivial preoccupation" with the "development of their political ideal and nothing more." Without rejecting the government's stated goals, the author warned that those in power—dissident Republicans and former Liberals at that time—had to live up to their ideals or lose the support of the *povo*.[123] The criterion applied to the government's performance here—the measure of improvement in common people's lives—was much closer to the core mission and identity of *A Gazetinha*.

From its first issue in 1891 to its last in 1900, *A Gazetinha* traded mainly in gossip about the scandalous behavior of unnamed but presumably identifiable city residents and complaints about the trials of daily life in Porto Alegre. The idea that the progress and justice promised by the Republic should extend also to the position and conditions of the *povo* was central to discussions of the regime in the paper. Its editors harangued authorities with complaints about abuses of workers by police and employers and the brutal and illegal forced recruitment of workers into the military.[124] The dismal material conditions of much of the *povo* were another source of irritation. When an outbreak of smallpox threatened the city in early 1892, for example, *A Gazetinha* advised the government to take decisive measures. The Hygiene Commission could not limit its actions to the disposal of the dead, the paper warned; without a forceful campaign to clean up streets and the homes of the poor, the "worrisome" situation would only get worse.[125] When such dramatic menaces did not loom over Porto Alegre, complaints focused on the lack of government aid to the city's poor residents in a time of accelerating inflation and subsequent misery. In one editorial, Aureliano de Abreu called on the government to set up a system of food warehouses as a means of ensuring a supply of basic necessities to the population and protecting against merchants' speculation.[126] Another writer expressed horror at bakeries' resistance to attempts to control bread prices; unless the government stepped in, he claimed, "we will find ourselves in the difficult contingency of working only for the bakers."[127]

Calls for protection from police and other official violence, and for basic material aid, were not abstract requests, but ones that arose from and responded to concrete living conditions of the *povo* in Porto Alegre. In making such demands, these self-appointed popular representatives conveyed a sense that they were citizens of the Republic and as such had certain rights.[128] When we look at a third area of complaints that the newspaper made to the Republican government in Porto Alegre, we see that this conception of citizens' rights was itself a conflict-laden construction. Much as they appealed to the state for protection of their physical safety and material conditions, the editors of *A Gazetinha* sought official action against perceived moral threats. Thus even while complaining at times of the oppressiveness of police actions, *A Gazetinha* called at other moments for stepped-up control over the vagrants, prostitutes, and other "idle people that [infest] the streets, plazas, and taverns of the city with damage to public morality and disrespect for the law."[129] Anyone who did not hold regular work qualified as a vagrant and was thus subject to verbal attack. In late 1892, for instance, an article called for a police crackdown on the peddlers, bootblacks, and others who congregated in the Praça da Alfândega (Customs Plaza) downtown and, according to the paper, "attack passersby, fight one against the other, some even drawing knives; in sum those vagrants are *monumental*, worthy of severe correction!"[130] However hardworking they may have been, prostitutes also received vitriolic criticism. Not only were their bordellos scenes of gambling, fights, and other immoralities and disorders, but their presence and unrestrained sexuality "contaminated" the city for good families.[131]

This attention to the fate of the decent segment of the *povo* also took the form of attacks against sexual immorality among plebeians in the gossip columns of *A Gazetinha*. Without giving names, but providing enough detail so that those involved (and possibly others) would recognize their targets, columnists chided such wrongdoers as young men of good family who romanced maids. Female sexuality, however, was the main target of these critiques, as evidenced by frequent remarks about married women caught in affairs; young girls who left the protection of their parents' homes to see their sweethearts; and, in short, any woman who dared refuse to keep her sexuality within the bonds of strict heterosexual monogamy and male control.[132]

The language of *A Gazetinha*'s recriminations mirrored, in large part, the rhetoric of elite moralization projects.[133] The editors of *A Gazetinha* may simply have shared that vision of the need to create a less unruly, more highly moralized people. It seems more likely, however, that their rhetoric reflected the distance they perceived between themselves and the crudest elements of the *povo;* the conspicuous participation of several of the paper's founders in the press and in "worker" associations may, in this case, have increased the distance. In their use of moralization rhetoric, these leaders revealed not only distance but also tension among sectors of the *povo*. By applying such moral standards to popular elements, these writers took on a great deal of subjective power—deciding, in effect, who fit into the definition of a good *povo* for Republican society and who fell into the category of those needing punishment or education. In so doing, they showed not only that readings of ideas associated with Republican projects existed among the *povo* but also that these readings were not "popular" in any simple sense. While calling for justice and governmental assistance for the *povo*, these men showed that they would not uncritically accept solidarity with all sectors. Instead, the *povo* for whom they fought was to be united on terms they would define.

The Afro-Brazilian workers' paper *O Exemplo* provides a similar but distinct case here. As with *A Gazetinha*, the editors of *O Exemplo* recognized the inequalities in Republican society and worked to better the lot of the *povo*. Their emphasis, however, was on the special conditions of Afro-Brazilians in Gaúcho society. In their inaugural issue, the editors made this stance clear, defining their program as "the defense of our class and the perfection of our mediocre knowledge."[134] The paper was far from the only representative of the Afro-Brazilian "class" in Porto Alegre; clubs such as the Club Guiné (Guinea Club), the Club Recreativo Operário (Worker's Recreational Club), and the venerable Sociedade Floresta Aurora (Dawn Forest Society) brought together Afro-Brazilians socially and were often—as at the "civic march" that celebrated the first month of the Republican regime—the public face of their community in Porto Alegre. *O Exemplo*, however, took a much more active role by taking on the "spiny" task of denouncing discrimination by those who "judge a man by the color of his epidermis."[135]

Positioning itself as the champion of this group, *O Exemplo* took on the responsibility of ensuring "the raising of our class," in large part by condemning the harsh treatment Afro-Brazilians received, particularly from the authorities. Distressingly frequent were complaints of harassment of Afro-Brazilians by army recruiters and the police.[136] Other examples of prejudice found their way into the paper's columns as well. When one Porto Alegre teacher put Afro-Brazilian students in a separate classroom, or when white politicians tried to block a mulatto's access to high-paying civil service jobs, *O Exemplo* stepped in with angry criticism.[137] At times, the editors went beyond this defensive posture, affirming the strength and special moral force of Africans and Afro-Brazilians. They declared that Afro-Brazilians would never commit the kinds of assaults they had witnessed whites make on orderly Afro-Brazilian groups.[138] More dramatically, these writers at times took pride in their origins in "Africa, nation of heroes."[139] Though, as a retrospective in a revived *O Exemplo* declared in 1930, the original paper had never sought "to mount battles between whites and blacks," it had persistently sought for its people a "place most deserving among civilized peoples."[140]

In a manner much like the efforts in *A Gazetinha*, the editors of *O Exemplo* placed limits on their advocacy of the group they chose to represent. In fact, this trait was even more evident in *O Exemplo*, which announced its intent to serve as a "disciplinary organ."[141] The paper's editors offered praise for the "decent folk" of their community, mentioning by name the "able teacher" who attended a church service and the "dignified young man" who had recently traveled with his fellow military workers of the War Arsenal, or drawing attention to the birthdays of a "well-considered citizen" and "Senhora Dona Ricarda Ribeiro, progenitor of the hardworking laborer Mariano Ribeiro."[142] At the same time, *O Exemplo* leveled the same charges against unruly or ignorant Afro-Brazilians that elites made, treating them as a moral contamination and suggesting campaigns (primarily of education) to remove any possible threat from such individuals; they expressed shame at those Afro-Brazilians whose behavior seemed to support racist sayings such as "there can't be a dance of blacks without trouble [*rolo*]."[143] Moreover, as in *A Gazetinha*, gossip columns in *O Exemplo* focused on sexual misconduct, particularly by women.[144] If anything, the Afro-Brazilian advocates were again more explicit than their "popular" colleagues at *A Gazetinha;* the former were, for instance, willing to proclaim that "the majority of the daughters of Eve are good for fire"—that is, are sinners—and "especially today, when [women] tend to conquer a certain sum of liberties that are tolerated in men" but that in women lead down "the road to dishonor."[145]

The Afro-Brazilian paper's moralization rhetoric, moreover, had its foundation in a more specific, racialized identity. Whereas the other popular newspaper generally called for the policing of disorder within the *povo* writ large, *O Exemplo*'s editors tended to stress the need for raising their racial "guild" to a moral level that justified Afro-Brazilians' search for greater rights and power in society. The effect of this rhetoric, however, paralleled what occurred with *A Gazetinha*. By defining, in a sense, which Afro-Brazilians were and were not good citizens, who was and was not worthy of rights in Republican society, *O Exemplo* implicitly accepted elements of an elite vision of the Republic. But this similar language had a different impact when used by Afro-Brazilians; it not only set up certain Afro-Brazilian members of the *povo* —the paper's editors—as arbiters of popular morality but also demonstrated again that plebeian demands for citizenship were complicated constructions. These men who took on the role of representatives of their race did not defend all Afro-Brazilians' rights and value but confined their support to "good" Afro-Brazilians. They thus strove for an improvement in Afro-Brazilians'—at least some Afro-Brazilians'—position in society by working with and manipulating the Republic's ruling entities and the ideas about the *povo* circulating within that society.

Beyond War

The fall of the *governicho* in June 1892 did not, of course, mark the end of partisan disputes in Porto Alegre and Rio Grande do Sul. Dissident Republicans and their "worker" allies continued to challenge PRR hegemony from 1893 through the end of the war in 1895 and, of course, well beyond that point.[146] Though the Castilhistas thus continued to face challenges from within the new politics that had sprung up since the 1880s, their major concern by 1893 had to be the armed threat that the Federal Party and its political bosses, from Silveira Martins to more local *caudilhos* like Gumercindo Saraiva, presented. Outcry against partisan violence, even murder, had begun in 1891 and accelerated as lines between the two sides—Castilhos's PRR and the national army that backed it versus the former Liberal and Conservative chieftains and the dissident Republicans who could stomach Gasparista command—became more sharply drawn. By late 1892, the sheer number of incidents meant that open hostilities had broken out, though declarations of war came only later.[147]

The outcome of the Federalist Revolt in 1895, like the regime change of late 1889, did not ultimately wreak profound destruction on the organization of social and political power, though both furthered transformations long underway. The ascension of the PRR in late 1889 and the affirmation of its rule by arms in 1895 were key moments in the rise of a new politics, fostered by elite parties and pushed always by changing associations among more plebeian sectors. Through these chronological markers, Porto Alegre saw an expansion of the boundaries around formal politics, as the PRR and several anti-Castilhista leagues fought ferociously for control over the government; in their battles, these elite forces regularly included sections of the *povo*. The PRR's victory in the Federalist Revolt quelled elite-led opposition, at least until the early years of the next century, and left the party rhetorically tied to support by and for "workers."[148] More to the point here, if it quavered a bit and sprang some leaks, the border around the political realm—around recognized, active membership in the nation—nevertheless held up. Elite parties, that is, welcomed some workers as political activists in the early Republic but also shut out the rest of the *povo* of Porto Alegre as they tried to reconstruct politics.

The story of the new politics therefore featured two main plotlines in the early years of the Republic, one featuring shifting coalitions between male workers and either Castilhistas or their partisan enemies and the other dominated by those plebeians, many of them reexcluded from citizenship, who refused to accept their place outside formal politics with equanimity. As part of these negotiations, new discursive currents, one abstractly popular and one specifically Afro-Brazilian, appeared. Along with "worker" groups that aligned with political parties, these latter protagonists created a new, popular realm in which community issues, including those of governance, received public attention. These various voices from outside the old elitist system—some of them accepted in official politics and others shut out—presented novel challenges to the geography of politics in the city.

Conclusion

LATE on the night of 18 January 1888, the young domestic servant Maria da Costa put an end to a conflict on the streets of Porto Alegre by referring to a doctrine that her social superiors would have considered subversive. Coming upon one of her female friends riding in a coach with another woman and two men, Maria accused the woman of deceit: hadn't the friend promised to spend the night with Maria? After hurling a few venomous insults at the woman, Maria turned, apparently to go on her way. Heading very slowly up the same road as the coach, she hindered its passage until the driver finally yelled at her to move. Unwilling to concede anything to her antagonists, Maria responded by turning to the man and asking "if the street did not belong to the King" (*se a rua não era do Rei*). To this question the driver could only offer quick assent. Most likely he wanted to avoid a flare-up of conflict. Especially as a plebeian who made his living by transporting goods and people in the city, however, he probably also accepted Maria's implication here —namely, that she or he or any member of the *povo* had a right to what historian Paulo Moreira has called a "relative liberty of movement and behavior" in the busy, often dirty, and at times violent public spaces of Porto Alegre's streets.[1] As the man tacitly acknowledged the validity of Maria's assertion of some form of plebeian autonomy in the city, the tense situation dissolved.[2]

Maria's declaration came in the midst of a series of transitions that shook the foundations of social and political relations not only in Porto Alegre but throughout Brazil. Within five months, slavery was phased out across the nation; in little more than a year, the widely admired stability of the Empire that had ruled Brazil since Independence in 1822 ended with the emergence of the First Republic. These transformations affected the Porto Alegre area in particular ways. Slavery's demise had little visible impact on the economy of the Gaúcho capital. On the other hand, in these years the region experienced a shift in its dominant political culture, from a variation on the seigneurial Liberalism that had characterized the Empire to a Positivism of a sort that gained control nowhere else in the Republic. Like other cities in Brazil, though, Porto Alegre found its official political spaces occupied as never before by individuals from outside the established elite.[3]

Set against the backdrop of these dramatic developments, the words of Maria da Costa remind us of what did and did not change in the years 1845 to 1895. In a sense, the street on which she walked, and the autonomy she claimed there, represented continuities that stretched through the period. From the middle to the end of the nineteenth century, that is, plebeian men and women strove to claim some forms of individual sovereignty. As the partisan landscape shifted around them, the Marias and Joãos and Felicidades of the *povo* fought persistently to win for themselves aspects of the kind of independence that only elite men enjoyed in their society. For most, the dream was to open up some breach of autonomy in a system of interlocking and seemingly inescapable relations of dependence and clientelism. The repertoire of strategies with which plebeians pursued this goal, and the meanings they attached to it, evolved, as we might expect, in keeping with the replacement of seigneurial Liberal by Positivist Republican dominance.[4] Still, for most Portoalegrenses, the Republic, like the Empire before it, left them inhabiting realms and carrying out struggles defined as nonpolitical, as outside the nation proper. Like that of Maria da Costa in the waning months of the Empire, these plebeians' status under Republican rule remained substantially similar to what they had known under the old Liberal and Conservative Parties of the Empire.

Others, though, found that the border around official politics stretched and became more porous in the late 1880s and into the 1890s. For some segments, particularly skilled male workers and aspiring entrepreneurs, loftier

Freedmen working as vendors on the streets of Porto Alegre, c. 1892. From Ronaldo Marco Bastos, *Porto Alegre: Um século de fotografia*, 1997.

political aims now lay within reach. Coming together through novel, collective identities, these men found in the rearrangements of power during the decadent Empire and the nascent Republic an opportunity to assert their rightful place in the body politic. Some men, mostly white and organized into groups with "worker" or "productive-class" identities, managed to ascend out of the *povo* and into formal politics. This led to cases of obvious individual social gain, as men like João Steenhagen went from positions as worker-entrepreneurs to places in political parties and state assemblies. The phenomenon went beyond these particular individuals, however; previously excluded sectors were entering official politics. Even some of those who remained outside the formal political process, moreover, participated in the broadening of associative activity and political discourse in the city, adding new and challenging elements to the "public" developing by the 1890s.

Both practical facts and ideological visions made this expansion of participation in formal politics possible. As we have seen, both the PRR and its enemies came to rely on certain segments of the populace for support in the increasingly bitter partisan battles of the late Empire and early Republic. In Rio Grande do Sul, where the mighty Liberal Party machine had become ever closer to the imperial government in the late 1880s, the arrival of the Republic was a major blow. With the old rulers' legitimacy in doubt and the new rulers lacking widespread support, societies of "workers"—a term that was loosely applied at the time and requires analysis in any study of the period—were able to gain a foothold in formal politics. The Positivist orientation of the Castilhistas and of some anti-Castilhista dissident Republicans, moreover, provided theoretical justification for bringing a broader portion of the population into the official public realm. Unlike the earlier hegemonic versions of Liberalism, the Positivist Republicanism of the 1880 and 1890s did not rest on individualist seigneurial conceptions of society. PRR plans did not, that is, derive from an understanding of social relations as based fundamentally on the power of the private patron over his dependents. Positivist Republicans thus shared little if any of the Liberals' anxiety about state power overwhelming seigneurial power. Indeed, against the Liberals' individualist seigneurial ideal, the Positivist Republicans posited a "progressive conservative" vision based on their interpretation of Auguste Comte's sociology. Although they were not interested in eliminating paternalistic or clientelistic relations between elites and plebeians (as they noted repeatedly), these Positivists proclaimed the need for a general reeducation of Gaúchos—masters and dependents alike—and for careful, state-led mobilization of elements of the *povo*. As the PRR organ *A Federação* declared less than three weeks after the fall of the Empire, "Much more so in the republican than in the monarchical system it is necessary to develop in the bosom of society the noble sentiments of veneration and tolerance, the only ones that can . . . guarantee the peace and happiness of nations."[5] PRR leaders dreamed that through the retraining and restructuring they would receive, plebeians and their social superiors alike could be made into productive elements in the reformulation of society.

We should not, however, be too quick to interpret the broadening of political participation in the late Empire and early Republic as a sign of the democratization of at least a corner of Brazil. PRR projects, after all, foresaw an "incorporation of the proletariat" with strict supervision from above—what Georges Sorel might have referred to as a "pedantocracy."[6] Moreover, as Hilda Sabato has remarked of Latin America generally, "the incorporation of relatively large sectors of the population in politically significant forms of organization and action . . . did not lead to the consolidation of political equality, and social and racial gaps between the few and the many remained a persistent reality."[7] In other words, the rise of associative activity and the push of some near- and nonelites into positions of influence in formal politics did not, as it would be easy to assume, add up to the birth of democracy.

At the same time, though, these developments did change the rules of the political game, most notably those governing the definition of what constituted true political behavior and who was capable of carrying it out. In a sense, the transition from the Liberal-dominated Empire to the Positivist-ruled Republic in Rio Grande do Sul moved, if it certainly did not erase, the line between formal and informal relations of power—between high and low politics, as it were. In this manner, the events of the last decades of the nineteenth century partially transformed the system of domination in Gaúcho society. The character of the new age, with a greater share of the populace engaged in a more authoritarian regime, thus presents us with a particular image—namely, that of change within continuity.

The challenge for historians of political culture in nineteenth-century Porto Alegre and of Brazil more broadly, then, must be dual. First, we have to address the profound problem that historian Steve J. Stern defines as "reconciling an undeniable sense of continuity that seems to render historical motion irrelevant, with an understanding of the historical motion that itself generates cycles of apparent repetition or continuity while transforming their social meaning and consequences."[8] In other words, we must tease out the changes hidden in visible continuity, in order to comprehend both the complexity that goes into the reproduction of patterns and the shifts that images of continuity obfuscate. At the same time, to get at both sides of this project, we have to appreciate the depth of conflicts within and beyond the walls of institutional power—and to recognize that these walls, too, are mobile and political constructions. Only by listening to both the loud proclamations of Liberal and Positivist orators and the softer protestations of plebeians in their daily lives, that is, can we find measured changes, and not just impersonal momentum, in the politics of nineteenth-century Brazilian society.

Abbreviations Used in Notes and Bibliography

AHMPA	Arquivo Histórico Municipal de Porto Alegre
AHRS	Arquivo Histórico do Rio Grande do Sul
ALP	Assembléia Legislativa Provincial
AN	Arquivo Nacional
Anais	*Anais [Annaes] da Assembléia Legislativa Provincial*
APERS	Arquivo Público do Estado do Rio Grande do Sul
BN/SM	Biblioteca Nacional, Seção de Manuscritos
Câm. Mun.	Câmara Municipal (city council)
Cód.	Códice (codex)
Corr.	Correspondência (correspondence)
CRB	Casa de Rui Barbosa
Del.	Delegado
EIA	*Estudos Ibero-Americanos* (Porto Alegre)
FCRB	Fundação Casa Rui Barbosa
FEE	Fundação de Economia e Estatística
HAHR	*Hispanic American Historical Review*
Interr.	Interrogatório (interrogation)
JLAS	*Journal of Latin American Studies*
l.	lata
LARR	*Latin American Research Review*
LBR	*Luso-Brazilian Review*
Leg.	Legislação (legislation)
m.	maço
Pres.	President (of Rio Grande do Sul)
proc.	processo crime (criminal case)
PUCRS	Pontifícia Universidade Católica do Rio Grande do Sul
r.	réu (masculine) / ré (feminine) / réus (plural) (defendant)

Relatório	*Relatório* (or Falla) *do Presidente da Província*
req. / Reqs.	requerimento (petition) / Requerimentos
RS	Rio Grande do Sul
Subdel.	Subdelegado
UFRGS	Universidade Federal do Rio Grande do Sul
V. Pres.	Vice President (of Rio Grande do Sul)

Notes

Introduction

1. The terms *Gaúcho* and *Riograndense* refer to a person or thing from Rio Grande do Sul.

2. "A Crise," *A Federação*, 9 June 1891, 1; "Amor, Ordem e Progresso," *A Federação*, 3 Dec. 1889, 1.

3. Hale, "Political and Social Ideas," and *The Transformation of Liberalism*. Cf. also Leopoldo Zea, *El positivismo;* Woodward, *Positivism in Latin America;* and Harp, *Positivist Republic*.

4. Positivists had significant sway in national regimes in Rio de Janeiro, Mexico City, and elsewhere, but only in Porto Alegre did Positivists construct a state based on Comtean principles and then govern it, though on a regional scale. PRR rule did, of course, face continued opposition even after the party's victory in the Federalist Revolt. See esp. Love, *Rio Grande do Sul;* Chasteen, *Heroes on Horseback;* Félix, *Coronelismo, borgismo e cooptação política;* and Dacanal and Gonzaga, *RS: Economia e política*.

5. José Honório Rodrigues, *Conciliação e reforma*, 20.

6. On emancipatory politics, cf. Chakrabarty, *Rethinking Working-Class History*, 219–30.

7. See Holanda, *Raízes do Brasil;* Rodrigues, *Conciliação e reforma;* Vianna, *Instituições políticas brasileiras*, and *Populações meridionais;* Mercadante, *A consciência conservadora;* Schwarz, *Ao vencedor as batatas;* Richard Graham, *Patronage and Politics;* Carvalho, *Cidadania no Brasil;* and Emília Viotti da Costa, "Introdução ao estudo," and *The Brazilian Empire*. Recently, Jurandir Malerba has tried to locate the origins of elites' conciliatory practices in the process of independence; see Malerba, *A corte no exílio*, 299 and passim.

8. Mercadante, *A consciência conservadora*.

9. See esp. Love, *Rio Grande do Sul;* Chasteen, *Heroes on Horseback;* Félix, *Coronelismo, borgismo e cooptação política;* Pinto, *Positivismo;* Pesavento, *A burguesia gaúcha;* and Bak, "Class, Ethnicity, and Gender," and "Labor, Community, and the Making of a Cross-Class Alliance."

10. For one critique of the older chronological choices and an excellent example of what a history across abolition can produce, see Hebe Maria Mattos, *Das cores do silêncio*.

11. Abèlés, "Anthropologie politique," 17, cited in Gledhill, *Power and Its Disguises*, 20. For a similar point about Brazil specifically, see Trindade, "Brasil em perspectiva," 352.

12. Emília Viotti da Costa, *The Brazilian Empire*, 1–52, and "Introdução."

13. For overviews, see Barman, *Brazil;* and Bethell and Carvalho, "1822–1850." The literature on individual rebellions is vast; fine revisionist examples include Kraay, "'As Terrifying as Unexpected'"; and Assunção, "Elite Politics and Popular Rebellion."

14. Cited in Bosi, "A escravidão," 6.

15. The phrase comes from Schwarz, *Ao vencedor as batatas*, and *Misplaced Ideas.* For rebuttals of his thesis, see, e.g., Bosi, "A escravidão"; Ortiz, *Cultura brasileira*, 27–35; and Maria Sylvia de Carvalho Franco, "As idéias estão no lugar."

16. Ilmar Rohloff de Mattos, *O tempo Saquarema;* cf. Fragoso and Florentino, *O arcaísmo como projeto.*

17. Richard Graham argues that as much as 50.6 percent of the male population age twenty-one or over may have participated in elections in the early 1870s; see *Patronage and Politics*, esp. chap. 4. Also see Love, "Political Participation in Brazil"; and Carvalho, *Teatro de sombras*, 139–43.

18. Cited in Bosi, "A escravidão," 4. See also Morgan, *American Slavery*, for a powerful description of the deep political links between Liberalism and slavery in North America.

19. Quoted by Martinho de Campos in 1882 and cited in Emília Viotti da Costa, *The Brazilian Empire*, 71. For works that emphasize the lack of ideological difference among parties in this period, see also Richard Graham, *Patronage and Politics;* Rodrigues, *Conciliação e reforma*; Mercadante, *A consciência conservadora*; and Emília Viotti da Costa, "Introdução ao estudo." Judy Bieber, by contrast, has argued that Liberal discourse became part of the definition of honorable identities for groups and identities in Minas Gerais; see Bieber, *Power, Patronage, and Political Violence*, and "A Visão do Sertão."

20. See Richard Graham, *Patronage and Politics*, esp. 16–33; cf. Alonso, *Idéias em movimento*, 61–64.

21. Chalhoub, *Machado de Assis*, 60–61.

22. Exceptions include protests against forced military conscription and the imposition of the metric system. See, e.g., Beattie, *Tribute of Blood;* Meznar, "The Ranks of the Poor"; Barman, "The Brazilian Peasantry."

23. On the 1868 crisis, see esp. Barman, *Citizen Emperor*, 217–25; Nabuco, *Um estadista do Império*, 1: 737–69.

24. On the regional nature and steps toward abolition, see esp. Emília Viotti da Costa, *Da senzala;* Conrad, *The Destruction;* and Toplin, *The Abolition of Slavery.* On the flight of slaves in São Paulo, see esp. Maria Helena P. T. Machado, *O plano e o pânico.* For an important revisionist take on the role of the Paulista planters, see Weinstein, "The Decline of the Progressive Planter."

25. Skidmore, *Black into White*, chap. 1; Kirkendall, *Class Mates;* João Cruz Costa, *O positivismo.*

26. Comte, *The Essential Comte;* Pickering, *Auguste Comte.* Cf. Hale, *The Transformation*, 29–31; and Harp, *Positivist Republic*, 10–21.

27. Sandra Lauderdale Graham, "The Vintem Riot"; Hahner, *Poverty and Politics*, chaps. 2–3; Nachman, "Positivism, Modernization."

28. For the argument that plebeian contributions made abolition a *revolutionary* moment, see Andrews, *Blacks and Whites*, 32–53.

29. Lessa, *A invenção republicana*, 46.

30. See esp. Carvalho, *Os bestializados*, and *A formação das almas;* Penna, *O progresso da ordem;* and Hahner, *Civilian-Military Relations.*

31. The regional literatures are too large to cite, but see a similar appeal in Bieber, *Power, Patronage, and Political Violence*, 6.

32. Gledhill, *Power and Its Disguises*, 12 (emphasis in original).

33. See Gramsci, *Selections from the Prison Notebooks*, 323–43 and passim.

34. This approach must take us beyond simply expanding the definition of what is political in a society, as called for by, e.g., Wood, "The Place of Custom."

35. See Anderson, *Imagined Communities*, chap. 4. On how Liberal and "Western" narratives of national histories exclude what they define as the "nonrational," see Chakrabakrty, *Provincializing Europe;* and Mehta, "Liberal Strategies." Specifically on the U.S. case, see Appleby, Hunt, and Jacob, *Telling the Truth*, 96.

36. Alonso, *Idéias em movimento*, 63.

37. Paz, *The Labyrinth of Solitude*, 22.

38. Carlos A. M. Lima, "Em certa corporação," 33; see also Chalhoub, *Visões da liberdade*, 253 and passim. On the range of logics that can inform popular culture and the negotiations contained within it, see, e.g., de la Peña, "La cultura política," 83–107; Martin, *Governance and Society;* Chambers, *From Subjects to Citizens;* and Mallon, *Peasant and Nation.*

39. Cited in Agambem, *Homo Sacer*, 11. Schmitt's notion of sovereignty fits well with anthropologist Roberto da Matta's distinction between individuals and citizens in modern Brazil; for da Matta, the ideal for Brazilians is not to be a citizen, bound by rules and regulations of the law, but to be an individual with the clout to rise above such restrictions. See, e.g., da Matta's classic essay "Você sabe com quem está falando? Um ensaio sobre a distinção entre indivíduo e pessoa no Brasil," in his *Carnavais, malandros e heróis*, 139–93.

40. Cited in Malerba, *Os brancos da lei*, 45.

41. Eduardo Silva, *As queixas*. 35.

42. See, e.g., Mallon, *Peasant and Nation;* Chambers, *From Subjects to Citizens;* Guardino, *Peasants, Politics, and the Formation;* Thurner, *From Two Republics;* Walker, *Cuzco and the Creation.* Also see the sweeping comparative work on the incorporation of working sectors in Latin America by Collier and Collier, *Shaping the Political Arena.*

43. Holanda, *Raízes do Brasil*, 182.

Chapter 1. "Our Compatriots Are Vagrants"

1. Rodrigues, *Conciliação*, 55, 64–66. Cf. Ilmar Rohloff de Mattos, *O tempo saquarema*, 110–11; and Barman, *Brazil*, 184–86.

2. Cód. II-32, 3, 4, BN/SM.

3. RS, Pres., *Relatório* (1846), 3–5.

4. ALP, 19 Oct. 1857, in *Correio do Sul,* 21 Oct. 1857, 2.

5. *O Mercantil,* 3 Aug. 1853, 1–3; "Os Presidentes de Provincia," *O Mercantil,* 4 Oct. 1851, 1; Piccolo, "Porto Alegre em 1873," 221–33, 226; Newton Luis Garcia Carneiro, *A identidade inacabada,* esp. 123–40.

6. On the emperor as the ultimate patron, see Richard Graham, *Patronage and Politics,* 40, 56–57, and "1850–1870," 160.

7. RS, Pres., *Relatório* (1846), 6.

8. ALP, 8 Nov. 1851, in *Correio de Porto Alegre,* 9 Nov. 1851, 1.

9. Alonso, *Idéias em movimento,* 63.

10. Kowarick, *Trabalho e vadiagem,* 115 and passim; Laura de Mello e Souza, *Desclassificados do ouro;* Pesavento, *Emergência.* For one especially clear example from Porto Alegre, see "Instrucção popular," *A Reforma,* 14 Nov. 1875, 2.

11. On the growth of such institutions in Porto Alegre, see Spalding, *Pequena história;* Macedo, *Porto Alegre;* and Moreira, "Entre o deboche."

12. The creation of a Beggars' Asylum in Porto Alegre was in fact a lengthy process. After discussions of the matter in 1857, asylum projects were relegated to the world of private charity reform. Under the guidance of the redoubtable Padre Cacique de Barros, a priest who ran several charitable institutions in the second half of the nineteenth century, construction began only in 1881. During the 1880s and 1890s, the project received some verbal support from local politicians but only limited government subsidies (though the original land had been granted by Emperor Dom Pedro II). After a series of delays, the Asylum was inaugurated officially in 1898. See "Asilo de mendigos," *A Federação,* 2 Jan. 1886, 1; "Asilo de Mendicidade," *A Federação,* 10 Jan. 1888, 1; "Asilo de mendigos em Pelotas," *A Federação,* 11 Jan. 1888, 1–2; and Macedo, *Os menores abandonados.* Two years earlier, politicians in Bahia had debated similar questions of public charity toward beggars; see Fraga Filho, *Mendigos,* 138–39.

13. "Assembléa provincial," *Correio do Sul,* 1 Nov. 1857, 3.

14. Langendonck, *Uma colônia,* 29. Saint-Hilaire had described the city similarly in 1820; see *Viagem ao Rio Grande do Sul,* 84.

15. Bauss, "Rio Grande do Sul"; Bell, "Early Industrialization," 403; Corcino Medeiros dos Santos, *Economia e sociedade do Rio Grande do Sul;* Alden, *Royal Government,* 59–275; Fernando Henrique Cardoso, "Rio Grande do Sul and Santa Catarina," 473–505.

16. Fernando Henrique Cardoso, *Capitalismo e escravidão,* 45, and "Rio Grande do Sul e Santa Catarina," 485–87.

17. Furtado, *The Economic Growth of Brazil,* 84–85.

18. Alden, "Late Colonial Brazil," 310–31; Magalhães, "Almanak," 71–72; Pedro Cezar Dutra Fonseca, *RS: Economia e conflitos políticos,* 13–14; Leitman, "O primeiro ciclo brasileiro"; Brown, "The Impact of American Flour Imports."

19. Chaves, *Memórias econômo-políticas,* 134–40; Schwartz, *Sugar Plantations,* 139.

20. On the rise of *charque,* see Fernando Henrique Cardoso, *Capitalismo e escravidão,* and "Rio Grande do Sul and Santa Catarina"; Bell, "Early Industrialization," and *Campanha Gaúcha;* and Bauss, "Rio Grande do Sul."

21. Bell, "Early Industrialization," and *Campanha Gaúcha,* 79 and passim.

22. RS, Pres., *Relatório* (1854), 52.

23. The debate over the nature of the Farroupilha—whether it was a separatist and republican revolution or merely an armed call for federalist reform within the Empire—has been long and heated, although at times less than instructive. Gutfreind, *A historiografia rio-grandense*, traces the development of the debate in detail; Padoin, *Federalismo gaúcho*, provides the most recent, lucid analysis of the various federalisms in the region around the time of the Farroupilha.

24. The following section draws primarily on Singer, *Desenvolvimento econômico*, 141–98. On the economy of the German colonies near Porto Alegre, see esp. Amado, *Conflito social*, 27–140; and Roche, *A colonização alemã.*

25. The lack of good roads gave added significance to river transportation; see Mulhall, *Rio Grande do Sul*, 32.

26. RS, Pres., *Relatório* (1853), 20.

27. Sérgio da Costa Franco, *Porto Alegre e seu comércio*, 30–31.

28. "A Crise da Provincia em Relação à Agricultura," *O Mercantil*, 5 May 1863, 2.

29. On trade by canoe and small boats, see proc. 828, r. Justino et al., m. 28, APERS; proc. 832, r. Antonio Luiz et al., m. 28, APERS; proc. 847, r. Simão Fructuozo, m. 29, APERS.

30. "Quadro das informações pedidas pela presidencia da provincia em portaria de 29-09-1864 para da execução ao aviso circular do ministéio dos negócios da Agricultura, Commercio e Obras Públicas, de 30-08 do mesmo anno," Corr. of Câm. Mun., Porto Alegre, m. 142, l. 135, AHRS.

31. Sérgio da Costa Franco, *Porto Alegre e seu comércio*, 55–57; Mulhall, *Rio Grande do Sul*, 5–7; *Catalogo da Exposição da Provincia . . . 1875*; *Catálogo da Exposição Brasileira-Alemã . . . Secção Brasileira.*

32. Avé-Lallemant, *Viagem pela província*, 377.

33. Célia Ferraz de Souza and Müller, *Porto Alegre*, 57–73, Sérgio da Costa Franco, *Porto Alegre e seu comércio*, 38–40; Dreys, *Notíticia descritiva*, 67–68; Isabelle, *Viagem ao Rio Grande do Sul*, 57; Sérgio da Costa Franco, *Porto Alegre: Guia histórico.*

34. *Synopse do recenseamento . . . 1890*, 103.

35. See, e.g., req. of João Birck, 13 Jan. 1852, Reqs., Colonização, m. 91, AHRS; Gans, *Presença teuta*, 21–93.

36. Mulhall, *Rio Grande do Sul*, 52.

37. This image gained popularity in the twentieth century and included a "whitewashing" of the region's mythic past, in which the racial characteristics of the Gaúcho changed, so that indigenous and African traits diminished or disappeared. On the evolution of this figure, see Meyer, *A prosa dos pagos*, 9–42.

38. *Recenseamento da população . . . 1872*, 17: 2. Hebe Maria Mattos argues that during the nineteenth century the term *pardo* was reserved for nonslaves; see Hebe Maria Mattos, *Das cores do silêncio*, 34–35. Other racial terms were also current in Porto Alegre during this period, including *mulato* (Afro-Brazilian, usually "darker" than a *pardo*), *crioulo* (Brazilian-born black), and *cabra* (literally, "goat"; a pejorative term for someone of mixed race).

39. Gans, *Presença teuta*, chap. 2.

40. Zanetti, "Calabouço urbano," 33–51.

41. *Recenseamento . . . 1872,* 17: 3, 6, 9, 12, 15, 18, 21; cf. Hünefeldt, *Paying the Price,* 1–2.

42. Hörmeyer, *O Rio Grande do Sul de 1850,* 99.

43. "Quadro das informações pedidas pela presidencia da provincia em portaria de 29-09-1864 para da execução ao aviso circular do ministéio dos negócios da Agricultura, Commercio e Obras Públicas, de 30-08 do mesmo anno," Corr. of Câm. Mun., Porto Alegre, m. 142, l. 135, AHRS.

44. Porto Alegre had *charqueadas,* but their number and volume of production were always miniscule relative to those of Pelotas. See "Mappa demonstrativo das charqueadas existentes na differentes freguesias do municipio da cidade de Porto Alegre, com declaração de seus proprietários e do numero de rezes, que se matarão nos 2 ultimos annos de 1854 e 1856," 27 Mar. 1856, Corr. of Câm. Mun., Porto Alegre, m. 138, l. 134, AHRS.

45. Holloway, "'A Healthy Terror,'" 674.

46. Richard Graham, *Patronage and Politics,* 33.

47. "Brades da opinião," *A Voz do Povo,* 1 Dec. 1852, 1; Piccolo, *Vida política,* 50–54, and "A política rio-grandense," 101–4; *O Mercantil,* 30 June 1863; "A política das ideias," *Propaganda,* 17 Jan. 1864, 1.

48. See esp. Newton Luis Garcia Carneiro, *A identidade,* 141–224; and Antunes, "Os partidos políticos," 2: 235–41.

49. ALP, 29 Oct. 1857, in *Correio do Sul,* 2 Nov. 1857, 1–2, and 3 Nov. 1857, 1–3. On the importance of the figure of the beggar, particularly the able-bodied beggar, in other societies characterized by a paternalist or seigneurial ethos, cf. Jütte, *Poverty and Deviance;* and Stanley, "Beggars Can't Be Choosers." On other regions of Brazil, see Holloway, *Policing Rio de Janeiro,* 131–34; and Fraga Filho, *Mendigos.*

50. ALP, 30 Oct. 1857, in *Correio do Sul,* 4 Nov. 1857, 1–2.

51. Ubatuba, ALP, 31 Oct. 1857, in *Correio do Sul,* 6 Nov. 1857, 1.

52. Caldre e Fião, ALP, 29 Oct. 1857, in *Correio do Sul,* 3 Nov. 1857, 1.

53. ALP, 31 Oct. 1857, in *Correio do Sul,* 8 Nov. 1857, 2; cf. ALP, 31 Oct. 1857, in *Correio do Sul,* 8 Nov. 1857, 1.

54. ALP, 31 Oct. 1857, in *Correio do Sul,* 6 Nov. 1857, 2.

55. Chaves, *Memórias,* 53–77.

56. Chaves, *Memórias,* 60, 61.

57. Chaves, *Memórias,* 62, 66–67.

58. Chaves, *Memórias,* 72–73. On the "whitening" thesis, see esp. Skidmore, *Black into White.*

59. Cf. Piccolo, "O discurso abolicionista no Rio Grande do Sul." Piccolo also mentions the more extreme antislavery position of Alexandre Luís, who tried to declare abolition and a republic in Rio Grande do Sul on three separate occasions between 1803 and 1831. A measure of his radical nature lay in his willingness to arm slaves to fight for their freedom. Cf. Laytano, *História da República,* 212–13.

60. On the diplomatic pressures the British imposed and on Brazilian elites' dis-

cussions of the matter, see esp. Bethell, *The Abolition;* Conrad, *The Destruction,* 20–29; and Emília Viotti da Costa, *Da senzala,* 70–85.

61. Curtin, *The Atlantic Slave Trade,* 29, cited in Conrad, *The Destruction,* 24.

62. Qtd. in Ilmar Rohloff de Mattos, *O tempo Saquarema,* 35.

63. In Slenes's estimation, Rio Grande do Sul and the rest of the South (Santa Catarina and Paraná) lost some 12,100 slaves through the interprovincial trade in the period 1851–72; see "The Demography and Economics," 140–41.

64. ALP, 31 Oct. 1857, in *Correio do Sul,* 8 Nov. 1857, 2.

65. ALP, 25 Nov. 1851, in *Correio de Porto Alegre,* 27 Nov. 1851, 1.

66. ALP, 13 Oct. 1852, in *O Mercantil,* 14 Oct. 1852, 1–3, and 15 Oct. 1852, 1. Ubatuba further declared, "I have not seen a single citizen who, however great a lover of the country he may be, has attempted to rid himself of his slaves out of humanitarian sentiments or to agree with the thought of the century; no one seeks to quit himself of a thing that he needs merely to march in conformity with certain ideas." See ALP, 13 Oct. 1852, in *O Mercantil,* 14 Oct. 1852, 3.

67. "Agricultura," *O Mercantil,* 28 Dec. 1853, 3.

68. ALP, 13 Oct. 1852, in *O Mercantil,* 14 Oct. 1852, 2.

69. ALP, 19 June 1848, in *O Commercio,* 26 June 1848, 3–5.

70. Lei n. 183, 18 Oct. 1850, Leis Provincias, RS, AN; cf. RS, Pres., *Relatório* (1852), 4. Similar prohibitions were often included in projects to set up colonies of national workers; for one such ban, see Projeto de Lei n. 20, ALP, 20 Oct. 1854, in *Tribuna Rio-Grandense,* 27 Oct. 1854, 1.

71. ALP, 25 Nov. 1851, in *O Correio de Porto Alegre,* 27 Nov. 1851, 1.

72. *A Reforma,* 16 June 1869, 2. The Provincial Assembly had previously debated and adopted specific regulations on slavery; those measures did not, however, have as their principal aim the gradual abolition of slavery itself. See, e.g., the rules on the use of slave workers in shipping: ALP, 7 Oct. 1852, in *O Mercantil,* 8 Oct. 1852, 1; ALP, 13 Oct. 1852, in *O Mercantil,* 14 Oct. 1852, 1–3; ALP, 18 Oct. 1847, in *O Commercio,* 28 Oct. 1847, 3. For a translation of the text of the Rio Branco Law, see Conrad, *The Destruction,* 305–9.

73. Caldre e Fião, "A Libertação das Crianças," *Revista do Parthenon . . . 1869* 1, no. 7 (Sept. 1869): 227–28; "Elemento servil," *A Reforma,* 7 Dec. 1871, 1.

74. "Manumissão," *A Reforma,* 29 Oct. 1869. Cf. "Emancipação," *A Reforma,* 7 Sept. 1870, 1; "Asylo de liberdade," *A Reforma,* 6 Dec. 1871, 1; and *Revista do Parthenon . . . 1869* 1, no. 6 (Aug. 1869): 200–201, and 1, no. 7 (Sept. 1869): 227–28.

75. "Luzo Brasileira," *A Reforma,* 3 Aug. 1875, 2.

76. "A escravatura. Fabio a Salustio," *Revista do Parthenon . . . 1872* 2, no. 1 (July 1872): 24; *Revista do Parthenon . . . 1869* 1, no. 9 (Nov. 1869): 2.

77. Caldre e Fião, "O escravo brasileiro," *Revista do Parthenon . . . 1869* 1, no. 5 (July 1869): 162. On Caldre e Fião's early anti-slave-trade activities, see Porto Alegre, *Homens illustres,* 44–46; and Cesar, "O Negro e a Colonização Rio-Grandense." On the participation of ex-slaves in the Paraguayan War, see esp. Kraay, "'The Shelter of the Uniform.'"

78. Cf. Achylles Porto Alegre, "O escravo fugitivo," *Revista do Parthenon . . . 1869* 1, no. 8 (Oct. 1869): 263; Schwarcz, *Retrato em branco e negro*, 163–221.

79. According to the Rio Branco Law, the freeborn children of slaves (*ingênuos*) were to remain in the service of their mothers' *senhores* until the children reached the age of twenty-one; as an alternative, *senhores* could receive financial compensation for releasing the children at the age of eight. See Conrad, *The Destruction*, 305.

80. "A escravatura. Fabio a Salustio," *Revista do Parthenon . . . 1872* 2, no. 2 (Aug. 1872): 55–56, and 2, no. 3 (Sept. 1872): 98–99.

81. "Asylo de liberdade," *A Reforma*, 6 Dec. 1871, 1.

82. RS, Pres., *Relatório* (1858), 39.

83. RS, Pres., *Relatório* (1864), 61.

84. RS, Pres., *Relatório* (1867), 3; Corr. of Câm. Mun., Porto Alegre, m. 143, l. 136, AHRS.

85. "A nova administração," *O Mercantil*, 5 May 1864, 1.

86. RS, Pres., *Relatório* (1853), rpt. in *O Mercantil*, 11 Oct. 1853 3; RS, Pres., *Relatório* (1854), 5.

87. Pesavento, *Emergência*, 39–40. Cf. Moreira, "Entre o deboche"; Gebara, *O mercado de trabalho livre;* and Lamounier, *Da escravidão*.

88. ALP, 30 Oct. 1857, in *Correio do Sul*, 6 Nov. 1857, 2.

89. RS, Pres., *Relatório* (1847), 12. For a very similar expression, see ALP, 20 Oct. 1854, in *Tribuna Rio-Grandense*, 28 Oct. 1854, 1–4.

90. ALP, 20 Oct. 1847, in *O Commercio*, 30 Oct. 1847, 3. See also President Cansansão de Sinimbú's judgment that "the care of the education of the people is the first duty of an enlightened Assembly": RS, Pres., *Relatório* (1854), 21. Also see RS, Pres., *Relatório* (1846), 10; ALP, 27 Oct. 1854, in *Tribuna Rio-Grandense*, 10 Nov. 1854, 1; ALP, 22 Oct. 1854, in *Correio do Sul*, 25 Oct. 1857, 1; "Instrucção publica," *A Reforma*, 4 Sept. 1870, 1; Comissão de Orçamento e Fazenda Provincial, *Anais*, 25 May 1880, 43.

91. ALP, 27 Oct. 1854, in *Tribuna Rio-Grandense*, 10 Nov. 1854, 1; "Instrucção publica," *A Reforma*, 4 Sept. 1870, 1. See also the 1877 speech by Representative Prestes Guimarães, *Anais* 1877, anexo, 1 May 1877, 132; Isabelle, *Viagem ao Rio Grande do Sul*, 62; RS, Pres., *Relatório* (1859), 23; "Instrucção popular," *A Reforma*, 14 Nov. 1875, 1–2.

92. Félix da Cunha demonstrated such a recognition when he objected that the Asylum would be constructed "with the heavy and assiduous labors that might destroy the effects of education and all the vices that generated it with laziness." See ALP, 29 Oct. 1857, in *Correio do Sul*, 3 Nov. 1857, 1.

93. RS, Pres., *Relatório* (1849), 2; ALP, 8 Nov. 1851, in *O Correio de Porto Alegre*, 9 Nov. 1851, 1; RS, Pres., *Relatório* (1846), 6; RS, Pres., *Relatório* (1861), 1: 3.

94. RS, Pres., *Relatório* (1855), 5. Cf. RS, Pres., *Relatório* (1862), 5. See also Oliveira Bello's earlier expressed opinion that "authority without force . . . is a body without spirit": RS, Pres., *Relatório* (1852), 8.

95. RS, Pres., *Relatório* (1862), 5; RS, Pres., *Relatório* (1851), 4. Even for Oliveira Bello, what made repression so indispensable was the lack of a proper education among the *povo;* see RS, Pres., *Relatório* (1855), 5–6.

96. Moreira, "Entre o deboche." Cf. Weber, "Códigos de posturas"; Giuliano, *Esboço histórico;* and Mauch, *Ordem pública e moralidade.*

97. Moreira, "Entre o deboche," 20. Similar legislation appeared in 1841, 1882, and 1888.

98. Moreira shows, e.g., that the funds set aside for the police in provincial budgets increased some 65 percent between 1868 and 1879 but then remained virtually stable until 1888. Partly because of the lack of funding, police institutions throughout the province remained in a "precarious" state that often drew sharp criticism from provincial leaders. Moreira, "Entre o deboche," 18–20.

99. See, e.g., "Regulamento do Corpo Policial," 31 Dec. 1869, Cód. Leg. 584, AHRS, Artigo 1, título 2, § 3, and artigos 111–64; cf. *O Mercantil,* 14 Aug. 1883, cited in Moreira, "Entre o deboche," 77.

100. As we will see in chap. 3, moreover, conflicts involving plebeians also demonstrated the popular classes' unwillingness to give way before the new projects of vigilance in their city. In their range of forms of resistance, they acted to preserve their own "other Porto Alegre," frustrating the main thrust of the second aim of the police reforms—more effective control over the existing *povo* itself.

101. Epaminondas de Arruda, *Anais,* 29 Apr. 1874, 41.

102. Holloway, "'A Healthy Terror,'" 650.

103. "Curso nocturno," *A Reforma,* 7 Aug. 1875, 1. Cf. "Aulas nocturnas," *A Reforma,* 17 Sept. 1875, 1; and RS, Pres., *Relatório* (1867), 20.

104. Câm. Mun. to Pres., 29 Mar. 1869, Corr. of Câm. Mun., Porto Alegre, m. 144, l. 136, AHRS; "Instrucção publica," *A Reforma,* 4 Sept. 1870, 1; "Instrucção popular," *A Reforma,* 14 Nov. 1875, 1–2; "Artes e officios, artes industriaes, e artes mechanicas," *A Reforma,* 19 June 1869, 2.

105. ALP, 21 Oct. 1854, in *Tribuna Rio-Grandense,* 31 Oct. 1854, 1–4.

106. Additamento to RS, Pres., *Relatório* (1848), 19; Projeto de lei n. 20, ALP, 20 Oct. 1854, in *Tribuna Rio-Grandense,* 27 Oct. 1854, 1. Cf. RS, Pres., *Relatório* (1847), 57–58.

107. RS, Pres., *Relatório* (1853), 30; RS, Pres., *Relatório* (1847), 11, 33–34. Cf. "Instituto de artifices," *Jornal do Commercio,* 1 Jan. 1882, 1.

108. "Regulamento de 25 de Fevereiro de 1848, determinando como se devem admittir e ser tratados os aprendizes menores do Arsenal de Guerra da Classe Provincial," Leg., 6.10, Rio Grande do Sul, cód. 568, 42–45, AHRS. See also lei n. 12, 19 Dec. 1837, Leg., 6.10, Rio Grande do Sul, cód. 570, 27–28, AHRS.

109. RS, Pres., *Relatório* (1867), 23.

110. RS, Pres., *Relatório* (1857), 53.

111. "Regulamento para o asylo das orfãs desvalidas e expostas da Santa Casa de Misericordia desta capital, com a invocação de Santa Leopoldina," RS, Pres., *Relatório* (1857), anexo 2, 3.

112. "Termo de declarações, Madre Directora do Asilo de Santa Leopoldina Maria Barbara da Trindade," 27 Apr. 1858, Polícia, Inquéritos, m. 2, AHRS.

113. Antonio de Azevedo Lima, *Synopse geographica,* 82–86.

114. Andrews, *Blacks and Whites,* esp. 50–51, 55–56.

Chapter 2. The Immigrant Solution and Its Problems, 1846–1880

1. [José Cândido Gomes], *Chronica*, 44.

2. Across Brazil, elites continued to dream of attracting European settlers even in regions where immigration schemes proved a dismal failure; see, e.g., Eisenberg, *The Sugar Industry*, 199–219.

3. Fernando Henrique Cardoso, *Capitalismo e escravidão*, 199.

4. Emília Viotti da Costa, *The Brazilian Empire*, 96–99.

5. The distinction is a fairly common one but appears in particularly rigorous form in Lando and Barros, "Capitalismo e colonização."

6. Cited in Beiguelman, *A formação do povo*, 57.

7. On early immigration schemes in the coffee region, see Emília Viotti da Costa, *The Brazilian Empire*, 94–124, and *Da senzala*, 99–152; Dean, *Rio Claro*, 88–123; Beiguelman, *A formação do povo*, 57–99; and Stein, *Vassouras*, 59–62. Holloway, *Immigrants on the Land*, analyzes the second wave of immigration in São Paulo and the evolving social relations of production in the coffee sector.

8. Lando and Barros, "Capitalismo e colonização," 21–22, and *A colonização alemã*, 22. On the strategic role of the region, see esp. Alden, *Royal Government*.

9. RS, Pres., *Relatório* (1854), 25.

10. RS, Pres., *Relatório* (1855), 23; cf. RS, Pres., *Relatório* (1856), 91.

11. Useful starting points for the study of German immigration include Amado, *Conflito social no Brasil;* Porto, *O trabalho alemão;* and Nogueira and Hutter, *A colonização.* On the Italians who became predominant in the mid-1870s, see Thales de Azevedo, *Italianos e gaúchos;* and Manfroi, *A colonização italiana.*

12. ALP, 25 Nov. 1851, in *O Correio de Porto Alegre*, 27 Nov. 1851, 1. Antônio Gonçalves Chaves added in 1847 that the inhabitants of the province "rarely take to the agricultural life," preferring ranching instead. See ALP, 6 Nov. 1847, in *O Commercio*, [31 Nov.] 1847, 1–2.

13. ALP, 26 Nov. 1852, in *O Mercantil*, 6–7 Dec. 1852, 1. A particularly clear link between the end of slavery and the introduction of *colonos* emerged in legislation to apply to immigration subsidies the revenues from a tax on the sale of slaves out of Rio Grande do Sul; see ALP, 13 Oct. 1852, in *O Mercantil*, 14 Oct. 1852, 1–3. It was, moreover, the desire to ensure that colonization would move the province away from the flaws of the slavery-based system that caused political leaders to try to keep slavery from entering the *colônias.* Despite occasional assertions to the contrary (*Relatório* [1852], 10), such legislation failed to prevent *colonos* from purchasing slaves and putting them to work on their properties. On the legislation, see lei n. 183, 18 Oct. 1850, Leis Provinciais, AN. On slaves in São Leopoldo, see, e.g., the ironic remarks in Alcides Lima, *História popular*, 98.

14. "A crise da provincia em relação à agricultura," *O Mercantil*, 5 May 1863, 3.

15. RS, Pres., *Relatório* (1856), 89.

16. RS, Pres., *Relatório* (1854), 25. Cf. ALP, 6 Nov. 1847, in *O Commercio*, 2 Dec. 1847, 1, and 31 Nov. 1847, 1–2.

17. See, e.g., RS, Pres., *Relatório* (1859), 75.

18. "Agricultura," *O Mercantil*, 28 Dec. 1853, 3. Ubatuba offered a very similar statement; ALP, 25 Nov. 1852, in *O Mercantil*, 27 Nov. 1852, 1; RS, Pres., *Relatório* (1859), 75.

19. ALP, 25 Nov. 1851, in *O Correio de Porto Alegre*, 27 Nov. 1851, 1.

20. RS, Pres., *Relatório* (1850), 23. Cf. ALP, 6 Nov. 1847, in *O Commercio*, [31 Nov. 1847], 1; and RS, Pres., *Relatório* (1861), 21.

21. ALP, 10 Nov. 1857, in *Correio do Sul*, 21 Nov. 1857, 1–2.

22. On Gaúcho officials' neglect of São Leopoldo in this period, see esp. Roche, *A colonização alemã*, 705 and passim; and Porto, *O trabalho alemão*, 142–57. In 1846, the colony of São Leopoldo was elevated to the status of *município* (municipality) and the urban center of the colony to that of *vila* (town).

23. On the rise of artisanal production and manufacturing, cf. Amado, *Conflito social*, 27–104, which provides the most sophisticated analysis of the growing economic complexity of the colony and the social effects of that development. See also Roche, *A colonização alemã*, 479–502; Singer, *Desenvolvimento econômico e evolução urbana*, 157–68; and Moure, "A inserção da economia imigrante."

24. ALP, 6 Nov. 1847, in *O Commercio*, [31 Nov.] 1847, 1.

25. ALP, 31 Oct. 1857, in *Correio do Sul*, 6 Nov. 1857, 1–2; RS, Pres., *Relatório* (1852), 12–13.

26. "Chronica de Porto Alegre," *O Mercantil*, 5–6 Oct. 1851, 3.

27. ALP, 26 Nov. 1852, in *O Mercantil*, 6–7 Dec. 1852, 1; Flores, in the Chamber of Deputies, 27 July 1875, rpt. in *A Reforma*, 3 Sept. 1875, 1–2. Cf. RS, Pres., *Relatório* (1852), 10–11.

28. ALP, 20 Oct. 1854, in *Tribuna Rio-Grandense*, 28 Oct. 1854, 1.

29. RS, Pres., *Relatório* (1847), 12.

30. "O Sr. Ministro da Agricultura e Lavoura," *A Reforma*, 31 Oct. 1869, 1. On projects to bring in Chinese contract workers during the last decades of slavery in Brazil, see Conrad, *The Destruction*, 33–34, 133. On elites' racial responses to these projects, cf. Célia Maria Marinho de Azevedo, *Onda negra*, 147–52.

31. "O Sr. Ministro da Agricultura e Lavoura," *A Reforma*, 31 Oct. 1869, 1.

32. Gaúcho elites associated the intelligence, industriousness, orderliness, and morality of Europeans with their race. On the evolution of forms of racism in Brazil, see esp. Skidmore, "Racial Ideas and Social Policy in Brazil," 7–36; and, specifically with regard to abolition and immigration in the Center-South, Célia Maria Marinho de Azevedo, *Onda negra*, 139–52.

33. "O Sr. Ministro da Agricultura e Lavoura," *A Reforma*, 31 Oct. 1869, 1.

34. Such calls appeared at times in the most powerful *fazenda* region—the coffee Center-South—during the last decades of slavery in Brazil; see Emília Viotti da Costa, *The Brazilian Empire*, 96–99. For a particularly strong example of these projects, see Rebouças, *Agricultura nacional*.

35. Amado, *Conflito social*, 51–52; Roche, *A colonização alemã*, 705–7; Lando and Barros, "Capitalismo e colonização," 29.

36. Roche, *A colonização alemã*, 706.

37. On the citizenship question in the twentieth century, see Gertz, "A construção de uma nova cidadania"; and Rambo, "Nacionalidade e cidadania."

38. Elites recognized the impossibility of attracting Europeans to work in the *charqueadas* in particular; see *Anais. Segunda sessão*, 25 May 1880, 43–46.

39. Cf. Porto, *O trabalho alemão*, 146 and passim; Amado, *Conflito social*, 51–52; Roche, *A colonização alemã*, 705–12.

40. ALP, 25 Oct. 1852, in *O Mercantil*, 27 Oct. 1852, 2.

41. *Anais. Primeira sessão*, 10 Nov. 1887, 41. On Koseritz's political evolution, see José Fernando Carneiro, *Karl von Koseritz;* and Oberacker, *Carlos von Koseritz*.

42. Roche, *A colonização alemã*, 101. On the effects of the Land Law, see esp. Emília Viotti da Costa, *The Brazilian Empire*, 78–93; Carvalho, *Teatro de sombras*, chap. 3; and Diacon, *Millenarian Vision*, 61–62.

43. ALP, 20 Oct. 1854, in *Tribuna Rio-Grandense*, 28 Oct. 1854, 1–4.

44. ALP, 27 Nov. 1852, in *O Mercantil*, 6–7 Dec. 1852, 2–3. For similar projects, particularly those using the United States as a model, cf. ALP, 25 Nov. 1851, in *O Correio de Porto Alegre*, 27 Nov. 1851, 1; RS, Pres., *Relatório* (1850), 23–25; and ALP, in *O Commercio*, 27 Nov. 1847, 1–4.

45. ALP, 26 Nov. 1852, in *O Mercantil*, 2 Dec. 1852, 1–2; ALP, 27 Nov. 1852, in *O Mercantil*, 6–7 Dec. 1852, 2–3.

46. "Importação de colonos," *O Mercantil*, 24 Nov. 1852, suplemento, 1.

47. ALP, 6 Nov. 1847, in *O Commercio*, 2 Dec. 1847, 1. Cf. RS, Pres., *Relatório* (1861), 21; Mariante's arguments in ALP, 25 Nov. 1851, in *O Correio de Porto Alegre*, 27 Nov. 1851, 2; and the speech by Flores in the Chamber of Deputies, rpt. in *A Reforma*, 3 Sept. 1875, 2.

48. Roche, *A colonização alemã*, 114–16. Thales de Azevedo, *Italianos e gaúchos*, 36–37, also stresses the tight financial straits through which the provincial government was passing in the early 1870s.

49. ALP, 13 Oct. 1852, in *O Mercantil*, 14 Oct. 1852, 3.

50. ALP, 10 Nov. 1857, in *O Mercantil*, 21 Nov. 1857, 1–2. Cf. the similar quotations from Fioravanti in Roche, *A colonização alemã*, 707.

51. Ubatuba (cf. Caldre e Fião), ALP, 21 Oct. 1854, in *Tribuna Rio-Grandense*, 31 Oct. 1854, 1–2.

52. Avé-Lallemant, *Viagem pela província*, 114.

53. Mulhall, *Rio Grande do Sul*, 52; cf. Avé-Lallemant, *Viagem pela província*, 111–14.

54. Amado, *Conflito social*, 44–45.

55. RS, Pres., *Relatório* (1851), 8–9.

56. ALP, 25 Oct. 1852, in *O Mercantil*, 27 Oct. 1852, 2.

57. ALP, 20 Oct. 1854, in *Tribuna Rio-Grandense*, 28 Oct. 1854, 1–4.

58. *Anais*, 22 July 1869, 68–71.

59. Richard Graham, "Os fundamentos da ruptura"; Bethell, *The Abolition of the Brazilian Slave Trade*.

60. RS, Pres., *Relatório* (1863), 8–9.

61. Pres. to Minister of the Empire, reservados n. 1 and n. 5, 29 Jan. 1863, Corr. to Pres., cód. A-2.16, AHRS; Police Chief to Pres., 27 Jan. 1863, Corr. da Secretaria de Polícia, Porto Alegre, m. 5, AHRS.

62. "O Kolonist," *A Reforma*, 9 Aug. 1853, 1.

63. *Anais*, 20 Sept. 1862, 2: 55–56; ALP, 25 Oct. 1852, in *O Mercantil*, 27 Oct. 1852, 1–2; ALP, 26 Oct. 1852, in *O Mercantil*, 28 Oct. 1852, 1; "Estudo da língua alemã," *A Reforma*, 5 Dec. 1875, 1; *Anais*, 10 Nov. 1887, 41.

64. ALP, 20 Oct. 1854, in *Tribuna Rio-Grandense*, 28 Oct. 1854, 1–4; ALP, 20 Oct. 1854, in *Tribuna Rio-Grandense*, 30 Oct. 1854, 1.

65. Thales de Azevedo also argues that elite frustration with German colonists was one of the factors that led officials to pursue Italian immigrants in the 1870s; see *Italianos e gaúchos*, 38.

66. ALP, 10 Nov. 1857, in *Correio do Sul*, 21 Nov. 1857, 1–2. Cf. "Importação de colonos," *O Mercantil*, 24 Nov. 1852, suplemento, 1; ALP, 20 Oct. 1854, in *Tribuna Rio-Grandense*, 28 Oct. 1854, 1–4.

67. ALP, 21 Oct. 1854, in *Tribuna Rio-Grandense*, 31 Oct. 1854, 1–4.

68. Even some of the most careful analyses of *colonos'* place in the province repeat this tendency in their treatment of early immigrants' political actions. Amado, e.g., attributes much of *colonos'* seeming passivity before Brazilian authorities to the tradition of subservience they had brought from Europe. See Amado, *Conflito social*, 51–53.

69. Cf. Amado, *Conflito social*, 48; and Biehl, "Jammerthal, the Valley of Lamentation."

70. See, e.g., req. of João Frederico Kringer, 16 Nov. 1833, IJJ^{9}451, AN; Pres. Manoel Antonio Galvão to Minister of Justice, 18 Jan. 1833, IJJ^{9}451, AN.

71. Píccolo, "Alemães e italianos," 579–80.

72. "Os jezuitas em São Leopoldo," *O Mercantil*, 11 Mar. 1864, 1; José Joaquim Rodrigues Lopes, "Considerações gerais, sobre a ex-Colônia de São Leopoldo em 1867," vol. 16, Cód. 809, Memórias, Coleção de Memórias e Outros Documentos, AN. Of the copious literature on the Muckers, the most useful works are Amado, *Conflito social*, and Biehl, "Jammerthal, the Valley of Lamentation," but see also the contending biases of Schupp, *Os "Mucker,"* and Petry, *O episódio do Ferrabraz*, and the attempt at a more balanced account of events in Domingues, *A nova face dos Muckers*.

73. Roche, *A colonização alemã*, 705–7; Oberacker, *Carlos von Koseritz*, 9–10.

74. Oberacker, *Carlos von Koseritz*, 9–10.

75. Gans, *Presença teuta*, 111–210.

76. Oberacker, *Carlos von Koseritz*, 15–17; Roche, *A colonização alemã*, 19, 710.

77. Oberacker, *Carlos von Koseritz*, 31–46; cf. Biehl, "Jammerthal, the Valley of Lamentation."

78. Amado, *Conflito social*, 27–104, lays out the increasing inequalities in Sao Leopoldo and uses them to explain the tensions that would ultimately produce the German Protestant Mucker movement that the provincial government would attempt to crush in 1873–74. In this regard, she provides rich, empirical support for the arguments of Maria Isaura Pereira de Queiroz, *O messianismo*, 220–30. Roche, *A coloniza-*

ção alemã, 557–600, on the other hand, treats the emergence of distinct social classes in colonies as by and large a conflict-free process.

79. Porto, *O trabalho alemão*, 152–58.

80. Roche, *A colonização alemã*, 710.

81. Piccolo, *Vida política no século 19*, 54. My political analysis derives in large part from this work; from Piccolo, *A política rio-grandense no II*, and "A política rio-grandense no Império"; and from Antunes, "Os partidos políticos no Rio Grande do Sul."

82. Emília Viotti da Costa, *The Brazilian Empire*, 53–77.

83. For examples of Liberal manipulations of the issue, see *Anais*, 22 Sept. 1862, 72–80, and 4 Oct. 1862, 174–79; "Silveira Martins," *A Reforma*, 25 July 1875, 1; "A interpellação," *A Reforma*, 6 Oct. 1875, 1; and Pesavento, "O imigrante na política rio-grandense," 156–68.

84. Gertz, *O perigo alemão*.

85. ALP, 14 Dec. 1888, in *Anais . . . 1888*.

86. [José Cândido Gomes], *Chronica de Porto-Alegre*, 16.

Chapter 3. The Politics of Everyday Life in the City

1. Isabelle, *Viagem to Rio Grande do Sul*, 68–69.

2. See Fernando Henrique Cardoso, *Capitalismo e escravidão*, esp. 125–53, on master-slave relations, and 239–69, on the problematic transformation of "objectified" slaves into free persons with abolition.

3. He concluded that only for a very few privileged slave artisans in the cities was a more profound understanding of, and reaction to, society's relations of power possible. See Fernando Henrique Cardoso, *Capitalismo e escravidão*, 125, 139, 148–50, 152, 239–69, 278–79. Cardoso's concentration on the especially harsh conditions of work in the *charqueadas* undoubtedly colored his vision of slavery in the region.

4. The literature is too vast to cite here. Useful places to start include Moreira, *Os cativos e os homens de bem*, and *Faces da liberdade;* Maestri Filho, *O escravo no Rio Grande do Sul;* Pesavento, *Emergência*, on Rio Grande do Sul; and the excellent historiographical essay in Schwartz, *Slaves, Peasants, and Rebels*, 1–38, on Brazil as a whole.

5. Chalhoub, *Visões da liberdade*, 40–43. Cf. Andrews, *Blacks and Whites*, 7–10; and Gorender, *A escravidão reabilitada*, 19–20, 144–45, 200–204.

6. On the shortcomings of resistance/accommodation models, see, e.g., Ortner, "Resistance and the Problem."

7. Diacon demonstrates the double-edged nature of patron-client relations in another southern region of Brazil; see *Millenarian Vision*, 10, 24–43.

8. On the more radical initiatives in and around Porto Alegre, see Kittleson, "The Problem of the People," chap. 2.

9. Proc. 1578, r. Felipe, m. 63, APERS.

10. Moreira, "Entre o deboche"; Zanetti, "Calabouço urbano," 90–91, 118–19. Cf. Pesavento, *Emergência*, which is less precise on the distinctions between state and private seigneurial power.

11. "Relatorio da Commissão encarregada de visitar as prisões e estabelecimentos de Caridade desta cidade," 17 Oct. 1831, Corr. of Câm. Mun., Porto Alegre, m. 125, l. 131, AHRS; req. of Rafael Ignacio Alves, 1850, Reqs., Polícia, m. 90, AHRS; Relatório diário, Quartel de Porto Alegre, 1859, Corpo Policial, m. 2, AHRS; Police Chief to Pres., 20 Sept. 1877, Polícia, Cód. 82, AHRS.

12. Câm. Mun. to Pres., 20 Oct. 1824, Corr. of Câm. Mun., Porto Alegre, m. 121, l. 130, AHRS. Cf. Câm. Mun. to Pres., 3 Oct. 1831, Corr. of Câm. Mun., Porto Alegre, m. 125, l. 131, AHRS; and an 1869 regulation limiting the number of lashes that could be applied to slaves: Police Chief to Del. of Porto Alegre, 24 Feb. 1869, Polícia, Cód. 240, AHRS.

13. Subdel. of 1st district to Pres., 8 Apr. 1847, Polícia, Subdelegacía de Polícia de Porto Alegre, m. 5, AHRS.

14. Luiz Carlos Soares, "Os escravos de ganho"; Marilene Rosa Nogueira da Silva, *Negro na rua;* Reis, *Death Is a Festival;* Kolchin, *American Slavery,* 74, 109–10, 128; Wade, *Slavery in the Cities,* 28–54; Hünefeldt, *Paying the Price of Freedom,* 111–17.

15. Proc. 841, r. Antonio Gonçalves Carneiro, m. 28, APERS; Rodrigues, *Atas do Conselho de Estado,* 4: 68–76. On the Council of State, see also Carvalho, *Teatro de sombras,* chap. 4. Gonçalves Carneiro later successfully petitioned the government for the return of his other slaves, several of whom had testified against him in what he called "the false imputation of the death of his other slave" André; see his req., 25 May 1852, Reqs., m. 91, AHRS.

16. Subdel. of 1st district to Pres., 8 Apr. 1847, Subdelegacia de Polícia, Porto Alegre, Polícia, m. 5, AHRS.

17. See, e.g., Police Chief to Pres., 20 Sept. 1877, Polícia, Cód. 82, AHRS; Relatórios diários, 1874, Força Policial, m. 2, AHRS; and "Presos sem culpa," *O Século,* 5 Oct. 1884, 2.

18. Diacon, *Millenarian Vision,* 25.

19. Proc. 1294, r. Manoel José Sanhudo e João Antonio dos Santos, m. 46, APERS; cf. proc. 1265, r. Amaro Francisco de Castro, m. 44, APERS.

20. See, e.g., Police Chief to Del. of Santa Maria, 10 Sept. 1868, Polícia, cód. 240, AHRS; Pres. to Police Chief, 3 June 1868, Polícia, cód. A.552, AHRS.

21. Proc. 862, r. Dionísio José dos Santos e Francisco Ribeiro, m. 29, APERS.

22. See, e.g., proc. 1248, r. Procópio Dias de Castro, m. 43, APERS; proc. 1009, r. José Francisco Seta Júnior, m. 34, APERS.

23. Proc. 1321, r. Tristão Pires de Lima, m. 48, APERS.

24. Proc. 831, r. Constantino, m. 28, APERS.

25. Meznar, "The Ranks of the Poor"; Beattie, *The Tribute of Blood;* J. Carlos Moré [Jean-Charles Moré], "Memoria sobre a organisação da Guarda Nacional na Província de São Pedro do Rio-grande do Sul," 1863, 16, 1, 16, BN/SM.

26. Proc. 1060, r. Manoel Rafael, escravo de Innocente Maciel Neto, Quinto, escravo de Antonio Pahim de Andrade et al., m. 35, APERS.

27. Cf. Chalhoub, *Visões da liberdade,* 253 and passim.

28. Proc. 1233, r. Januário, Jerônimo, e João, m. 43, APERS.

29. Termo de interr. e perguntas feitas a preta Maria, 8 Apr. 1846, Polícia, Inquéritos, m. 2, AHRS; cf. Auto de perguntas feito a Verediana, 30 Mar. 1874, Polícia, Inquéritos, m. 4, AHRS.

30. Proc. 821, r. Antonio Clemente Suzano, m. 28, APERS; proc. 844, r. Joanna, m. 28, APERS; req. of Florência, 15 Mar. 1861, Reqs., Grupo Escravos, m. 98, AHRS; Hünefeldt, *Paying the Price*, 63–85.

31. Auto de perguntas feito to preto Felipe, 1 Dec. 1869, Polícia, Inquéritos, m. 3, AHRS; proc. 1230, r. Luiz Manoel da Silva Rosa, m. 43; Auto de perguntas feito a Francisco, 17 Jan. 1863, Polícia, Inquéritos, m. 3, AHRS.

32. Subdel. of 2d district of Triunfo to Police Chief, 28 Apr., 13 June, 13 July, 10 Sept., and 9 Nov. 1866, Delegacia de Polícia, m. 32, AHRS; RS *Relatório* (1859), 5.

33. Police Chief to Pres., 16 Jan. 1863, Secretaria de Polícia, m. 7, AHRS; Police Chief to Pres., 9 Jan. 1863, Secretaria de Polícia, m. 5, AHRS; Autos de perguntas feito a Manoel e Francisco, 17 Jan. 1863, Polícia, Inquéritos, m. 3, AHRS.

34. Proc. 1255, r. Francisco Caetano dos Santos, m. 44, APERS.

35. On the "translation" of plebeian projects into the language of the dominant culture, see Chalhoub, *Visões da liberdade*, esp. 65; and Roseberry, "Hegemony and the Language of Contention."

36. Interr. feito to preto crioulo escravo de Antonio Manoel de Azambuja, 9 Nov. 1869, Polícia, Inquéritos, m. 3, AHRS.

37. On the legal provisions for the liberation of a slave against the wishes of his or her master, see Malheiro, *A escravidão no Brasil*, 1: 94–102. As noted by the Council of State in the case of the slave André, punishment by the *senhor* did not appear among the accepted reasons for such emancipation.

38. Interr. feito to preto crioulo escravo de Antonio Manoel de Azambuja, 9 Nov. 1869, Polícia, Inquéritos, m. 3, AHRS. For another suggestion of the rejection of the use of irons, see Police Chief to Pres., 25 July 1863, Secretaria de Polícia, m. 5, AHRS.

39. Auto de perguntas feito a Luiza, 18 Apr. 1874, Polícia, Inquéritos, m. 4, AHRS; *O Século*, 6 July 1884 (the article first appeared in *O Rio-Grandense*, 6 Oct. 1876). Cf. Autos de perguntas feitos a Genoveva, Leopoldina, Rufina, 11 Nov. 1865; and Autos de perguntas feitos a D. Ursula Clara de Lima, João Antonio de Azevedo, Antonio Simões Pereira, 22 Nov. 1865, Polícia, Inquéritos, m. 3, AHRS.

40. Autos de perguntas feitos a Genoveva, Leopoldina, Rufina, 11 Nov. 1865, and Autos de perguntas feitos a D. Ursula Clara de Lima, João Antonio de Azevedo, Antonio Simões Pereira, 22 Nov. 1865, both Polícia, Inquéritos, m. 3, AHRS.

41. See, e.g., Auto de perguntas feito a Israel Benedito de Paiva, 30 Mar. 1874, Polícia, Inquéritos, m. 4, AHRS. In several cases, slaves put forward an even worse scenario in which punishment came as a result of *senhores'* own crimes. Masters in these incidents, that is, beat slaves to keep them from revealing the murders or thefts the masters themselves had committed. Cf. Auto de perguntas feito to preto João, 5 Oct. 1869, Polícia, Inquéritos, m. 3, AHRS; Auto de perguntas feito a Francisco, 1 May 1873, Polícia, Inquéritos, m. 4, AHRS.

42. Proc. 1397, r. Bolivar do Larre Pinto, m. 53, APERS.

43. Proc. 1002, r. Rita, m. 34, APERS; proc. 824, r. Eva, m. 28, APERS.

44. Auto de perguntas feito a Verediana, 30 Mar. 1874, Polícia, Inquéritos, m. 4, AHRS.

45. Auto de perguntas feito a Luiza, 18 Apr. 1874, Polícia, Inquéritos, m. 4, AHRS; Auto de perguntas feito a Leopoldina, 11 Nov. 1865, Polícia, Inquéritos, m. 3, AHRS.

46. Article 4 of the Rio Branco Law states in regard to the right of peculium: "The slave is permitted to form a saving fund from what may come to him through gifts, legacies, and inheritances, and from what, by consent of his owner, he may obtain by his labour and economy." Furthermore, §2 of that same article recognizes the slave's right to apply that sum to the purchase of his or her freedom: "The slave who, through his savings, may obtain means to pay his value has a right to freedom." The text of the Rio Branco Law appears in translation in Conrad, *The Destruction*, 305–9.

47. Malheiro, *A escravidão no Brasil*, 1: 61–65, cited passages on 62–63; Conrad, *Children of God's Fire*, 267–73.

48. Manuela Carneiro da Cunha, "Silences of the Law."

49. As early as the second decade of the nineteenth century, we see slaves attempting to force their owners to free them in return for a sum of money; see req. of Manoel, 17 June 1811, Reqs., Grupo Escravos, m. 4, AHRS; req. of Maria, 27 Aug. 1814, Reqs., Grupo Escravos, m. 11, AHRS.

50. Req. of Belisário, 24 Feb. 1872, Reqs., Grupo Escravos, m. 156, AHRS; Of. of Police Chief to Pres., 17 Sept. 1877, Polícia, cód. 82, AHRS; req. of João Rodrigues, 8 Aug. 1855, Reqs., Grupo Polícia, m. 93, AHRS. Cf. Manoel de Oliveira Paes to Pres. Joaquim Antão Fernandes Leão, 31 Mar. 1860, Marinha, Delegacia da Capitania do Porto, m. 64, l. 539, AHRS.

51. Proc. 1236, r. Joaquim Vieira da Cunha e Silvana, m. 43, APERS; Police Chief to Subdel. of 2d district of capital, 29 Nov. 1871, Polícia, cód. 241, AHRS. Stanley J. Stein similarly found that Africans who possessed knowledge of divination, curing, and broad links to the supernatural world served as "a potential focal point of resistance to the slave system imposed by the master"; see Stein, *Vassouras*, 196–209.

52. Proc. 1267, r. José, m. 44, APERS.

53. Chalhoub, *Visões da liberdade*, 250, and "Slaves, Freedmen and the Politics of Freedom."

54. *Colleção das Leis e Resoluções da Província . . . 1857*, 87, Leg. Provincial, cód. 579, AHRS; Câm. Mun. to Pres., 18 Sep. 1856, artigos 92 and 108, Corr. of Câm. Mun., Porto Alegre, m. 138, l. 134, AHRS. Porto Alegre's first *código de posturas* (municipal code) appeared in 1829; new codes and major revisions appeared in 1831, 1837, 1844, 1847, and 1857. See the Livro de Registro das Posturas Municipais de 1829 até 1888, AHMPA; *Colleção das Leis e Resoluções da Província do Rio Grande do Sul. XIII Volume. 2a. sessão da 7a. Legislatura. 1857* (Typographia do Mercantil, 1858), 87, Leg. Provincial, Cód. 579, AHRS; Câm. Mun. to Pres., 18 Sept. 1856, Corr. of Câm. Mun., Porto Alegre, m. 138, l. 134, AHRS.

55. In much of the rest of Brazil, *batuque* refers simply to Afro-Brazilian dances; in Porto Alegre and Rio Grande do Sul, however, it refers to Afro-Brazilian religious practice, including but not exclusively dances. *Candomblé* (or at times *candombé*, as in

Coruja) is in normal usage here an equivalent term. Cf. Laytano, *Folclore*, 198; *Colleção das Leis e Resoluções da Província . . . 1857*, 87, Leg. Provincial, cód. 579, AHRS; Câm. Mun. to Pres., 18 Sept. 1856, artigos 48 and 122, Corr. of Câm. Mun., Porto Alegre, m. 138, l. 134, AHRS; Câm. Mun. to Vice Pres., 13 Nov. 1829, Corr. of Câm. Mun., Porto Alegre, m. 123, l. 131, AHRS.

56. See capítulo 42, 1831 código, Livro de Registro das Posturas.

57. Capítulos 19–21, 35, 1831 código, Livro de Registro das Posturas; Câm. Mun. to Pres., 18 Sept. 1856, artigos 80–81, 97, 102, Corr. of Câm. Mun., Porto Alegre, m. 138, l. 134, AHRS. Such legislation was certainly not unique to Porto Alegre or to Brazil; cf. Algranti, *O feitor ausente*, 50–51; and Wade, *Slavery in the Cities*, 80–110.

58. Police Chief to Pres., 21 and 25 Nov. 1833, Chefatura de Polícia, m. 7, AHRS.

59. Moreira, "Entre o deboche," 80–121; proc. 823, r. Rodrigo, m. 28, APERS; proc. 831, r. Constantino, m. 28, APERS; proc. 832, r. Antonio Luiz, Bebiano Jozé Carneiro da Fontoura et al., m. 28, APERS; proc. 844, r. Joanna, m. 28, APERS; proc. 1249, r. Rafael and Gregório, m. 44, APERS; Quartel do Comando da Força Policial, Porto Alegre, Relatórios Diários, 1874, Força Policial, m. 2, AHRS.

60. Cf. Holloway, *Policing Rio de Janeiro*, which provides an excellent account of the development of mechanisms of state control and some forms of resistance to them in the imperial capital.

61. Cf. the portrayals of the city in Mazeron, *Reminiscências*, and *Notas para a historia;* and Coruja, *Antigualhas*.

62. Hörmeyer, *O Rio Grande do Sul*, 79.

63. Coruja, *Antigualhas*, 37–38.

64. [José Cândido Gomes], *Chronica de Porto-Alegre*, 10; cf. Mazeron, *Reminiscências*, 66.

65. Laytano, *Festa de Nossa Senhora dos Navegantes*.

66. Gresele, "A irmandade dos negros," 18–19; Barea, "Histórico da Egreja," 13. Cf. Nara H. N. Machado, "A Igreja de N.S. do Rosário dos Pretos," 191–92; and Castanho and Nunes, "A Confraria de Nossa Senhora."

67. Coruja, *Antigualhas*, 27. On the transfer of the patron's day and the building of the Church of the Brotherhood of the Rosary (completed in 1827), see Gresele, "A Irmandade dos negros," 28, 31–33. Karasch argues forcefully, in fact, that Afro-Brazilians in early nineteenth-century Rio de Janeiro used the forms of Catholic ritual in their *irmandades* but adopted the content of such rituals in a range of partial and "heterodox" ways; see *Slave Life*, 254–301, esp. 254–61.

68. On social assistance programs, see Gresele, "A irmandade dos negros," 36; Russell-Wood, *The Black Man*, 150–55; and Maria Inês Côrtes de Oliveira, *O liberto*, 81–83. Specifically in relation to funerary practices, see Reis, *Death Is a Festival*.

69. Gresele, "A irmandade dos negros," 32.

70. Luccock, *Notas sobre o Rio-de-Janeiro*, 127–28.

71. Hörmeyer, *O Rio Grande do Sul*, 79.

72. Hörmeyer, *O Rio Grande do Sul*, 79.

73. Herskovits, "The Southernmost Outposts," 213–14.

74. This take on religious syncretism relies on the analysis of Karasch in *Slave Life*.

75. Req. to Subdel. of 1st district of Porto Alegre, 21 Dec. 1850, Reqs., Grupo Polícia, m. 90, AHRS; Laytano, *Festa de Nossa Senhora dos Navegantes*, 42; [José Cândido Gomes], *Chronica de Porto-Alegre*, 9; Spalding, *Pequena história*, 237.

76. Gresele also noted scornfully that "in the heart of the Irmandade, no one sinned for an excess of piety." See Gresele, "A irmandade dos negros," 11.

77. Req. to Subdel. of Police of 1st district of Porto Alegre, 21 Dec. 1850, Reqs., Grupo Polícia, m. 90, AHRS.

78. Req. to Police Chief, 30 Aug. 1849, Reqs., Grupo Polícia, m. 89, AHRS. The spelling of *cocumbi* varied, appearing also as *quicumbe* or *cucumbe*.

79. Because of their concern with preventing disturbances, police officials preferred that Afro-Brazilian dances take place outside of the most highly populated zones of the city. Cf. the response attached to req. to Subdel. of Police of 1st district of Porto Alegre, 21 Dec. 1850, Reqs., Grupo Polícia, m. 90, AHRS, in which one official states, "it seems to me convenient that [the *quicumbi*] take place where it will not bother the neighborhood." Also see the response to req. to Police Chief, 9 Apr. 1850, Reqs., Grupo Polícia, m. 90, AHRS.

80. On these "theatrical dances," see Karasch, *Slave Life*, 247–99 (the phrase is hers); Marina de Mello e Souza, *Reis negros;* and Bastide, *The African Religions*, 120–24.

81. Miller, "Central Africa," 42 n. 33.

82. Of. do Police Chief à Câm Mun desta Capital, 4 May 1872, Polícia, cód 250, AHRS; Police Chief to Subdel. of São Gabriel, 21 Feb 1867, Polícia, cód 252, AHRS. On the historical figure of Rainha Ginga, see Miller, "Central Africa."

83. Req. to Police Chief, 19 Feb. 1850, Reqs., Grupo Polícia, m. 90, AHRS.

84. Coruja, *Antigualhas*, 26–27; Ferreira, *Imagens sentimentais*, 94.

85. Autos de perguntas feitos a Matildes Lebania Pereira dos Santos, Manoel Fernandes Talhada, e o africano João, 27 Oct. 1858, Polícia, Inquéritos, m. 2, AHRS.

86. In colonial Brazil, accusations of heterodoxy and specifically of witchcraft were not generally directed against African and Afro-Brazilian practices. See Laura de Mello e Souza, *O diabo na Terra de Santa*.

87. Proc. 859, r. João, m. 29, APERS; cf. proc. 1236, r. Joaquim Vieira da Cunha e Silvana, m. 43, APERS.

88. Unnumbered proc., r. Andreza do Rosario, m. 41, APERS.

89. Proc. 1261, r. Fidelis, m. 44, APERS. Some of the practices labeled witchcraft may, in fact, have reflected Afro-Brazilian or other forms of popular medicine. See Chalhoub, *Cidade febril*. Also see the suggestive rejection of popular cures by a Gaúcho physician in "Exposição à Humanidade," *O Porto-Alegrense*, 11 June 1849, 1–2.

90. Proc. 859, r. João, m. 29, APERS. The choice of hiding or revealing religious practices was not always, however, guided only by security concerns. At times, the religious meaning of a particular site dictated that rituals be held there. The most striking example of this appeared outside the city of Santa Maria, where the "holy waters" of a small river attracted surprising numbers of worshippers; see *O Porto-Alegrense*, 11 June 1849, 1–3.

91. Compare Karasch, *Slave Life,* 254 and passim.

92. Corrêa, "Panorama das religiões," 13–14.

93. Pesavento, "Lugares malditos."

94. Both Mattoso and Maria Inês Côrtes de Oliveira assert that the precise ethnic distinctions that marked earlier membership in *irmandades* faded through the eighteenth and nineteenth centuries. See Mattoso, *To Be a Slave,* 128–32; Oliveira, *O liberto,* 80–81; and Karasch, *Slave Life,* 82–88, 298.

95. In 1851, the jewels that had adorned the image of Nossa Senhora da Conceição (Our Lady of the Conception) in Porto Alegre's Central Church were stolen by a freedman (whose legal status was challenged by a *senhor* from Alegrete). Four members of the *irmandade* of Nossa Senhora da Conceição testified at the trial, including the brotherhood's treasurer and legal agent (*procurador*). All of the four were *pardo* artisans (two shoemakers or shoe repairmen, one goldsmith, and one outfitter) born in other provinces (two from Rio de Janeiro and one each from Minas Gerais and Bahia). See proc. 836, r. Antonio Ferreira de Lacerda and Antonio Ribeiro, m. 28, APERS. Coruja described the *irmandade* as being made up "almost completely of *pardos*"; see Coruja, *Antigualhas,* 37. Nossa Senhora da Conceição was in fact the special patron of *pardos;* see Karasch, *Slave Life,* 269.

96. On *condição,* see esp. Richard Graham, *Patronage and Politics.*

97. Proc. 957, r. Marcelino, m. 32, APERS. On the importance of hats as signs of status, see Fraga Filho, *Mendigos, moleques e vadios,* 83.

98. Salles, *Guerra,* 63.

99. Proc. 1499, r. Salome Suzano Escalara, m. 58, APERS; cf. proc. 1234, r. Miguel Alves de Carvalho, m. 43, APERS.

100. Proc. 1219, r. Serafim Floriano, m. 42, APERS.

101. Proc. 1270A, r. Antonio José Godinho, m. 45, APERS.

102. Proc. 1322, r. João Alves Pedroso, m. 48, APERS. Cf. Moreira, *Faces da liberdade,* 69–71. On authorities' general concern about such veterans, see Circular to Delegates, 3 Nov. 1870, Polícia, cód. 241, AHRS. On other soldiers' hostility to foreigners, see Chief of Police to Pres., Porto Alegre, 8 Apr. 1879, Polícia, cód. 88, AHRS.

103. Moreira, "Entre o deboche," 80–121.

104. Proc. 1737, r. Francisco Barbosa Forquine, m. 70, APERS; Chief of Police to Del., Porto Alegre, 12 Oct. 1870, Polícia, cód. 241, AHRS.

105. Circular to Del., 3 Nov. 1870, Polícia, cód. 241, AHRS; Chief of Police to Subdel., Belém, 23 Sept. 1871, Polícia, cód. 241, AHRS.

106. Proc. 1358, r. Ildefonso Ferreira de Azevedo Lopes, m. 51, APERS.

107. *O Mercantil,* 31 May 1878.

108. Police Del. to Commander of Detachment of Sixth Infantry Battalion, Pelotas, 31 Dec. 1871, Delegacia de Polícia, m. 10, AHRS.

109. Dr. Luiz da Silva Flores, Dr. José Alves Nogueira da Silva, and Dr. Francisco Ferreira d'Abreu to Pres., 21 Apr. 1850, IJJ⁹451, AN.

110. Proc. 1295, r. Augusto Rebello, Cassiano, João Francisco Barbosa e Paulino Lopes, m. 46, APERS; proc. 832, r. Antonio Luiz et al., m. 28, APERS.

111. For examples of freedpersons rented out, either by their *senhores* or by themselves, see proc. 866, r. Luiz Teixeira da Silva, m. 29, APERS; proc. 1013, r. Maria Ignacia, m. 34, APERS.

112. Masters' power to reenslave was a constant threat, but one that they seem rarely to have tried to apply. Cf. Chalhoub, *Visões da liberdade*, 131–43; Manuela Carneiro da Cunha, *Antropologia*, 123–44; and Malheiro, *A escravidão no Brasil*, 1: 128–43.

113. For examples in the *processos*, see proc. 817, r. José Ferreira Santos, m. 28, APERS; proc. 1226, r. João Correia Fontes, m. 42, APERS; proc. 1237, r. Leonor Justina da Silva, m. 43, APERS. Cf. on Porto Alegre in a later period, Claudia Fonseca, "Pais e filhos na família popular"; and on other areas of nineteenth-century Brazil, Dias, *Power and Everyday Life*, 126–27.

114. Proc. 866, r. Luiz Teixeira da Silva, m. 29, APERS.

115. Proc. 913, r. Florencio, m. 31, APERS; proc. 975, r. Marianno Joaquim, m. 33, APERS.

116. Proc. 820, r. José Joaquim Garcês Cabelleira, m. 28, APERS; unnumbered proc., r. Andreza do Rosário, m. 41, APERS; proc. 837, r. Francisco e José, m. 28, APERS.

117. Proc. 818, r. Francisco Joaquim Garcês Cabelleira, m. 28, APERS; proc. 820, r. José Joaquim Garcês Cabelleira, m. 28, APERS; cf. proc. 1239, r. Gregório Ribeiro do Valle, m. 43, APERS.

118. Proc. 1230, r. Luiz Manoel da Silva Rosa, m. 43, APERS. Cf. also proc. 1293, r. Manoel Florencio da Conceição, m. 46, APERS, in which a veteran of the Paraguayan War attacked a man who had treated him with "arrogance" and called him "black" (*negro*).

119. Proc. 863, r. Luiz Weber, m. 29, APERS; [José Cândido Gomes], *Chronica de Porto-Alegre*, 54. See also proc. 1235, r. Pedro Licht, m. 43, APERS; proc. 975, r. Marciano Joaquim, m. 33, APERS; and proc. 858, r. Francisco Alves Monteiro, m. 29, APERS.

120. Proc. 974, r. Izidro de Souza, m. 33, APERS.

121. On allegations of spreading scandal through *pasquins*, see proc. 1222, r. Antonio Luiz Pereira de Oliveira, m. 42, APERS; and proc. 1459, r. Marcelino Francisco de Barcellos, m. 56, APERS.

122. Cf. proc. 813, r. Manoel Gomes da Silva, m. 29, APERS; proc. 816, r. Candido Ribeiro Moreira, m. 28, APERS; proc. 833, r. Antonio Joaquim dos Santos, m. 28, APERS; proc. 848, r. Manoel José Sueiro, m. 29, APERS; proc. 870, r. Victoria, m. 29, APERS; and proc. 1193, r. José dos Passos Júnior, m. 41, APERS.

123. Proc. 976, r. Theodoro Pereira da Silva, m. 33, APERS; proc. 1010, r. Joaquim, m. 34, APERS; proc. 1210, r. Laurindo Nery da Cruz, m. 42, APERS; proc. 1239, r. Gregório Ribeiro do Valle, m. 43, APERS; proc. 1250, r. João do Prado, m. 44, APERS; proc. 1281, r. Januário Antonio Fernandes, m. 45, APERS.

124. Proc. 854, r. João Fidelis, m. 29, APERS. Apparently the woman was more committed to *felicidade* than to fidelity. Cf. proc. 943, r. Manoel, m. 32, APERS, for another male slave's attempt to control his woman; and Sandra Lauderdale Graham, *Caetana Says No*, esp. 62.

125. Stern, *The Secret History*, 180.

126. Proc. 863, r. Luiz Weber, m. 29, APERS; see the similar attempt to sidestep provocations in proc. 833, r. Antonio Joaquim dos Santos, m. 28, APERS.

127. On the role of mediators in defusing conflicts, see proc. 1461, r. Joaquim Gonçalves de Faria, m. 56, APERS; proc. 1479, r. Manoel José do Bomfim, m. 57, APERS; and proc. 1473, r. Francisco Antonio Carrilho, m. 57, APERS. For examples of men who sought out official intervention instead of facing their tormentors directly, see proc. 833, r. Antonio Joaquim dos Santos, m. 28, APERS; and proc. 813, r. José Rodrigues da Silva, m. 28, APERS.

128. Cf. Chalhoub, *Trabalho, lar e botequim*, esp. 223–24.

129. Stern makes a strong, related case, specifically with regard to the culture of macho play that characterized plebeian men's interactions in late colonial Mexico. He argues that the jousting and challenging in which men engaged were in fact inseparable from an impulse toward solidarity; see *The Secret History*, chap. 7.

130. Esteves, *Meninas perdidas*, 115–205. See also Caulfield and Esteves, "50 Years of Virginity."

131. Esteves, *Meninas perdidas*, 139.

132. Stern has argued persuasively for the existence of codes other than the much discussed honor/shame complex, rather than simple individual attempts to maneuver within that ideological system. See Stern, *The Secret History*, 11–20. Cf. Kuznesof, "Sexual Politics, Race and Bastard-Rearing"; and Stavig, "'Living in Offense of Our Lord.'"

133. Proc. 817, r. José Ferreira Santos, m. 28, APERS.

134. Cf. proc. 1208, r. José Domingues Almeida, m. 41, APERS; proc. 1220, r. João Antonio de Carvalho, m. 42, APERS; proc. 1226, r. João Correia Fontes, m. 42, APERS; proc. 853, r. Luiz Antonio Machado da Rosa e Militão Moreira de Araujo Silva, m. 29, APERS.

135. Besides the cases cited in the previous note, see the bigamy trial of Francisco José d'Oliveira, which included a brother who placed himself in charge of defending his sister's honor. Proc. 857, r. Francisco José d'Oliveira, m. 29, APERS.

136. Proc. 1253, r. Antonio Candido Gomes, m. 44, APERS; proc. 1219, r. Serafim Floriano, m. 42, APERS. On Rio de Janeiro, see Sandra Lauderdale Graham, *House and Street*; Esteves, *Meninas perdidas*, esp. 43–54; and Caulfield, *In Defense of Honor*.

137. In 1869, one schoolgirl seems to have chosen the strategy of hiding a pregnancy and possibly killing the child as a way of preserving her honor; see proc. 1197, r. Leocádia Balbina da Costa, m. 41, APERS. On "private pregnancy," see Twinam, "Honor, Sexuality, and Illegitimacy," esp. 125–34, 155 n. 46.

138. Caulfield in particular argues that women's expressions of sexual desire were anathema to elite officials; see Caulfield, *In Defense of Honor*; and Caulfield and Esteves, "50 Years of Virginity," 62.

139. This prevailing code did put some limits on men's acceptable sexual behavior. Bigamy and pederasty, e.g., were clearly off-limits. See proc. 857, r. Francisco José d'Oliveira, m. 29, APERS; and proc. 829, r. Izidro José da Silva, m. 28, APERS.

140. Proc. 1441, r. Lourenço Luiz Vieira, m. 55, APERS; proc. 1443, r. Joaquim José dos Santos, m. 55, APERS.

141. Proc. 833, r. Antonio Joaquim dos Santos, m. 28, APERS.

142. Proc. 1237, r. Leonor Justina da Silva, m. 43, APERS.

143. Esteves, *Meninas perdidas*, 134–40. Other studies demonstrate that plebeian women in São Paulo and Rio de Janeiro did not live according to the stereotyped honor/shame formula, though they do not comprehensively reconstruct the codes by which women of the *povo* lived. Cf. Dias, *Power and Everyday Life;* and Soihet, *Condição feminina*, 303–15.

144. Proc. 1440, r. Saturnino Antonio da Veiga, m. 55, APERS.

145. Proc. 1193, r. José dos Passos Júnior e Mathias Guethnaner, m. 41, APERS. Cf. proc. 1253, r. Antonio Candido Gomes, m. 44, APERS.

146. Proc. 852, r. Manoel José Vieira, m. 29, APERS; cf. proc. 1261, r. Fidelis, m. 44, APERS.

147. Men of the *povo* also tried to impose their patriarchal authority on other men. Thus the former soldier José Francisco d'Avila reacted harshly when his nephew Felisbino Gonçalves da Silva, a man fifty-four years of age, greeted him impudently. Pulling Felisbino aside, José "asked if that was how you greeted men with beards on their faces, with an '*ora viva*' [a highly informal salutation], that was what the devil had said when he saw that part of his mother." See proc. 1215, r. Felisbino Gonçalves da Silva, m. 42, APERS.

148. Proc. 849, r. José João Corrêa, m. 29, APERS; proc. 865, r. José Antonio Botelho, m. 29, APERS. On the dual nature of honor—as open to all but tied to social hierarchies—see Stern, *The Secret History*, 14–16, 168–69, 180.

149. Proc. 829, r. Izidro José da Silva, m. 28, APERS.

150. Moreira, "Entre o deboche," 158–84. On women's mobility and the importance of female-headed households in São Paulo, see Dias, *Power and Everyday Life*, esp. 15–20.

151. Unnumbered proc., r. Andreza do Rosario, m. 41, APERS; and see proc. 1013, r. Maria Ignacia, m. 34, APERS, which describes a freedwoman who knifed a female slave she suspected of trying to steal her man.

152. Cf. Chalhoub, *Trabalho, lar e botequim*, 143–46.

Chapter 4. Blurring the Lines of Public Politics

1. Cf. Moura, *Cocheiros e carroceiros.*

2. Proc. 1519, r. José Velho, m. 59, APERS.

3. *Acta dos trabalhos do Centro Abolicionista em Porto Alegre, aos 7 de Setembro de 1884*, AHMPA, 1. This image of emancipation as the redemption of slaves was common in discussions in 1883–84. As part of the celebrations of 7 Sept. 1884, the city renamed a large park previously known as the Campo do Bom Fim (and later known as Farroupilha Park, in honor of the 1835–45 Farroupilha Revolution) "Park of the Redemption" in honor of the abolitionist movement; see Sérgio da Costa Franco, *Porto Alegre: Guia histórico*, 163–67.

4. See the speech by Joaquim Pedro Salgado on 26 Apr. 1886 in *Anais. 2a. Sessão*, 1886, 134.

5. *O Século*, 13 Jan. 1884, 4.

6. See Zanetti, "Calabouço urbano," 33–51; cf. Bell, *Campanha Gaúcha*, 44–53.

7. Smith, *Do Rio de Janeiro*, 142.

8. Smith, *Do Rio de Janeiro*, 182–86.

9. On patronage in the Empire, see esp. Richard Graham, *Patronage and Politics;* and Bieber, *Power, Patronage, and Political Violence.* On the "ideological" nature of Gaúcho politics, see Love, *Rio Grande do Sul*, 73.

10. Assis Brasil, *Dois discursos*, 26.

11. The central provision of the Rio Branco Law declared free all children born to slave mothers.

12. When the Liberal leader Gaspar Silveira Martins returned to Porto Alegre in 1883 and invited his "co-religionaries" to join in an emancipationist campaign, the Liberal *Gazeta de Porto Alegre* pointed to the moment as a chance to reveal to the public a reunited party; see Bakos, *RS: Escravismo e abolição*, 113. On the split between Liberal factions led by Silveira Martins and Manuel Luís Osório, see Love, *Rio Grande do Sul*, 21–24; and Piccolo, *A política rio-grandense*, 99–112.

13. Orico, *Silveira Martins*, 175; Silveira Martins, *Silveira Martins*, 275. Cf. *O Cruzeiro*, 2 Nov. 1880, 2, cited in Toplin, *The Abolition of Slavery*, 187–88; and the 4 Apr. 1884 speech by the Liberal Itaquy in *Anais. 2a. sessão*, 1884, 48–51.

14. Silveira Martins, *Discursos parlamentares*, 341–43; Silveira Martins, *Silveira Martins*, 277; Orico, *Silveira Martins*, 176–77.

15. "Emancipação servil," *Jornal do Commercio*, 3 Feb. 1882, 1; Bakos, *RS: Escravismo e abolição*, 106–8, 114–15; Conrad, *The Destruction*, 203–4.

16. "Avante Porto Alegre," *A Reforma*, 15 Aug. 1884, 1, cited in Fernando Henrique Cardoso, *Capitalismo e escravidão*, 224.

17. Bakos, *RS: Escravismo e abolição*, 111, 117–18. Cf. "A questão do elemento servil," parts 4 and 5, *O Conservador*, 18 and 19 Aug. 1884, 1; and Fernando Henrique Cardoso, *Capitalismo e escravidão*, 227–28, 230.

18. Piccolo, "A política rio-grandense no Império," 109.

19. "Movimento Republicano," *O Conservador*, 18 Aug. 1884, 1.

20. "A questão do elemento servil IV," *O Conservador*, 18 Aug. 1884, 1; "O abolicionismo e o Sr. Silveira Martins," *O Conservador*, 11 Oct. 1884, 1; "E é abolicionista," *O Conservador*, 18 Sept. 1884, 2; "Digno exemplo," *O Conservador*, 21 Aug. 1884, 2.

21. "A questão do elemento servil II," *O Conservador*, 12 Aug. 1884, 1; "O programa do novo gabinete," *O Conservador*, 26 June 1884, 1; "Abolicionistas e escravocratas," *O Conservador*, 31 Jan. 1882, 2.

22. "A questão do elemento servil XI," *O Conservador*, 28 Aug. 1884, 1; "A questão do elemento servil II," *O Conservador*, 12 Aug. 1884, 1.

23. See the note on *A Voz do Escravo*, an abolitionist paper established in Pelotas, in *O Século*, 23 Jan. 1881, 3; and "Liberdade," *O Século*, 20 July 1884, 3.

24. "O açoite official," *O Século*, 27 Apr. 1884, 2; "O Sr. Chefe de Policia," *O Século*, 20 Feb. 1881, 4; "Degradante scena," *O Século*, 17 July 1881, 3.

25. Announcements of abolitionist parties and benefits, along with articles by Miguelina de Werna on the progress of the organization of the kermis, appeared weekly in *O Século* during Aug. and Sept. 1884.

26. Pinto, *Positivismo*, 9–10, and "Contribuição ao estudo," 58–101; Love, *Rio Grande do Sul*, 28–31.

27. Kirkendall, *Class Mates*, 68, 74, 159; Sérgio da Costa Franco, *Júlio de Castilhos*, 15–22.

28. Rosa, *Julio de Castilhos*, 1: 58–59; "O público," *A Imprensa*, 5 Mar. 1882, 1; "Os Republicanos," *O Século*, 15 June 1884, 3; "Dissidencia Republicana," *O Século*, 22 June 1884, 2; Porto Alegre's response, *O Século*, 29 June 1884, 2.

29. *Convenção Republicano de 23 de fevereiro; Annaes do Congresso Republicano Rio-Grandense. Primeira sessão;* Boeira, "O Rio Grande do Sul," 36.

30. *Convenção Republicano de 23 de fevereiro*, 20; Love, *Rio Grande do Sul*, 27; Bakos, *RS: Escravismo e abolição*, 83.

31. "Um appello," *A Federação*, 6 Aug. 1884, 1, rpt. in Rosa, *Julio de Castilhos*, 2: 249–50.

32. "A liberdade victoriosa," *A Federação*, 16 Aug. 1884, 1, rpt. in Rosa, *Julio de Castilhos*, 2: 230.

33. "O governo e o abolicionismo," *A Federação*, 28 May 1884, 1, and "O governo e o abolicionismo II," *A Federação*, 29 May 1884, 1, both rpt. in Rosa, *Julio de Castilhos*, 2: 225–31; "A solução do dilema," *A Federação*, 28 July 1884, 1, and "A abolição no Rio Grande," *A Federação*, 1 Aug. 1884, 1, both rpt. in Mozart Pereira Soares, *Júlio de Castilhos*, 52–56.

34. Cf. "O problema politico," *A Federação*, 27 July 1887, 1, which uses Comte's theory to condemn a Liberal argument that slavery in Brazil had been "a social necessity."

35. *Convenção Republicano de 23 de fevereiro*, 8, 40; Love, *Rio Grande do Sul*, 36 and passim.

36. Moreira, "Os contratados," 222–23. The limit of seven years was based on provisions of the Free Womb Law of 28 Sept. 1871, which had set a similar limit on the services for which a slave might contract with third parties or with one or more *senhores* when the slave belonged to joint owners and had been granted manumission by one of them. Such services were to indemnify the master or masters for the loss of their slave. See the translation of that law in Conrad, *The Destruction*, 305–9, esp. article 4, nos. 3 and 4.

37. Just two other provinces, Ceará on 25 Mar. 1884 and Amazonas on 10 July 1884, declared abolition before the Gaúcho emancipationists.

38. Conrad, *The Destruction*, 307. See the lists of arrests for the year 1886, esp. those for "theft of services," in Polícia, Cód. 103, AHRS.

39. *Jornal do Commercio*, 29 Aug. 1882, cited in Moreira, "Os contratados," 213.

40. See article 4 of the law, in Conrad, *The Destruction*, 305–9; cf. Malheiro, *A escravidão*, 1: 94–102.

41. For Gaúcho contemporaries' explicit assertions of the nonpartisan nature of abolitionism, see "Manifestação popular," *A Reforma*, 1 Aug. 1884, 2; Bakos, *RS: Escravismo e abolição*, 61, 127; and Emília Viotti da Costa, *Da senzala*, 432.

42. On the irruption of women's political cultures in abolitionist and other nineteenth-century politics in the United States, see Baker, "The Domestication of Politics."

43. The *Acta dos trabalhos do Centro Abolicionista* gives a celebratory account of the contributions of many of these organizations and also of the role of the press (with the exception of *O Conservador*). On the abolitionist activities of the Partenon Literário, see Zilberman, "O Partenon Literário"; and Monti, *O abolicionismo*, 61–65. The newspapers of the day contained many detailed descriptions of specific acts of the various associations that were freeing slaves. On the Masons, see *O Século*, 8 June 1884, 3; and Bakos, *RS: Escravismo e abolição*, 41–43. On the Sociedade Rio Branco, see *O Conservador*, 9 July 1883, 3; and *O Século*, 17 Aug. 1884, 2.

44. Spalding, "O Centro Abolicionista," 199 and passim.

45. Spalding, "O Centro Abolicionista," 193. Like the charity bazaars, the street-by-street liberation of Porto Alegre followed a pattern established by abolitionist groups in the northeastern city of Fortaleza; cf. Girão, *A abolição no Ceará*, 87–88, 158–60.

46. Spalding, "O Centro Abolicionista," 188–91.

47. "Instituto de artifices," *Jornal do Commercio*, 1 Jan. 1882, 1; "A caridade," *Colibri*, 8 May 1887, 1; RS, Pres., *Relatório* (1857), appendix; "As irmãs de charidade," *O Século*, 16 Jan. 1881, 1; "Associação das mães cristãs," *O Conservador*, 20 Oct. 1888, 1; Pedro Maia Soares, "Feminismo."

48. *Jornal do Commercio*, 1 Aug. 1884, cited in Monti, *O abolicionismo*, 85–86. Cf. Hahner, *Emancipating the Female Sex*, 38–39; and Moraes, *A campanha abolicionista*, 23–24, 37, 42.

49. *O Século*, 11 Nov. 1880, 3.

50. *O Século*, 23 Mar. 1884, 2.

51. Examples of women's groups include Sociedade Redemptora (founded in 1870) and Associação Protetora dos Escravos (1882) in São Paulo; Avé (1884) in Recife; and Cearenses adoras (1882) in Fortaleza. See Hahner, *Emancipating the Female Sex*, 38–40; Mott, *Submissão e resistência*, 77–79; Moraes, *A campanha abolicionista*, 41; Girão, *A abolição no Ceará*, 136, 201–2; and Spalding, "O Centro Abolicionista," 199.

52. Spalding, "O Centro Abolicionista," 189, 191–93.

53. *Jornal do Commercio*, 14 Aug. 1884, cited in Monti, *O abolicionismo*, 91.

54. H. Martins, "A Propaganda," *Jornal do Commercio na Kermesse*, 7 Sept. 1884, 1. Names of the women organizers appear in Spalding, "O Centro Abolicionista," 200. Cf. Weimar, *O trabalho escravo*, 97–100.

55. Spalding, "O Centro Abolicionista," 199.

56. Conrad, *The Destruction*, 208.

57. *Jornal do Commercio na Kermesse*, 7 Sept. 1884, 4.

58. Conrad, *The Destruction*, 208.

59. H. Martins, "A Propaganda," *Jornal do Commercio na Kermesse*, 7 Sept. 1884, 1; Porto Alegre, "A tendeira," *Jornal do Commercio na Kermesse*, 7 Sept. 1884, 4.

60. *O Século*, 6 July 1884, 2; *O Rio-Grandense*, 6 Oct. 1876. Cf. "Parece incrível," *O Mercantil*, 9 June 1883, 2.

61. "Scenas da escravidão," *O Mercantil*, 8 June 1883, 2.

62. "Encarcerados," *O Século*, 24 Aug. 1884, 2; "Às authoridades," *O Século*, 20 July 1884, 2; "Presos sem culpa," *O Século*, 5 Oct. 1884, 2.

63. Vieira, *A musa moderna*, 75–79.

64. *Jornal do Commercio na Kermesse*, 7 Sept. 1884, 3.

65. "Um pai no tempo da escravidão," *O Mercantil*, 28 Aug. 1883, 1; cf. "A mulher brasileira é esclavocrata [*sic*]?" *O Mercantil*, 17 Mar. 1884, 1.

66. Cf. Emília Viotti da Costa, *The Brazilian Empire*, 247–65. I develop these ideas more fully in "'Campaign All of Peace and Charity'" and "Women and Notions of Womanhood."

67. Qtd. in Girão, *A abolição no Ceará*, 136.

68. In 1885, some 22,709 slaves remained in the province; see RS, Pres., *Relatório* (1886), 177–78. For the last numbers available for Porto Alegre prior to final abolition, which may have included slaves brought in after the 1883–84 movement, see *O Mercantil*, 4 Jan. 1887, 3; "População escrava," *O Mercantil*, 28 June 1888, 2; *A Federação*, 31 Mar. 1887, 2; "Resumo" annexed to RS, Pres., *Relatório* (1888), 30–32; and Conrad, *The Destruction*, 209, 285.

69. "Quilombolas," *O Mercantil*, 8 Nov. 1879, 2.

70. Interim Police Chief to V. Pres., 11 Sept. 1887, Secretaria de Polícia, m. 20, AHRS.

71. For police responses to newspapers' reports of abuses, see "Auto de exhumação e autopsia no cadáver da parda Virgínia," 21 July 1886, Polícia, Inquéritos, m. 5, AHRS; Police Chief to Pres., 29 Apr. 1885, Secretaria de Polícia, m. 19, AHRS; and Police Chief to Pres., 17 Sept. 1877, Polícia, Cód. 82, AHRS.

72. "Sevicias," *A Federação*, 21 Dec. 1887, 2.

73. "Uma infeliz," *O Mercantil*, 20 Jan. 1887, 2; "Auto de perguntas e corpo de delito feito no pardo Fermino," 26 Nov. 1887, Delegacia de Polícia de Rio Pardo, m. 21, AHRS.

74. Proc. 1563, r. Ricardo José Pereira, m. 61, APERS.

75. Police Chief to Pres., 1 May 1885, Secretaria de Polícia, m. 19, AHRS.

76. *A Federação*, 13 May 1887, 2; for a similar case, see "Acautelem-se!" *O Conservador*, 29 Dec. 1883, 2.

77. "Digno de applausos," *O Mercantil*, 30 May 1887, 2.

78. To Pres., 16 Feb. 1887, Polícia, Cód. 107, AHRS.

79. Proc. 1682, r. Ernesto Francisco de Paula, m. 68, AHRS.

80. Interim Police Chief to Pres., 19 Mar. 1884, Secretaria de Polícia, m. 16, AHRS.

81. Police Chief to Pres., 23 Feb. 1885, Secretaria de Polícia, m. 19, AHRS. See also similar reports on 5 Feb., 18 Mar., and 19 Mar. 1884, Polícia, Cód. 107, AHRS.

82. Police Chief to Pres., 16 June 1887, Polícia, Cód. 107, AHRS.

83. Proc. 1629, r. Leopoldo Bier, m. 65, APERS.

84. Police Chief to Pres., 17 Jan. 1885, Secretaria de Polícia, m. 19, AHRS.

85. Proc. 1535, r. Manoel Ignacio Pavão, m. 60, APERS; proc. 1600, r. Manoel Ignacio Pavão, Joana de Oliveira Eiras, Antonio Capita, Olegario Rollim, and José Fereira, m. 63, APERS; Police Chief to Pres., 17 Jan. 1885, and annexed letter from substitute Subdel. from district of Belém to Del., Secretaria de Polícia, m. 19, AHRS; RS, Pres. *Relatório* (1885), 13.

86. "Protesto," *O Conservador*, 4 Mar. 1888, 4.

87. "Deshumanidade," *O Mercantil*, 1 Aug. 1883, 2; "Deshumanidade," *O Mercantil*, 2 Aug. 1883, 2.

88. Proc. 1682, r. Ernesto Francisco de Paula, m. 68, APERS. See also "Por um escravo," *O Mercantil*, 25 Feb. 1887, 2; the master's response in "Por um escravo," *O Mercantil*, 26 Feb. 1887, 2; and *A Federação*, 22 Dec. 1887, 2, in which a *senhor* claims that one of his employees, not himself, had beaten the *contratado* Manoel Joaquim.

89. Proc. 1556, r. Theodoro de Oliveira Ramos, Antonio Oliveira Ramos, José Antonio da Silva, Marcolino da Silva, and Henrique Gomes Ribeiro, m. 61, APERS; "A sociedade libertadora Esperança e Caridade," *O Século*, 14 Dec. 1884, 2–3. Also see Moreira's detailed analysis in *Os cativos*, esp. 126–37.

90. On emancipations made by the Irmandade de Nossa Senhora do Rosário, see Gresele, "A irmandade dos negros"; and Bakos, *RS: Escravismo e abolição*, 41. Proc. 1556, r. Theodoro de Oliveira Ramos et al., m. 61, APERS, contains the statutes of Esperança e Caridade, as well as fascinating complaints against the directors by several members. As Paulo Moreira has also demonstrated in *Os cativos*, these records show that the society consisted of a directorate of free (mostly artisan) benefactors and a membership of slaves; according to its statutes, members were to deposit money in the treasury of the organization, which would apply the sums to the purchase of individual members when their contributions exceeded their value. See also *O Século*, 14 Dec. 1884, 2–3; *O Mercantil*, 2 July 1883, 3; *O Mercantil*, 16 July 1883, 2; and *O Mercantil*, 6 Oct. 1883, 2.

91. On the collective actions by groups of slaves on São Paulo *fazendas*, see Dean, *Rio Claro*, 143–49; Emília Viotti da Costa, *Da senzala*, 335–42; Conrad, *The Destruction*, 245–47; Célia Maria Marinho de Azevedo, *Onda negra*, 201–11; and Maria Helena P. T. Machado, *O plano e o pânico*.

92. RS, Pres., *Relatório* (1887), 71.

93. See, e.g., Polícia, Cód. 98, 100–102, AHRS; reports of "Prisões," in *O Conservador*, 22 and 25–28 May, 2 and 11 June 1886; J-058, Livro de rol de culpados do cartório do Jury, Porto Alegre, 1883–88, 25.

94. "Secretaria de policia," *A Federação*, 3 May 1887, 2.

95. "Prisões," *O Conservador*, 20 Feb. 1887, 2.

96. Cf. the daily reports in Polícia, Cód. 102–12; and Moreira, "Os contratados," 219–21.

97. *Anais. 2a. sessão*, 4 Apr. 1884, 48–51.

98. Originally published in the *Jornal do Commercio*, these poems were collected in Vieira, *A musa moderna*.

99. Vieira, *A musa moderna*, 17–18.

100. Vieira, *A musa moderna*, 73–74.

101. RS, Pres., *Relatório* (1885), 6; RS, Pres., *Relatório* (1887), 13, 37; RS, Pres., *Relatório* (1888), 25. Cf. also the defense of a young freedman in proc. 1578, r. Felipe, m. 63, APERS.

102. Azevedo [pseud. "Fiscal Honorário"], "Coisas municipais," *A Federação*, 28 Jan. 1886, 1. The identity of "Fiscal" comes from Porto Alegre, *Homens illustres*, 285.

Also see the similar language in "Asylo de Sta. Thereza," *A Reforma*, 11 Aug. 1886, 2; and "Instituto de Artifices," *Jornal do Commercio*, 1 Jan. 1882, 1.

103. *A Federação*, 7 Jan. 1885, cited in Bakos, *RS: Escravismo e abolição*, 123–24. Although the Centro failed to follow through on this plan, others pushed for popular education; see RS, Pres., *Relatório* (1885), 108.

104. *Anais. Primeira sessão*, 11 Nov. 1885, 94–95, and 28 Oct. 1885, 20. Cf. RS, Pres., *Relatório* (1888), 22–23; and the speech by Joaquim Pedro in *Anais*, 14 Apr. 1884, 76–78. Cf. also Albino Pereira Pinto in *Anais. Primeira sessão*, 9 Nov. 1887, anexo, 3, 65.

105. "Os emancipados," *O Mercantil*, 20 Aug. 1887, 1–2.

106. Leg., Cód. 614, Ato 84, 3 Sept. 1886, AHRS; "Apparato bellico," *A Reforma*, [11] Nov. 1886, 1–2. Cf. Moreira, "Entre o deboche," chap. 1.

107. The budget provided for the police force by the Provincial Assembly for these years was as follows:

1879–80	451:015$890 réis
1880–81	410:233$000 réis
1881–82	483:000$000 réis
1888	475:645$000 réis

See Leg., Cód. 596, lei 1220, AHRS; Leg., Cód. 601, lei 1259, AHRS; Leg., Cód. 601, lei 1344, AHRS; Leg., Cód. 615, lei 1688, AHRS; and Moreira, "Entre o deboche," 19. The number of members of the police force actually dropped from a high of 1,059 in 1878–89 to 795 in 1881–83 and 719 in 1888. See Leg., Cód. 596, lei 1148, AHRS; Leg., Cód. 601, leis 1245, 1306, and 1378, AHRS; and Leg., Cód. 615, lei 1753, AHRS.

108. "Boa medida," *O Mercantil*, 30 Jan. 1888, 1; "Contractados," *O Conservador*, 28 Jan. 1888, 2.

109. "A criadagem," *A Federação*, 12 June 1885, 2.

110. "Serviço domestico," *A Federação*, 1 Feb. 1886, 1.

111. "Serviço domestico," *A Federação*, 8 Feb. 1886, 2.

112. "Serviço domestico," *A Federação*, 10 Mar. 1886, 1.

113. "Serviço domestico," *A Federação*, 19 Feb. 1886, 2.

114. For the regulations set up in other cities, see Bakos, "Regulamentos"; and Moreira, "Entre o deboche," 235–37.

115. Regulamento sent to Pres., 22 Sept. 1886, Corr. of Câm. Mun., Porto Alegre, m. 149, l. 137, AHRS. Cf. Additivo to artigo 10. do codigo de posturas de Porto Alegre, Leg. Provincial, Cód. 615, AHRS; and Barbosa, *O processo legislativo*, 210–11.

116. RS, Pres., *Relatório* (1887), 10, in Corr. of Câm. Mun., Porto Alegre, m. 150, l. 137, AHRS.

117. 19 Dec. 1887, Corr. of Câm. Mun., Porto Alegre, m. 150, l. 137, AHRS.

118. Corr. of Câm. Mun., Porto Alegre, m. 150, l. 137, AHRS; Moreira, "Entre o deboche," 238.

119. Câm. Mun. to Pres., 2 June 1888, Corr. of Câm. Mun., Porto Alegre, m. 150, l. 137, AHRS.

120. Porto Alegre, Câm. Mun., *Annaes*, 22 Jan. 1890, 3–4, and 9 Aug. 1890, 24; Secretary of Police to Governor, Cód. 120, Polícia, 2 July 1890, AHRS.

121. Moreira, "Entre o deboche," 232.

Chapter 5. "A Strange Vision of Popular Movement"

1. Sérgio da Costa Franco, *Júlio de Castilhos*, 55; Moritz, *Acontecimentos politicos*, 26.

2. Sérgio da Costa Franco, *Júlio de Castilhos*, 59–61; manifesto of Justo de Azambuja Rangel, ousted vice president of Rio Grande do Sul, 16 Nov. 1889, in *Almanak litterario . . .1891*, 227–28.

3. Love, *Rio Grande do Sul*, 40.

4. Manifesto of Joaquim Pedro Salgado, Joaquim Pedro Soares, and Joaquim Antonio Vasques, 21 Nov. 1889, in *Almanak litterario . . . 1891*, 230–31. Many notable Conservative leaders such as Silva Tavares had joined the PRR earlier in 1889.

5. *Almanak litterario . . . 1891*, 230–31.

6. Pacheco, *O cidadão está nas ruas;* Bak, "Class, Ethnicity, and Gender," and "Labor, Community, and the Making of a Cross-Class Alliance."

7. Cf. Alonso, *Idéias em movimento*, 259.

8. Pinto, *Positivismo;* Trindade, "Aspectos políticos," 125.

9. Silveira Martins, *Silveira Martins*, 70, cited in Love, *Rio Grande do Sul*, 24.

10. Boeira, "O Rio Grande do Sul de Auguste Comte."

11. Fontoura, *Memórias*, 34–35.

12. Love, *Rio Grande do Sul;* Chasteen, *Heroes on Horseback;* Félix, *Coronelismo, borgismo*. Cf. Sérgio da Costa Franco, *Júlio de Castilhos;* and Baretta, "Political Violence," on the role of ideology in the realignments of patronage in the countryside; Baretta counters Franco's denial that ideology played any part in the conversion of some local bosses to Castilhism.

13. See, e.g., Richard Graham, *Patronage and Politics*.

14. Pesavento, *O imaginário da cidade*, 263; Hahner, *Poverty and Politics*, 35.

15. Fontoura, *Memórias*, 6.

16. Comte, *System of Positive Polity*, 1: 136.

17. Comte, *The Essential Comte*, 227, and *System of Positive Polity*, 1: 153.

18. *Diário Oficial*, 14 Feb. 1889, cited in Ligia Ketzer Fagundes, Kummer, Stephanou, and Pesavento, *Memória da indústria*, 24–25.

19. Rodríguez, *Castilhismo*, 8.

20. Cf. "A crise," *A Federação*, 9 June 1891, 1.

21. "As classes productoras," *A Federação*, 27 Sept. 1889, 1; cf. "Pensões e reformas dos operarios," *A Federação*, 10 Sept. 1891, 1. Like Comte, the PRR also thought the existing economic elite required moral reeducation.

22. "Columna dos operarios," *A Federação*, 17 Jan. 1889, 2.

23. "Reunião de operarios," *A Federação*, 26 Apr. 1889, 2; "Columna dos operarios," *A Federação*, 18 Jan. 1889, 2.

24. "Liga Agrícolo-Industrial," *A Federação*, 5 Feb. 1889, 2.

25. Singer, *Desenvolvimento econômico*, 141–98.

26. Pesavento, "República velha gaúcha," 201; Baretta, "Political Violence," 28.

27. *Catálogo da Exposição Brasileira-Alemã*, 1–360 (section on Brazilian producers).

28. Mulhall, *Rio Grande do Sul*, 5–7; Sérgio da Costa Franco, *Porto Alegre e seu comércio*, 55–57; *Catálogo da Exposição da Provincia*, 3–5; *Catálogo da Exposição Brasileira-Alemã*, 246–47.

29. Baretta, "Political Violence," 69; Roche, *A colonização alemã*, 2: 506. Cf. Pesavento, *A burguesia gaúcha*, 20–47.

30. Proc. 1711, r. Marcilio Dias, m. 69, APERS; proc. 1785, r. João de Oliveira e Silva Filho, m. 73, APERS.

31. Gans, *Presença teuta*, 52–72, provides lists of German-owned establishments by street in 1850–89.

32. Bakos, *Porto Alegre e seus eternos intendentes*, 18.

33. The War Arsenal, for instance, employed children as "minor apprentices" and women through a putting-out system.

34. *Democracia Social*, 16 July 1893, 1, rpt. in Marçal, *Primeiras lutas*, 131.

35. Gans, *Presença teuta*, 86; Baretta, "Political Violence," 66–78; "Pela Patria," *A Federação*, 30 Nov. 1889, 2.

36. See, e.g., *O Operario*, 17 May 1885, 1; *Diário Oficial*, 14 Feb. 1889, rpt. in Ligia Ketzer Fagundes, *Memória da indústria*, 24–25; *A Federação*, 5 Sept. 1887, 2; *O Productor*, 21 Aug. 1889, 1.

37. Petersen, "*Que a União*," 31–32; Cláudia Pons Cardoso, "O importante papel"; Moacyr Flores, "A educação da mulher"; "O Operario," *O Operario*, 20 Jan. 1889, 1. Cf., on a later period, Bak, "Class, Ethnicity, and Gender."

38. "13 de Maio," *A Federação*, 13 May 1889, 1.

39. Cf. "A mashorca do sr. João Alfredo," *A Federação*, 2 Jan. 1889, 1; "A guerra de raças," *A Federação*, 10 May 1889, 1; and "A abolição e a republica," *A Federação*, 13 May 1889, 1.

40. "Communicado," *A Federação*, 19 Feb. 1889, 2; "Lição a brancos e negros," *A Federação*, 23 Jan. 1889, 1.

41. Pesavento, *A burguesia gaúcha*, 61–63; Marçal, *Primeiras lutas*, 11; Rio Grande do Sul, *Actos . . . 1882*, 6–21; Petersen, "*Que a União*," 34–53.

42. Marçal, *Primeiras lutas*, 12; Rio Grande do Sul, *Actos . . . 1882*, 44–92, 338–58.

43. See, e.g., Aluísio Azevedo, *Mulatto*.

44. "Classe caixeiral," *O Athleta*, 26 July 1885, 2–3; "Fechamento de portas," *O Athleta*, 20 Sept. 1885, 1.

45. See, e.g., "A observancia do domingo," *O Mercantil*, 18 Sept. 1853, 2.

46. Sérgio da Costa Franco, *Porto Alegre e seu comércio*, 80–84.

47. *A Federação*, 5 Sept. 1887, 2. The *O Operario* that appeared in 1885 may simply have changed ownership during the year; see also *O Pampeiro*, *O Girondino*, and *O Productor* (which also had a German-language edition).

48. *O Operario*, 17 May 1885.

49. Petersen, "*Que a União*," 51–53; "O Operario," *O Operario*, 20 Jan. 1889, 1.

50. "As classes operarias," *O Girondino*, 4 July 1889, 1–2.

51. Richard Graham, *Patronage and Politics;* Love, "Political Participation in Brazil"; Carvalho, *Teatro de sombras*, 139–43.

52. *Catálogo da Exposição Brasileira-Alemã*, 322–33.

53. *O Conservador*, 4 July 1889, 1.

54. Gans, *Presença teuta*, 66.

55. Even the Conservative Party showed itself capable of referring to the Workers' Union as a "distinguished society"; see *O Conservador*, 17 July 1889, 2.

56. "Eleição de 31 de Agosto," *O Productor*, 21 Aug. 1889, 1; "As classes operarias," *O Girondino*, 4 July 1889, 2; Moritz, *Acontecimentos*, 8–10. *O Operario*, though, hesitated longer than the PRR in its attacks against Silva Só; cf. "A eleição," *O Operario*, 20 Jan. 1889, 2.

57. "As classes operarias," *O Girondino*, 4 July 1889, 2; "Liga Agrícolo-Industrial," *A Federação*, 5 Feb. 1889, 2; "Protesto," *A Federação*, 10 Jan. 1889, 2; "Industrialistas e operarios," *A Federação*, 14 Jan. 1889, 2–3.

58. "Protesto," *A Federação*, 10 Jan. 1889, 2; "As classes operarias," *O Girondino*, 4 July 1889, 1–2; "O deputado operario," *O Conservador*, 4 July 1889, 1.

59. Rpt. in Piccolo, *Vida política*, 64.

60. Baretta, "Political Violence," 30–35.

61. "Columna dos operarios," *A Federação*, 17 Jan. 1889, 2; "Liga Agrícolo-Industrial," *A Federação*, 28 May 1889, 2.

62. *Almanak litterario . . . 1889*, 213.

63. "Successos de hontem," *Jornal do Commercio*, 5 Feb. 1892, 2.

64. Proc. 1787, r. Coronel João Pinto da Fonseca Guimarães et al., m. 73, APERS.

65. Romero, *Provocações*, 401–16, cited in Lessa, *A invenção*, 46; cf. Angela Maria de Castro Gomes, *A invenção*, 21 and passim.

66. Moraes qtd. in Carvalho, *Os bestializados*, 24.

67. On Porto Alegre in this period, see esp. Pacheco, *O cidadão;* Pesavento, *A burguesia gaúcha;* Baretta, "Political Violence"; and Petersen, "*Que a União*." Cf. also Carvalho, *Os bestializados;* Penna, *O progresso da ordem;* Assunção, "Elite Politics and Popular Rebellion"; Ribeiro, *A liberdade em construção;* Schultz, *Tropical Versailles;* and Chalhoub, "Slaves, Freedmen and the Politics of Freedom."

68. "O jubilo popular," *A Federação*, 18 Nov. 1889, 1. Francophiles in search of reasons to protest the Brazilian monarchy, the PRR earlier that year had organized a demonstration commemorating the fall of the Bastille; see "Festejos," *O Conservador*, 13 July 1889, 2; and "A festa republicana," *O Conservador*, 15 July 1889, 1.

69. Pacheco, *O cidadão*, 56–58.

70. Pacheco, *O cidadão*, 58–68; Medeiros, *Escola Militar*, 59.

71. "A marcha cívica," *A Federação*, 16 Dec. 1889, 1, in Pacheco, *O cidadão*, 88–90.

72. "Pela Patria," *A Federação*, 30 Nov. 1889, 2.

73. Love, *Rio Grande do Sul*, 40–41; Sérgio da Costa Franco, *Júlio de Castilhos*, 60–66.

74. Sérgio da Costa Franco, *Júlio de Castilhos*, 65; LAI to Governor, 13 Feb. 1890, RB MF75, FCRB.

75. Pesavento, *A burguesia gaúcha*, 139.

76. Júlio de Castilhos, Antão de Faria, Homero Baptista, Assis Brasil, and Ernesto Alves, "Manifesto sobre a 'questão bancaria," in Rosa, *Julio de Castilhos*, 2: 295–302; Baretta, "Political Violence," 37–39, 65–78.

77. "Dr. Demetrio Ribeiro," *A Federação*, 3 Mar. 1890, 1, in Pesavento, *A burguesia gaúcha*, 140.

78. "De sol a sol," *O Athleta*, 9 Mar. 1890, 3–4; "Discursos proferidos no banquete oferecido ao dr. Demétrio Ribeiro quando de sua estada no Rio Grande do Sul," *A Federação*, 4 Mar. 1890, 1, in Pesavento, *A burguesia gaúcha*, 140.

79. Sérgio da Costa Franco, *Júlio de Castilhos*, 65–67; Moritz, *Acontecimentos politicos*, 47–63.

80. *Almanak litterario . . . 1892*, 26, also cited in Pacheco, *O cidadão*, 71–72.

81. Gen. Frota et al. to Provisional Government, 30 Apr. 1890, RB MF75, FCRB; Pacheco, *O cidadão*, 71–74.

82. Moritz, *Acontecimentos politicos*, 77.

83. *A Federação*, 7 May 1890, in Teixeira, *A revolução*, 107.

84. Teixeira, *A revolução*, 106–7; *A Reforma*, 7 May 1890; *A Federação*, 7 and 8 May 1890, in Pacheco, *O cidadão*, 76–79; Moritz, *Acontecimentos politicos*, 78–79.

85. This paragraph draws on Pacheco, *O cidadão*, 80–86; Sérgio da Costa Franco, *Júlio de Castilhos*, 72; and esp. on the articles from *O Mercantil* and *A Federação* transcribed in Moritz, *Acontecimentos politicos*, 79–101.

86. Sérgio da Costa Franco, *Júlio de Castilhos*, 76.

87. Sérgio da Costa Franco, *Júlio de Castilhos*, 76.

88. Trindade, "Aspectos políticos," 131; Moritz, *Acontecimentos politicos*, 139–43; Love, *Rio Grande do Sul*, 42; Sérgio da Costa Franco, *Júlio de Castilhos*, 76.

89. Trindade, "Aspectos políticos," 133.

90. Moritz, *Acontecimentos politicos*, 196–201.

91. *O Rio Grande*, 21 Oct. 1890, 1; Pacheco, *O cidadão*, 111–14.

92. *O Rio Grande*, 22 Oct. 1890, 1.

93. Pacheco, *O cidadão*, 116–17.

94. "Liga Operaria," *A Federação*, 3 and 26 Dec. 1890, 1.

95. "Liga Operaria," *A Federação*, 6 Dec. 1890, 1; Pacheco, *O cidadão*, 119–21.

96. See, e.g., "A grande naturalização," *A Federação*, 16 Dec. 1889, 1; "Ainda a liberdade religiosa," *A Federação*, 1 July 1890, 1; "Protesto," *A Federação*, 14 May 1892, 2.

97. Love, *Rio Grande do Sul*, 45; Sérgio da Costa Franco, *Júlio de Castilhos*, 97.

98. There was some minor dissension within the PRR on the degree of authority granted to the executive, but concerns of party unity apparently silenced such doubts. See, e.g., *Annaes do Congresso Constituinte*, esp. Título II, caps. 1–2, Título III, and Título VI of the final version of the state constitution, 97–100. See Pinto, "The Positivist Discourse," 209–11, on the constitution and its similarities to the Apostolate's plan.

99. Sérgio da Costa Franco, *Getúlio Vargas*, 36–37.

100. "A projecto de Constituição do Estado, IV," *A Reforma,* 4 July 1891, 1; cf. Castro, *A república que a revolução destruiu,* 62.

101. "Caveat, populus," *A Reforma,* 8 July 1891, 1; "14 de Julho," *A Reforma,* 14 July 1891, 1; "A obra," *A Reforma,* 23 July 1891, 1; "É grave!" *A Reforma,* 1 Sept. 1891, 1; "Dictador," *A Reforma,* 21 July 1891, 1.

102. Assis Brasil, *Do governo presidencial;* "Jacobinismo," *A Reforma,* 21 July 1891, 1.

103. Orico, *Silveira Martins,* 394.

104. Sérgio da Costa Franco, *Júlio de Castilhos,* 104; cf. Moritz, *Acontecimentos politicos,* 241.

105. Love, *Rio Grande do Sul,* 47.

106. Love, *Rio Grande do Sul,* 47–49; Moritz, *Acontecimentos politicos,* 241–51.

107. *O Mercantil,* 12 Nov. 1891, in Moritz, *Acontecimentos politicos,* 258–62.

108. Love, *Rio Grande do Sul,* 48–49; Sérgio da Costa Franco, *Júlio de Castilhos,* 110–13.

109. Trindade, "Aspectos políticos," 135.

110. "Operarios!" and "Meeting," *L'Avvenire,* 7 Mar. 1892, 1; "Meeting operario" and "L'Avvenire," *A Federação,* 4 Apr. 1892, 2; Borges, *Italianos,* 73.

111. "Os successos," *Jornal do Commercio,* 6 Feb. 1892, 2; "Successos de hontem," *Jornal do Commercio,* 5 Feb. 1892, 2. Cf. Sérgio da Costa Franco, *Júlio de Castilhos,* 117–22.

112. On Kappel as an effective patron, cf. "Uma festa do trabalho," *A Reforma,* 10 Dec. 1891, 2.

113. Proc. 1711, r. Marcilio Dias, m. 69, APERS; proc. 1785, r. João de Oliveira e Silva Filho, m. 73, APERS.

114. Sérgio da Costa Franco, *Júlio de Castilhos,* 130.

115. "A obra," *A Reforma,* 23 July 1891, 1.

116. *Almanak litteraria . . . 1892,* 44; the income redistribution provision appears as point 29. Cf. Petersen, "*Que a União,*" 86–88.

117. "Gremios dos Artistas," *A Federação,* 7 Mar. 1892, 1; Petersen, "*Que a União,*" 95–96; Marçal, *Primeiras lutas,* 61–63.

118. It is possible, of course, that these groups were simply unable to attract elite allies.

119. Chatterjee, *The Politics,* 59–60.

120. On "Zé Povo" or "Zé Povinho," see, e.g., the cartoon on the cover of *O Século* on 25 June 1882, in which the Liberals are depicted as inviting the *povo* (in the figure of Zé Povinho) to a feast before elections and then booting them out immediately thereafter. Cf. also Marcos A. da Silva, *Caricata República.*

121. "A classe operaria porto-alegrense," *A Gazetinha,* 15 Jan. 1893, 1.

122. Mauch, *Ordem pública,* 52–53.

123. "Pelas esquinas," *A Gazetinha,* 10 Apr. 1892, 4; cf. "A Republica," *A Gazetinha,* 15 Nov. 1891, 1.

124. "Notas da semana," *A Gazetinha,* 28 Feb. 1892, 3; "Pelas esquinas," *A Gazetinha,* 10 Jan. 1892, 2; "Apanhados," *A Gazetinha,* 29 Nov. 1891, 3.

125. "Actualidade," *A Gazetinha,* 24 Jan. 1892, 1.

126. "A carestia," *A Gazetinha,* 3 Apr. 1892, 1. A similar call was made soon after in Pelotas; see "Cooperativa," *O Operario* (Pelotas), 1 May 1892, 1. See also complaints that speculation and corruption by figures linked to the municipal government were depriving the *povo* of basic water and sewage services: "Pelas esquinas," *A Gazetinha,* 24 Jan. 1892, 2; "Hydraulica Guahybense," *A Gazetinha,* 31 Jan. 1892, 1; "Pelas esquinas," *A Gazetinha,* 31 Jan. 1892, 2.

127. "Pelas esquinas," *A Gazetinha,* 6 Dec. 1891, 2.

128. On similar demands of citizens' rights made in Rio de Janeiro in 1900–1910, cf. Eduardo Silva, *As queixas do povo.*

129. "Vagabundagem," *A Gazetinha,* 7 Feb. 1892, 1. See also Mauch, *Ordem pública,* 60–66.

130. "Apanhados," *A Gazetinha,* 20 Dec. 1891, 3. Cf. esp. the humorous poem "Semana do vadio," *A Gazetinha,* 24 Jan. 1892, which describes the week of a vagrant as a series of excuses not to work.

131. "Apanhados," *A Gazetinha,* 20 Dec. 1891, 3.

132. See "Apanhados," *A Gazetinha,* 8 Nov. 1891, 3; 15 Nov. 1891, 3; 13 Dec. 1891, 3; and 20 Dec. 1891, 3.

133. For examples of elite rhetoric, see Police Chief to Governor, 4 Jan. 1893, Polícia, Cód. 125, AHRS; Pres. of the Junta Municipal to Secretary of State, 14 Apr. 1890, Corr. da Junta Municipal, m. 355, l. 121 vert., AHRS; "Chronica medica," *Folha Nova,* 25 Oct. 1892, 2. Cf. Mauch, *Ordem pública,* 69–126; and Pesavento, *Emergência,* and "Lugares malditos."

134. *O Exemplo,* 12 Nov. 1892, 1.

135. *O Exemplo,* 12 Nov. 1892, 1. Cf. Bratzel and Masterson, "O Exemplo," 587–88.

136. "Escandalo," *O Exemplo,* 12 Mar. 1893, 1, and "Por um vexame," *O Exemplo,* 12 Mar. 1893, 2, both qtd. in Fernando Henrique Cardoso, *Capitalismo e escravidão,* 253.

137. "A quem toca," *O Exemplo,* 8 Jan. 1893, 1, and "Pelo dever," *O Exemplo,* 23 July 1893, 1, both in Fernando Henrique Cardoso, *Capitalismo e escravidão,* 253, 255. Cf. also the letter from Júlio Nehemias, who complained of the common assumption that Afro-Brazilians were vagrants and incapable of having solid family relations: "Communicado," *A Federação,* 19 Feb. 1889, 2.

138. "Mais um vexame," *O Exemplo,* 1 Jan. 1893, 1, in Fernando Henrique Cardoso, *Capitalismo e escravidão,* 254–55 n. 25.

139. "Cuba," *O Exemplo,* 3 Nov. 1895, 2, in Fernando Henrique Cardoso, *Capitalismo e escravidão,* 268 n. 55.

140. *O Exemplo,* 2 Jan. 1930, 1; *O Exemplo,* 8 Jan. 1893, qtd. in Bratzel and Masterson, "O Exemplo," 589.

141. "Nossos detractors," *O Exemplo,* 30 Apr. 1893, 1.

142. "Festividades" and "Picnic," *O Exemplo,* 11 Dec. 1892, 3; *O Exemplo,* 30 Apr. 1893, 3.

143. "Desagradavel," *O Exemplo,* 30 Apr. 1893, 1–2; "Actualidade," *O Exemplo,* 25 June 1893, 1, in Fernando Henrique Cardoso, *Capitalismo e escravidão,* 255.

144. See, e.g., "Pauladas," *O Exemplo*, 11 Dec. 1892, 4; "Burlesqueando," *O Exemplo*, 20 Apr. 1893, 4.

145. "Farpas," *O Exemplo*, 30 Apr. 1893, 3–4.

146. See esp. Rüdiger, "O proletariado gaúcho."

147. Love, *Rio Grande do Sul*, chap. 3; Chasteen, *Heroes on Horseback*.

148. On later challenges to the PRR from rival parties, see Love, *Rio Grande do Sul;* and Pedro Cezar Dutra Fonseca, *RS: Economia e conflitos*. On the PRR's tense relationship with workers, see esp. Bak, "Class, Ethnicity, and Gender," and "Labor, Community, and the Making of a Cross-Class Alliance"; Bilhão, *Rivalidades;* and Bodea, *A greve geral de 1917*.

Conclusion

1. Moreira, "Entre o deboche," 54–55.

2. Proc. 1681, r. Maria da Costa, m. 68, APERS.

3. Hahner, *Poverty and Politics*, esp. chap. 3; Sandra Lauderdale Graham, "The Vintem Riot"; Penna, *O progresso*, 173–85.

4. The concept of "repertoire" comes from Charles Tilly, cited in Guardino, *Peasants, Politics, and the Formation*, 7; and Forment, *Democracy*, 433, esp. n. 27.

5. "Amor, ordem e progresso," *A Federação*, 3 Dec. 1889, 1.

6. Berlin, *Against the Current*, 315.

7. Sabato, "On Political Citizenship," 1314.

8. Stern, "Tricks of Time," 150.

Bibliography

Archives

PORTO ALEGRE

Arquivo Histórico do Rio Grande do Sul
Arquivo Histórico Municipal de Porto Alegre
Arquivo Público do Rio Grande do Sul
Assembléia Legislativa do Rio Grande do Sul/Solar dos Câmaras
Biblioteca Pública
Instituto Histórico e Geográfico do Rio Grande do Sul
Museu de Comunicação Social Hipólito José da Costa

RIO GRANDE

Biblioteca Rio-Grandense

RIO DE JANEIRO

Arquivo Nacional
Biblioteca Nacional
Casa de Rui Barbosa
Instituto Histórico e Geográfico Brasileiro

Newspapers

PORTO ALEGRE

O Athleta, 1885–86, 1890
O Commercio, 1847–48
O Conservador, 1879–89
Correio de Porto Alegre, 1849, 1851
Correio do Sul, 1857, 1859–60
O Exemplo, 1892–95, 1930
A Federação, 1885–93
Folha Nova, 1892–93
A Gazeta da Tarde, 1895

A Gazetinha, 1891–98
O Girondino, 1889
A Imprensa, 1881–82
Jornal do Comércio, 1879, 1882, 1889–90
Mercantil/O Mercantil, 1852–53, 1861–65, 1878–84, 1887–88
O Operario, 1885, 1889
O Pampeiro, 1886
O Porto-Alegrense, 1849
O Productor, 1889
A Propaganda, 1864
A Reforma, 1869–71, 1875, 1886, 1891
O Rio-Grandense, 1846
O Século, 1880–87
Tribuna Rio-Grandense, 1854
A Voz do Povo, 1852

OTHERS

O Operario (Pelotas), 1892
A Ordem (Jaguarão), 1884–87
A Voz do Escravo (Pelotas), 1881

Published Primary Sources

Almanak litterario e estatistico do Rio Grande do Sul, organizado por Alfredo Ferreira Rodrigues. 1889–93. Pelotas, Porto Alegre, and Rio Grande: Carlos Pinto & Comp., 1888–[92].

Annaes do Congresso Constituinte do Estado do Rio Grande do Sul (1891). 2d ed. Porto Alegre: Officinas Graphicas d'A Federação, 1929.

Annaes do Congresso Republicano Rio-Grandense. Primeira sessão periodica. 1883. Porto Alegre: Typ. de Gundlach & Cia., 1883.

Annaes do Congresso Republicano Rio-Grandense. Terceira sessão periodica. 1885. Porto Alegre: Oficinas typographicas d'A Federação, 1885.

Annuario da Provincia do Rio Grande do Sul publicado sob a direcção de Graciano Alves de Azambuja. 1885, 1889, 1892. Porto Alegre: Gundlach & Cia., 1884, 1888, 1891.

Assis Brasil, Joaquim Francisco de. *Democracia representativa: Do voto e do modo de votar.* Rio de Janeiro: Typ. de G. Leuzinger & Filhos, 1893.

———. *A democracia representativa na República (Antologia).* Ed. Vicente Barreto. Brasília: Câmara dos Deputados, 1983.

———. *Dictadura, parlamentarismo, democracia.* [Porto Alegre]: Livraria do Globo, 1908.

———. *Do governo presidencial na república brasileira.* Lisbon: Companhia Nacional Editora, 1896.

———. *Dois discursos pronunciados na Assembleia Legislativa da Provincia do Rio Grande do Sul.* Porto Alegre: Officinas typographicas da Federação, 1886.

———. *História da República Riograndense.* Porto Alegre: Estante Rio-Grandense União de Seguros/Companhia Rio-Grandense de Artes Gráficas, 1982.

———. *Idéias políticas de Assis Brasil.* Ed. Paulo Brossard. Brasília: Senado Federal; Rio de Janeiro: FCRB/MinC, 1989.

Avé-Lallemant, Robert. *Viagem pela província do Rio Grande do Sul (1858).* Trans. Teodoro Cabral. Belo Horizonte: Ed. Itatiaia; São Paulo: Ed. da Universidade de São Paulo, 1980.

Azevedo, Aluísio. *Mulatto.* Trans. Murray Graeme MacNicoll. Austin: University of Texas Press, 1990.

Barbosa, Eni, ed. *O processo legislativo e a escravidão negra na província de São Pedro do Rio Grande do Sul: Fontes.* Porto Alegre: Assembléia Legislativa do Estado do Rio Grande do Sul/CORAG, 1987.

Bastos, Ronaldo Marcos. *Porto Alegre: Um século de fotografia.* CD-ROM. Canoas: Editora da ULBRA, 1997.

Beschoren, Maximiliano. *Impressões de viagem na Província do Rio Grande do Sul.* Porto Alegre: Martins Livreiro, 1989.

Brasiliense [de Almeida e Melo], Américo. *Os programas dos partidos e o Segundo Império.* Brasília: Senado Federal; Rio de Janeiro: FCRB/MEC, 1979.

Caldre e Fião, José Antonio do Vale. *O corsário: Romance rio-grandense.* 1849. 6th ed. Porto Alegre: Movimento, 1985.

———. *A divina pastora: Romance.* 1847. Porto Alegre: RBS, n.d.

Camargo, Antonio Eleutherio de. *Quadro estatistico e geographico da Provincia de S. Pedro do Rio Grande do Sul.* Porto Alegre: Typ. do Jornal do Commercio, 1868.

Canstatt, Oscar. *Brasil—terra e gente.* 2d ed. Trans. Eduardo de Lima Castro. Rio de Janeiro: Conquista, 1975.

Castilhos, Júlio de. *Idéias políticas de Júlio de Castilhos.* Ed. Paulo Carneiro. Brasília: Senado Federal; Rio de Janeiro: FCRB, 1982.

Catálogo da Exposição Brasileira-Alemã em Porto Alegre, Provincia de S. Pedro do Rio Grande do Sul (Brasil). 1881. Porto Alegre: Typographia da Deutsche Zeitung, 1881.

Catálogo da Exposição da Provincia de S. Pedro do Rio Grande do Sul em 1875. N.p., n.d.

Chaves, Antonio José Gonçalves. *Memórias ecônomo-políticas sobre a administração pública do Brasil.* Porto Alegre: Companhia União de Seguros Gerais, 1978.

Christie, William Dougal. *Notes on Brazilian Questions.* London and Cambridge: MacMillan and Co., 1865.

Convenção republicana de 23 de fevereiro. Porto Alegre: Typographia de Gundlach and Comp., 1882.

Coruja, Antonio Álvares Pereira. *Antigualhas: Reminiscências de Porto Alegre.* Porto Alegre: Companhia União de Seguros Gerais, 1983.

Couty, Louis. *A escravidão no Brasil.* Rio de Janeiro: FCRB, 1988.

Despatches from United States Consuls in Rio Grande do Sul, 1829–97. 7 vols. Microfilm. Washington, D.C.: The National Archives, National Archives and Records Services, General Services Administration, 1957.

"Documentos relativos à historia da capitania, depois provincia, de S. Pedro do Rio

Grande do Sul, compilados e copiados na secretaria do governo em Porto Alegre, de ordem do conselheiro barão Homem de Mello, ex-presidente da mesma provincia." *Revista do Instituto Historico, Geographico e Ethnographico do Brasil* 40 (1877): 191–298; 41 (1878): 273–386; 42 (1879): 5–90, 105–56.

Dreys, Nicolau. *Notícia descritiva da Província do Rio Grande de S. Pedro do Sul.* Porto Alegre: Editora Nova Dimensão/Editora da PUCRS, 1990.

Fundação de Economia e Estatística. *De Província de São Pedro a Estado do Rio Grande do Sul: Censos do RS, 1803–1950.* Porto Alegre: FEE, 1981.

[Gomes, José Cândido]. *Chronica de Porto-Alegre.* Porto Alegre: Typographia d'O Mercantil, 1855.

Hörmeyer, Joseph. *O Rio Grande do Sul de 1850: Descrição da Província do Rio Grande do Sul no Brasil meridional.* Trans. Heinrich A. W. Bunse. Porto Alegre: D. C. Luzzatto Editores/EDUNISUL, 1986.

Isabelle, Arsène. *Emigração e colonização na província brasileira do Rio Grande do Sul, na República Oriental do Uruguai e em toda a bacia do Prata.* Trans. Belfort de Oliveira. Rio de Janeiro: Gráfica Editora Souza, 1950.

———. *Viagem ao Rio Grande do Sul (1833–1834).* Trans. and ed. Dante de Laytano. Porto Alegre: Martins Livreiro Editor, 1983.

Itaquy, Egydio Barbosa Oliveira. *Monarchia federal. Politica do Augusto Senador Gaspar Silveira Martins. Candidatura provincial.* Porto Alegre: Estabelecimento Typographico de Gundlach & Cia., 1886.

Jansen, Carlos. *O patuá: Novela gauchesca (1879–1880).* Porto Alegre: Gabinete de Pesquisa de História do Rio Grande do Sul/Instituto de Filosofia e Ciências Humanas da UFRGS, 1974.

Langendonck, Madame van. *Uma colônia no Brasil.* Florianópolis: Ed. Mulheres; Santa Cruz do Sul: EDUNISC, 2002.

Leonino, Arthur. *Impressões de viagem; O Rio Grande do Sul tal qual é.* Rio de Janeiro: Typ. de G.Leuzinger & Filhos, 1881.

Lima, Alcides. *História popular do Rio Grande do Sul.* 3d ed. Porto Alegre: Martins Livreiro Editor, 1983.

Lima, Antonio de Azevedo. *Almanak administrativo, commercial e industrial rio-grandense para 1874.* Porto Alegre: Typ. do Jornal do Commercio, [1873].

———. *Synopse geographica, historica e estatista do municipio de Porto Alegre.* Porto Alegre: Estab. Typ. de Gundlach & C., 1890.

Luccock, John. *Notas sôbre o Rio-de-Janeiro e partes meridionais do Brasil tomadas durante uma estada de dez anos nesse país, de 1808 a 1818.* Trans. Milton da Silva Rodrigues. 2d ed. São Paulo: Livraria Martins Editora, n.d.

Magalhães, Manoel Antonio de. "Almanak da vila de Porto Alegre, com reflexões sobre o estado da capitania do Rio Grande do Sul." *Revista do Instituto Historico, Geographico, e Ethnographico do Brasil* 30 (1867): 43–74.

Malheiro, Perdigão. *A escravidão no Brasil: Ensaio histórico, jurídico, social.* 2 vols. 3d ed. Petrópolis: Vozes; Brasília: Instituto Nacional do Livro, 1976.

Mawe, John. *Travels in the Interior of Brazil, Particularly in the Gold and Diamond Districts of that Country by Authority of the Prince Regent of Portugal; Including a Voyage to the Rio de la Plata, and an Historical Sketch of the Revolution of Buenos Ayres.* London: Longman, Hurst, Rees, Orme, and Brown, 1812.

Mello, Francisco Ignácio Marcondes Homem de. "Indice chronologico dos factos mais notaveis da historia da capitania, depois provincia, de S. Pedro do Rio Grande do Sul." *Revista do Instituto Historico, Geographico e Ethnographico do Brasil* 42 (1879): 113–40.

Mulhall, Michael George. *Rio Grande do Sul and Its German Colonies.* London: Longmans, Green, and Co., 1873.

Nabuco, Joaquim. *O eclypse do abolicionismo.* Rio de Janeiro: n.p., 1886.

———. *Um estadista do Império.* 2 vols. 5th ed. Rio de Janeiro: Topbooks, 1997.

Pinheiro, José Feliciano Fernandes (Visconde de São Leopoldo). *Anais da província de São Pedro: História da colonização alemã no Rio Grande do Sul.* 4th ed. Petrópolis: Vozes; Brasília: Instituto Nacional do Livro, 1978.

Porto Alegre. Municipal Council. *Annaes da Camara Municipal da Cidade de Porto Alegre de Janeiro a Dezembro de 1890.* Porto Alegre: Typographia á vapor do Jornal do Commercio, 1890.

Porto Alegre, Apolinário. *Paisagens: Contos.* Porto Alegre: Movimento; Brasília: MinC/Pró-Memória/Instituto Nacional do Livro, 1987.

Posturas policiaes da Camara Municipal da Cidade de Porto Alegre approvadas pelo Conselho Geral da Provincia. Porto Alegre: Typographia do Commercio, 1847.

Qorpo Santo [José Joaquim de Campos Leão]. *Enciclopédia ou seis mezes de uma enfermidade.* Porto Alegre: Typografia Qorpo Santo, 1877.

———. *As relações naturais e outras comédias.* Ed. Guilhermino Cesar. Porto Alegre: Edições Faculdade de Filosofia da UFRGS, 1969.

Rebouças, André. *Agricultura nacional: Estudos economicos, propaganda abolicionista e democratica.* Rio de Janeiro: A. J. Lamoureux & Co., 1883.

Recenseamento da população do Império do Brasil a que se procedeu no dia 10. de agosto de 1872. 19 vols. Rio de Janeiro: Directoria Geral de Estatística, 1873–76.

Relatorio apresentado pela Directoria de Estatistica em 31 de julho de 1895 annexo ao relatorio do Secretario de Estado dos Negocios do Interior e Exterior de 15 de agosto de 1895. Porto Alegre: Oficinas Typographicas d'A Federação, 1896.

Revista do Parthenon Litterario. Ano de 1869 (Separata da Revista do Instituto Histórico e Geográfico do Rio Grande do Sul). Porto Alegre: Oficinas Gráficas da Imprensa Oficial, 1951.

Revista do Parthenon Litterario. Ano de 1872 (Separata da Revista do Instituto Histórico e Geográfico do Rio Grande do Sul). Nos. 117 a 120. Porto Alegre: Oficinas Gráficas da Imprensa Oficial, 1953.

Rio Grande do Sul. *Actos do Governo da Provincia do Rio Grande do Sul de 1882.* Porto Alegre: Officinas Typographicas de Carlos Echenique, 1908.

Rio Grande do Sul. Legislative Assembly. *Anais.* 1866–67, 1871–77, 1879–80, 1884–85.

Rio Grande do Sul. President. *Relatório* [*Falla* in 1867; by Vice President in 1857]. 1846–89.

Rodrigues, José Honório, ed. *Atas do Conselho de Estado*. 13 vols. Brasília: Senado Federal, 1973–78.

Saint-Hilaire, Auguste de. *Viagem ao Rio Grande do Sul*. Trans. Adroaldo Mesquita da Costa. Porto Alegre: ERUS/Martins Livreiro Editor, 1987.

Seidler, Carl. *Dez anos no Brasil*. Trans. Bertholdo Klinger. Belo Horizonte: Ed. Itatiaia; São Paulo: Ed. da Universidade de São Paulo, 1980.

Silveira Martins, Gaspar da. *Discursos parlamentares*. Brasília: Câmara dos Deputados, 1979.

Smith, Herbert Huntington. *Do Rio de Janeiro a Cuyabá: Notas de um naturalista*. São Paulo: Companhia Melhoramentos de S. Paulo, 1922.

Synopse do recenseamento de 31 de dezembro de 1890. Rio de Janeiro: Oficina da Estatística, 1898.

Teixeira, Mucio S. Lopes. *A revolução do Rio Grande do Sul, suas causas e seus effeitos*. Porto Alegre: Jornal do Commercio, 1893.

Vieira, Damasceno. *A musa moderna*. Porto Alegre: Typ. do Jornal do Commercio, 1885.

Villalba, Epaminondas [Raul Villa-Lobos]. *A Revolução Federalista no Rio Grande do Sul (Documentos e commentarios)*. Rio de Janeiro: Laemmert & Ca. Editores, 1897.

Secondary Sources

Abèlés, Marc. "Anthropologie politique de la modernité." *L'Homme* 121 (1992): 15–30.

Abreu, Florencio de. *A Constituinte e o projecto de constituição da República Rio-Grandense (ensaio histórico)*. Porto Alegre: Typographia do Centro, 1930.

———. *Ensaios e estudos históricos*. Rio de Janeiro: Irmãos Pongetti, 1964.

Agamben, Giorgio. *Homo Sacer: Sovereign Power and Bare Life*. Trans. Daniel Hiller-Roazen. Stanford: Stanford University Press, 1998.

Alden, Dauril. "Late Colonial Brazil." In Bethell, *Colonial Brazil*, 284–343.

———. *Royal Government in Colonial Brazil, with Special Reference to the Administration of the Marquis of Lavradio, Viceroy, 1769–1779*. Berkeley: University of California Press, 1968.

Algranti, Leila Mezan. *O feitor ausente: Estudo sobre a escravidão urbana no Rio de Janeiro*. Petrópolis: Vozes, 1988.

Alonso, Angela. *Idéias em movimento: A geração 1870 na crise do Brasil-Império*. São Paulo: Paz e Terra, 2002.

Alves, Francisco das Neves, and Luiz Henrique Torres, org. *Pensar a Revolução Federalista*. Rio Grande: Editora da Fundação Universidade de Rio Grande, 1993.

Amado, Janaína. *Conflito social no Brasil: A revolta dos "Mucker," Rio Grande do Sul, 1868–1898*. São Paulo: Edições Símbolo, 1978.

Anderson, Benedict. *Imagined Communities: Reflections on the Origin and Spread of Nationalism*. 2d ed. London: Verso, 1993.

Andrade, Maria José de Souza. *A mão de obra escrava em Salvador, 1811–1860*. São Paulo: Corrupio; [Brasília]: CNPq, 1988.

Andrews, George Reid. *Blacks and Whites in São Paulo, Brazil, 1888–1988.* Madison: University of Wisconsin Press, 1991.

Antunes, Paranhos. "Os partidos políticos no Rio Grande do Sul (1822–1889): Gênese e desdobramento histórico desde a proclamação da Independência à República." In *Anais do Primeiro Congresso de História e Geografia Sul Rio-Grandense,* 2: 215–66. Porto Alegre: Livraria do Globo, 1936.

Appelbaum, Nancy P. *Muddied Waters: Race, Region, and Local History in Colombia, 1846–1948.* Durham: Duke University Press, 2003.

Appelbaum, Nancy P., Anne S. Macpherson, and Karin Alejandra Rosemblatt, eds. *Race and Nation in Modern Latin America.* Chapel Hill: University of North Carolina Press, 2003.

Appleby, Joyce, Lynn Hunt, and Margaret Jacob. *Telling the Truth about History.* New York: W. W. Norton, 1994.

Aragão, R. Batista. *Escravidão e abolicionismo.* Fortaleza: IOCE, 1988.

Arend, Silvia Maria Favero. *Amasiar ou casar? A família popular no final do século XIX.* Porto Alegre: Editora da Universidade/Prefeitura de Porto Alegre, 2001.

Arrom, Silvia Marina. *The Women of Mexico City, 1790–1857.* Stanford: Stanford University Press, 1985.

Assunção, Matthias Röhrig. "Elite Politics and Popular Rebellion in the Construction of Post-Colonial Order: The Case of Maranhão, Brazil (1820–41)." *JLAS* 31 (1999): 1–38.

Azevedo, Célia Maria Marinho de. *Onda negra, medo branco: O negro no imaginário das elites—século XIX.* Rio de Janeiro: Paz e Terra, 1987.

Azevedo, Thales de. *Italianos e gaúchos: Os anos pioneiros da colonização italiana no Rio Grande do Sul.* Porto Alegre: A Nação/Instituto Estadual do Livro, 1975.

Bak, Joan L. "Class, Ethnicity, and Gender in Brazil: The Negotiation of Workers' Identities in Porto Alegre's 1906 Strike." *LARR* 35 (2000): 83–123.

———. "Labor, Community, and the Making of a Cross-Class Alliance in Brazil: The 1917 Railroad Strikes in Rio Grande do Sul." *HAHR* 78 (1998): 179–227.

———. "Political Centralization and the Building of the Interventionist State in Brazil: Corporatism, Regionalism and Interest Group Politics in Rio Grande do Sul, 1930–1937." *LBR* 21 (1985): 9–25.

Baker, Paula. "The Domestication of Politics: Women and American Political Society, 1780–1920." *American Historical Review* 89 (1984): 620–47.

Bakos, Margaret Marchiori. "O imigrante europeu e o trabalho escravo no Rio Grande do Sul." In *Anais do IV Simpósio de História da Imigração e Colonização Alemã no Rio Grande do Sul,* 399–405. [São Leopoldo]: Museu Histórico Visconde de São Leopoldo/Instituto Histórico de São Leopoldo, 1987.

———. *Porto Alegre e seus eternos intendentes.* Porto Alegre: EDIPUCRS, 1996.

———. "Regulamentos sobre o serviço dos criados: Um estudo sobre o relacionamento estado e sociedade no Rio Grande do Sul (1887–1889)." *EIA* 1–2 (1983): 125–36.

———. "Repensando o processo abolicionista sul-rio-grandense." *EIA* 14 (1988): 117–38.

———. *RS: Escravismo e abolição*. Porto Alegre: Mercado Aberto, 1982.

———. "Sobre a mulher escrava no Rio Grande do Sul." *EIA* 16 (1990): 47–56.

Barea, Monsenhor José. "Histórico da Egreja de N. S. do Rosário de Porto Alegre." Unpublished ms.

Baretta, Sílvio Rogério Duncan. "Political Violence and Regime Change: A Study of the 1893 Civil War in Southern Brazil." Ph.D. diss., University of Pittsburgh, 1985.

Barman, Roderick J. *Brazil: The Forging of a Nation, 1798–1852*. Stanford: Stanford University Press, 1988.

———. "The Brazilian Peasantry Reexamined: The Implications of the Quebra-Quilo Revolt, 1874–1875." *HAHR* 57 (1977): 401–24.

———. *Citizen Emperor: Pedro II and the Making of Brazil, 1825–91*. Stanford: Stanford University Press, 1999.

Barreto, Abeillard. *Primórdios da imprensa no Rio Grande do Sul*. Porto Alegre: Comissão Executiva do Sesquicentenário da Revolução Farroupilha, Subcomissão de Publicações e Concursos, [1986].

Barroso, Carmen, and Albertina Oliveira Costa, eds. *Mulher, mulheres*. São Paulo: Cortez/Fundação Carlos Chagas, 1983.

Bastide, Roger. *The African Religions of Brazil: Toward a Sociology of the Interpenetration of Civilizations*. Trans. Helen Sebba. Baltimore: Johns Hopkins University Press, 1978.

Bauss, Rudy. "Rio Grande do Sul in the Portuguese Empire: The Formative Years, 1777–1808." *The Americas* 39 (1983): 519–35.

Beattie, Peter. *The Tribute of Blood: Army, Honor, Race, and Nation in Brazil, 1864–1945*. Durham: Duke University Press, 2001.

Becker, Klaus. "O episódio dos 'Muckers'." In *Enciclopédia Rio-Grandense*, 2: 83–114. Porto Alegre: Sulina, 1968.

Beiguelman, Paula. *A formação do povo no complexo cafeeiro: Aspectos políticos*. 2d ed. São Paulo: Pioneira, 1977.

———. *Formação política do Brasil*. 2d ed. São Paulo: Pioneira, 1976.

Bell, Stephen. *Campanha Gaúcha: A Brazilian Ranching System, 1850–1920*. Stanford: Stanford University Press, 1998.

———. "Early Industrialization in the South Atlantic: Political Influences on the *Charqueadas* of Rio Grande do Sul before 1860." *Journal of Historical Geography* 19 (1993): 399–411.

Bello, José Maria. *A History of Modern Brazil, 1889–1964*. Trans. James L. Taylor. Stanford: Stanford University Press, 1966.

Bento, Cláudio Moreira. *O negro e descendentes na sociedade do Rio Grande do Sul (1635–1975)*. Porto Alegre: Grafosul/Instituto Estadual do Livro/DAC/SEC, 1976.

Bergstresser, Rebecca Baird. "The Movement for the Abolition of Slavery in Rio de Janeiro, Brazil, 1880–1889." Ph.D. diss., Stanford University, 1973.

Berlin, Isaiah. *Against the Current: Essays in the History of Ideas*. Ed. Henry Hardy. Princeton: Princeton University Press, 2001.

Bernd, Zilá, and Margaret M. Bakos. *O negro: Consciência e trabalho*. Porto Alegre: Editora da Universidade/UFRGS, 1991.

Bethell, Leslie. *The Abolition of the Brazilian Slave Trade.* Cambridge: Cambridge University Press, 1970.

———, ed. *Brazil: Empire and Republic, 1822–1930.* Cambridge: Cambridge University Press, 1989.

———, ed. *Colonial Brazil.* Cambridge: Cambridge University Press, 1987.

Bethell, Leslie, and José Murilo de Carvalho. "1822–1850." In Bethell, *Brazil: Empire and Republic,* 45–112.

Bieber, Judy. *Power, Patronage, and Political Violence: State Building on a Brazilian Frontier, 1822–1889.* Lincoln: University of Nebraska Press, 1999.

———. "A *Visão do Sertão:* Party Identity and Political Honor in Late Imperial Minas Gerais, Brazil." *HAHR* 81 (2001): 309–42.

Biehl, João Guilherme. "Jammerthal, the Valley of Lamentation: *Kultur,* War, Trauma and Subjectivity in Nineteenth-Century Brazil." *Journal of Latin American Cultural Studies* 8 (1999): 171–98.

Bilhão, Isabel Aparecida. *Rivalidades e solidariedades no movimento operário: Porto Alegre, 1906–1911.* Porto Alegre: EDIPUCRS, 1999.

Bodea, Miguel. *A greve geral de 1917 e as origens do trabalhismo gaúcho.* Porto Alegre: L&PM, 1979.

Boeira, Nelson. "O Rio Grande de Auguste Comte." In Dacanal and Gonzaga, *RS: Cultura e ideologia,* 34–59.

Borges, Stella. *Italianos: Porto Alegre e trabalho.* Porto Alegre: EST Edições, 1993.

Bosi, Alfredo. "A escravidão entre dois liberalismos." *Estudos Avançados* 3 (1988): 4–39.

Boxer, C. R. *The Golden Age of Brazil, 1695–1750: Growing Pains of a Colonial Society.* Berkeley: University of California Press, 1962.

Bratzel, John F., and Daniel M. Masterson. "O Exemplo: Afro-Brazilian Protest in Porto Alegre." *The Americas* 33 (1977): 585–92.

Brown, Gregory G. "The Impact of American Flour Imports on Brazilian Wheat Production: 1808–1822." *The Americas* 47 (1991): 315–36.

Butler, Kim D. *Freedoms Given, Freedoms Won: Afro-Brazilians in Post-Abolition São Paulo and Salvador.* New Brunswick: Rutgers University Press, 1998.

Caldeira, Teresa Pires do Rio. *A política dos outros: O cotidiano dos moradores da periferia e o que pensam do poder e dos poderosos.* São Paulo: Editora Brasiliense, 1984.

Cardoso, Cláudia Pons. "O importante papel das mulheres sem importância: Porto Alegre 1889–1910." Master's thesis, PUCRS, 1995.

Cardoso, Fernando Henrique. *Capitalismo e escravidão no Brasil meridional: O negro na sociedade escravocrata do Rio Grande do Sul.* 2d ed. Rio de Janeiro: Paz e Terra, 1977.

———. "Rio Grande do Sul e Santa Catarina." In Holanda, *História Geral da Civilização Brasileira,* 2: 473–505.

Cardoso, Fernando Henrique, and Octávio Ianni. *Cor e mobilidade social em Florianópolis.* São Paulo: Editora Nacional, 1960.

Carneiro, José Fernando. "O Império e a colonização no Rio Grande do Sul." *Fundamentos da Cultura Rio-Grandense,* 4th ser., 61–96. Porto Alegre: Faculdade de Filosofia da Universidade do Rio Grande do Sul, 1960.

———. *Karl von Koseritz.* Porto Alegre: Instituto Estadual do Livro, 1959.

Carneiro, Newton Luis Garcia. *A identidade inacabada: O regionalismo político no Rio Grande do Sul*. Porto Alegre: EDIPUCRS, 2000.

Carvalho, José Murilo de. *Os bestializados: O Rio de Janeiro e a República que não foi*. São Paulo: Companhia das Letras, 1987.

———. *Cidadania no Brasil: O longo caminho*. Rio de Janeiro: Civilização Brasileira, 2001.

———. *A construção da ordem: A elite política imperial*. Rio de Janeiro: Editora Campus, 1980.

———. *A formação das almas: O imaginário da República no Brasil*. São Paulo: Companhia das Letras, 1990.

———. *Teatro de sombras: A política imperial*. São Paulo: Vértice/Editora Revista dos Tribunais; Rio de Janeiro: Instituto Universidade de Pesquisas do Rio de Janeiro, 1988.

Castanho, Mara Regina, and Mara Regina Nunes. "A Confraria de Nossa Senhora do Rosário e São Benedito em Porto Alegre." In *Cultura afro-brasileira*, ed. Moacyr Flores, 37–46. Porto Alegre: Escola Superior de Teologia São Lourenço de Brindes, 1980.

Castro, Sertório de. *A república que a revolução destruiu*. 2d ed. Brasília: Editora Universidade de Brasília, 1982.

Caulfield, Sueann. *In Defense of Honor: Sexual Morality, Modernity, and Nation in Early-Twentieth-Century Brazil*. Durham: Duke University Press, 2000.

Caulfield, Sueann, and Martha de Abreu Esteves. "50 Years of Virginity in Rio de Janeiro: Sexual Politics and Gender Roles in Political and Popular Discourse, 1890–1940." *LBR* 30 (1993): 47–74.

Cesar, Guilhermino. "O Batuque Proibido." *Correio do Povo*, Caderno de Sábado, 3 April 1976, 3.

———. *História da literatura do Rio Grande do Sul (1737–1902)*. Rio de Janeiro, Porto Alegre, São Paulo: Editora Globo, 1956.

———. "O Negro e a Colonização Rio-Grandense." *Diário de Notícias*, suplemento, 17 August 1958, 2.

———. "As Posturas e o Negro." *Correio do Povo*, Caderno de Sábado, 10 April 1976, 3.

Chakrabarty, Dipesh. *Provincializing Europe: Postcolonial Thought and Historical Difference*. Princeton: Princeton University Press, 2000.

———. *Rethinking Working-Class History: Bengal 1890 to 1940*. Princeton: Princeton University Press, 1989.

Chalhoub, Sidney. *Cidade febril: Cortiços e epidemias na corte imperial*. São Paulo: Companhia das Letras, 1996.

———. *Machado de Assis, historiador*. São Paulo: Companhia das Letras, 2003.

———. "Medo branco de almas negras: Escravos, libertos e republicanos na cidade do Rio." *Revista Brasileira de História* 8 (1988): 83–106.

———. "Slaves, Freedmen and the Politics of Freedom in Brazil: The Experience of Blacks in the City of Rio." *Slavery and Abolition* 10 (1989): 64–84.

———. *Trabalho, lar e botequim: O cotidiano dos trabalhadores no Rio de Janeiro da Belle Époque*. 2d ed. Campinas: Editora da Unicamp, 2001.

———. *Visões da liberdade: Uma história das últimas décadas da escravidão na corte.* São Paulo: Companhia das Letras, 1990.

Chalhoub, Sidney, Gladys Ribeiro, and Martha de R. Esteves. "Trabalho escravo e trabalho livre na cidade do Rio: Vivência de libertos, 'galegos' e mulheres pobres." *Revista Brasileira de História* 5 (1984–85): 85–116.

Chambers, Sarah C. *From Subjects to Citizens: Honor, Gender, and Politics in Arequipa, Peru, 1780–1854.* University Park: Pennsylvania State University Press, 1999.

Chasteen, John Charles. "Background to Civil War: The Process of Land Tenure in Brazil's Southern Borderland, 1801–1893." *HAHR* 71 (1991): 732–60.

———. *Heroes on Horseback: A Life and Times of the Last Gaucho Caudillos.* Albuquerque: University of New Mexico Press, 1995.

———. "Trouble between Men and Women: Machismo on Nineteenth-Century *Estancias.*" In *The Middle Period in Latin America: Values and Attitudes in the 17th–19th Centuries,* ed. Mark D. Szuchman, 123–40. Boulder: Lynne Rienner, 1989.

Chatterjee, Partha. *The Politics of the Governed: Reflections on Popular Politics in Most of the World.* New York: Columbia University Press, 2004.

Chiavenatto, Julio José. *Genocídio americano: A Guerra do Paraguai.* 22d ed. São Paulo: Editora Brasiliense, 1988.

Collier, Ruth Berins, and David Collier. *Shaping the Political Arena: Critical Junctures, the Labor Movement, and Regime Dynamics in Latin America.* Princeton: Princeton University Press, 1991.

Comte, Auguste. *The Essential Comte.* Ed. Stanislav Andreski. New York: Harper and Row, 1974.

———. *The Positive Philosophy.* Trans. Harriet Martineau. New York: AMS Press, 1974.

———. *System of Positive Polity.* 4 vols. London: Longmans, Green, and Co., 1875.

Conrad, Robert E. *The Destruction of Brazilian Slavery, 1850–1888.* Berkeley: University of California Press, 1971.

———, ed. *Children of God's Fire: A Documentary History of Slavery in Brazil.* Princeton: Princeton University Press, 1983.

Constantino, Núncia Santoro de. *O italiano da esquina: Imigrantes na sociedade porto-alegrense.* Porto Alegre: Escola Superior de Teologia e Espiritualidade Franciscana, 1991.

Corrêa, Norton Figueiredo. *O batuque do Rio Grande do Sul: Antropologia de uma religião afro-rio-grandense.* Porto Alegre: Editora da Universidade/UFRGS, n.d.

———. "Panorama das religiões afro-brasileiras do Rio Grande do Sul." In Oro, *As religiões afro-brasileiras do Rio Grande do Sul,* 9–46.

Costa, Emília Viotti da. *The Brazilian Empire: Myths and Histories.* 2d ed. Chapel Hill: University of North Carolina Press, 2000.

———. *Crowns of Glory, Tears of Blood: The Demerara Slave Rebellion of 1823.* New York: Oxford University Press, 1994.

———. *Da senzala à colônia.* 3d ed. São Paulo: Brasiliense, 1989.

———. "Introdução ao estudo da emancipação política do Brasil." In *Brasil em perspectiva,* ed. Carlos Guilherme Mota, 75–139. São Paulo: Difusão Européia do Livro, 1968.

Costa, João Cruz. *A History of Ideas in Brazil: The Development of Philosophy in Brazil and the Evolution of National History.* Trans. Suzette Machado. Berkeley: University of California Press, 1964.

———. *O positivismo no Brasil: Notas sobre a história do positivismo do Brasil.* São Paulo: Companhia Editora Nacional, 1956.

Cunha, Ernesto Antonio Lassance. *O Rio Grande do Sul: Contribuição para o estudo de suas condições economicas.* Rio de Janeiro: Imprensa Nacional, 1908.

Cunha, Manuela Carneiro da. *Antropologia do Brasil: Mito, história, etnicidade.* São Paulo: Brasiliense/Editora da Universidade de São Paulo, 1986.

———. "Silences of the Law: Customary Law and Positive Law on the Manumission of Slaves in 19th-Century Brazil." *History and Anthropology* 1, no. 2 (1985): 427–43.

Cunha, Rui Vieira da. "Escravos rebeldes em Porto Alegre." *Mensário do Arquivo Nacional* 9 (1978): 9–14.

Curtin, Philip D. *The Atlantic Slave Trade: A Census.* Madison: University of Wisconsin Press, 1969.

Dacanal, José Hildebrando, ed. *RS: Imigração e colonização.* Porto Alegre: Mercado Aberto, 1980.

Dacanal, José Hildebrando, and Sergius Gonzaga, eds. *RS: Cultura e ideologia.* Porto Alegre: Mercado Aberto, 1980.

———, eds. *RS: Economia e política.* Porto Alegre: Mercado Aberto, 1979.

Damsceno, Athos. *Imprensa caricata do Rio Grande do Sul no século XIX.* Porto Alegre: Editora Globo, 1962.

Damasceno Vieira, Athos. *O Carnaval porto-alegrense no século XIX.* Porto Alegre: Livraria do Globo, 1970.

da Matta, Roberto. *Carnavais, malandros e heróis: Para uma sociologia do dilema brasileiro.* 4th ed. Rio de Janeiro: Zahar Editores, 1983.

———. *A casa e a rua: Espaço, cidadania, mulher e morte no Brasil.* Rio de Janeiro: Editora Guanabara, 1987.

Davis, David Brion. *Slavery and Human Progress.* New York: Oxford University Press, 1984.

Dean, Warren. *Rio Claro: A Brazilian Plantation System, 1820–1920.* Stanford: Stanford University Press, 1976.

de la Peña, Guillermo. "La cultura política entre los sectores populares de Guadalajara." *Nueva Antropología* 11 (1990): 83–107.

Diacon, Todd A. *Millenarian Vision, Capitalist Reality: Brazil's Contestado Rebellion, 1912–1916.* Durham: Duke University Press, 1991.

Dias, Maria Odila L. da Silva. *Power and Everyday Life: The Lives of Working Women in Nineteenth-Century Brazil.* Trans. Ann Frost. New Brunswick: Rutgers University Press, 1995.

Dillenberg, Sérgio Roberto. *A imprensa em Porto Alegre de 1845 a 1870.* Porto Alegre: Sulina/ARI, 1987.

Docca, Souza. *O sentido brasileiro da Revolução Farroupilha.* Porto Alegre: Livraria do Globo, 1935.

Domingues, Moacyr. *A nova face dos Muckers*. São Leopoldo: Rotermund, 1977.
Drescher, Seymour. "Brazilian Abolition in Comparative Perspective." *HAHR* 68 (1988): 429–60.
Duarte, Olympio. *Excavações históricas*. Porto Alegre: Globo, 1933.
DuBois, Ellen Carol. *Feminism and Suffrage: The Emergence of an Independent Women's Movement in America, 1848–1869*. Ithaca: Cornell University Press, 1978.
Eisenberg, Peter L. *The Sugar Industry in Pernambuco: Modernization without Change, 1840–1910*. Berkeley: University of California Press, 1974.
Ericksen, Nestor. *O sesquicentenário da imprensa rio-grandense*. Porto Alegre: Sulina, 1977.
Esteves, Martha de Abreu. *Meninas perdidas: Os populares e o cotidiano do amor no Rio de Janeiro da Belle Époque*. Rio de Janeiro: Paz e Terra, 1989.
Fagundes, Ligia Ketzer, Lizete Kummer, Maria Stephanou, and Sandra Jatahy Pesavento. *Memória da indústria gaúcha: Das origens a 1930*. Porto Alegre: Editora da Universidade/UFRGS, FEE, 1987.
Fagundes, Morivalde Calvet. *História da Revolução Farroupilha*. 2d ed. Caxias do Sul: Editora da Universidade de Caxias do Sul; Porto Alegre: Martins Livreiro, 1985.
Faoro, Raymundo. *Os donos do poder: Formação do patronato político brasileiro*. 2 vols. 7th ed. Rio de Janeiro: Globo, 1987.
Félix, Loiva Otero. *Coronelismo, borgismo e cooptação política*. Porto Alegre: Mercado Aberto, 1987.
Ferreira, Athos Damasceno. *Imagens sentimentais da cidade*. Porto Alegre: Livraria do Globo, 1940.
Ferreira Filho, Arthur. *História geral do Rio Grande do Sul, 1503–1964*. 3d ed. Rio de Janeiro, Porto Alegre, and São Paulo: Editora Globo, 1965.
Florentino, Manolo, and José Roberto Góes. *A paz das senzalas: Famílias escravas e tráfico atlântico, Rio de Janeiro, c. 1790–c. 1850*. Rio de Janeiro: Civilização Brasileira, 1997.
Flores, Hilda Agnes Hübner, ed. *Porto Alegre: História e cultura*. Porto Alegre: Martins Livreiro Editor, 1987.
Flores, Moacyr. "A educação da mulher na propaganda republicana positivista." *EIA* 20 (1994): 119–30.
———. *Modelo político dos farrapos: As idéias políticas da revolução farroupilha*. Porto Alegre: Mercado Aberto, 1988.
———, ed. *Cultura afro-brasileira*. Porto Alegre: Escola Superior de Teologia São Lourenço de Brindes, 1980.
Flory, Thomas. *Judge and Jury in Imperial Brazil, 1808–1871: Social Control and Political Stability in the New State*. Austin: University of Texas Press, 1981.
———. "Race and Social Control in Independent Brazil." *JLAS* 9 (1977): 199–224.
Fonseca, Claudia. "Pais e filhos na família popular (início do século XX)." In *Amor e família no Brasil*, ed. Maria Angela d'Incao, 95–128. São Paulo: Contexto, 1989.
Fonseca, Pedro Cezar Dutra. *RS: Economia e conflitos políticos na República Velha*. Porto Alegre: Mercado Aberto, 1983.

Fonseca, Rosa Maria Benicio da. "A questão servil: Análise dos pronunciamentos dos deputados gaúchos nas sessões da Assembléia Legislativa Provincial, 1883–1887." UFRGS, curso de especialização em história do Rio Grande do Sul, n.d.

Fontoura, João Neves da. *Memórias*. Vol. 1, *Borges de Medeiros e seu tempo*. Rio de Janeiro: Editora Globo, 1958.

Forment, Carlos A. *Democracy in Latin America, 1760–1900*. Vol. 1, *Civic Selfhood and Public Life in Mexico and Peru*. Chicago: University of Chicago Press, 2003.

Fraga Filho, Walter. *Mendigos, moleques e vadios na Bahia do século XIX*. São Paulo: Hucitec; Salvador: Editora da Universidade Federal da Bahia, 1995.

Fragoso, João, and Manolo Florentino. *O arcaísmo como projeto: Mercado atlântico, sociedade agrária e elite mercantil em uma economia colonial tardia: Rio de Janeiro, c. 1790–c. 1840*. Rio de Janeiro: Civilização Brasileira, 2001.

Franco, Maria Sylvia de Carvalho. *Homens livres na ordem escravocrata*. 3d ed. São Paulo: Kairós, 1983.

———. "As idéias estão no lugar." *Cadernos de Debate* 1 (1976): 61–64.

Franco, Sérgio da Costa. *Gente e espaços de Porto Alegre*. Ed. Universidade/UFRGS, 2000.

———. *Getúlio Vargas e outros ensaios*. Porto Alegre: Ed. Universidade/UFRGS, 1993.

———. *Júlio de Castilhos e sua época*. 2d ed. Porto Alegre: Editora da Universidade/UFRGS/MEC/SESu/PROEDI, 1988.

———. *Porto Alegre: Guia histórico*. 2d ed. Porto Alegre: Editora da Universidade/UFRGS, 1992.

———. *Porto Alegre e seu comércio*. Porto Alegre: Associação Comercial de Porto Alegre, 1983.

———. *Porto Alegre sitiada (1836–1840): Um capítulo da Revolução Farroupilha*. Porto Alegre: Editora Sulina, 2000.

———. "O sentido histórico da Revolução de 1893." In *Fundamentos da Cultura Rio-Grandense*, 5th ser., 191–216. Porto Alegre: Faculdade de Filosofia da Universidade do Rio Grande do Sul, 1962.

Freitas, Décio. *O capitalismo pastoril*. Porto Alegre: Escola Superior de Teologia São Lourenço de Brindes, 1980.

———. "Farrapos: Uma rebelião federalista." In Freitas et al., *A Revolução Farroupilha*, 110–21.

———. "O gaúcho: O mito da 'produção sem trabalho'." In Dacanal and Gonzaga, *RS: Cultura e ideologia*, 7–24.

Freitas, Décio, et al. *A Revolução Farroupilha: História e interpretação*. Porto Alegre: Mercado Aberto, 1985.

Freyre, Gilberto. *O escravo nos anúncios de jornais brasileiros do século XIX*. 2d ed. São Paulo: Ed. Nacional; Recife: Instituto Joaquim Nabuco de Pesquisas Sociais, 1979.

———. *Order and Progress: Brazil from Monarchy to Republic*. Trans. Rod W. Horton. New York: Alfred A. Knopf, 1970.

———. *Sobrados e mucambos: Decadência do patriarcado rural e desenvolvimento do urbano*. 2 vols. 3d ed. Rio de Janeiro: Editora José Olympio, 1961.

Furtado, Celso. *The Economic Growth of Brazil: A Survey from Colonial to Modern Times.* Trans. Ricardo W. de Aguiar and Eric Charles Drysdale. Berkeley: University of California Press, 1965.

Gans, Magda Roswita. *Presença teuta em Porto Alegre no século xix (1850–1889).* Porto Alegre: Editora da UFRGS/ANPUH/RS, 2004.

Gebara, Ademir. *O mercado de trabalho livre no Brasil (1871–1888).* São Paulo: Brasiliense, 1986.

Genovese, Eugene D. *Roll, Jordan, Roll: The World the Slaves Made.* New York: Vintage, 1976.

———. *The World the Slaveholders Made: Two Essays in Interpretation.* 2d ed. Middletown: Wesleyan University Press, 1988.

Gertz, René. "A construção de uma nova cidadania." In Mauch and Vasconcellos, *Os alemães*, 29–40.

———. *O perigo alemão.* Porto Alegre: Ed. da Universidade/UFRGS, 1991.

Giacomini, Sonia Maria. *Mulher e escrava: Uma introdução histórica ao estudo da mulher negra no Brasil.* Petrópolis: Vozes, 1988.

Ginzberg, Lori D. *Women and the Work of Benevolence: Morality, Politics, and Class in the 19th-Century United States.* New Haven: Yale University Press, 1990.

Girão, Raimundo. *A abolição no Ceará.* 2d ed. Fortaleza: Secretaria de Cultura do Ceará, 1969.

Giuliano, João. *Esboço histórico da organização da polícia no Rio Grande do Sul.* Porto Alegre: Oficinas Gráficas da Imprensa Oficial, 1957.

Gledhill, John. *Power and Its Disguises: Anthropological Perspectives on Politics.* 2d ed. London: Pluto Press, 2000.

Gomes, Angela Maria de Castro. *A invenção do trabalhismo.* 2d ed. Rio de Janeiro: Relume Dumará, 1994.

Gonzaga, Sergius, and Luís Augusto Fischer, eds. *Nós, os gaúchos.* 2d ed. Porto Alegre: Editora da Universidade/UFRGS, 1993.

Gorender, Jacob. *A escravidão reabilitada.* São Paulo: Editora Ática, 1990.

Graf, Márcia Elisa de Campos. *Imprensa periódica e escravidão no Paraná.* Curitiba: Secretaria de Estado da Cultura e do Esporte, 1981.

Graham, Richard. "1850–1870." In Bethell, *Brazil: Empire and Republic*, 113–60.

———. *Britain and the Onset of Modernization in Brazil, 1850–1914.* Cambridge: Cambridge Latin American Studies, 1968.

———. "Os fundamentos da ruptura de relações diplomáticas entre o Brasil e a Grã-Bretanha em 1863: 'A Questão Christie.'" *Revista de História* (São Paulo) 8 (1962): 117–38, 379–402.

———. *Patronage and Politics in Nineteenth-Century Brazil.* Stanford: Stanford University Press, 1990.

———, ed. *The Idea of Race in Latin America, 1870–1940.* Austin: University of Texas Press, 1990.

Graham, Sandra Lauderdale. *Caetana Says No: Women's Stories from a Brazilian Slave Society.* Cambridge: Cambridge University Press, 2002.

———. *House and Street: The Domestic World of Servants and Masters in Nineteenth-Century Rio de Janeiro.* Cambridge: Cambridge University Press, 1988.

———. "Slavery's Impasse: Slave Prostitutes, Small-Time Mistresses, and the Brazilian Law of 1871." *Comparative Studies in Society and History* 33 (1991): 669–94.

———. "The Vintem Riot and Political Culture: Rio de Janeiro, 1880." *HAHR* 60 (1980): 431–49.

Gramsci, Antonio. *An Antonio Gramsci Reader: Selected Writings, 1916–1935.* Ed. David Forgacs. New York: Schocken Books, 1988.

———. *Selections from the Prison Notebooks.* Ed. and trans. Quintin Hoare and Geoffrey Nowell Smith. New York: International Publishers, 1971.

Gresele, Ottilia. "A irmandade dos negros em Porto Alegre (como se fazia a defesa e promoção da classe em outros tempos)." *Estudos Leopoldenses* 6 (1968): 3–38.

Guardino, Peter. *Peasants, Politics, and the Formation of Mexico's National State: Guerrero, 1800–1857.* Stanford: Stanford University Press, 1996.

Guimarães, Lucia Maria Paschoal, and Maria Emilia Prado, eds. *O liberalismo no Brasil imperial: Origens, conceitos e prática.* Rio de Janeiro: Revan/UERJ, 2001.

Gutfreind, Ieda, *A historiografia rio-grandense.* Porto Alegre: Editora da Universidade/UFRGS, 1992.

———. "Rio Grande do Sul, 1889–1896: A proclamação da República e a reação liberal através de sua imprensa." Master's thesis, PUCRS, 1979.

Haberly, David T. "Abolitionism in Brazil: Anti-Slavery and Anti-Slave." *LBR* 9 (1972): 30–46.

Hagen, Acácia Maria Maduro, and Paulo Roberto Staudt Moreira, eds. *Sobre a rua e outros lugares: Reinventando Porto Alegre.* Porto Alegre: Caixa Econômica Federal, 1995.

Hahner, June E. *Civilian-Military Relations in Brazil, 1889–1898.* Columbia: University of South Carolina Press, 1969.

———. *Emancipating the Female Sex: The Struggle for Women's Rights in Brazil, 1850–1940.* Durham: Duke University Press, 1990.

———. *Poverty and Politics: The Urban Poor in Brazil, 1870–1920.* Albuquerque: University of New Mexico Press, 1986.

Hale, Charles A. "Political and Social Ideas in Latin America, 1870–1930." In *Latin America: Economy and Society, 1870–1930*, ed. Leslie Bethell, 225–99. Cambridge: Cambridge University Press, 1989.

———. *The Transformation of Liberalism in Late Nineteenth-Century Mexico.* Princeton: Princeton University Press, 1989.

Harp, Gillis J. *Positivist Republic: Auguste Comte and the Reconstruction of American Liberalism, 1865–1920.* University Park: Pennsylvania State University Press, 1995.

Hasslocher, Gaston Mazeron. *Notas para história de Porto Alegre.* Porto Alegre: Barcellos, Bertaso & Cia., 1928.

Hersh, Blanche Glassman. "The 'True Woman' and the 'New Woman' in Nineteenth-Century America: Feminists-Abolitionists and a New Concept of True Womanhood." In *Woman's Being, Woman's Place: Female Identity and Vocation in American History*, ed. Mary Kelley, 271–82. Boston: G. K. Hall & Co., 1979.

Herskovits, Melville J. "The Southernmost Outposts of New World Africanisms." In *The New World Negro: Selected Papers in Afroamerican Studies*, ed. Frances S. Herskovits, 199–216. Bloomington: Indiana University Press, 1966.
Holanda, Sérgio Buarque de. *História geral da civilização brasileira*, vols. 2–3. São Paulo: Difusão Européia do Livro, 1964, 1967.
———. *Raízes do Brasil*. 26th ed. São Paulo: Companhia das Letras, 1995.
Holloway, Thomas H. "The Brazilian 'Judicial Police' in Florianópolis, Santa Catarina, 1841–1871." *Journal of Social History* 20 (1987): 733–56.
———. "'A Healthy Terror': Police Repression of Capoeiras in Nineteenth-Century Rio de Janeiro." *HAHR* 69 (1989): 637–76.
———. *Immigrants on the Land: Coffee and Society in São Paulo, 1886–1934*. Chapel Hill: University of North Carolina Press, 1980.
———. *Policing Rio de Janeiro: Repression and Resistance in a 19th-Century City*. Stanford: Stanford University Press, 1993.
Hünefeldt, Christine. *Paying the Price of Freedom: Family and Labor among Lima's Slaves, 1800–1854*. Berkeley: University of California Press, 1994.
Ianni, Octavio. *As metamorfoses do escravo: Apogeu e crise da escravatura no Brasil meridional*. 2d ed. São Paulo: Hucitec; Curitiba: Scientia et Labor, 1988.
Iglesias, Francisco. "Vida política, 1848/1868." In Holanda, *História geral da civilização brasileira*, 2: 9–112.
Janotti, Maria de Lourdes Mônaco. *Os subversivos da República*. São Paulo: Brasiliense, 1986.
Jardim, Jorge Luiz Pastorisa. "Comunicação e militância: A imprensa operária do Rio Grande do Sul (1892–1923)." Master's thesis, PUCRS, 1990.
Joseph, Gilbert M., ed. *Reclaiming the Political in Latin American History: Essays from the North*. Durham: Duke University Press, 2001.
Joseph, Gilbert M., and Daniel Nugent, eds. *Everyday Forms of State Formation: Revolution and the Negotiation of Rule in Modern Mexico*. Durham: Duke University Press, 1994.
Jütte, Robert. *Poverty and Deviance in Early Modern Europe*. Cambridge: Cambridge University Press, 1994.
Karasch, Mary C. *Slave Life in Rio de Janeiro, 1808–1850*. Princeton: Princeton University Press, 1987.
Kirkendall, Andrew J. *Class Mates: Male Student Culture and the Making of a Political Class in Nineteenth-Century Brazil*. Lincoln: University of Nebraska Press, 2002.
Kittleson, Roger A. "'Campaign All of Peace and Charity': Gender and the Politics of Abolitionism in Porto Alegre, Brazil, 1879–1888." *Slavery and Abolition* 22 (2001): 83–108.
———. "The Problem of the People: Popular Classes and the Social History of Ideas in Porto Alegre, Brazil, 1846–1893." Ph.D. diss., University of Wisconsin, Madison, 1997.
———. "Women and Notions of Womanhood in Brazilian Abolitionism." In *Gender and Slave Emancipation in the Atlantic World*, ed. Diana Paton and Pamela Scully. Durham: Duke University Press, 2005.

Kolchin, Peter. *American Slavery, 1619–1877*. New York: Hill and Wang, 1993.

Kowarick, Lúcio. *Trabalho e vadiagem: A origem do trabalho livre no Brasil*. São Paulo: Brasiliense, 1987.

Kraay, Hendrik. "'As Terrifying as Unexpected': The Bahian Sabinada, 1837–1838." *HAHR* 72 (1992): 501–27.

———. *Race, State, and Armed Forces in Independence-Era Brazil: Bahia, 1790s–1840s*. Stanford: Stanford University Press, 2001.

———. "'The Shelter of the Uniform': The Brazilian Army and Runaway Slaves, 1800–1888." *Journal of Social History* 29 (1996): 637–57.

———, ed. *Afro-Brazilian Culture and Politics: Bahia, 1790s to 1990s*. Armonk, N.Y.: M. E. Sharpe, 1998.

Kuznesof, Elisabeth Anne. "Sexual Politics, Race and Bastard-Rearing in Nineteenth-Century Brazil: A Question of Culture or Power?" *Journal of Family History* 16 (1991): 241–60.

Lagemann, Eugenio. "Imigração e industrialização." In Dacanal, *RS: Imigração e colonização*, 114–34.

Lamounier, Maria Lúcia. *Da escravidão ao trabalho livre (a lei de locação de serviços de 1879)*. Campinas: Papirus, 1988.

Landes, Joan B. *Women and the Public Sphere in the Age of the French Revolution*. Ithaca: Cornell University Press, 1988.

Lando, Aldair M., and Eliane C. Barros. "Capitalismo e colonização—os alemães no Grande do Sul." In Dacanal, *RS: Imigração e colonização*, 9–46.

———. *A colonização alemã no Rio Grande do Sul: Uma interpretação sociológica*. 2d ed. Porto Alegre: Movimento, 1981.

Lanna, Ana Lúcia D. *A transformação do trabalho: A passagem para o trabalho livro na Zona da Mata Mineira, 1870–1920*. 2d ed. Campinas: Editora da UNICAMP, 1989.

Lara, Sílvia Hunold. *Campos da violência: Escravos e senhores na Capitania do Rio de Janeiro, 1750–1808*. Rio de Janeiro: Paz e Terra, 1988.

Lavrin, Asunción, ed. *Sexuality and Marriage in Colonial Latin America*. Lincoln: University of Nebraska Press, 1989.

Laytano, Dante de. *Festa de Nossa Senhora dos Navegantes: Estudo de uma tradição das populações Afro-Brasileiras de Pôrto Alegre*. [Porto Alegre]: Comissão Estadual de Folclore do Rio Grande do Sul, 1955.

———. *Folclore do Rio Grande do Sul: Levantamento dos costumes e tradições gaúchas*. 2d ed. Caxias do Sul: Editora da Universidade de Caxias do Sul; Porto Alegre: Escola Superior de Teologia São Lourenço de Brindes/Nova Dimensão, 1987.

———. *História da República Rio-Grandense (1835–1845)*. 2d ed. Porto Alegre: Sulina/ARI, 1983.

Lazzari, Alexandre. *Coisas para o povo não fazer: Carnaval em Porto Alegre (1870–1915)*. Campinas: Editora da Unicamp/Cecult, 2001.

Leal, Elisabete. "Mulher e família na virada do século—o discurso d'A Federação." In Hagen and Moreira, *Sobre a rua: Reinventando Porto Alegre*, 19–49.

Leal, Victor Nunes. *Coronelismo: The Municipality and Representative Government in Brazil*. Trans. June Henfrey. Cambridge: Cambridge University Press, 1977.

Leitman, Spencer. "Negros farrapos: Hipocrisia racial no sul do Brasil no século XIX." In Freitas et al., *A Revolução Farroupilha*, 61–78.

———. "O primeiro ciclo brasileiro de trigo e a Guerra dos Farrapos." *Revista do Instituto Histórico e Geográfico Brasileiro* 307 (1975): 58–74.

———. *Raízes sócio-econômicas da Guerra dos Farrapos: Um capítulo da história do Brasil no século XIX*. Trans. Sarita Linhares Barsted. Rio de Janeiro: Edições Graal, 1979.

Lessa, Renato. *A invenção republicana: Campos Sales, as bases e a decadência da Primeira República brasileira*. São Paulo: Vértice, Editora Revista dos Tribunais; Rio de Janeiro: Instituto Universitário de Pesquisas do Rio de Janeiro, 1988.

Levine, Robert M. "Elite Perceptions of the *Povo*." In *Modern Brazil: Elites and Masses in Historical Perspective*, ed. Michael L. Conniff and Frank D. McCann, 209–24. Lincoln: University of Nebraska Press, 1989.

———. *Pernambuco in the Brazilian Federation, 1889–1937*. Stanford: Stanford University Press, 1978.

Lewin, Linda. *Politics and Parentela in Paraíba: A Case Study of Family-Based Oligarchy in Brazil*. Princeton: Princeton University Press, 1987.

Lima, Carlos A. M. "Em certa corporação: Politizando convivências em irmandades negras no Brasil escravista (1700-1850)." *História: Questões e Debates* (Curitiba) 30 (1999): 11–38.

Lima, Solimar Oliveira. "Resistência e punição de escravos em fontes judiciais no Rio Grande do Sul: 1818–1833." Master's thesis, PUCRS, 1994.

Lins, Ivan Monteiro de Barros. *História do positivismo no Brasil*. São Paulo: Companhia Editora Nacional, 1964.

Loner, Beatriz Ana. "Operários e participação no início da República: O caso de Pelotas e Rio Grande." *EIA* 22 (1996): 71–89.

Love, Joseph L. "Political Participation in Brazil, 1881–1969." *LBR* 7 (1970): 3–24.

———. *Rio Grande do Sul and Brazilian Regionalism, 1882–1930*. Stanford: Stanford University Press, 1971.

———. *São Paulo in the Brazilian Federation, 1889–1937*. Stanford: Stanford University Press, 1980.

Love, Joseph L., and Bert J. Barickman. "Rulers and Owners: A Brazilian Case Study in Comparative Perspective." *HAHR* 66 (1986): 743–65.

Love, Joseph L., and Nils Jacobsen, eds. *Guiding the Invisible Hand: Economic Liberalism and the State in Latin American History*. New York: Praeger, 1988.

Luebke, Frederick C. *Germans in Brazil: A Comparative History of Cultural Conflict during World War I*. Baton Rouge: Louisiana State University Press, 1987.

Macedo, Francisco Riopardense de. *Os menores abandonados e o Padre Cacique de Barros*. Porto Alegre: n.p., 1982.

———. *Porto Alegre, história e vida da cidade*. Porto Alegre: Editora da UFRGS, 1973.

Machado, Maria Helena P. T. *Crime e escravidão: Trabalho, luta e resistência nas lavouras paulistas (1830–1888)*. São Paulo: Brasiliense, 1987.

———. *O plano e o pânico: Os movimentos sociais na década da abolição*. Rio de Janeiro: Editora UFRJ/EDUSP, 1994.

Machado, Nara H. N. "A Igreja de N.S. do Rosário dos Pretos." *EIA* 16 (1990): 189–96.

Maestri Filho, Mário. *O escravo gaúcho: Resistência e trabalho*. Porto Alegre: Editora da Universidade/UFRGS, 1993.

———. *O escravo no Rio Grande do Sul: A charqueada e a gênese do escravismo gaúcho*. Porto Alegre: Escola Superior de Teologia São Lourenço de Brindes; Caxias do Sul: Universidade de Caxias do Sul, 1984.

———. *Quilombos e quilombolas em terras gaúchas*. Porto Alegre: Escola Superior de Teologia São Lourenço de Brindes; Caxias do Sul: Universidade de Caxias do Sul, 1979.

Magalhães, Elisabeth K. C. de, and Sonia Maria Giacomini. "A escrava ama-de-leite: Anjo ou demônio?" In *Mulher, mulheres*, ed. Carmen Barroso and Albertina Oliveira Costa, 73–88. São Paulo: Cortez/Fundação Carlos Chagas, 1983.

Malerba, Jurandir. *Os brancos da lei: Liberalismo, escravidão e mentalidade patriarcal no Império do Brasil*. Maringá: Editora da Universidade Estadual de Maringá, 1994.

———. *A corte no exílio: Civilização e poder no Brasil às vésperas da independência (1808 a 1821)*. São Paulo: Companhia das Letras, 2000.

Mallon, Florencia E. *The Defense of Community in Peru's Central Highlands: Peasant Struggle and Capitalist Transition, 1860–1940*. Princeton: Princeton University Press, 1983.

———. "Exploring the Origins of Democratic Patriarchy in Mexico: Gender and Popular Resistance in the Puebla Highlands." In *Women of the Mexican Countryside, 1850–1990*, ed. Heather Fowler-Salamini and Mary Kay Vaughan, 3–26. Tucson: University of Arizona Press, 1994.

———. *Peasant and Nation: The Making of Postcolonial Mexico and Peru*. Berkeley: University of California Press, 1995.

Manfroi, Olívio. *A colonização italiana no Rio Grande do Sul: Implicações econômicas, políticas e culturais*. Porto Alegre: Grafosul/Instituto Estadual do Livro/DAC/SEC, 1975.

Marçal, João Batista. *Primeiras lutas operárias no Rio Grande do Sul*. Porto Alegre: Globo, 1985.

Martin, Cheryl English. *Governance and Society in Colonial Mexico: Chihuahua in the Eighteenth Century*. Stanford: Stanford University Press, 1996.

Mattos, Hebe Maria. *Das cores do silêncio: Os significados da liberdade no sudeste escravista—Brasil século XIX*. 2d ed. Rio de Janeiro: Nova Fronteira, 1998.

———. *Escravidão e cidadania no Brasil monárquico*. Rio de Janeiro: Jorge Zahar, 2000.

Mattos, Ilmar Rohloff de. *O tempo Saquarema: A formação do estado imperial*. 2d ed. São Paulo: Editora Hucitec, 1990.

Mattoso, Katia M. de Queirós. *To Be a Slave in Brazil, 1550–1888*. Trans. Arthur Goldhammer. New Brunswick: Rutgers University Press, 1986.

Mauch, Cláudia. "Colônia Africana: Criminalidade e controle social (Porto Alegre, 1888–1900)." Photocopy.

———. *Ordem pública e moralidade: Imprensa e policiamento urbano em Porto Alegre na década de 1890*. Santa Cruz do Sul: EDUNISC/ANPUH-RS, 2004.

Mauch, Cláudia, and Naira Vasconcellos, eds. *Os alemães no sul do Brasil: Cultura, etnicidade e história*. Canoas: Editora da ULBRA, 1994.

Mazeron, Gaston Hasslocher. *Notas para a historia de Porto Alegre*. Porto Alegre: Barcellos, Bertaso & Cia., 1928.

———. *Reminiscências de Porto Alegre*. Porto Alegre: Livraria Selbach, n.d.

Medeiros, Laudelino T. *Escola Militar de Porto Alegre (1853–1911): Significado cultural*. Porto Alegre: Editora da Universidade/UFRGS, 1992.

Mehta, Uday. "Liberal Strategies of Exclusion." *Politics and Society* 18 (1990): 427–54.

Mercadante, Paulo. *A consciência conservadora no Brasil: Contribuição ao estudo da formação brasileira*. Rio de Janeiro: Editora Saga, 1965.

Meyer, Augusto. *A prosa dos pagos*. 3d ed. Rio de Janeiro: Presença; Brasília: Instituto Nacional do Livro, 1979.

Meznar, Joan E. "The Ranks of the Poor: Military Service and Social Differentiation in Northeast Brazil, 1830–1875." *HAHR* 72 (1992): 335–51.

Midgley, Clare. *Women against Slavery: The British Campaigns, 1780–1870*. London: Routledge, 1992.

Miller, Joseph C. "Central Africa during the Era of the Slave Trade, c. 1490s–1850s." In *Central Africans and Cultural Transformations in the American Diaspora*, ed. Linda M. Heywood, 21–69. Cambridge: Cambridge University Press, 2002.

Monti, Verônica A. *O abolicionismo: Sua hora decisiva no Rio Grande do Sul—1884*. Porto Alegre: Martins Livreiro Editor, 1985.

Moraes, Evaristo de. *A campanha abolicionista (1879–1888)*. Rio de Janeiro: Livraria Editora Leite Ribeiro, 1924.

Moreira, Paulo Roberto Staudt. *Os cativos e os homens de bem: Experiências negras no espaço urbano. Porto Alegre—1858–1888*. Porto Alegre: EST Edições, 2003.

———. "Os contratados: Uma forma de escravidão disfarçada." *EIA* 16 (1990): 211–24.

———. "As crias da casa." In *Histórias de trabalho*, ed. Ana Lúcia Vellinho D'Angelo, 133–42. Porto Alegre: UE/Porto Alegre, 1995.

———. "Entre o deboche e a rapina: Os cenários sociais da criminalidade popular em Porto Alegre (1868–1888)." Master's thesis, UFRGS, 1993.

———. *Faces da liberdade, máscaras do cativeiro: Experiências de liberdade e escravidão, percebidas através das cartas de alforria—Porto Alegre (1858–1888)*. Porto Alegre: Arquivo Público do Estado/EDIPUCRS, 1996.

Morgan, Edmund S. *American Slavery, American Freedom: The Ordeal of Colonial Virgina*. New York: W. W. Norton, 1975.

Moritz, Gustavo. *Acontecimentos políticos no Rio Grande do Sul 89–90–91*. Porto Alegre: Tipografia Thurmann, 1939.

Mott, Maria Lucia de Barros. *Submissão e resistência: A mulher na luta contra a escravidão*. 2d ed. São Paulo: Contexto, 1991.

Moura, Ana Maria da Silva. *Cocheiros e carroceiros: Homens livres no Rio de senhores e escravos*. São Paulo: Editora Hucitec, 1988.

Moure, Telmo. "A inserção da economia imigrante na economia gaúcha." In Dacanal, *RS: Imigração e colonização*, 91–113.

Nachman, Robert G. "Positivism, Modernization and the Middle Class in Brazil." *HAHR* 57 (1977): 1–23.

Neves, Lúcia Maria Bastos Pereira dos. *Corcundas e constitucionais: A cultura política da independência (1820–1822)*. Rio de Janeiro: Revan/FAPERJ, 2003.

Nishida, Mieko. *Slavery and Identity: Ethnicity, Gender, and Race in Salvador, Brazil, 1808–1888*. Bloomington: Indiana University Press, 2003.

Nogueira, Arlinda Rocha, and Lucy Maffeir Hutter. *A colonização em São Pedro do Rio Grande do Sul (1824–1889)*. Porto Alegre: Editora Garatuja/Instituto Estadual do Livro/DAC/SEC, 1975.

Nonato, Raimundo. *História social da abolição em Mossoró*. [Mossoró]: n.p., 1983.

Oberacker, Carlos H., Jr. *Carlos von Koseritz*. São Paulo: Anhambi, 1961.

Oliveira, Andradina de. *A Mulher Riograndense. 1a. série. Escriptoras Mortas*. Porto Alegre: Oficinas Graphicas da Livraria Americana, 1907.

Oliveira, Clóvis Silveira de. *Porto Alegre: A cidade e sua formação*. Porto Alegre: Gráfica e Editora Norma, 1985.

Oliveira, Maria Inês Côrtes de. *O liberto: O seu mundo e os outros*. São Paulo: Corrupio; [Brasília]: CNPq, 1988.

Orico, Osvaldo. *Silveira Martins e sua época*. Porto Alegre: Livraria do Globo, 1935.

Oro, Ari Pedro, ed. *As religiões afro-brasileiras do Rio Grande do Sul*. Porto Alegre: Editora da Universidade/UFRGS, 1994.

Ortiz, Renato. *Cultura brasileira e identidade nacional*. 3d ed. São Paulo: Brasiliense, 1985.

Ortner, Sherry B. "Resistance and the Problem of Ethnographic Refusal." *Comparative Studies in Society and History* 37 (1995): 173–93.

Osório, Joaquim Luís. *Partidos políticos no Rio Grande do Sul: Período republicano*. 2d ed. Porto Alegre: Assembléia Legislativa, 1992.

Pacheco, Ricardo de Aguiar. *O cidadão está nas ruas: Representações e práticas acerca da cidadania republicana em Porto Alegre (1889–1891)*. Porto Alegre: Editora da Universidade/UFRGS, 2001.

Padoin, Maria Medianeira. *Federalismo gaúcho: Fronteira platina, direito e revolução*. São Paulo: Companhia Editora Nacional, 2001.

Pang, Eul-Soo. *Bahia in the First Brazilian Republic: Coronelismo and Oligarchies, 1889–1934*. Gainesville: University of Florida Press, 1979.

Paz, Octavio. *The Labyrinth of Solitude*. Trans. Lysander Kemp. New York: Grove Press, 1961.

Pedro, Joana Maria, et al. *Negro em terra de branco: Escravidão e preconceito em Santa Catarina no século XIX*. Porto Alegre: Mercado Aberto, 1988.

Peixoto, Eduardo Marques. "Questão Maurer. Os Mukers." *Revista do Instituto Historico e Geographico Brasileiro* 68 (1907): 393–505.

Penna, Lincoln de Abreu. *O progresso da ordem: O florianismo e a construção da República*. Rio de Janeiro: Sette Letras, 1997.

Pesavento, Sandra Jatahy. *A burguesia gaúcha: Dominação da capital e disciplina do trabalho (RS: 1889–1930)*. Porto Alegre: Mercado Aberto, 1988.

———. *O cotidiano da República: Elites e povo na virada do século*. Porto Alegre: Editora da Universidade/UFRGS, 1990.

———. *Emergência dos subalternos: Trabalho livre e ordem burguesa*. Porto Alegre: Editora da Universidade/UFRGS, 1989.

———. "Farrapos, liberalismo e ideologia." In Freitas et al., *A Revolução Farroupilha*, 5–29.

———. *O imaginário da cidade: Visões literárias do urbano—Paris, Rio de Janeiro, Porto Alegre*. Porto Alegre: Editora da Universidade/UFRGS, 1999.

———. "O imigrante na política rio-grandense." In Dacanal, *RS: Imigração e colonização*, 156–94.

———. "Lugares malditos: A cidade do 'outro' no Sul brasileiro (Porto Alegre, passagem do século XIX ao século XX)." *Revista Brasileira de História* 19 (1999): 195–216.

———. *Os pobres da cidade: Vida e trabalho 1880–1920*. Porto Alegre: Editora da Universidade/UFRGS, 1994.

———. "República velha gaúcha: 'Estado autoritário e economia.'" In Dacanal and Gonzaga, *RS: Economia e política*, 193–228.

———. *RS: Agropecuária colonial e industrialização*. Porto Alegre: Mercado Aberto, 1983.

———, ed. *Memórias Porto Alegre: Espaços e vivências*. Porto Alegre: Editora da Universidade/Prefeitura de Porto Alegre, 1991.

Petersen, Sílvia Regina Ferraz. "As greves no Rio Grande do Sul (1890–1919)." In Dacanal and Gonzaga, *RS: Economia e política*, 277–327.

———. "A mulher na imprensa operária gaúcha da século XIX." *Revista de História* (Porto Alegre) 1 (1986–87): 83–110.

———. *"Que a União Operária seja nossa pátria!" História das lutas dos operários gaúchos para construir suas organizações*. Santa Maria: Editoraufsm; Porto Alegre: Ed. Universidade/URFGS, 2001.

Petersen, Sílvia Regina Ferraz, and Maria Elizabeth Lucas. *Antologia do movimento operário gaúcho, 1870–1937*. Porto Alegre: Ed. Universidade/UFRGS/tchê!, 1992.

Petry, Leopoldo. *O episódio do Ferrabraz: Documentos para o estudo da história dos "Mucker" do Ferrabraz*. 2d ed. São Leopoldo: Casa Editora Rotermund, 1966.

Pezat, Paulo Ricardo. "A conquista da liberdade pelo negro: Consenso e contra-senso." *EIA* 16 (1990): 231–40.

Piccolo, Helga Iracema Landgraf. "Alemães e italianos no Rio Grande do Sul: Fricções inter-étnicas e ideológicas no século XIX." In *A presença italiana no Brasil*, ed. Luis A. de Boni, 2: 577–93. Porto Alegre: Escola Superior de Teologia; Turin: Fondazione Giovanni Agnelli, 1990.

———. "O discurso político na Revolução Farroupilha." *Revista de História* (Porto Alegre) 1 (1986–87): 39–53.

———. "Escravidão, imigração e abolição: Considerações sobre o Rio Grande do Sul do século XIX." In *Anais da VIII Reunião da Sociedade Brasileira de Pesquisa Histórica*, 53–62. São Paulo: [Sociedade Brasileira de Pesquisas Históricas], 1989.

———. "O parlamento nacional e a Revolução Farroupilha." *Estudos Leopoldenses* 21 (1985): 7–155.

———. "A política rio-grandense no Império." In Dacanal and Gonzaga, *RS: Economia e política*, 93–117.

———. *A política rio-grandense no II Império (1868–1882)*. Porto Alegre: Gabinete de Pesquisa de História do Rio Grande do Sul/Instituto de Filosofia e Ciências Humanas, UFRGS, 1974.

———. "Porto Alegre em 1873: A imprensa liberal da capital como fonte de estudo para a política provincial." *Revista do Instituto de Filosofia e Ciências Humanas* 4 (1976): 221–33.

———. "A resistência escrava no Rio Grande do Sul." In *Cadernos de Estudo* 6. Porto Alegre: UFRGS, 1992.

———. "A resistência escrava no Rio Grande do Sul: Reação ou afirmação?" *EIA* 16 (1990): 241–52.

———. "Século XIX: Alemães protestantes no Rio Grande do Sul e a escravidão." In *Anais da VIII Reunião da Sociedade Brasileira de Pesquisa Histórica*, 103–7. São Paulo: [SBPH], 1989.

———. *Vida política no século 19: Da descolonização ao movimento republicano*. Porto Alegre: Editora da Universidade/UFRGS, 1991.

Pickering, Mary. *Auguste Comte: An Intellectual Biography*. Vol. 1. New York: Cambridge University Press, 1993.

Pinto, Celi Regina Jardim. "Contribuição ao estudo da formação do Partido Republicano Rio-Grandense (1882–1892)." Master's thesis, UFRGS, 1979.

———. *Positivismo: Um projeto político alternativo (RS: 1889–1930)*. Porto Alegre: L&PM, 1986.

———. "The Positivist Discourse of the Republican Party of Rio Grande do Sul: A Successful Political Project in the Brazilian Old Republic." Ph.D. diss., University of Essex, 1986.

Porto, Aureliano. *O trabalho alemão no Rio Grande do Sul*. Porto Alegre: Estabelecimento Gráfico Sta. Terezinha, 1934.

Porto Alegre, Achylles. *História popular de Porto Alegre*. Porto Alegre: Unidade Editorial Porto Alegre, 1994.

———. *Homens illustres do Rio Grande do Sul*. Porto Alegre: Livraria Selbach, n.d.

———. *Paizagens mortas*. Porto Alegre: Livraria do Globo, 1922.

Prado Júnior, Caio. *The Colonial Background of Modern Brazil*. Trans. Suzette Machado. Berkeley: University of California Press, 1967.

Queiroz, Maria Isaura Pereira de. *O messianismo no Brasil e no mundo*. São Paulo: Dominus, 1965.

Queiroz, Suely Robles Reis de. *Os radicais da República*. São Paulo: Brasiliense, 1986.

Rago, Margareth. *Os prazeres da noite: Prostituição e códigos da sexualidade feminina em São Paulo (1890–1930)*. Rio de Janeiro: Paz e Terra, 1991.

Rambo, Arthur Blasio. "Nacionalidade e cidadania." In Mauch and Vasconcellos, *Os alemães*, 43–53.

Ramos Escandón, Carmen. "Señoritas porfirianas: Mujer e ideología en el México progresista, 1880–1910." In *Presencia e transparencia: La mujer en la historia de México*, ed. Carmen Ramos Escandón, 143–61. Mexico City: El Colegio de México, 1987.

Reis, João José. *Death Is a Festival: Funeral Rites and Rebellion in Nineteenth-Century Brazil.* Trans. H. Sabrina Gledhill. Chapel Hill: University of North Carolina Press, 2003.

———. "A greve negra de 1857 na Bahia." *Revista USP* 18 (1993): 7–29.

———. *Slave Rebellion in Brazil: The Muslim Uprising of 1835 in Bahia.* Trans. Arthur Brakel. Baltimore: Johns Hopkins University Press, 1993.

Reis, João José, and Eduardo Silva. *Negociação e conflito: A resistência negra no Brasil escravista.* São Paulo: Companhia das Letras, 1989.

Retamozo, Aldira Correa, et al. *O papel da mulher na Revolução Farroupilha.* Porto Alegre: tchê!, n.d.

Ribeiro, Gladys Sabina. *A liberdade em construção: Identidade nacional e conflitos antilusitanos no Primeiro Reinado.* Rio de Janeiro: Relume Dumará/FAPERJ, 2002.

Roche, Jean. *L'administration de la province du Rio Grande do Sul de 1829 a 1847.* Porto Alegre: Universidade do Rio Grande do Sul, Faculdade de Filosofia, 1961.

———. *A colonização alemã e o Rio Grande do Sul.* 2 vols. Porto Alegre: Editora Globo, 1969.

Rodrigues, José Honório. *Conciliação e reforma no Brasil: Um desafio histórico-cultural.* 2d ed. Rio de Janeiro: Nova Fronteira, 1982.

Rodríguez, Ricardo Vélez. *Castilhismo: Uma filosofia da República.* Porto Alegre: Escola Superior de Teologia São Lourençco de Brindes; Caxias do Sul: Universidade de Caxias do Sul, 1980.

Romero, Sylvio. *O Castilhismo no Rio Grande do Sul.* Porto: Officinas do Commercio do Porto, 1912.

———. *Provocações e debates.* Porto: Livraria Chardron, 1910.

Rosa, Othelo. *Julio de Castilhos (perfil biographico e escriptos politicos).* Porto Alegre: Globo, 1930.

Roseberry, William. "Hegemony and the Language of Contention." In *Everyday Forms of State Formation: Revolution and the Negotiation of Rule in Modern Mexico,* ed. Gilbert M. Joseph and Daniel Nugent, 355–66. Durham: Duke University Press, 1994.

Rüdiger, Francisco Ricardo. "O proletariado gaúcho e a Revolução Federalista." *EIA* 17 (1991): 37–46.

Russell-Wood, A. J. R. "Late Colonial Brazil, 1750–1808." In *Colonial Brazil,* ed. Leslie Bethell, 284–343. Cambridge: Cambridge University Press, 1987.

———. "Prestige, Power and Piety in Colonial Brazil: The Third Orders of Salvador." *HAHR* 69 (1989): 61–89.

Russomano, Victor. *História constitucional do Rio Grande do Sul, 1835–1930.* 2d ed. Porto Alegre: Assembléia Legislativa do Estado do Rio Grande do Sul, 1976.

Sabato, Hilda. *The Many and the Few: Political Participation in Republican Buenos Aires.* Stanford: Stanford University Press, 2001.

———. "On Political Citizenship in Nineteenth-Century Latin America." *American Historical Review* 106 (2001): 1290–1315.

Sachs, Emanie. *"The Terrible Siren": Victoria Woodhull (1838–1927).* New York: Harper and Brothers Publishers, 1928.

Saes, Décio. *A formação do estado burguês no Brasil (1888–1891)*. Rio de Janeiro: Paz e Terra, 1985.

Salles, Ricardo. *Guerra do Paraguai: Escravidão e cidadania na formação do exército*. Rio de Janeiro: Paz e Terra, 1990.

Sanhudo, Ary Veiga. *Porto Alegre crônicas da minha cidade*. Porto Alegre: Editora Movimento/Instituto Estadual do Livro, 1975.

Santos, Corcino Medeiros dos. *Economia e sociedade do Rio Grande do Sul: Século XVIII*. São Paulo: Editora Nacional; Brasília: Instituto Nacional do Livro/Fundação Nacional Pró-Memória, 1984.

Santos, Guarani. *A violência branca sobre o negro no Rio Grande do Sul, 1725–1889*. Porto Alegre: Livraria Ponto Negro Brasileiro, n.d.

Santos, Ronaldo Marcos dos. *Resistência e superação do escravismo na província de São Paulo (1885–1888)*. São Paulo: Instituto de Pesquisas Econômicas/Fundação Instituto de Pesquisas Econômicas, 1980.

Santos, Wanderley Guilherme dos. *Cidadania e justiça: A política social na ordem brasileira*. Rio de Janeiro: Campus, 1979.

Schmidt, Benito Bisso. *Um socialista no Rio Grande do Sul: Antônio Guedes Coutinho (1868–1945)*. Porto Alegre: Ed. Universidade/UFRGS, 2000.

Schneider, Regina Portella. *A instrução pública no Rio Grande do Sul, 1770–1889*. Porto Alegre: Editora da Universidade/UFRGS/EST Edições, 1993.

Schultz, Kirsten. *Tropical Versailles: Empire, Monarchy, and the Portuguese Royal Court in Rio de Janeiro, 1808–1821*. New York: Routledge, 2001.

Schupp, Ambrósio. *Os "Mucker": A tragédia histórica do Ferrabrás*. 4th ed. Porto Alegre: Martins Livreiro-Editor, 1993.

Schwarcz, Lília Moritz. *Retrato em branco e negro: Jornais, escravos e cidadãos em São Paulo no final do século XIX*. São Paulo: Companhia das Letras, 1987.

Schwartz, Stuart B. *Slaves, Peasants, and Rebels: Reconsidering Brazilian Slavery*. Urbana: University of Illinois Press, 1992.

———. *Sugar Plantations in the Formation of Brazilian Society: Bahia, 1550–1835*. Cambridge: Cambridge University Press, 1985.

Schwarz, Roberto. *Misplaced Ideas: Essays on Brazilian Culture*. London: Verso, 1992.

———. *Ao vencedor as batatas: Forma literária e processo social nos inícios do romance brasileiro*. 3d ed. São Paulo: Livraria Duas Cidades, 1988.

Scott, James C. *Domination and the Arts of Resistance: Hidden Transcripts*. New Haven: Yale University Press, 1990.

Silva, Adhemar Lourenço da, Jr. "Povo! Trabalhadores! Tumultos e movimento operário." Master's thesis, UFRGS, 1994.

Silva, Eduardo. *As queixas do povo*. Rio de Janeiro: Paz e Terra, 1988.

———. *Prince of the People: The Life and Times of a Brazilian Free Man of Colour*. Trans. Moyra Ashford. London: Verso, 1993.

Silva, Elmar M. da. "Ligações externas da economia gaúcha." In Dacanal and Gonzaga, *RS: Economia e política*, 55–91.

Silva, Leonardo Dantas, ed. *A abolição em Pernambuco*. Recife: Fundação Joaquim Nabuco/Editora Massangana, 1988.

Silva, Marcos A. da. *Caricata República: Zé Povo e o Brasil*. São Paulo: Marco Zero, 1990.
Silva, Marilene Rosa Nogueira da. *Negro na rua: A nova face da escravidão*. São Paulo: HUCITEC; Brasília: CNPq, 1988.
Silveira Martins, José Júlio. *Silveira Martins*. Rio de Janeiro: Typ. São Benedicto, 1929.
Singer, Paul. *Desenvolvimento econômico e evolução urbana: Análise da evolução econômica de São Paulo, Blumenau, Pôrto Alegre, Belo Horizonte e Recife*. São Paulo: Editora Nacional/Editora da USP, 1968.
Skidmore, Thomas E. *Black into White: Race and Nationality in Brazilian Thought*. New York: Oxford University Press, 1974.
———. "Racial Ideas and Social Policy in Brazil, 1870–1940." In Graham, *The Idea of Race*, 7–36.
Slenes, Robert Wayne. "The Demography and Economics of Brazilian Slavery: 1850–1888." Ph.D. diss., Stanford University, 1975.
———. *Na senzala, uma flor: Esperanças e recordações na formação da família escrava*. Rio de Janeiro: Nova Fronteira, 1999.
Soares, Luiz Carlos. "Os escravos de ganho no Rio de Janeiro do século XIX." *Revista Brasileira de História* 8 (1988): 107–42.
Soares, Mozart Pereira. *Júlio de Castilhos*. Porto Alegre: Instituto Estadual do Livro, 1991.
Soares, Pedro Maia. "Feminismo no Rio Grande do Sul: Primeiros apontamentos (1835–1945)." In *Vivência: História, sexualidade e imagens femininas*, ed. Maria Cristina A. Bruschini and Fúlvia Rosemberg, 1: 121–51. São Paulo: Brasiliense, 1980.
Soihet, Rachel. *Condição feminina e formas de violência: Mulheres pobres e ordem urbana, 1890–1920*. Rio de Janeiro: Forense Universitária, 1989.
Souza, Célia Ferraz de, and Dóris Maria Müller. *Porto Alegre e sua evolução urbana*. Porto Alegre: Ed. da Universidade/UFRGS, 1997.
Souza, Laura de Mello e. *Desclassificados do ouro: A pobreza mineira no século XVIII*. 2d ed. Rio de Janeiro: Edições Graal, 1986.
———. *O diabo e a Terra de Santa Cruz: Feitiçaria e religiosidade popular no Brasil colonial*. São Paulo: Companhia das Letras, 1986.
Souza, Marina de Mello e. *Reis negros no Brasil escravista: História da Festa de Coroção do Rei Congo*. Belo Horizonte: Editora UFMG, 2002.
Spalding, Walter. "O Centro Abolicionista." *Anais do III Congresso Sul-riograndense de história e geografia*, 2: 187–201. Porto Alegre: Instituto Histórico e Geográfico do Rio Grande do Sul, 1940.
———. *Construtores do Rio Grande*. 3 vols. Porto Alegre: Sulina, 1969–73.
———. *A epopéia farroupilha (pequena história da Grande Revolução, acompanhada de farta documentação da época—1835–1845)*. Rio de Janeiro: Editora do Exército, 1963.
———. *A grande mestra (Ana Aurora do Amaral Lisboa)*. Porto Alegre: Sulina, 1953.
———. *Pequena história de Porto Alegre*. Porto Alegre: Sulina, 1967.
———. *A Revolução Farroupilha*. 3d ed. São Paulo: Editora Nacional; Brasília: Editora Universidade de Brasília, 1982.
Sperb, Angela Tereza. "Autos do processo dos Mucker: Nova fonte para o estudo do

episódio do Ferrabraz." In *Anais do IV Simpósio de História da Imigração e Colonização Alemã no Rio Grande do Sul*, 239–48. [São Leopoldo]: Museu Histórico Visconde do São Leopoldo/Instituto Histórico de São Leopoldo, 1987.

Stanley, Amy Dru. "Beggars Can't Be Choosers: Compulsion and Contract in Postbellum America." *Journal of American History* 78 (1992): 128–59.

Stavig, Ward. "'Living in Offense of Our Lord': Indigenous Sexual Values and Marital Life in the Colonial Crucible." *HAHR* 75 (1995): 597–622.

Stein, Stanley J. *Vassouras: A Brazilian Coffee County, 1850–1900*. 2d ed. Princeton: Princeton University Press, 1985.

Stern, Steve J. *The Secret History of Gender: Women, Men, and Power in Late Colonial Mexico*. Chapel Hill: University of North Carolina Press, 1995.

———. "Tricks of Time: Colonial Legacies and Historical Sensibilities in Latin America." In *Colonial Legacies: The Problems of Persistence in Latin American History*, ed. Jeremy Adelman, 135–50. New York: Routledge, 1999.

Telles, Norma. "Rebeldes, escritoras, abolicionistas." *Revista de História* (São Paulo) 120 (1989): 73–83.

Tenorio Trillo, Mauricio. *Argucias de la historia: Siglo XIX, cultura y "América Latina."* Mexico City: Editorial Paidós, 1999.

Thompson, E. P. *The Making of the English Working Class*. New York: Vintage, 1966.

———. "Patrician Society, Plebeian Culture." *Journal of Social History* 7 (1974): 382–405.

Thurner, Mark. *From Two Republics to One Divided: Contradictions of Postcolonial Nationmaking in Andean Peru*. Durham: Duke University Press, 1997.

Thurner, Mark, and Andrés Guerrero, eds. *After Spanish Rule: Postcolonial Predicaments of the Americas*. Durham: Duke University Press, 2003.

Toplin, Robert Brent. *The Abolition of Slavery in Brazil*. New York: Atheneum, 1972.

Torres, João Camillo de Oliveira. *O positivismo no Brasil*. 2d ed. Petrópolis: Vozes, 1957.

Trindade, Hélgio. "Aspectos políticos do sistema partidário republicano rio-grandense (1882–1937)." In Dacanal and Gonzaga, *RS: Economia e política*, 119–91.

———. "Brasil em perspectiva: Conservadorismo liberal e democracia bloqueada." In *Viagem incompleta. A experiência brasileira (1500–2000): A grande transação*, ed. Carlos Guilherme Mota, 349–80. 2d ed. São Paulo: Editora SENAC São Paulo, 2000.

———. *Poder legislativo e autoritarismo no Rio Grande do Sul, 1891–1937*. Porto Alegre: Sulina, 1980.

Twinam, Ann. "Honor, Sexuality, and Illegitimacy in Colonial Spanish America." In Lavrin, *Sexuality and Marriage in Colonial Latin America*, 118–55.

Uricoechea, Fernando. *The Patrimonial Foundations of the Brazilian Bureaucratic State*. Berkeley: University of California Press, 1980.

Varela, Alfredo. *História da grande revolução: O cyclo farroupilha no Brasil*. 6 vols. Porto Alegre: Livraria do Globo, 1933.

———. *Riogrande do Sul: Descripção physica, historica e economica*. Pelotas and Porto Alegre: Livraria Universal, 1897.

Vellinho, Moysés. *Brazil South: Its Conquest and Settlement*. Trans. Linton Lomas Barrett and Marie MacDavid Barrett. New York: Alfred A. Knopf, 1968.

Vianna, Francisco José de Oliveira. *Instituições políticas brasileiras*. 2 vols. 3d ed. Rio de Janeiro: Record, 1974.

———. *Populações meridionais do Brasil: História, organização, psicologia*. 5th ed. Rio de Janeiro: José Olympio Editora, 1952.

Volpato, Luiza Rios Ricci. *Cativos do sertão; Vida cotidiana e escravidão em Cuiabá, 1850–1888*. São Paulo: Editora Marco Zero; Cuiabá: Editora da Universidade Federal de Mato Grosso, 1993.

Wade, Richard C. *Slavery in the Cities: The South 1820–1860*. London, Oxford, and New York: Oxford University Press, 1964.

Walker, Charles F. *Cuzco and the Creation of Republican Peru, 1780–1840*. Durham: Duke University Press, 1999.

Warren, Richard A. *Vagrants and Citizens: Politics and the Masses in Mexico City from Colony to Republic*. Wilmington, Dela.: Scholarly Resources, 2001.

Weber, Beatriz Teixeira. *As artes de curar: Medicina, religião, magia e positivismo na República Rio-Grandense—1889–1928*. Santa Maria: Ed. da UFSM; Bauru: EDUSC/Editora da Universidade do Sagrado Coração, 1999.

———. "Códigos de posturas e regulamentação do convívio social em Porto Alegre no século XIX." Master's thesis, UFRGS, 1992.

Weimar, Günter. *O trabalho escravo no Rio Grande do Sul*. Porto Alegre: Sagra/Editora da UFRGS, 1991.

Weinstein, Barbara. "Brazilian Regionalism." *LARR* 17 (1982): 262–76.

———. "The Decline of the Progressive Planter and the Rise of Subaltern Agency: Shifting Narratives of Slave Emancipation in Brazil." In Joseph, *Reclaiming the Political in Latin American History*, 81–101.

Williams, Raymond. *Marxism and Literature*. New York: Oxford University Press, 1977.

Witter, Nikelen Acosta. *Dizem que foi feitiço: As práticas da cura no sul do Brasil (1845 a 1880)*. Porto Alegre: EDIPUCRS, 2001.

Wood, Andy. "The Place of Custom in Plebeian Political Culture: England, 1550–1800." *Social History* 22 (1997): 46–60.

Woodward, Ralph Lee, ed. *Positivism in Latin America, 1850–1900: Are Order and Progress Reconciliable?* Lexington, MA: D. C. Heath and Company, 1971.

Zanetti, Valéria. "Calabouço urbano: Escravos e libertos em Porto Alegre (1840–1860)." Master's thesis, PUCRS, 1994.

Zea, Leopoldo. *El positivismo en México*. Mexico City: Fondo de Cultura Económica, 1968.

Zilberman, Regina. "O Partenon Literário: Literatura e discurso político." In *O Partenon Literário: Poesia e prosa—antologia*, ed. Carmen Consuelo Silveira Zilberman and Carlos A. Baumgarten, 25–42. Porto Alegre: Escola Superior de Teologia São Lourenço de Brindes/Instituto Cultural Português, 1980.

Index

Abèlés, Marc, 3
abolition. *See* slavery, abolition of
Abolitionist Center of Porte Alegre (Centro Abolicionista de Porto Alegre), 129–33, 143, 216n43
Abreu, Aureliano de, 177–78
Africa, 180; end of slave trade from, 29–31; influence of, 95–97, 99–100
Africans, 106; in Porto Alegre population, 20–21; racism against, 14, 40, 55–56. *See also* Afro-Brazilians
Afro-Brazilians, 102, 106, 179; dances and rituals of, 98, 207n55, 209n79, 209n90; newspaper of workers, 179–81; police and, 90–91, 98, 209n79; as political participants, 157, 175; racism against, 40, 55–56; rejection of conditional emancipation by, 141; religion of, 92–101
Agricultural-Industrial League (LAI, or Liga Agrícolo-Industrial): formation of, 154–55; PRR support by, 165, 168; as workers' organization, 160–62, 176; Workers' Union and, 159–60
agriculture, 30, 57; in Center-South, 59–60; *charque* (dried beef) production in, 16–17, 38, 121, 204n3; export, 59; immigrants in, 50–53, 59–60, 67, 72–73; market, 18–19, 155; ranchers and, 17, 38, 126; in Rio Grande do Sul, 16–17, 161; slave labor in, 21–22, 30, 51–53, 121, 204n3; training for, 36, 43
Albuquerque, Viscount of, 5–6
Alencar, José de, 4
Alonso, Angela, 14–15
Americo, Sebastião, 101
Andrea, Francisco José de Souza Soares de, 41
André (slave), 78–79, 85
Argentina, 17
artisans, 21, 53; job associations representing, 158–59; in Porto Alegre, 18, 155–56
Artisans' Guild (Grêmio dos Artistas), 176
Asilo de Santa Leopoldina, 44
assimilation. *See* immigrants, assimilation of
Assis Brasil, Joaquim Francisco, 125–26, 166, 171–72
"asylums of liberty" *(asilos de liberdade)*, 35–36
authoritarianism, 3; of Castilhos and PRR, 10, 168; of Deodoro, 172
autonomy: difficulty of establishing, 79; as goal, *vs.* dependency, 9–10, 15, 193n39; of immigrant colonies, 68–69; of immigrants, 48, 64–66; plebeian, 89, 116, 183; as plebeian goal, 39, 41, 45, 76, 81–84; religious freedom as, 90, 101
Azevedo, Alfredo de, 159–60

Bank of Emissions (Banco Emissor), 167, 171
banks, issuing currency, 165–67, 171
Barbosa, Rui, 165
Barcellos, Israel Rodrigues, 23–24, 62
Barcelos, Ramiro (Fortes de), 125–26, 160, 167
Barros, Cacique de, 194n12
Becker, Luiz, 139
Beggars' Asylum (Asilo de Mendicidade): creation of, 194n12; criticism of, 198n92; in elites' attempt to refashion plebeians, 15–16, 24–27, 44; ideology of vagrancy and, 39–40; relation of slavery and abolition to, 30–31, 33, 36
begging, 27–28. *See also* vagrancy
Belisário (slave), 87–88

Bello, Luís Alves Leite de Oliveira, 41, 63, 198n94, 198n95
Benedita, patron-client relations of, 76–77, 81
Bier, Leopoldo, 138
Bittencourt, Carlos Machado de, 168
Bittencourt, Felipe Lopes de, 104
Bittencourt, José Bernardino da Cunha, 65, 67
Boeira, Nelson, 152
Brazil, 66; avoidance of revolution, 1, 4; immigrants' loyalty to, 65–66; as nation-state, 4–5. *See also* Empire, Brazilian; First Republic, Brazilian
Brazilian exceptionalism, myth of, 4
Britain, 29, 66
Britto, Sá, 40
Brummers, 70
Buenos Aires, 16

Cabelleira, José Joaquim Garcês, 107
Campo do Bom Fim (Parque da Redenção), 99, 213n3
Canto, Mariano José do Filho, 138
Capistrano, João, 61
Capitalismo e escravidão no Brasil meridional (Cardoso), 75
capitalists: as "independent producers," 165, 169; workers forming labor party separate from, 173
Cardoso, Fernando Henrique, 75
Carneiro, Antonio Gonçalves, 78, 85, 205n15
Cassal, Barros, 166–69, 172
Castilhos, Júlio de: Deodoro and, 172; dissident Republicans and, 168–70; and end of Empire, 149–50; opposition to, 168–70, 174; philosophy of, 154, 168, 170; power of, 165, 171–75; PRR and, 152–53, 169–70, 173–74, 181–82; in state government, 164–66, 168, 170–72
Catholicism: blending of other religious practices with, 101, 208n67; lay brotherhoods in, 92–94; plebeians' heterodox practices outside, 95–101; in popular culture, 91–94; religious freedom for others and, 69, 123; as state religion, 58–59, 69
Caxias, Duke of (Luiz Alves de Lima e Silva), 13–14
Center-South: coffee plantations in, 6–7, 29–30; immigrants and, 49–50, 59–60; influence in national government, 12, 59; Rio Grande do Sul supplying, 16, 50
Chalhoub, Sidney, 6, 75
Chasteen, John, 152
Chatterjee, Partha, 176
Chaves, Antonio José Gonçalves, 28–29
Chaves, Pedro Rodrigues Fernandes (Baron of Quaraim), 23–24
Chinese immigrants, discrimination against, 56–57
Christie Affair, 66
Church of Our Lady of the Rosary, 94
Cintra, Saião Lobato de Ulhôa, 52
citizenship: autonomy *vs.*, 193n39; for immigrants, 58, 60–61, 69; obstacles to, 9, 69; plebeians', 10, 183; worthiness for, 159, 178–79, 181
Civil Guard (Military Brigade), 165, 174
class, social, 5, 92
class hierarchy, 4. *See also* social order
class interests: job associations representing workers, 157–59; political parties and, 176
clientelism, 6, 90, 174; after emancipation, 118–19, 142–43; autonomy *vs.* dependency in, 105–6, 184; patron-client relations in, 76–77, 79–80; plebeians' rights in, 80–84; plebeians trying to use patron-client relations, 84–86, 102–3; political parties and, 9, 186. *See also* paternalism
Club Caixeiral (Store Clerks' Club), 158
coffee growers: dependence on slavery, 6–7, 29–30; immigrants and, 49, 58
Colégio de Santa Tereza, 44
colonies, of immigrants. *See* immigrant colonies
colonization, internal, 43, 67–68
colonos. *See* immigrants
Comte, Auguste: Castilhos and PRR using ideology of, 152–54, 170–71; Positivism of, 7, 152–54; Republicans' respect for, 1, 126
Conceição, Clara Joaquina da, 115–16
Conceição, Zeferina Maria da, 111–13
Conservatives, 150, 182, 222n55; abolition and, 123–25, 128; divisiveness among,

124–25; Liberals and, 5–6, 23; Liberals *vs.*, 5, 24, 124, 128
constitution: of Empire, 58–59; of Rio Grande do Sul, 152–54
contract workers *(parceria)*, 50–51, 59
Corrêa, Norton, 101
Coruja, Antonio Álvares Pereira, 92–93, 99
Costa, Cândido, 167–68
Costa, Emília Viotti da, 4, 49, 72
Costa, Francisco Xavier da, 177
Costa, Marcos Antonio da, 119
Costa, Maria da, 183–84
Counter-League (Contra-Liga), 23–24
coup d'état: attempt, in Rio Grande do Sul, 173–74; First Republic formed by, 7–8
culture: blending of, 69–70, 99–100; popular, 90–94
Cunha, Félix Xavier da, 13–14, 24; on Beggars' Asylum, 25–26, 198n92; proposals for reform by, 71–72
Cunha, Joaquim Vieira da, 89
Cunha, Manuela Carneiro da, 87

da Matta, Roberto, 193n39
dances, Afro-Brazilian, 90, 96–100, 209n79, 209n90
Deutsche Zeitung (newspaper), 66

economy: bank-of-issue proposal in, 165–67; effects of immigration in, 17, 57–58, 62–63; effects of slavery in, 28–29, 32; expectations of immigrants in, 51–54, 73; of immigrant colonies, 70–71, 155; of Porto Alegre, 17–19, 70–71, 155–56; of Rio Grande do Sul, 16–18, 38–39
education: in elites' attempt to refashion plebeians, 37, 40, 43–45; for freeborn citizens, 35–37; for immigrants, 65–67, 69; for labor and morality, 143–44, 153–54, 186–87
elections, 159; accusations of fraud in, 169; direct presidential rejected, 171; participation in, 5, 192n17
elites, 30, 42, 173; abolition and, 27, 33–34, 123–25, 127–29, 135; ambivalence about immigrants, 47, 57–58, 60–63; *colono*, 71; criticisms of slavery by, 28, 32–33, 56–57, 121, 126; dissatisfaction with immigrants, 63–65, 72; divisiveness among, 6–7, 10, 13–14, 23–24, 122–23, 135–36; on education, 40, 43–45, 143–44; effects of slavery on morality of, 133–34; efforts to refashion plebeians, 14–16, 24–27, 37–38, 41–45, 54–55, 91; in emancipation movement, 120–21, 128–32; expectations of immigrants, 37–38, 47–49, 51–54, 73; freedpersons and, 34–37, 76–78, 143–45; on internal colonization proposals, 67–68; maintaining social order, 2–3, 35, 39, 125, 139; new power relations of, 150–51, 156; in patron-client relations, 79–80, 142–43; plebeian resistance to, 31–32, 39; on poverty, 24–27; regional, 5, 13–14, 17; regulation of master-servant relations of, 145–48; relations with immigrants, 9, 50, 59, 68–69, 70–71, 72–73; relations with plebeians, 10, 41–42, 79; relations with slaves, 78–79; self-image of, 19; threats to, 5, 10, 58, 65–66; using state social-control functions, 41–42, 77–78
emancipation: activism for, 7, 214n12; conditional, 127–28, 135, 141–42, 144; patron-client relations after, 118–19, 142–43; in Porto Alegre, 120, 129–33; seen as redemption, 213n3; slaves' petition to authorities for, 86–88; slaves' savings funds for, 86–87, 207n46; voluntary, 197n66, 216n45. *See also* Free Womb Law; slavery, abolition of
emancipation funds, 140–41, 216n43, 218n90
emancipation movement, 121; feminization of, 122–23, 128–32, 134, 216n51
emancipation organizations, 129–33, 216n43, 216n45, 216n51
Empire, Brazilian, 2; creation of, 3, 5, 7; end of, 3, 126–27, 149, 184; finances of, 50–51, 164
Estado Oriental (Uruguay), 16–17
Esteves, Martha, 111, 114
Estudante, O. *See* Gomes, José Cândido ("O Estudante")
ethnic groups: associations of, 21, 157–58, 164; in manufacturing, 21–22; as political participants, 157, 173–74; in Porto Alegre population, 20–21
Exemplo, O (newspaper), 179–81

family: effects of slavery on, 133–34; nation as, 6, 13–14; plebeians' rights to, 81–82, 135
Fanfa, Ignacio Furtado, 108, 110
Faria, Antão de, 167, 168
Farroupilha Revolution, 3; effects of, 12, 38, 41–42, 51, 61; isolation of Porto Alegre in, 70; nature of, 195n23; Republicans and, 13, 125; women's role in, 130
federalism, Republic violating principles of, 165
Federalist Party (Partido Federalista), 173
Federalist Revolt, 163, 182; PRR victory in, 2, 150, 152, 182
Federal Party, *vs.* PRR, 171, 181–82
Federal Republican Party (Partido Republicano Federal), as anti-Castilhos, 169
Félix, Loiva, 152
Ferreira, Athos Damascena, 99
Ferreira, Damazia Joaquina, 81
Fião, Antonio do Vale Caldre e, 43, 62; in Beggars' Asylum debate, 25–26; on freedpersons, 27–28; on internal colonization, 67–68; supporting abolition, 33–35
Fidelis, João, 109–10
Fioravanti, Antonio Ângelo Christiano, 53, 64
First Republic, Brazilian, 3, 165, 184; celebrations of, 163–64; competing visions of, 153–54, 171; formed by military coup, 7–8; new politics of, 162–63, 182; political inclusiveness of, 11, 151; political struggle for control of, 150, 157, 167
Fonseca, General Deodoro da, 163, 165, 168, 172
Fontoura, João Neves da, 153
Fortes, Candida, 133
Fortes, João Pereira da Silva Borges, 14–15, 64
França, Serafim dos Anjos, 80
Franco, Sérgio da Costa, 172
freedpersons: efforts to help, 27–28, 33, 137–38; elites and, 34–35, 141, 144–45, 167; failure to complete contracted service, 141–42; patron-client relations of, 76–77, 105–6; threat of reenslavement of, 106, 211n112; training for, 35–37, 143–44
Free Womb (Rio Branco) Law (1871), 33, 35, 214n11; politics around, 36, 123; service provisions of, 127–28, 198n79, 215n36; slaves' savings funds under, 86–87, 127
Frota, Júlio Anacleto Falcão da, 166–67

Galvão, Manoel Antonio, 40
Gay, Maria Jesuína, 131–32
Gazetinha, A (newspaper), 176–79
gender, 102; feminization of emancipation movement, 122–23, 128–32, 134; honor and, 108–14; in plans for education of plebeians, 44–45; of political participants, 156–57
gender relations, men's honor and, 115
gender roles: among plebeians, 109–10; emancipation movement and, 130–32
General Association of Workers (Allgemeiner Arbeiter Verein), 176
German Beneficient Society (Deutscher Hilfsverein), 157
Gledhill, John, 8
Goerisch, Francisco, 173
"Golden Law" (1888), 7
Gomes, José Cândido ("O Estudante"), 27, 72–73; on religious practices, 92, 99; on runaway slaves, 46–47
government, 92; abolition and, 29, 126; Center-South dominance's in national, 12, 59; immigration and, 61, 68–70; levels of, 13, 126; national, 13, 24, 174; performance of criticized, 177–78; plebeians and, 42, 79–80, 88–89, 194n12; regulation of master-servant relations by, 84–85, 146–48; social-control functions of police, 77–79; subsidizing immigration, 62–63, 68
government buildings, in Porto Alegre, 19
Graham, Richard, 5
Gramsci, Antonio, 8
Guimarães, Valentim, 134
Gusmão, A. Soares Amaya de, 147

Haensel, Frederico, 71
Hale, Charles, 2
Held, João Maria von, 159–60, 169, 176
Herskovits, Melville, 95–96
Herzog, Franz, 155, 156, 176
Historical Liberal Party, 24, 71
Holanda, Sérgio Buarque de, 11
Holloway, Thomas, 22, 42
honor: among plebeians, 115–17; gender

and, 108–11; sexuality and, 111–14, 212n137; violence and, 113–15
honor/shame complex, 111–15, 117, 213n143
Hörmeyer, Joseph, 92, 94–95
households: domestic servants in, 145–46; slaves in, 21, 85–86
housing: of plebeians, 21, 105, 116; of slaves, 90–91, 105

ideology of vagrancy, 15, 39–40. *See also* vagrancy
immigrant colonies, 47; economy of, 70–71, 155; government support for, 50–51; granted *município* status, 71, 201n22; isolation of, 60–61, 66–69; slavery in, 200n13. *See also* São Leopoldo
immigrants, 20; assimilation of, 64–70, 72–73; culture of, 69–71; discrimination against Chinese, 56–57; economy of, 17, 50–51, 70–71; elite ambivalence about, 47, 57–58, 61–63, 65–66, 72; elite dissatisfaction with, 63–65, 72; elite expectations of, 14, 43, 47–49, 51–55, 73; elites hoping to replace slave labor with, 32, 37–38, 49–52, 200n13; ethnicity of, 67, 108; German, 18, 48, 57, 60–61, 67, 70, 169, 203n78; Italian, 18, 57, 60–61; jobs for, 50–51, 72–73; land for, 61–63; loyalty to Brazil questioned, 65–66; plebeians *vs.*, 14, 53–54, 67–68; in politics, 61, 170, 173; Portuguese, 67; racism in preference for European, 40, 55–56, 201n32; role in social order, 9, 60–61; work ethic of, 54–55
immigration, 29, 61; government subsidies for, 62–63, 68
"independent producers," 165–66, 169
industry, 25, 36; *charque* (dried beef) production as, 16–17, 38, 121; ethnic groups in, 21–22; immigrants and, 51, 53, 155; in Porto Alegre, 18–19, 155–56; in Rio Grande do Sul, 16–17, 161
Irmandade de Nossa Senhora do Rosário (Brotherhood of Our Lady of the Rosary), 93, 96–97, 141, 218n90
Isabelle, Arsène, 74–75
Itaqui, Egydio Barbosa Oliveira, 142

Jesús, Joan Guedes de, 114–15
José, Dionísio, 80
José, Maria, 97–98

Kappel, Simão, 174
Karasch, Mary C., 208n67
Koseritz, Carlos [Karl] von, 61, 70; slaves of, 136, 141–42
Kowarick, Lúcio, 15

labor: associations, 157–59, 164; in Beggars' Asylum debate, 25–27; complaints about shortage and surplus of, 38–39; conditions of, 82–83, 135; by immigrants, 32, 37–38, 49–52, 54–55, 200n13; for industry, 156; regulation of master-servant relations in, 145–48; by slaves, 21–22, 31–32, 37–38, 49–52, 121, 200n13; training for, 35–36, 43–45, 143–44, 153–54
LAI. *See* Agricultural-Industrial League (LAI, or Liga Agrícolo-Industrial)
land, 61–63, 79
language, immigrants', 65, 67
Latin America: Brazil as unlike rest of, 5; immigrants to, 47
lay brotherhoods, 102, 141; Afro-Brazilians in, 96; ethnic distinctions in, 210n94, 210n95; plebeian participation in, 92–94
Laytano, Dante de, 92–93
League (Liga), 23–24, 165
Leoni, Francisco Colombo, 173, 176
Leopoldina (slave), 85–86
Lessa, Renato, 7
liberalism: as antidemocratic, 5, 8; contradictions within, 4; nonelites' autonomy under, 9–10; Positivism *vs.*, 2–3, 184
Liberal Party: abolition proposals of, 33, 36
Liberals, 150; abolition and, 123–24, 128–29; alliances of, 160–61, 182; as antidemocratic, 5, 8; Conservatives and, 5–6, 23; dominance in province, 123, 186; forming Historical Liberal Party, 24; plebeian relations with, 171, 224n120; political culture of, 5, 8–9, 22–23, 151–52; power of, 152–53, 162, 164–65, 173; proposals for reform, 71–72; in Provincial Assembly, *161;* PRR *vs.*, 152–53, 161, 172–73, 182; on religious freedom, 123
Liberation Society (Sociedade Libertadora), 36

Lima, Carlos A. M., 9
Lima, José Rodrigues, 144
Lima, Tristão Pires de, 80
Love, Joseph, 152
Luccock, John, 94–95
Luís, Alexandre, 196n59
Luís, Francisco, 10

Malheiro, Perdigão, 86–88
manufacturing. *See* industry
Mariante, Antonio Joaquim da Silva, 40, 54–55
Martins, Gaspar Silveira, 24, 71–72, 152; on emancipation, 123–24, 214n12; exile of, 164–65, 172–73; PRR *vs.*, 181–82; Silva Só allying with, 160–61; slaves of, 85, 132; state government and, 172–73
masculinity, 107–10
Mattos, Hebe Maria, 195n38
Mattos, Ilmar Rohloff de, 5
Mauch, Cláudia, 177
Memórias ecônomo-políticas sobre a administração pública no Brasil (Gonçalves Chaves), 28–29
Mendonça, João Jacintho de, 62–63
merchants, 71, 161
Mesquita, Francisco José de, 156, 166, 170
military, 80, 144; politics and, 7–8, 164, 168; sale of uniforms from, 104–5; status from service in, 103–5, 159; violence against soldiers, 136–37
Minas Gerais, 6, 16
mining, 16
miscegenation, 29
Moçambique, Lúcio and Antonio, 142
monarchy, 4; removal of, 7, 149
Monteiro, Vitorino, 175
Moraes, Evaristo de, 162
morality: education for, 153–54; effects of slavery on, 29, 33–34, 132–34; emancipation movement and, 128–32, 134; immigrants', 54–56; looseness of criticized, 178–79, 180–81; plebeians', 45, 54–55, 95; of police, 42; slaves', 31–34, 36–37, 52. *See also* honor/shame complex
Moreira, Paulo, 116, 218n90; on police, 77, 199n98; on repression, 41–42; on resistance by plebeians, 142, 148
Muckers, 69
mutual aid societies, 157

nation: as antidemocratic, 9; as family, 6, 13–14
National Union (União Nacional), 169
nativism, 72
naturalization, for immigrants, 59
Nelson, Maria Luiza, 85
Neri, Felippe, 27–28, 30
newspapers, 164; for Afro-Brazilian workers, 179–81; for "independent producers," 169; of labor associations, 158–59, 221n47; master-slave relations and, 136, 139, 145–46; for *povo*, 176–79; Republican, 154–55, 163–64

Oliveira, Antônio da Costa e, 103–4
Oliveira, Otaviano Manoel de, 177
Osório, Manuel Luís, 24, 71

Pacheco, Ricardo, 163
Paiva, Ernesto, 172
Paraguayan War (1865–1870), 3, 18–19, 130; effects of, 38–39, 98, 155; military service in, 34, 103–5
parliamentarianism, 171
partisan politics, 71, 175; taking emancipation movement out of, 128–29; workers' representatives in, 160–61. *See also* political parties; politics; *specific political parties*
Passos, José dos, Júnior, 114–15
paternalism: nation as family under, 6, 28; plebeians under, 44, 76; slaves under, 28, 78–79, 140–41. *See also* clientelism
patriarchy, among plebeians, 115–17, 213n147
patronage, 6, 9–10; political parties and, 5, 122
patron-client relations. *See* clientelism
Pedro, Dom, II, 5
Pedroso, João Alves, 104
Pelotas, Viscount of, 164, 166
Pelotas (city), 17, 19
Pesavento, Sandra, 39, 153, 165
Petersen, Silvia, 159
Pinto, Celi, 125–26
plebeians, 151; autonomy of, 9–10, 38, 45, 76, 183–84; commonalities among, 21; control over, 12–13, 41, 79, 90–91,

138–39; education of, 40, 43–45; elite efforts to refashion, 14–16, 24–27, 37–38, 41–45, 54, 91; free *vs.* slave, 105–6, 119–20; *A Gazetinha* newspaper for, 176–79; hierarchies among, 102–8, 175, 213n147; honor of, 108–11, 115–17; honor/shame complex of, 111–14, 213n143; immigrants *vs.*, 53–54, 67–68; living conditions of, 82–83, 177–80; in patron-client relations, 76–77, 79–81, 102–3; police and, 79, 137–39; political involvement by, 162, 174–75, 184–87; political parties and, 153–54, 162, 169, 171, 224n120; racism among, 106–8; regulation of master-servant relations of, 145–48; relations with state, 9, 12–13, 88–89, 136–37; religion of, 92–101; repression of, 41–42, 198n94, 198n95; resistance by, 39, 91, 135, 148, 199n100; solidarity among, 6, 75–76, 102–5, 137–38, 212n129; struggle for rights by, 80–82; trying to improve working conditions, 82–83. *See also* workers
police: budget for, 199n98, 219n107; *A Gazetinha* criticizing, 177–78; master-servant relations and, 80, 147; religious practices and, 99–101, 209n79; repression of plebeians by, 41–42, 88–89, 138–39, 178; slaves seeking help from, 85, 87–88, 137–38; social-control function of, 77–79, 91, 96–97, 99–101, 144, 199n100
political culture, 3; of Liberals, 5, 8–9, 22–23, 151–52; popular, 75, 90, 102–5; in Republic, 162–63
political parties, 150; Agricultural-Industrial League as, 154–55; contention among, 122–25, 127, 162–63; mobilization of masses by, 166–68; PRR *vs.* other, 126; in Rio Grande do Sul, 151–52; similarity of, 5–6; workers' relations with, 159, 163, 169, 175–76. *See also specific parties*
politics: elite power over, 14–15, 58–59, 150–51; as exclusionary and elitist, 2, 5, 8–10, 22–23, 157, 171; greater involvement in, 70–71, 184–87; immigrant participation in, 48, 61, 70–71; increasing inclusiveness of, 3, 10–11, 150–51, 154, 162–63, 175; job associations in, 158–59; over abolition, 120–21, 135; participation in, 3–4, 7–8, 156–57, 187; plebeian involvement in, 174–75; reform of, 71–72; renegotiation of, 7, 12, 162–63, 182; scientific, 2. *See also* partisan politics
Ponche Verde, Treaty of, 61
poor. *See* plebeians
Porto Alegre: elite divisiveness in, 23–24; growth of, 19–20, 155; population of, 20, 20–21; slave population in, 22, 121
Porto Alegre, Apolinário, 126, 132
Portugal, independence from, 2, 4
Portuguese Beneficient Society (Sociedade Portuguesa de Beneficência), 157
Positivism, 10, 186; influence of, 7, 170–71, 191n4; PRR and, 126, 150, 153–54; rise of, 1–2, 152, 184; tenets of, 1, 8, 11, 165
poverty: Beggars' Asylum debate over, 24–27; of plebeians, 105, 116
power relations, 2; changing with Liberal to Positivist shift, 3–4, 187; *vs.* Politics, 3, 8, 11. *See also* clientelism
Praiera (rebellion), 12
Prates, Fidêncio, 55, 67
productive classes. *See* "independent producers"
Progressive Liberal Party (Partido Liberal Progressista), 23–24
PRR. *See* Rio Grandense Republican Party (PRR, or Partido Repubicano Rio-Grandense)

race: in Church activities, 92, 210n95; in coup d'état attempt, 174; in Porto Alegre population, 20–21; terms for, 195n38; whitewashing of history, 195n37
racism: against Africans and Afro-Brazilians, 40; among plebeians, 102, 106–8; in elites' preference for European immigrants, 55–56, 201n32; *O Exemplo* criticizing, 179–80; PRR complaints about, 157
rebellions, renegotiating politics after, 12
reform, 121, 195n23; education, 40; in efforts to refashion plebeians, 15–16; Liberal proposals for, 33, 71–72; of slavery, *vs.* abolition, 33, 124

religion: Afro-Brazilian dances and rituals of, 207n55, 209n90; heterodox, 95–101, 209n86; immigrants', 58–59, 69; plebeians' practices, 95–102; police control of, 96–97, 99–101; popular, 91–94; in slave-master relationships, 89–90; social-control function of, 41, 94–95. *See also* Catholicism
religion, freedom of, 90, 170; immigrants promised, 58–59; Liberals on, 72, 123
repression, of plebeians, 37, 41, 198n94, 198n95
Republic. *See* First Republic, Brazilian
Republicans, 6; abolition and, 124–25, 128; dissident, 168–70, 172–74, 181; ideology of, 1, 11, 152; plebeians and, 145, 184; Positivism of, 1, 186; power of, 162, 164–65, 167; in Rio Grande do Sul *vs.* rest of Brazil, 150–51; Workers' Union and, 159–60. *See also* Rio Grandense Republican Party (PRR)
revolution, Brazil's avoidance of, 1, 4, 127
Ribas, Taborda, 145–46
Ribeiro, Demétrio, 153–54; leaving PRR, 168; rejecting government's bank-of-issue plan, 165–66
rights: for Afro-Brazilians, 181; Federalists and, 171; Liberals and, 71–72; plebeians asserting, 9–10, 76, 80–84, 96–99, 178; property, 124–25, 134; for slaves, 82–83, 86–88, 127–28. *See also* religion, freedom of; voting, right of
Rio Branco Law. *See* Free Womb (Rio Branco) Law (1871)
Rio de Janeiro, 6–7, 21; slave population in, 23
Rio Grande (city), 16–20
Rio Grande do Sul, 13–14; abolition in, 6, 28, 30; Castilhos's power in, 172, 174–75; Center-South *vs.*, 59–60; coup d'état attempt in, 173–74; economy of, 16, 161–62; elites of, 17, 30; government of, 24, 172, 196n59; immigrants in, 50, 59–60; national government and, 13–14; political parties in, 151–52; population, 20; Republicans in, 150–51, 173–74; slave population in, 22, 121, 217n68; state constitution of, 170–71; *vs.* rest of Brazil, 8, 17, 150–51
Rio Grandense Republican Party (PRR, or Partido Republicano Rio-Grandense), 123; abolitionism of, 125–27; on bank-of-issue plan, 166–67; Castilhos and, 169–70; control of state institutions, 165, 171–72; dissident Republicans *vs.*, 168–70, 181–82; and end of Empire, 126–27, 149–50, 163; Federalists *vs.*, 171, 181–82; goals of, 1, 10, 157; as innovative, 125–26; LAI and, 154–55, 161; mobilization of masses by, 166–68; opposition to, 160, 166, 171; platform of, 157, 186–87; Positivism of, 126, 153–54; power of, 3, 164–65, 168, 173–74, 223n98; in Rio Grande do Sul, 149–51; support for, 153, 156, 186; victory in Federalist Revolt, 150, 152, 182; vision for Republic, 153–54. *See also* Republicans
Rio Pardo, 19, 46–47
Roche, Jean, 59
Rodrigues, José Honório, 2, 13
Rosa, Luiz Manoel da Silva, 107–8
Rosário, Andreza do, 116
Rosas, Juan Manuel de, 3
Roth, Guilherme, 159–60

Sabato, Hilda, 187
Salgado, Joaquim Pedro, 129
Salvador, slave population in, 21, 23
Sanhudo, Manoel José, 79
Santos, Antonio Joaquim dos, 113–14
Santos, Francisco Caetano dos, 83
Santos, João Antonio dos, 79
Santos, Joaquim José dos, 113
Santos, José Ferreira, 111–13
Santos, Matildes Lebania Pereira dos, 99–100
São Leopoldo: economy of, 53, 70–71; granted *município* status, 71, 201n22; immigrant colony at, 18–19, 50–51, 53, 68; success of colonization in, 62–63
São Paulo: immigrants in, 49–50, 58; slavery in, 6–7
Saraiva, Gumercindo, 181
Schmitt, Benito Bisso, 193n39
Second Empire, stability of, 5
seigneurial relations. *See* clientelism; patronage
sexuality: honor and, 111–14, 212n137; limits on, 212n139; looseness criticized, 178–79, 180–81
Silva, Paulino Ferreira da, 137
Silva, Pedro Firmiano da, 105

Silveira, Manoel Francisco da, 102–3
Sinimbú, João Lins Vieira Cansansão de, 17–18, 51
slavery, 4, 16, 184, 200n13; brutality in, 106, 132–33; effects on economy, 28–29, 32; effects on morality, 29, 33–34, 36–37, 133–34; elite criticisms of, 28, 32–33, 56–57, 121, 126; elite divisiveness about, 6–7, 135–36; harshness of, 74, 204n3; loss of family in, 81–82, 133; master-slave relations after emancipation from, 118–19, 142–43; proper relations within, 27–28, 84–86, 89–90; punishment in, 83–86, 89, 205n12, 206n41; reform *vs.* abolition of, 124; replacing labor of, 30–31, 52–53, 200n13; resistance to, 31–32, 75; revolts against, 31–32, 74–75; threat of reenslavement of freedpersons, 106, 211n112
slavery, abolition of, 2–3; declaration of, 120, 123, 215n37; elites on, 27, 30; government's proposed role in, 29; indemnification in, 124–25, 127–28, 130, 215n36; politics over, 120–21, 123–24; proposals for, 28–29, 33, 126–27, 196n59; at provincial *vs.* federal level, 126; reasons for, 28–29, 33–34, 132–33. *See also* emancipation; Free Womb Law
slaves, 157; definitions of "disorder," 90–91; other plebeians and, 75–76, 105–6, 137–38; petition to authorities for emancipation, 86–88; population of, 21, 22–23, 121, 217n68; proper relations of, 80, 84–86; punishment of, 136–38; regulation of treatment of, 78–79, 85, 136–38, 205n12, 206n37; resistance by, 46–47, 82–83, 135, 196n59; savings funds of, 86–87, 140–41, 207n46; treatment of, 82–86; using elite divisiveness about slavery, 135–36; work for, 21–22, 82–83
slave trade: end of African, 29–31, 52; interprovincial, 30, 197n63
Slenes, Robert, 30
Smith, Herbert Huntington, 121–22
Só, José Manoel da Silva, 159–62
social institutions: in attempt to refashion plebeians, 15–16, 44; for freeborn children, 36
social order: after emancipation, 34–35, 127–28; efforts to maintain, 25–27, 123, 139; efforts to maintain during abolition, 30, 32–33, 125, 128–29, 135; elites having to share power in, 150–51; immigrants in, 48–50, 58, 60–61, 63–66, 73; master-servant relations in, 76–77, 139, 145–48; methods of maintaining, 41–45, 94–95; plebeians in, 76, 90–91; PRR on, 127, 153–54, 186; punishment in, 83–86, 89; state participation in, 77–79, 145–48; threats to, 39, 48–50, 57, 141
Socialist Party manifesto, 176
sociology, Comte on, 7
Soledade, Nicolau Tolentino da, 173, 176
Souza, Laura de Mello e, 15
Souza, Manoel Marques de (Baron of Porto Alegre), 24
Souza, Semiana Joaquina de, 116
state institutions, PRR control of, 171–72
state militia (Civil Guard), 165, 174
Steenhagen, João von, 155–56, 176, 185–86
Stein, Stanley J., 207n51
Stern, Steve J., 110, 187, 212n129
Suzano, Antonio Clemente, 81

tariff, special, 161–62, 171
Tavares, Francisco da Silva, 167–68
Torres, Joaquim José Rodrigues, 30
trade, 5; Rio Grande in, 16–18; tariff's effects on, 161–62; through Porto Alegre, 18–19, 155. *See also* slave trade
transportation: of immigrants, through Porto Alegre, 18–19, 155; for Rio Grande, 17–18
Trindade, Hélgio, 172
Triunfo, 19

Ubatuba, Manoel Pereira da Silva, 27–28; on abolition, 31–33, 197n66; on immigrants, 51, 64
United States, 40, 63

vagrancy, 40; in Beggars' Asylum debate, 25–27; elite fear of, 39, 142–43, 178; plebeians' accused of, 37, 54–55, 145–46. *See also* ideology of vagrancy

Vasconcellos, Emílio de Andrade, 136
Velho, José, 118–20
Vergueiro, Nicolau, 51
Vicente, Manoel, 136
Vieira, Damasceno, 133, 142–43
Vieira, Lourenço Luiz, 113
Vieira, Manoel José, 115–16
"Vintem" riots, 7
violence, 4, 79, 182; among plebeians, 106–8, 116; honor and, 109, 113–14; in slavery, 82–83, 89, 106; against soldiers, 136–37
voting, right of, 59, 159

War Arsenal, Porto Alegre's, 19, 44, 155, 164, 221n33
Weber, Luiz, 108, 110
Werna, Miguelina de, 125, 131
Werna Bilstein, Miguel de, 125
witchcraft: accusations of, 116, 207n51; against masters, 89, 207n51; medicine called, 209n86, 209n89; police repressing, 99–101
workers, 165; definition of, 160; identity as, 176–77, 185; newspapers of,S 159, 179–81; organizations of, 154–55, 157–59, 176; political involvement by, 174–75; political parties and, 163, 169, 171, 175–76; political parties of, 154–55, 173; representation for, 157–62. *See also* plebeians
Workers' Center (Centro Operário), 169, 176
Workers' League (Liga Operária), 169–70
Workers' Union (Sociedade Beneficente União Operária), 159–60, 165, 222n55

Zanetti, Valéria, 77
Zaniratti, Guelfo, 156, 169